HANDBOOK OF HUMOR AND PSYCHOTHERAPY
Advances in the Clinical Use of Humor

Edited by
William F. Fry, Jr., MD and
Waleed A. Salameh, PhD

Professional Resource Exchange, Inc.
Sarasota, Florida

Hardbound Edition ISBN: 0-943158-19-2
Library of Congress Catalog Number: 86-062714

The proofreader for this book was Janet Nunez, the
production supervisor was Debbie Worthington, the
graphics coordinator was Judy Warinner, the typist was
Lois Hartz, the cover designer was Bill Tabler, and the
printer was BookCrafters.

My grateful dedication is to all those contributing to my life being such a rich and exciting adventure.

William F. Fry, Jr.

I would like to dedicate this book to my family, where I first learned to appreciate and enjoy the gift of humor. To my father, Anthony, for his amusing Tarzan stories. To my mother, Espérance, for her radiant smile. To my brother, Wael, for his boundless repertoire of striking impersonations that have invariably summoned my laughter.

Waleed A. Salameh

BIOGRAPHIES

William F. Fry, Jr., MD, is a behavioral scientist and clinical psychiatrist, based from 1953 to 1983 in Menlo Park, California, and since 1983 in Nevada City, California. His pre-medical education took place at Bowdoin College; Grinnell College; University of Cincinnati; and University of Oregon. His medical education was achieved at the University of Southern California and the University of Cincinnati with a doctorate in medicine awarded in 1949. He also had the pleasure of participating in a teaching program at the University of Oslo, Norway. Dr. Fry served his internship at The Queen's Hospital, Honolulu, Hawaii, and his psychiatric residency with the Veterans Administration Hospital, Menlo Park, California. His residency included training at the Menlo Park VA facility, VA hospitals in San Francisco and Oakland, Cowell Clinic at University of California, Berkeley, and Langley Porter Clinic in San Francisco. In 1953, he began his professional career as both a scientist and clinical therapist. His research work began with participation as an original member of the Gregory Bateson Communication project. That affiliation existed from 1953 to 1962. It was during this participation that his long-term commitment to the study of humor began. It was also during that association that his involvement with the initiation of Family Therapy studies and the Mental Research Institute took place. Dr. Fry's humor research has been the source of material for two previous books: *Sweet Madness: A Study of Humor* (1963) and *Make 'em Laugh*, with Melanie Allen, PhD (1976). Numerous articles, book chapters, speaking engagements, and educative experiences have also resulted from this research. The wide range of Dr. Fry's research interests has made it possible for him to interface with a very large number of other humor scholars throughout the world, providing him the opportunity of bringing together many people with similar objectives and interests.

Dr. Fry is a Diplomate of the American Board of Psychiatry and a Life Fellow of the American Psychiatric Association. He has had service in both the U.S. Army and the U.S. Naval Reserve. He has functioned as consultant for numerous mental health facilities. He is Associate Clinical Professor, with the Department of Psychiatry, Stanford University School of Medicine. He has been, since 1964, Director of the International Gelotology Institute.

Waleed A. Salameh, PhD, is a licensed clinical and consulting psychologist in private practice and Director of the San Diego Institute for Integrative Short-Term Psychotherapy. Dr. Salameh obtained his BA degree from the University of Michigan, his MA from Duquesne University in Pittsburgh, Pennsylvania, and his PhD in clinical psychology from the University of Montreal in 1981. He received his clinical training at the Queen Elizabeth Hospital of Montreal and the Montreal General Hospital, working in both inpatient and outpatient psychotherapeutic settings. After completing a post-graduate training program specializing in short-term psychotherapy at the McGill University Institute of Short-Term Dynamic Psychotherapy, Dr. Salameh accepted the position of clinical psychologist with the California Department of Mental Health. Following this appointment, he entered full-time private practice. He is the author of over 70 professional articles and presentations, a stress reduction handbook, as well as four book chapters in the areas of psychotherapy and effective communication. He is currently working on a forthcoming volume entitled *Integrative Short-Term Psychotherapy (ISTP): The Origination of Human Change.*

Dr. Salameh's clinical practice focuses on using the psychotherapeutic approach he has developed, Integrative Short-Term Psychotherapy (ISTP), in working with individuals, couples, families, and groups. As a consultant for various mental health settings, Dr. Salameh has conducted numerous workshop training experiences in the ISTP therapeutic model and in Humor Immersion Training[TM], a training system he has elaborated to facilitate humor development skills.

Dr. Salameh holds a certification in Psychotherapy from the Quebec, Canada, Corporation of Psychologists, and currently serves as an oral commissioner with the State of California Psychology Examining Committee. In 1985, he was awarded the Milton H. Erickson Institute of San Diego Scholarly Author Award in recognition of his contributions to the field of hypnotic and strategic interventions.

PREFACE

There are a finite number of specifically identifiable things that can make life not only livable, but also delightful, rich, and desirable. One of the most readily available of these is humor. The creation of humor is a natural capacity of mankind. It is a part of our genetic template and is found throughout the human race. This natural and ubiquitous creation of humor is met on all sides by that hearty and complex response that is known as mirth. Together, these two--the creation and its response--provide some of the most pleasureful and stimulating, even illuminating moments during the course of a lifetime. This benefit to humanity, which is found in humor and mirth, is available to individuals alone as well as to people relating together in the course of communal activities.

Our challenge is to refine the expression of this powerful combination in its most positive aspects. Humor is a resource to be cherished, cultivated, and conserved. However, the value of humor to the psychotherapeutic process has been both unintentionally and deliberately ignored. Undaunted by this omission in the evolution of science, several courageous "mavericks" have pursued theoretical and experiential investigations of the numerous ways in which humor and mirth can help attain therapeutic goals. A substantial body of useful information has been developed that can provide guidance and inspiration to others in the mental health professions. Each author included here is a pioneer of sorts in that he or she has advanced beyond the conventional extents of contemporary science and become familiar with novel, unique, and sometimes controversial experience. It has been the objective of this handbook to bring together as much of this valuable information as is practicable into one reference source.

Our initial acknowledgment is an expression of appreciation to these scientists: for their willingness to labor at the task of combining their information into a communicable form by ordering and summarizing innumerable therapeutic moments; for their patience in the face of editorial demands; for their understanding and support during the lengthy search for a courageous, imaginative, and talented publisher for the book; and for the energy and creativity that made it possible for them to accumulate this information in the first place.

This acknowledgment does not diminish our regard for other scientists in this field, whose work for one reason or another is not included here. Our second appreciation, then, is for all those others who are progressively expanding the knowledge of how humor can benefit the therapeutic process.

Appreciation is also felt and expressed to those who have given us material assistance or moral support during this venture. This list includes various members of our respective families, including Mrs. Elizabeth S. Fry, Mr. Anthony Salameh, Mrs. Esperance Salameh, Dr. Wael Salameh, Mr. and Mrs. Alfred Catrib, and other friends. Dr. William Henry gave valuable editorial suggestions at a formative point during our project. Communications with Drs. Viktor Frankl, Julius Heuscher, Harvey Mindess, and Bernard Tetreau were productively stimulating. The production of this book was anticipated by the publication in *The Sciences*, journal of the New York Academy of Sciences, of a version of the chapter written by Dr. Jeffrey H. Goldstein. That publication was arranged by Cheryl S. Cohen, Managing Editor, *The Sciences*, and occurred in the August, 1982 (Vol. 22, #6) issue of the journal.

Editing was significantly aided by the secretarial assistance of Mrs. Elizabeth S. Fry and Ms. Sandra Slad. The editorial guidance of our publishers at Professional Resource Exchange, Inc., Drs. Lawrence G. Ritt and Peter A. Keller, was creative, effective, and necessary. Finally, our grateful regards go to Debbie Worthington, production supervisor at Professional Resource Exchange. Her patience, remarkable organizational talents, and continuous attention to details are manifested throughout this volume.

W.F.F. and W.A.S.

TABLE OF CONTENTS

Table of Contents

INTRODUCTION

It was a hot August day in Los Angeles, California, 1979. William Fry and I were attending the Second International Conference on Humor and had met for lunch in Japantown. As usual our conversation drifted to humor, a topic of longstanding research interest for him and an area of clinical interest for me. As a clinician, I was concerned about the paucity of available literature with respect to the psychotherapeutic uses of humor. I proposed to William Fry that we co-edit a nuts-and-bolts handbook for clinicians clarifying the applications of humor in everyday clinical work. He agreed to join me in this project, and the kernel of the present volume was planted.

Nevertheless, my voyage into humorland had started some time earlier. It began with an unceasing admiration for some individuals I encountered in different walks of life who seemed to possess a balsamic and spontaneously communicated sense of humor; it was propelled by my fascination with the creative and emotionally regenerative aspects of the humor experience. My interest in humor was simultaneously paralleled by a clinical interest in the area of personality development, having been keenly interested in the psychogenesis and development of that psychological formation we call personality. The term "personality" seemed to refer to a sometimes idiosyncratic assemblage of characteristics that make a statement about an individual. Relatedly, I asked myself the question: "Why do some individuals choose to make a humorous statement?" Subsequently, when the time came to design a PhD dissertation project in clinical psychology at the University of Montreal, my parallel interests in humor and personality development converged in the decision to conduct a PhD research project on the personality characteristics, childhood backgrounds, and creative process of stand-up comedians. I opted to study stand-up comedians because they were clearly interested in making a humorous statement. In order to collect my research data, I traveled to New York City, San Francisco, and Los

Angeles to test and interview stand-up comics. Many hours were spent at stand-up comedy clubs watching the professional creators of humor in action as they performed their comic routines. Among other things, my research with stand-up comedians and comediennes filled me with respect for the potency of humor in reconciling opposites, soothing wounds, helping individuals adjust in healthy ways, and inspiring refreshing solutions to stagnant problems. However, as a clinician I was interested in exploring how these curative dimensions can be transferred into the psychotherapeutic arena. During that period I had begun my doctoral clinical internship at the Montreal General Hospital, a teaching hospital of McGill University. I worked in the department of psychiatry under the supervision of chief psychologist Allen Surkis, PhD, a masterful clinician who introduced me to clinical hypnosis, psychodrama, and the area of indirect communication. Allen Surkis possessed a unique sense of humor, and encouraged my nascent explorations in the therapeutic utilization of humor. Following the completion of my doctoral internship, I enlisted in a post-graduate training program in the principles and technique of short-term psychotherapy, offered by McGill University's Institute of Short-Term Dynamic Psychotherapy under the direction of Habib Davanloo, MD. Davanloo impressed me as an intense, relentless clinician who would leave no stone unturned in the quest to effect constructive patient change. My training experiences with Surkis and Davanloo led to the fermentation of another cardinal question, which in this instance took the form of a clinical challenge: "Would it be possible to combine the intensity and drive of short-term psychotherapy with the intensity and drive of humor?" I was not yet ready to answer that critical question. I needed further field exposure as a clinical practitioner.

I began my clinical career as a practicing psychotherapist in 1980. My day-to-day clinical work with different patients inculcated me with a realistic sense of what the process of change is about and how it can be best facilitated. I pursued additional advanced training in different models of short-term psychotherapy and in the work of Milton Erickson. I listened to patients. My psychotherapeutic perspective and clinical technique started to jell. I started to discern what sorts of approaches worked best. It became increasingly apparent to me that the patients I worked with were most responsive to a treatment approach that included less obfuscation, less density, less time in treatment than is traditionally thought to be ideal, less therapist unresponsiveness, and less solemnity. On the other hand, effective treatment approaches seemed to include more focusing on specific patient issues, more analyzing of the actual interactions occurring between therapist and patient during therapy sessions, more simplicity and explicitness in defining the patient's problem areas, more expression of emotional material during the course of treatment, more use of imagery and metaphor to illustrate both dilemmas and alternatives, more enlisting of the patient's own constructive conscious and unconscious resources to catalyze change, more therapist transparency, and more humor. The result of my labors at determining what works in psychotherapy is a new clinical approach, Integrative Short-Term Psychotherapy (ISTP), which is presented in Chapter 10 of this volume. Furthermore, I have elaborated a new technology for humor development, the Humor Immersion Training^{TM} workshops, also discussed in Chapter 10. In HIT workshops, individuals learn specific humor building skills for utilization in both professional and personal contexts.

And the voyage continues. For myself, and for my friend and colleague William Fry, this handbook represents both a culmination of 7 years of effort as well as a signpost in our individual professional journeys in the humor field. Furthermore, the handbook also serves as a forum for the work of the contributors and their distinctive therapeutic perspectives. Recent developments in the psychotherapies are examined and the important role of humor in diverse clinical approaches is extensively covered. That humor finds a welcome place in all these approaches reflects both a recognition and a growing acceptance of the clinical relevance of this new therapeutic tool. The handbook presents techniques for using humor in working with adults, children, families, and groups, buttressing technical aspects with rich clinical vignettes.

I hope you will find the handbook helpful in your work and relevant to your clinical interests. Beyond the fresh ideas and new technical information, I also hope that the handbook will invite more humor into your life. Despite all the limitations and swarming contradictions of human existence, the invaluable gift of a laugh or the gentle touch of a healing smile can still brighten and recharge the days of our lives.

-Waleed A. Salameh

Through the years, since the inception in 1953 of my scientific interest in humor and the concomitant beginning of my practice as a clinical psychiatric therapist, I made a concerted effort to avoid mingling my clinical work and my basic humor research. I believed that such separation of clinical and research activities would provide a broader base of professional experience and catalyze both my scientific development and my personal maturation. I believed that this conscious division would encourage amalgamations at unconscious levels. I reasoned that this combination of conscious exposures and unconscious ferment would result in a multiple benefit of progressively increasing my store of specific information and enhancing the expansion of general human wisdom available to guide my decisions and enrich my life.

In my youth and early adult years, I was a somewhat silly person and I recognized it, and was mightily interested in overcoming that almost congenital disadvantage in as many ways as I could reasonably introduce into my circumstances. It is certainly possible that this programming of conscious and unconscious processes and levels may have been yet another example of that silliness of mine. Nevertheless, it seems to have worked in several ways, and I have become used to being continuously thrilled by discoveries of new lodes of information and knowledge. Expansions of wisdom provide me with a sense of life being a true gift and the old silliness, which I now understand to have been rooted largely in a romantic philosophy having many manifestations, including musical preferences, is much diminished, even to the point that I now only infrequently find myself embarrassed by naivety or a limited horizon of awareness.

It might appear that this schizoid approach to a professional career would be rather difficult to accomplish. This was not the case until just a few years prior to the publication of this book. My objective of maintaining separate lives in clinical work and in basic humor research was aided by several compelling historic conditions. One of these entails the trend in earlier years to consider humor too frivolous, tangential, or insignificant for it to have any implications for the clinical therapeutic process. Humor was even regarded as disruptive, diversionary, and perhaps destructive in the therapeutic context. It was considered irresponsible to introduce humorous material into the treatment relationship. Responding mirthfully to humorous sallies by patients was held to be questionable if one were truly dedicated to advancing the patient's welfare. Several authors of following chapters in this volume refer to specific instances of this negative view of humor in therapy.

I must say that, although I maintained this clinical/research separation, and although the general orthodox view of humor in therapy was unfavorable, a unique set of clinical experiences during the late 1950's and the early 1960's laid the groundwork for my subsequent personal acceptance of the possibility of clinical value in humor. These experiences occurred during participation in the Gregory Bateson Schizophrenic Communication Research Project and in the establishment by Donald D. Jackson of the Mental Research Institute in Palo Alto, California. They were focused almost exclusively on family therapy--developing theory, exploring practice and specific therapeutic techniques, assaying the range of family therapy applications, and training ourselves and others.

Although I did not introduce humor techniques into my family therapy work, following the dictum mentioned above, I soon found it impossible to avoid or ignore the humor that is usually a generous portion of family interaction in therapy. Humor in the family therapy context is such a potent element of family interaction that it demands therapeutic attention. This experience made me more receptive to the value of humor for the general therapeutic process. A potentiality was created, making it possible to see in later years that although I would continue to do clinical work and basic humor research apart from one another, professionals elsewhere could be establishing important bodies of knowledge and experience wherein humor was recognized for its clinical benefits.

Another historic factor made it comparatively easy for me to carry on two separate professional lives as clinician and researcher. This was the primitive state of humor research. Basic humor research has truly been basic, in each sense of the word. Humor research had little to offer to the clinician and his or her treatment procedures; my humor research had little to offer. I was quite able to conduct my research studies without thought of their possible clinical implications, because at the level where I was operating there were no, or very few, direct clinical implications. Even the field of experimental psychology, probably the science most advanced in humor studies, was at such a rudimentary stage in its humor research that very little could be readily translated into clinical significance.

Much was understood about humor as a cultural phenomenon, as a source of entertainment and pleasure, as a literary tradition; but the science of humor had been much neglected. I stepped into humor research at a level during which clinical considerations were remote. My research questions were concerned with theoretical and technical issues: experimental design, matters having to do with laboratory instrumentation, and the significant challenge of stimulating mirth in experimental settings.

I was hacking at a veritable wilderness--one with demand for innovation and flexibility, one with rich and undeveloped prospects, but not one offering seething stimulation for translation into clinical possibility. And so I was madly happy, busy with all this experimentation, rooting into the howling wilderness, as my ancestors of 300 years before had done in a more actual, less metaphoric sense. I had the courage, or folly, to be a research pioneer. But my vision was not sufficient to see beyond demands of doing science onto a vista involving humor in clinical transactions and therapeutic relationship until just a few years before publication of this book.

Consider my surprise when, during the late 1970's, people whom I respected began to converse with me and ruminate about humor being used as a treatment procedure. Some of this speculation arose in response to several of the messages presented by my friend, psychologist Harvey Mindess, in his book *Laughter and Liberation*, published in 1971. One of the important subjects discussed in that book was the hope-promoting and hope-expanding power of humor. Several people talking with me reasoned that, because hope and humor are so closely allied and because the need for hope is intense in the clinical context, humor should have some unexplored clinical benefits.

As my research studies became more widely known and my circle of humor conversants enlarged, I became one of the nexus points of an international humor studies underground network, and I began to hear more specific ideas, speculations, observations, opinions, even experiences with therapeutic uses and values of humor. Much of this material was concerned with humor in group settings--traditional group therapy, T-groups, Gestalt groups, Sensitivity Training, groups associated with more radical forms of therapy, such as Primal Scream, EST, The Family. A rich source of humor-in-therapy thought and experience have been the powerful and dynamic meetings of the international Alcoholics Anonymous. Family therapy continued to be a lively arena for the operation of humor in therapeutics, confirming our early impressions.

An event that catalyzed the humor-in-therapy field was the publication, in 1979, of publisher Norman Cousins's personal account of the role humor played in his recovery from physical disease. Although not a document dealing with psychotherapy, *Anatomy of an Illness* had an enormously stimulating impact on all sorts of clinicians, including that traditionally conservative group, the medical professionals. Its stimulation was enhanced by public enthusiasm for clinical humor expressed on several occasions by world-famous heart surgeon, Norman Shumway. The stimulation was reinforced when psychiatrist George Vaillant reported, in his book *Adaptation to Life*, that the results of the 40 years Harvard Grant Study indicated the appropriateness of listing humor as one of the five mature human coping mechanisms.

Thus, during the early 1980's, I was contacted by increasing numbers of people with clinical affiliations and commitments who were interested in exploring the deliberate use of humor as a therapeutic tool. It is striking that a relatively high proportion of these people were nurses, technicians, or others involved in institutional health care--hospitals, convalescent homes, long-term care facilities, rest and retirement homes. Many of these persons expressed a deep frustration with several aspects of the traditional systems of institutional care and approached from different viewpoints the question of whether humor could provide supplementary or even alternative components to long-term health care.

My networking in the humor field was greatly aided by the initiation in 1976 of a series of international conferences on humor studies. These conferences brought together authorities and enthusiasts from many different countries for 3 to 5 day exchanges of ideas and experiences in many diverse fields of humor. The first conference took place at the University of Wales, Cardiff, Wales (1976); then two were held in the United States at Los Angeles (1979) and Washington, DC (1982). A fourth conference was sponsored by the University of Tel Aviv, Israel (1984), a fifth at University College, Cork, Ireland (1985), and a sixth (1987) by Arizona State University. During participation in these conferences, I became aware of some personal blind spots in my overview of the humor world.

I discovered that humor-in-therapy had not been limited to speculation, opinion, and questions. During some of those years of my rigorous isolation of humor from clinical practice, there had been a number of clinicians forging a body of experience and/or theory on the values of humor for the therapeutic process. Several of these were mental health practitioners, such as psychiatrists John Schimel and Herman Staples, dealing with the emotional and mental problems of adolescent patients. But I found that this innovative ferment was not limited to adolescent psychiatry. It was expanding into many other areas of therapeutics, and substantially so in several instances. A number of pioneers were already probing humor-in-therapy values to establish various clinical protocols, assemblages of techniques, rating of applicability, limitation, and indication. Most of the scientists contributing to this book were among that progressive group.

When Waleed Salameh, for whom I had functioned as doctoral consultant, approached me with his interest in documenting the existence and extent of this innovative development in clinical humor, I was sufficiently informed of its magnitude to react with enthusiasm and pleasure--and with no small amount of ironic awareness that after all those years of splendid separateness, my two professional lives were coming to a rapprochement in a creative project containing the potentiality for many present and future benefits in health care. The compilation of this volume, although it subsequently turned out to be a very lengthy and energy-consuming project, seemed to be a highly worthwhile activity in which we could take satisfaction for having contributed not only specific information to our fellow professionals, but also formalization in this otherwise amorphous dynamism.

At an earlier point in this essay, I wrote that perhaps keeping separate my two professional activities (humor research and clinical psychiatry) might have been a manifestation of my silliness. I do not believe that now. However, it was rather silly of me not to realize early that these two would have to meet somewhere down the line and not to prepare myself for that inevitable rapprochement. I knew the power of humor in human relationships; I was a precocious apostle of the richness and strength of humor in human life. I was fully aware that, although humor can be destructive when used for hostile purposes, humor contributes emotional and even physical benefit in many ways and in many human circumstances.

I believed in the value of humor both in individual personal life and in the lifetime experiences that bring people together in common purpose and common endeavor. I believed in humor as a creative catalyst allowing humans to expand into the farthest reaches of their potentialities more frequently than with most other elements of life. It was silly of me that I did not anticipate that someday I would be co-editing a book recording and presenting this new, significant, and beneficial therapeutic discipline.

-William F. Fry, Jr.

Two more issues deserve mention at this juncture:

1. *Disclaimer*: In keeping with the ethical considerations regarding case presentations, we have asked all contributors to adhere to the requirement of patient confidentiality. Consequently, the names of all patients discussed in this handbook have been fictionalized. Secondary case details have also been changed, and all personally identifying information has been removed. Any possible similarities in name or detail to past or current treatment cases are unintended and purely coincidental. Secondly, it should be pointed out that the type of humor referred to in this volume is a constructive, empathic humor, which is totally unrelated to sarcasm, racist or sexist humor deformations, put-downs, and other abuses of humor. Thirdly, the ideas presented by each contributor are based on his or her own clinical work,

and may not be automatically applicable in all cases and with all patients. Psychotherapy students, interns, and trainees would be well-advised to consult with their supervisors as to how and when to introduce humor into their psychotherapeutic interventions. Specialized workshop training in the appropriate clinical uses of humor is suggested for those therapists or students interested in developing their clinical skills in this area.

2. *Handbook Organization*: Except for the beginning theoretical chapter and the closing chapter, all handbook chapters are organized in six major sections. We believe that this organizational structure will make for a sense of continuity and enhance congruousness while allowing the reader to compare the unique features in each contributor's work. The chapters are generally organized in six sections as follows:

a. Theoretical Perspective--The authors' rationale for using humor in psychotherapy. How their system evolved. Their theoretical model and clinical insights.

b. Technique--How the authors use humor in day-to-day work with a variety of patients.

c. Pertinent Uses--Appropriate and inappropriate uses of humor. Ways to modify techniques for your own practice. Indications and contraindications for using humor in psychotherapy.

d. Clinical Presentation--Illustrations of the authors' techniques in action.

e. Sythesis--A summary of the major tenets of the authors' clinical perspective.

f. References--Bibliographic documentation of the authors' perspective to facilitate further study by the reader.

We have written a brief commentary to accompany each chapter, introducing the reader to the chapter's distinct coordinates and specifying what we found to be unique elements in each contributor's approach.

-William F. Fry, Jr. and Waleed A. Salameh

THERAPEUTIC EFFECTS
OF LAUGHTER

Jeffrey H. Goldstein

Dr. Goldstein is one of the foremost contemporary humor scholars. In this chapter he provides a detailed review of the diverse attitudes about laughter and humor held by philosophers, scientists, and clinicians from the time of Aristotle up to the present. He describes the co-existence of both positive and negative views of the therapeutic value of laughter and humor. In searching for a synthesis to resolve this apparent discrepancy, he explores a wide range of experimental data regarding the psychological and physiological impact of humor and laughter. Dr. Goldstein completes his chapter with a three-dimensional conclusion:

1. That laughter and humor are complex phenomena and have complex effects on the other aspects of human functioning, with the result that their effects can usually be beneficial, but under certain circumstances may be detrimental.
2. That the quality of life is palpably enhanced by a sense of humor, if not its quantitative duration.
3. While the weight of the existing psychophysiological evidence favors laughter as a beneficial phenomenon, more research is clearly needed to examine the long-term effects of laughter and humor on emotional and physical health.

Dr. Goldstein's rich theoretical review invites further scientific thinking and clinical research on the subject of laughter and humor. He simultaneously identifies unanswered research questions in this rapidly developing field of inquiry and suggests technical tools for investigating such questions. We trust that these questions will soon receive proper empirical consideration.

Dr. Goldstein is a social and research psychologist. He is presently Professor of Psychology at Temple University in Philadelphia, Pennsylvania. His publications include The Psychology of Humor (1972) and the Handbook of Humor Research (Vols. 1 & 2) (1983), both co-edited with Dr. Paul E. McGhee.

✻   ✻   ✻

1

Despite our limited knowledge of the mechanisms underlying humor and laughter, the belief is widespread that laughter is beneficial to one's physical and psychological well-being. Although this may be true, it would be a mistake to accept this position without sound empirical support.

Thirty or 40 years ago, the suggestion that laughter or any other positive emotion had medical or psychiatric benefits would have been laughable. Only since the end of the Second World War did westerners come to think that stress and anxiety might have somatic consequences. To suggest the antithesis of this--that laughter, relaxation, or joy could have therapeutic effects--was nearly unthinkable. However, throughout history there have been those who have believed that positive emotions, humor among them, were not just enjoyable but *vital*.

There are fads in medicine and behavioral science just as in literature, art, and styles of dress. Today it is fashionable to attribute healing and restorative powers to laughter. The current popularity of the healthy laughter notion owes much to Norman Cousins's 1979 book, *Anatomy of an Illness*. Partly as a result of this book, and partly as a result of the rise of holistic medicine in the past decade, physicians are more likely than ever to work with their patients, to disclose more information about illness and recovery, and to think about humor and other sources of emotional comfort as part of treatment. A resulting concern is that the patient will be seen as responsible for his or her affliction or failure to recover--that by not having the will to live, the proper outlook on life, or a sufficient sense of humor, the patient will be seen to suffer willfully. However, despite Cousins's belief that laughter was a necessary ingredient in his rather remarkable recovery from what appears to have been ankylosing spondylitis, the scientific evidence for this claim is lacking. I do not wish to dispute the claim here, I merely want to encourage the search for supporting evidence.

Whenever a belief suddenly comes into vogue, and this is perhaps more true in science than elsewhere--it is wise to examine its origins and history. Certainly when something as ephemeral as laughter is considered responsible for "miraculous" cures, we should probably examine how this belief developed.

EARLY BELIEFS ABOUT LAUGHTER

It is difficult to imagine that only within the last 100 years or less has laughter in public been socially acceptable. For much of Western history laughter was thought to be impolite at best, sinful at worst.

NEGATIVE VIEWS OF LAUGHTER

It was the tendency of physicians in the Middle Ages to locate each emotion in some organ of the body. The seat of love was the heart and the seat of laughter was the spleen, probably because laughter was viewed as a "low" form of behavior. "By identifying laughter with the spleen rather than the brain or heart, let alone spirit, the rational and religious values of a comic sensitivity were easily dismissed" (Hyers, 1981, p. 18).

Even as now, there were attempts during the Middle Ages to reconcile medicine with the prevailing morality. In 1676, Robert Barclay wrote in "Apology for the True Christian Divinity," "It is not lawful to use games, sports, plays, nor among other things comedies among Christians, under the notion of recreations, since they do not agree with Christian silence, gravity and sobriety; for laughing, sporting, gaming, mocking, jesting, vain talking, etc., is not Christian liberty, nor harmless mirth" (1676/1969). This of course is consistent with the locus of laughter in the spleen. The Pilgrim settlers to America likewise looked upon laughter with disdain and permitted it only when it would serve to illustrate a moral lesson.

In a well-known letter to his son written in 1748, Lord Chesterfield advised, "Lord Laughter is the mirth of the mob, who are only pleased with silly things; for true Wit or good Sense never excited a laugh since the creation of the world. A man of parts and fashion is therefore only seen to smile, but never heard to laugh."

In 1794 the German philosopher, George Friedrich Meier, noted that religion (and philosophy) were not appropriate objects of laughter. "We are never to jest on or with things which, on account of their importance or weight, claim our utmost seriousness. There are things...so great and important in themselves, as never to be thought of and mentioned but with much sedateness and solemnity. Laughter on such occasions is criminal and indecent...For instance, all jests on religion, philosophy, and

3

the like important subjects" (quoted in Hyers, 1981). Richard Hurd (1811) wrote that laughter "obscures truth, hardens the heart, and stupefies the understanding."

In Victorian England, although girls and women were permitted to smile in deference or to giggle at the slightest suggestion of impropriety, they were not to laugh with glee. They could be embarrassed but not happy. (Today, of course, they may be happy but not embarrassed.) Writing during the reign of Queen Victoria, George Vasey (1877) argues that children laugh, not out of any sense of joy or humor, but because they have been tickled as infants:

> Now it cannot fail to have been observed by all those who are not absolutely blind or mentally deficient that the operation of tickling is invariably commenced at a very early period of infancy, and children are thus taught and accustomed to laugh even before they have begun to think. Thus they learn to laugh, not because they like it, or because they are pleased, but solely because they are tickled. (pp. 28-29)

In other words, if children were not tickled before they were able to think they would not laugh as adults. According to Vasey, children's laughter is "...nothing more nor less than spasmodic and involuntary contractions and dilatations of the pectoral muscles and the lungs, excited into action by absurd ticklings and stupid monkey tricks" (pp. 32-33).

In 1905 Freud considered it increasingly credible that humor was a reflection of underlying anxiety, bitterness, or unspoken hostility. He proposed that laughter stemmed from repressed aggressive and sexual impulses, and thus could be seen as an expression of them.*

---

*Freud was careful to distinguish jokes that were hostile or sexual in nature from what we might call "pure humor." About the latter, Freud wrote: "Humour has in it a <u>liberating</u> element. But it has also something fine and elevating, which is lacking in the other two ways of deriving pleasure from intellectual activity. Obviously, what is fine about it is the triumph of narcissism, the ego's victorious assertion of its own vulnerability. It refuses to be hurt by the arrows of reality or to be compelled to suffer. It insists that it is impervious to wounds dealt by the outside world, in fact, that these are merely occasions for affording it pleasure. This last trait is a fundamental characteristic of humor" (1928, p. 2).

Writing in 1905, as well, Sir Arthur Mitchell said that because laughter was beyond bodily control it must represent "a state of mental disorder--keeping always in view the singular and irrational character of the phenomena of laughter. When this prolonged laughter had ceased, I think we should be justified in calling what had happened a transitory fit of mental disorder" (p. 52).

POSITIVE VIEWS OF LAUGHTER

Although Freud distinguished between hostile wit and benign humor, he was certainly not the first to recognize that at least some laughter might be indicative of the absence of underlying pathology. As early as the 13th century, Henri de Mondeville, a surgeon, proposed that laughter be used as an aid to recovery from surgery. He believed that negative emotions could interfere with recovery. "The surgeon must forbid anger, hatred, and sadness in the patient, and remind him that the body grows fat from joy and thin from sadness" (cited in Moody, 1978, p. 29).

From the time of Aristotle, laughter has been recommended as a means of strengthening the lungs and furthering the health of the whole organism. Mulcaster, a 16th century physician, wrote that laughter was a physical exercise and, as such, was healthy, that is, health-giving. He wrote that laughter could help those who have cold hands and cold chests and are troubled with melancholia, because "it moveth much aire in the breast, and sendeth the warmer spirites outward."

In one of the most thoughtful and complete analyses of laughter, the French physician, Laurent Joubert (1579/1979), still working within the framework of the humoral theory, presented several views on the origins and functions of laughter that are still in use, though in slightly different form. Like Aristotle, Joubert saw laughter as arising from "a defect or ugliness that is not painful or destructive." The ugliness incites sadness while its relative painlessness incites joy. These contrary emotions are said to stir the heart in alternating contractions and dilatations, sadness causing the contractions and joy the dilatations. This to-and-fro movement is transferred to the diaphragm, leading to the rapid breathing we call "hearty laughter."

According to Joubert (1579/1979), the consequences of laughter are beneficial, and can be seen in the face and eyes. He writes:

> Is it not in the face, and especially in the eyes which (laughter) moves so freely that nothing surpasses it? Is it not there that it shows itself and appears most favorably, rendering these parts more than charming? Certainly there is nothing that gives more pleasure and recreation than a laughing face, with its wide, shining, clear, and serene forehead, eyes shining, resplendent from any vantage point, and casting fire as do diamonds; cheeks vermilion and incarnate, mouth flush with the face, lips handsomely drawn back..., chin drawn in, widened, and a bit recessed...."

Specific references to the healthful effects of laughter scatter the philosophical and medical literature of the 18th and 19th centuries. Immanuel Kant wrote in *Critique of Judgment* (1790) that "In the case of jokes, we feel the effect of this slackening in the body by the oscillation of the organs, which promotes the restoration of equilibrium and has a favorable influence upon health." Herbert Spencer (1860) proposed that laughter was a mechanism for releasing excess tension, and therefore was an important restorative mechanism. This view of laughter as a tension-reduction process is influential even today, though without a great deal of empirical evidence to sustain it at this juncture.

Sully (1902) proposed that laughter was not only "good exercise," but also reduced unpleasant tension and promoted digestion. Gottlieb Hufeland, a 19th century German professor, said:

> Laughter is one of the most important helps to digestion with which we are acquainted; and the custom in vogue among our ancestors, of exciting it by jesters and buffoons, was founded on true medical principles. Cheerful and joyous companions are invaluable at meals. Obtain such, if possible, for the nourishment received amid mirth and jollity is productive of light and healthy blood. (quoted in Hyers, 1981, p. 20)

These various statements by physicians and philosophers are further reinforced by James Walsh (1928), an American physician, who added that the beneficial effects of laughter are mediated by psychological effects:

> The best formula for the health of the individual is contained in the mathematical expression: health varies as the amount of laughter...Laughter makes one expansive in outlook and is very likely to give the feeling that the future need not be the subject of quite so much solicitude as is usually allowed for it. The effect of laughter upon the mind not only brings relaxation with it, so far as mental tension is concerned, but makes it also less prone to dreads and less solicitous about the future. This favorable effect on the mind influences various functions of the body and makes them healthier than would otherwise be the case.

TOWARD RECONCILIATION

When opinions reflect such extremes--the belief that laughter is evil and symptomatic and the belief that it is health-giving and beneficial--it is probably safe to conclude that there is some validity in each position. There is considerable evidence that laughter can indicate underlying, and perhaps unconscious, hostility and conflict. There is also a good deal of evidence that laughter can reflect self-acceptance, joy, inner strength, and adjustment. In other words, laughter is ambiguous in its capacity to reflect extremes of attitude and adjustment. We do not yet know enough about laughter and humor to state just how such reflection comes about or how to distinguish reliably between healthy laughter and malevolent laughter. However, there are some important clues in the literature.

On the basis of current psychological evidence, laughter does not always indicate or promote well-being. It will take the experience and sensitivity of the clinician to determine when laughter is called for and what it signifies. We already know some of the *contraindications of humor and laughter* and also have available some promising techniques for further studying this issue. For example, Pollio, Mers, and Lucchesi (1972) have tape-recorded laughter in different situations and examined

7

the tapes with an oscilloscope, permitting measurement of the latency, amplitude, and duration of laughter. There are characteristic laugh patterns for different types of humor and for different individuals. Some individuals expel a great deal of air and reach an early, explosive "laugh peak," while the laughter of others builds gradually over several seconds. For example, it is possible using this technique to determine what it is about "canned laughter" in television situation-comedies that sounds so unnatural. Pollio and his colleagues have shown that it is the very short latency and early maximum amplitude that, in contrast to natural laughter, make canned laughter sound artificial. This method may enable us to examine "unnatural" or "forced" laughter to determine whether it is accompanied by stress or tension and when it is a genuine expression of underlying positive affect. Fry (1977b) has also examined respiratory patterns in mirth and noted that laughter can be highly idiosyncratic with respect to inspiration, expiration, and interval pauses, modified by various parameters.

If laughter is to serve either as an indicator or promoter of physical and psychological well-being, it will be necessary to distinguish "pathological" laughter from "beneficial" laughter; to distinguish laughter associated with joy from laughter arising from embarrassment, fear, and hostility; and to refrain from treating laughter as a monolithic entity. Some of what is already known about pathological and beneficial laughter is reviewed below.

LAUGHTER AS INDICATIVE OF PATHOLOGY

Laughter does not always indicate an underlying positive mood or reflect a state of adjustment or physical well-being. Instead it may reflect psychological, social, or physical malaise.

Psychologically, laughter may indicate self-deprecation, hostility toward others--as in racist joking, defensiveness, closed-mindedness--or a preoccupation with scatology or sex. I would not want to label these attitudes and dispositions "pathological," but only wish to point out that psychologists have often treated laughter as a reflection of underlying attitudes, affects, and cognitions and that these attitudes, feelings, and thoughts may not always be those we think of as healthy or desirable.

Laughter may also be an effective device for reducing stress (Lefcourt & Martin, 1986; Martin & Lefcourt, 1983; Schill & O'Laughlin, 1984). Laughter may decrease autonomic arousal, lowering heart and respiration rates. However, in two studies there was no significant relationship found between appreciation of nonsense, hostile, or sexual jokes and high or low scores on Beck's Depression Inventory (Safranek & Schill, 1982; Scogin & Merbaum, 1983). It is conceivable that laughter or spontaneous joking can be used as an indication of general level of stress or anxiety, though the content and social nature of joking must also be taken into account.

The failure to laugh may convey as much information as laughter itself. Levine and Redlich (1955), for example, report the tendentious nature of *not* laughing. People who suffer from impaired sexual functioning, for example, may fail to see the point in a sexual joke.

Socially, laughter and humor may drive a wedge between individuals, creating a chasm where only a gap had existed. A hostile or pointed remark that makes another person or group of people the butt of a joke may make communication between individuals more difficult (Goldstein, 1976). Although humor may be used as a means of communication between individuals, as a way of making oneself vulnerable to another, it may also be used defensively as a barrier to communication. Likewise, a person may use humor as a tactic of ingratiation, as a way of manipulating another person and his or her feelings, or as a means of social control (Fine, 1983; Martineau, 1972). Filling a conversation with jokes and witty remarks can be a way of not participating in conversation, a way of psychologically closing oneself off from the ongoing proceedings (Kane, Suls, & Tedeschi, 1977).

Physically there are many instances when laughter indicates underlying pathology. Black (1982, 1984), Duchowny (1983), and Moody (1978) review many of these. In three neurological disorders--pseudobulbar palsy, amyotrophic lateral sclerosis ("Lou Gehrig's disease"), and multiple sclerosis--there is a distinctive type of "aberrant" laughter. Sudden outbursts of laughter often occur, but the laughter is beyond the control of the patient and does not reflect any underlying sense of elation.

Likewise, a form of epilepsy known as gelastic epilepsy involves a dull, hollow, and clearly inappropriate laughter. In a review of the literature, Gascon and Lombroso (1971) note that as early as 1873 it was recognized that an epileptic episode may manifest itself as laughter. Among 10 patients who suffered gelastic seizures seen by Gascon and Lombroso, two distinct types appeared. For half the cases the laughter consisted only of the motor components with its normal affective accompaniment. In these patients, the evidence suggested a diencephalic lesion. In the five cases in which there appeared a lesion in the temporal lobe, there was more affect associated with the laughter. In these latter cases, the seizure was usually preceded by a distinct, often pleasurable aura, experienced by the patient as mirth. Black (1982) notes that gelastic epilepsy in childhood is often due to tumors of the hypothalamus. Duchowny (1983) distinguishes two types of gelastic seizure involving laughter, those in which the hypothalamus is involved and those with limbic system involvement. The characteristics of these two types are shown in Table 1. Hypothalamic attacks include brief episodes of elementary laughter, whereas the laughter during limbic seizures is typically more varied.

A review of pathological laughter and brain disorders by Ironside (1956) notes that pathological laughter "is

TABLE 1: GELASTIC SEIZURES – HYPOTHALAMIC VERSUS LIMBIC

	Hypothalamic	Limbic
Quality of laughter	Simple	Complex
Emotional correlate	Absent	Variable
Consciousness	Lost	Variable
Postictal amnesia	Yes	Variable
Autonomic dysfunction	Prominent	Variable
Associated behaviors	Rare	Running; crying
EEG	General spike wave	Focal temporal spikes

From "Pathological Disorders of Laughter" by M. S. Duchowny in Handbook of Humor Research. Applied Studies (Vol. 2, p. 100) by P. E. McGhee and J. H. Goldstein (Eds.), 1983, New York: Springer-Verlag. Copyright © 1983.

most frequent in diseases of both hemispheres interfering with cortico-hypothalamic and cortico-bulbar tracts" (p. 603). Alzheimer's disease and Pick's disease, also known as "presenile dementias," wherein the patient suffers from "early senility," are often accompanied by a change in the sense of humor. There is frequently an increased tendency to crack silly jokes, an inability to take serious matters seriously, and a kind of facetiousness in the patient's remarks. Furthermore, there are acute conditions, such as ethyl alcohol poisoning, that can result in inappropriate, excessive, or uncontrollable laughter.

It is generally clear in all these examples that the laughter does not genuinely reflect an underlying sense of joy or elation, that it is not under the patient's conscious control, and that it is inappropriate to the social situation in which it occurs. This implies that "healthy" or normal laughter does reflect a sense of mirth, is to some degree under cognitive control, and is appropriate to the situation.

LAUGHTER AS INDICATIVE OF HEALTH

"Laughter and humor have been hailed as good for the body because they restore homeostasis, stabilize blood pressure, oxygenate the blood, massage the vital organs, stimulate circulation, facilitate digestion, relax the system, and produce a feeling of well-being" (Keith-Spiegel, 1972, p. 5). Despite these often-repeated claims, there is remarkably little research to support them (Robinson, 1977, 1983). It is striking how few studies there are on the long-term medical or psychological consequences of laughter and humor. There are surely a dozen studies of pathological laughter in the neurological and psychiatric literature for every study of healthy laughter. Of course, there are many studies of humor and laughter--over a thousand by last count (Goldstein et al., 1977). There are studies that examine preference for one type of humor over another, studies of personality and intelligence and their relation to humor, and so on. These may prove useful in understanding the role of humor in health, but there is only a handful of studies that directly examine the long-term effects of humor or the physiological consequences of repeated or prolonged laughter.

Perhaps the best documented studies examine the correlates of laughter that can be measured most readily, namely, heart rate, skin conductance, and respiration. As early as the turn of the century, Angell and Thompson noted that "A hearty laugh, causing sudden and violent changes in the breathing curve, is accompanied by the sharpest and most marked vaso-dilation, as tested by capillary pulse drawing; though in one case the opposite effect of constriction was produced" (as quoted in Sully, 1902, p. 33).

Sully wrote in 1902 that the movements of laughter suddenly interrupt the rhythmic flow of respiration and that, because these spasms may temporarily weaken the organism, laughter might have important functions for the survival of the species. Otherwise, he argued, it would not have developed or persisted in its present form. This point was reiterated more recently by Fry (1977a).

Modern studies of the physiological effects of laughter tend to monitor heart rate or skin conductance (and in one study [Chapman, 1976] the tension of the frontalis muscle) just prior to, during, and immediately following laughter. In most of these studies, arousal or tension is found to increase during the presentation of a joke, cartoon, or riddle, to increase further during laughter itself, and to be followed by a decrease in autonomic arousal to or below the initial tonus level. This pattern has been observed repeatedly, using different measures of arousal and different kinds of humor-producing stimuli (e.g., Averill, 1969; Brody, 1983; Fry, 1979; Goldstein et al., 1975; Langevin & Day, 1972; Levi, 1963; McGhee, 1983; Sekeres & Clark, 1980; Svebak, 1977).

These studies tend to support those theories of laughter, such as Berlyne's (1972), that emphasize humor's tension-reducing (or, occasionally, tension-maintaining) properties. However, most of these studies do not characterize or explain the tension that is presumably reduced through laughter. In psychoanalytic theories, the tension is seen to be the product of unconscious impulses and repressions. In cognitive and social psychological theories, it is thought to result from interpersonal or intergroup conflict, from socially facilitated arousal, and may even be induced by what Berlyne has referred to as the "collative properties" of the joke itself. Collative variables include incongruity, novelty, and surprise. What is less in dispute is the typical finding in the psychophysiological studies of laughter that arousal, from whatever source or however interpreted, may be reduced through laughter.

A few studies have examined humor appreciation in brain-damaged patients (Brownell et al., 1983; Gardner et al., 1975; Prigatano & Pribram, 1981; Svebak, 1982). These studies lead to the conclusion that the right cerebral hemisphere is particularly critical in understanding and hence in appreciating humor.

All the studies referred to above have examined laughter only in experimental settings. Studies that examine the long-term consequences of chronic and repeated instances of laughter are nearly nonexistent (Mantell & Goldstein, 1985). For centuries laughter has been considered good exercise, and we know that laughter does not deplete the amount of oxygen in peripheral blood (Fry & Stoft, 1971). What we do not know is whether those who laugh regularly--many times a day, for example--are more healthy and better adjusted than those who do not.

Some of the recent popular books on humor imply that it will unquestionably lead to a healthy and prolonged life. Cousins (1979), for example, notes approvingly the longevity, sense of humor, and love for Baroque music of Albert Schweitzer and Pablo Casals. As far as I can determine from a cursory reading of biographies and recent necrologies, comedians and comic writers do not live any longer than other people, such as the writers of serious drama, artists, or politicians. It would be surprising if they did. These accounts fail to note that *the quality of life is surely enhanced by a sense of humor and not necessarily its duration.*

Laughter may actually be related in several ways to longevity. Fry (1979) notes that of the major heart attack risks that have been identified (cigarette smoking, obesity, diabetes, hypertension, stress, hypercholesteremia, lack of exercise), laughter is clearly related to the reduction of stress and to physical exercise, and may be related to hypertension. We know that the "Type A personality," characterized by seriousness, stress, concern with time, impatience, and hostility (Friedman & Rosenman, 1974), has a greater incidence of heart attack than the "Type B personality," in whom a sense of humor may displace anger, anxiety, and hostility (Mantell & Goldstein, 1985). We know, too, that people who are in a good mood, who are aroused as by adrenaline, are more apt to experience laughter and mirth than those who are unaroused or depressed, as by a tranquilizer such as chlorpromazine (Schachter & Wheeler, 1962).

In his introduction to Cousins's book, Rene Dubos (as well as Cousins and others) speculated that the newly-discovered pituitary secretions known as endorphins are related to laughter and its beneficial effects. Endorphins are chemically related to opiates, such as heroin and morphine, and act to reduce pain and instill feelings of elation. It has recently been shown, for instance, that long-distance runners experience a state of euphoria that is related to the amount of Beta-endorphin in their bloodstreams. Laughter may act on the endocrine system, the pituitary gland in particular, to produce not only a reduction in physical stress and pain, but a sense of euphoria as well. It should be emphasized, though, that data confirming the role of Beta-endorphin in laughter have yet to be collected.

SUMMARY AND CONCLUSIONS

The focus of this chapter has reflected what I offer as the present state of knowledge of the therapeutic effects of laughter. It has dealt more with anecdotes and proclamations than with data because there are a great many beliefs, both positive and negative, presented in the literature, and relatively little hard evidence concerning the effects of laughter and humor. Nevertheless, one can note a qualitative difference even in the kinds of unsubstantiated claims for laughter reported here. Those statements about the negative, even evil, consequences of laughter tend to be moral proclamations that emphasize the lack of decorum and "primitive, uncontrollable" nature of laughter. The focus of the critical arguments against laughter stems more from philosophy and early psychology than from medicine and physiology, even though there are statements by medieval and Victorian physicians on the inappropriateness and coarseness of laughter. Even these statements emanate from a philosophical rather than a purely medical position. Positive claims for laughter are more likely to stem from a physiological perspective and, in the 20th century, from a psychological one as well.

A review of the claims and evidence for and against laughter as therapeutic leads to the conclusion that laughter cannot be regarded as a single undifferentiated phenomenon. It does not always stem from the same psychological, physiological, or social conditions and does not always have the same psychological, physiological, or social consequences. A distinction must be made between: (a) healthy laughter and humor, which reflects a particular psychological outlook, a lack of tendentiousness (in the Freudian sense of expressing sexual and aggressive impulses), and an underlying sense of positive affect; and (b) the laughter that is reflective of anger and hostility or no affect at all. Techniques for distinguishing these varieties of laughter already exist, though the search for simpler identifying characteristics of different types of laughter and humor is needed. Just as medical students learn to identify the sounds of irregular heartbeats, perhaps they may become sensitized to the sounds of irregular patterns of laughter.

The weight of the psychophysiological evidence is in favor of laughter as a beneficial phenomenon among normal individuals. Laughter of brief duration is capable of reducing autonomic arousal. Whether there is chronically less anxiety, stress, or arousal among those whose laughter is more prolonged or frequent is not known. Recent efforts have been made to introduce humor among college students (Scheff et al., 1984) and in residential homes for the elderly (Andrus Volunteers, 1983) as a means of reducing stress. The results of these studies are still pending. The program of research by Lefcourt and Martin (1986) provides additional support for the role of humor in reducing stress.

Given the high cost of most biomedical research, it would require only a trivial amount of funding to study the long-term consequences of laughter and humor on health, longevity, and recovery from trauma, such as depression, coronary disease, or surgery. What is most striking about the literature on laughter and health is how far our convictions exceed our knowledge.

REFERENCES

Andrus Volunteers. (1983). *Humor: The Tonic You Can Afford*. Los Angeles: Andrus Gerontology Center, University of Southern California.

Averill, J. R. (1969). Autonomic response patterns during sadness and mirth. *Psychophysiology, 5*, 399-414.

Barclay, R. (1969). Apology for the true Christian divinity. In C. Hyers (Ed.), *Holy Laughter: Essays on Religion in the Comic Perspective*. New York: Seabury. (Original work published 1676)

Berlyne, D. E. (1972). Humor and its kin. In J. H. Goldstein & P. E. McGhee (Eds.). *The Psychology of Humor* (pp. 43-60). New York: Academic Press.

Black, D. W. (1982). Pathological laughter: A review of the literature. *Journal of Nervous & Mental Disease, 170,* 67-71.

Black, D. W. (1984). Laughter. *Journal of the American Medical Association, 252,* 2995-2998.

Brody, R. (1983). Anatomy of a laugh. *American Health,* Nov/Dec, 43-47.

Brownell, H. H., Michel, D., Powelson, J., & Gardner, H. (1983). Surprise but not coherence: Sensitivity to verbal humor in right-hemisphere patients. *Brain and Language, 18,* 20-27.

Chapman, A. J. (1976). Social aspects of humorous laughter. In A. J. Chapman & H. C. Foot (Eds.), *Humor and Laughter* (pp. 115-185). London: Wiley.

Cousins, N. (1979). *Anatomy of an Illness.* New York: Norton.

Duchowny, M. S. (1983). Pathological disorders of laughter. In P. E. McGhee & J. H. Goldstein (Eds.), *Handbook of Humor Research. Applied Studies* (Vol. 2, pp. 84-108). New York: Springer-Verlag.

Fine, G. A. (1983). Sociological approaches to the study of humor. In P. E. McGhee & J. H. Goldstein (Eds.), *Handbook of Humor Research. Basic Issues* (Vol 1., pp. 159-181). New York: Springer-Verlag.

Freud, S. (1928). Humour. *International Journal of Psychoanalysis, 9,* 1-6.

Freud, S. (1960). *Jokes and Their Relation to the Unconscious* (J. Strachey, Trans.). New York: Norton. (Original work published 1905)

Friedman, M., & Rosenman, R. H. (1974). *Type A Behavior and Your Heart.* New York: Knopf.

Fry, W. F. (1977a). The appeasement function of mirthful laughter. In A. J. Chapman & H. C. Foot (Eds.), *It's a Funny Thing, Humour* (pp. 23-26). Oxford: Pergamon Press.

Fry, W. F. (1977b). The respiratory components of mirthful laughter. *Journal of Biological Psychology, 19,* 39-50.

Fry, W. F. (1979). Humor and the cardiovascular system. In H. Mindess & J. Turek (Eds.), *The Study of Humor: Proceedings of the 2nd International Humor Conference* (pp. 55-61). Los Angeles: Antioch College.

Fry, W. F., & Stoft, P. E. (1971). Mirth and oxygen saturation levels of peripheral blood. *Psychotherapy & Psychosomatics, 19,* 76-84.

Gardner, H., Ling, P. K., Flamm, L., & Silverman, J. (1975). Comprehension and appreciation of humorous material following brain damage. *Brain, 98,* 399-412.

Gascon, G. G., & Lombroso, C. T. (1971). Epileptic (gelastic) laughter. *Epilepsia, 12,* 63-76.

Goldstein, J. H. (1976). Theoretical notes on humor. *Journal of Communication, 26,* 104-112.

Goldstein, J. H., Harman, J., McGhee, P. E., & Karasik, R. (1975). Test of an information-processing model of humor: Physiological response changes during problem- and riddle-solving. *Journal of General Psychology, 92,* 59-68.

Goldstein, J. H., McGhee, P. E., Smith, J. R., Chapman, A. J., & Foot, H. C. (1977). Humour, laughter and comedy: A bibliography of empirical and nonempirical analyses in the English language. In A. J. Chapman & H. C. Foot (Eds.), *It's a Funny Thing, Humour* (pp. 469-507). Oxford: Pergamon Press.

Hurd, R. (1811). *The Works of Richard Hurd.* London: Cadell & Davis.

Hyers, C. (1981). *The Comic Vision and the Christian Faith.* New York: Pilgrim Press.

Ironside, R. (1956). Disorders of laughter due to brain lesions. *Brain, 79,* 589-609.

Joubert, L. (1979). *Treatise on Laughter* (G. DeRocher, Trans.) University, AL: University of Alabama Press. (Original work published in 1579)

Kane, T. R., Suls, J. M., & Tedeschi, J. T. (1977). Humour as a tool of social interaction. In A. J. Chapman & H. C. Foot (Eds.), *It's a Funny Thing, Humour* (pp. 13-16). Oxford: Pergamon Press.

Kant, I. (1790). *Critique of Judgment.* Berlin: Lagarde.

Keith-Spiegel, P. (1972). Early conceptions of humor: Varieties and issues. In J. H. Goldstein & P. E. McGhee (Eds.), *The Psychology of Humor* (pp. 4-39). New York: Academic Press.

Langevin, R., & Day, H. I. (1972). Physiological correlates of humor. In J. H. Goldstein & P. E. McGhee (Eds.), *The Psychology of Humor* (pp. 129-142). New York: Academic Press.

Lefcourt, H. M., & Martin, R. A. (1986). *Humor and Life Stress: Antidote to Adversity.* New York: Springer-Verlag.

Levi, L. (1963). The urinary output of adrenalin and noradrenalin during pleasant and unpleasant emotional states. *Psychosomatic Medicine, 27,* 403-419.

Levine, J., & Redlich, F. C. (1955). Failure to understand humor. *Psychoanalytic Quarterly, 24,* 560-572.

Mantell, M., & Goldstein, J. H. (1985). *Humour and the Coronary-Prone Behavior Pattern.* Paper presented at 5th International Conference on Humour, Cork, Ireland.

Martin, R. A., & Lefcourt, H. M. (1983). Sense of humor as a moderator of the relation between stressors and mood. *Journal of Personality and Social Psychology, 45,* 1313-1324.

Martineau, W. H. (1972). A model of the social functions of humor. In J. H. Goldstein & P. E. McGhee (Eds.), *The Psychology of Humor* (pp. 101-125). New York: Academic Press.

McGhee, P. E. (1983). The role of arousal and hemispheric lateralization in humor. In P. E. McGhee & J. H. Goldstein (Eds.), *Handbook of Humor Research. Basic Issues* (Vol. 1, pp. 13-37). New York: Springer-Verlag.

Meier, G. F. (1947). *Thoughts on Jesting.* Austin: University of Texas Press. (Original work published in 1794)

Mitchell, A. (1905). *About Dreaming, Laughing and Blushing.* Edinburgh: William Green.

Moody, R. A. (1978). *Laugh after Laugh.* Jacksonville, FL: Headwaters Press.

Mulcaster, R. (1887). *Positions.* London: Bernard & Quick. (Original work published in 1581)

Paskind, H. A. (1932). Effect of laughter on muscle tone. *Archives of Neurology & Psychiatry, 28,* 623-628.

Pollio, H. R., Mers, R., & Lucchesi, W. (1972). Humor, laughter, and smiling: Some preliminary observations of funny behaviors. In J. H. Goldstein & P. E. McGhee (Eds.), *The Psychology of Humor* (pp. 211-239). New York: Academic Press.

Prigatano, G. P., & Pribram, K. H. (1981). Humor and episodic memory following frontal versus posterior brain lesions. *Perceptual & Motor Skills, 53,* 999-1006.

Robinson, V. M. (1977). *Humor and the Health Professions.* Thorofare, NJ: Slack.

Robinson, V. M. (1983). Humor and health. In P. E. McGhee & J. H. Goldstein (Eds.), *Handbook of Humor*

Research. Applied Studies (Vol. 2, pp. 109-128). New York: Springer-Verlag.

Safranek, R., & Schill, T. (1982). Coping with stress: Does humor help? *Psychological Reports, 51,* 222.

Schachter, S., & Wheeler, L. (1962). Epinephrine, chlorpromazine, and amusement. *Journal of Abnormal and Social Psychology, 65,* 121-128.

Scheff, T., White, S., Camarena, P., Nuzum, N., Kosh, S., & White, C. (1984). *Laughter and Stress.* Santa Barbara: The Laughter Project, University of California.

Schill, T., & O'Laughlin, S. (1984). Humor preference and coping with stress. *Psychological Reports, 55,* 309-310.

Scogin, F. R., & Merbaum, M. (1983). Humorous stimuli and depression: An examination of Beck's premise. *Journal of Clinical Psychology, 39,* 165-169.

Sekeres, R. E., & Clark, W. R. (1980). Verbal, heart rate, and skin conductance responses to sexual cartoons. *Psychological Reports, 47,* 1227-1232.

Spencer, H. (1860). The physiology of laughter. *Macmillan's Magazine. 1,* 395-402.

Sully, J. (1902). *Essays on Laughter.* New York: Longmans, Green.

Svebak, S. (1977). Some characteristics of resting respiration as predictors of laughter. In A. J. Chapman & H. C. Foot (Eds.), *It's a Funny Thing, Humour* (pp. 101-104). Oxford: Pergamon Press.

Svebak, S. (1982). The effect of mirthfulness upon amount of discordant right-left occipital EEG alpha. *Motivation and Emotion, 6,* 133-143.

Vasey, G. (1877). *The Philosophy of Laughter and Smiling* (2nd ed.). London: Burns.

Walsh, J. J. (1928). *Laughter and Health.* New York: Appleton.

HUMOR IN PSYCHOTHERAPY:
A SHIFT TO A
NEW PERSPECTIVE

Barbara Killinger

In this chapter, Dr. Barbara Killinger raises significant theoretical issues related to the psychotherapeutic uses of humor. These are issues derived, in large part, from her original research in this area. Her clinical approach, as delineated in this chapter, emphasizes gentleness and therapeutic sensitivity to patient needs. She underscores the importance of the therapist's maturity as a moderating personality variable in using humor, helping thus to insure that humor will not be used carelessly but rather in a way that is beneficial for patients. Dr. Killinger's technique of "verbal picture painting" may be of particular interest for verbally oriented therapists who prefer the palace of the palate to the pallet of the palette.

Dr. Killinger is a clinical psychologist in private practice in Toronto, Canada. She is the author of the chapter, "The Place of Humour in Adult Psychotherapy" in A. J. Chapman and H. C. Foot (Eds.), It's a Funny Thing, Humour (1977).

❋   ❋   ❋

THEORETICAL PERSPECTIVE

Laughter erupting and floating out of the therapy room--laughter and tears, both ends of the emotional spectrum--what could be more natural? Or so I thought. As a psychology intern I became fascinated with the role humor was playing in psychotherapy, especially with two deeply disturbed, but very bright patients who had buried their sense of humor (Killinger, 1977). Both lacked the will to live and had attempted suicide several times;

previous psychotherapy had failed to produce significant changes. The rediscovery of their capacity to receive and initiate humor in the sessions seemed to be a turning point in their search for health. The objectivity gained by viewing their world through humor allowed positive attitudes towards life situations to emerge.

Through these and similar experiences, it became apparent that the humor I had spontaneously begun using in psychotherapy appeared to release clients from a narrow, ego-centered focus while loosening rigid, circular thinking. Thought processes that had become ruminatively stale and closed were interrupted through humor, and new, fresh perspectives emerged.

Imagine my surprise when I read Kubie's (1971) paper on "The Destructive Potential of Humor in Psychotherapy." Counter to the experiences of this budding therapist, Kubie warned that the use of humor by the psychiatrist is potentially destructive to the therapeutic relationship, especially when used by inexperienced therapists in the early stages of psychoanalysis. Kubie's chief objections centered around therapist humor diverting or blocking free association, causing patient confusion as to whether the therapist is serious, mocking, joking, or masking his or her own hostilities. Further, Kubie stated that humor can be a form of self-display or exhibitionism, or a defense against dealing with psychological pain, and can blunt self-observing and correcting mechanisms in the therapist. When humor is at the patient's expense, Kubie warned, it may be seen as mockery, no matter how serious, compassionate, or educational the intent. Angry feelings may be blocked, and the patient may feel constrained to join in to prove his or her own sense of humor, or defend against accepting the importance of the symptoms to evade the acceptance of help. Only as the patient gains a deeper understanding and insight into himself or herself and domination over unconscious processes can an experienced therapist use a gentle and sympathetic humor to facilitate the incorporation of new insights. Kubie (1971) stated that "even if it could be demonstrated beyond a question that the use of humor *late* in therapy is safe in the hands of the experienced, how can the inexperienced be dissuaded from imitating too early so easy, seductive, and self-gratifying a device?" (p. 866).

Stimulated by this striking contrast between my own observations and Kubie's strong warnings, I began a review of the literature on humor. This search revealed almost no empirical data specifically on how humor is used in psychotherapy, although humor was acknowledged to be useful and facilitative to the therapeutic process (Poland, 1971; Rosenheim, 1974). Most experimental studies made use of written jokes or cartoons, and results could not be generalized to all humor. The few humor and psychotherapy studies, although interesting and imaginative, were often anecdotal and lacking in methodological rigor, or failed to provide any sound theoretical base (Killinger, 1976). Kaneko (1971) had developed a research model for examining the role of humor in psychotherapy, but no research had been done to test the model.

Subsequently, I decided to dedicate my doctoral study (Killinger, 1976) to a clarification of whether the use of humor by the therapist is a facilitative skill, or one that serves destructive tendencies by inhibiting or blocking the therapeutic process. Early and later therapy and inexperienced and experienced therapist variables were introduced. Humor incidents (laughter and nonlaughter) and randomly-selected nonhumorous control statements were identified, extracted, coded, and analyzed by trained judges from auditory tapes of 85 sessions of ongoing psychotherapy. These judges also recorded frequency of humor used by each therapist. Statements were assessed on therapist's intent and facilitativeness of outcome for the client by pairs of independent judges who were blind to the purpose or subject under study. Because the use of humor is usually spontaneous rather than premeditative, "intent" was used in its sense of purpose or objective to accomplish or attain. *Intent* was assessed in terms of (a) Direction of Communication (other-directed vs. self-focused), (b) Manner of Delivery (nondefensive vs. defensive), and (c) Content of Communication (relevant vs. irrelevant). *Outcome* was evaluated from client's statements after the therapist's intervention and was judged on (a) Content (whether client exploration and understanding was facilitated as a result of the humorous intervention), and (b) Attitude of Client towards the Therapist (whether a positive attitude was facilitated based on content and voice quality judgments). The study's design is described in detail elsewhere (Killinger, 1977).

During this empirical investigation I developed a special system of humor classification. Initially I defined humor in its broadest sense, inclusive of wit and humor creation. Its occurrence was identified behaviorally by affect and defined as "laughter humor": laughter behavior or verbal report of amusement by either participant in response to the therapist's verbalization. The therapist's humorous intervention could take the form of one or more of the seven categories adapted from those identified by Landis and Ross (1933). Additional descriptions from Koestler (1974) were chosen to clarify each category. Kaneko's (1971) identification of humor "by description" included all humor techniques, and these were entered in brackets under appropriate categories. It was emphasized, however, that an incident may fit under several categories or descriptions. The following categories proved all-inclusive and reliable:

1. *Exaggeration or simplification.* An over- or understatement of fact, thoughts, feelings, sensations, and so on, often used for emphasis (i.e., dramatization, imitation, mock seriousness, nonsense, absurdity, slapstick).
2. *Incongruity.* Where any two frames of reference are made to yield a comic effect by associating them or hooking them together, usually with the infusion of an impulse, however faint, of aggression or apprehension (i.e., form vs. content; undertones vs. overtones; metaphorical vs. literal meaning; professional vs. common sense logic; trivial vs. exalted; incompatible codes of behavior or rule--such as play on words, ideas, puns, irony, satire, paradox, mock seriousness).
3. *Unexpectedness or surprise.* Some surprising fact, thought, idea, or feeling is presented that is different from or opposite to what the listener expected to hear (i.e., play on words, ideas, incredulous disbelief, analogy, metaphor, dramatization, paradox).
4. *Revelation of truth.* A person projects himself or herself into the situation in question with a consequent exposure of his or her own unrevealed thoughts, feelings, and ideas to the listener (i.e., metaphor, analogy, allusion, dramatization).
5. *Superiority or ridicule.* A person feels superior and consequently puts others down by mocking their appearance or behavior. Superiority feelings result from seeing the inability of others to handle situations adequately that appear simple to the

observer; or from perceiving others as deformed, foreign, or different, thus deviating from the accepted norms of society. A mixture of aggression and apprehension may take the form of malice, contempt, the veiled cruelty of condescension, or the absence of sympathy with the victim; or it may be sublimated and no longer conscious or evident as in highly sophisticated, civilized humor (i.e., teasing, joshing, bantering, poking fun, mimicry, joking, laughing at oneself, imitation, dramatization, satire, irony, derision, ethnic or in-group stories, regional stories).

6. *Repression or release.* A person may release tension aroused by thoughts and feelings around subjects such as fear or sex, or a person may release feelings such as pleasure and happiness that he or she is experiencing concerning the listener's situation (i.e., laughing at oneself, hostile joke, dirty joke, sexual joke, smut, obscenity).

7. *Word play.* A person uses nonsensical logic, comic verse, or play on words, such as alliterations, puns, or rhyming (i.e., punning, nonsense, foolishness, mock seriousness, clowning, smoke screen--casting everything in comic form, slapstick, absurdity, double entendre, farce, accident--or slip-of-tongue).

My study's strictly behavioral definition of humor proved incomplete. While listening to therapy tapes to be used for training raters to recognize humor statements, I became aware that this definition failed to capture a more subtle, creative, clever type of humor where there was no overt, audible laughter response. It was hypothesized later that smiling could occur as a response that would not be detected by auditory tapes.

A "nonlaughter" category of humor was therefore devised where one of the seven categories of humor was used in the form of a figure of speech, or some clever, unusual, or original phrasing of words that allowed one to play with the ideas or thoughts presented. Such statements were judged as humorous by the criteria of originality, emphasis, or economy devised by Koestler (1974) to evaluate whether humor was good, bad, or indifferent. Therapists' statements were further assessed by the following criteria:

1. *Originality.* If the humor provides the essential element of surprise that cuts across our expectations by its use of originality, uniqueness, or cleverness.
2. *Emphasis.* If it has tension-accumulating effects through various techniques of suggestive emphasis, such as exaggeration, simplification, repetition, or implosion.
3. *Economy.* If it has implicit hints instead of explicit statements, and calls for "extrapolation, interpolation, and transposition" of the material.

Findings from the study (Killinger, 1976) showed no significant differences in humor frequency related to therapist experience, suggesting that experience-level may not be the key factor in determining how often humor is used. Rather, the level of maturity as well as developmental and environmental influences may be more important considerations in using humor. The absence of significant differences between early and later therapy occasions was an unexpected finding as more humor was anticipated in later therapy sessions. Two possible explanations could be postulated with respect to this finding: (a) the interval between early and late may not have been great enough, or (b) therapists may have been less cautious with university students of above-average intelligence and sophistication. In this setting the accepted norm of humor appreciation could argue for a more consistent use of humor by the therapist.

Therapist *Intent* results supported the hypothesis that therapists focused on clients, stayed with the topic of the interaction, and communicated in a nondefensive manner. This would suggest that humor is effectively used to convey ideas or intention. Humor as a facilitative tool to communicate a positive therapist-client attitude also received support with no significant differences in *Outcome* Attitude means. Similarly, Content mean scores also registered on the facilitative end of the scale, showing positive client exploration after the humor statement. Although the author has never argued that humor is more facilitative than any other effective therapeutic technique such as empathy, genuineness, and so forth, the study's results indicated that therapist nonhumorous "control statements" judged for Content (whether client exploration and understanding was facilitated) showed mean scores significantly more positive than those for "laughter humor."

An examination of nonhumorous control statements revealed that approximately one-third involved questions, whereas far fewer humor statements contained questions. It may be that more directive, purposeful, clarifying, or inquiring types of statements, rather than statements cloaked in humor, were interpreted by raters as making a more definite contribution to client exploration. Because questions can be very facilitative in furthering exploration, it was suspected that the effectiveness of questions might be largely responsible for the relatively high Content ratings on control statements. Further analyses showed that questions, questions plus statements, or both combined, compared to nonquestions, did not differentially affect humor and control Content ratings. However, Attitude scores showed significant differences. Humor with no questions added produced a more positive rating than control statements containing questions plus statements, whereas straight question mean ratings compared favorably with nonquestions in facilitativeness.

It is possible that the form the communication takes, be it humorous or nonhumorous, question or statement, may not be as important as the way it is delivered, for example, voice quality of the therapist. Also, the most frequently used technique of superiority or ridicule that usually produced "laughter humor" and rarely was used in the more purposeful or metaphoric "nonlaughter humor" was found to be less facilitative than mean scores for all occasions of laughter humor. This may have affected the Outcome results, and would suggest that a cautionary note would be indicated against the use of this technique to further client exploration.

What theoretical differences lie behind the categories of laughter and nonlaughter humor? When do people laugh, smile, or remain silent in response to humor? Koestler's (1974) separation of thought and emotion may explain why overt laughter, a giggle, or a smile may or may not be a response to the more subtle, intellectual type of humor. The re-creative act of perceiving such humor often forces one to leap mentally from one associative context to a mutually incompatible frame of reference (i.e., "A masochist is a person who likes a cold shower in the morning so he takes a hot one" [p. 5]). Emotions cannot suddenly change direction to keep step with reasoning when a sudden switch of ideas leads to a different

27

type of logic. "It is emotion deserted by thought that is discharged in laughter" (p. 7). Koestler states that most theorists would agree that an element of aggressiveness or apprehension always underlies the emotions discharged in laughter. However, these feelings tend to be sublimated or masked in the subtler types of humor, and malice or an absence of sympathy may be combined with affection in friendly teasing.

Koestler's theories suggest an energy model for determining whether a person will laugh aloud or smile as a response to humor. The amount of energy and tension invested and built-up within the listener depends in part on whether content is intellectual and subtle, or emotion-laden and blatant. Intellect rather than emotion is more involved when problem-solving skills are being taxed to expose an incongruity, or transpose a scene to fit into one's own frame of reference. Thus when intellectual energy is required for interpretation, emotional energies may be insufficient to trigger the laughter response.

Yet another factor is whether the client senses enough trust to feel free from threat to participate in the humor. The therapist's intentions or motives in delivering a covert humorous message must be perceived to be in the client's best interests. Otherwise, fear and distrust will override the humorous element in the message, and tension will prevail. In my study, therapists struggling to capture the essence of what the client was feeling or thinking often seemed to keep a certain distance emotionally in order to gain a perspective on the client's experiencing. They used a more intellectual type of humor in which objects or happenings were used to describe a person's situation. A patient was expounding on her ambivalence around the future of her love affair:

Therapist: OK. I'm feeling there's an expectation on myself. I can let myself off the hook, but...(*pause*) it's not quite like a ping-pong ball for you. "I hope that things get better. I'm afraid things won't get better. I think things will get better. I don't think things will get better." You bounce back and forth from a hope to a fear!

At times the clients also seemed to keep emotionally distant as listeners who were judging whether the therapist really understood their thoughts and feelings. With energies absorbed in trust issues, clients would be less likely to enter fully into humor, and laughter would be less likely to occur as a result. Furthermore, the issue of whether a client is physically ill, fatigued, depressed, severely disturbed, or psychotic has serious implications for whether he or she will feel like laughing, or even understand the humorous intent of the story.

An important theoretical question is whether or not effective therapists use humor in psychotherapy. Although humor as a therapeutic tool has come under empirical investigation only recently, a positive sense of humor has long been accepted as indicative of good emotional health, and indeed a sign of maturity. For Freud, the ability to produce or appreciate humor was seen as a condition of maturity, thus mirroring the triumph of the pleasure principle and narcissism over stressful environmental situations (O'Connell et al., 1969). Because the most effective therapist is said to be the person who possesses the quality of maturity (Carkhuff & Berenson, 1967; Rogers, 1961), a mature therapist is more likely to use humor naturally in the therapeutic setting as well as in other environments. The aspects of maturity that are of special relevance to humor are the ability of mature individuals to laugh at themselves, accept their own limitations and those of others, and view their personal weaknesses from a humorous standpoint (Heath, 1965).

Therapeutic effectiveness is closely tied in with other qualities of maturity. Mature persons possess a broad perspective based on life experiences that enables them to view their own and others' problems in a larger context, to be open and flexible, and to be able to see alternate points of view. Because the mature person is an integrated individual who has attained self-acceptance, self-respect, self-trust, and self-discipline, he or she is usually able to communicate these values to others (Freeman & Greenwald, 1961; Heath, 1965). I believe that whether humor is used in a facilitative, therapeutic way depends more on the level of maturity of the therapist than on his or her level of clinical experience as suggested by Kubie (1971). This maturity also safeguards the client by insuring that humor will be used therapeutically.

The effective therapist suspends his or her own interests in favor of understanding the client's perceptions of the problem he or she is experiencing (Carkhuff & Berenson, 1967; Rogers, 1961). Therefore any humor used by an effective therapist is likely to be conveying a message to the client, rather than be focused on the therapist's concerns. The context of humor is also expected to center on the client's situation, rather than diverting attention away. The mature therapist's own ego strength and lack of defensiveness enable him or her to use humor in a relaxed and supportive way to convey genuine interest, understanding, and concern. There is no need to be defensive or ridiculing, and the therapist may share personal weaknesses or doubt in a humorous vein.

Humor seems best described as an interactive personal experience that occurs between client and therapist. Its potential lies in its utilization as a tool to enable people to view their problems from a new perspective. As Rosenheim (1974) suggests, humor serves to broaden clients' self-awareness by improving their ability to view themselves and others more objectively and to develop fuller affective reactions. When clients experience emotional difficulties or feel "stuck" in a situation, they are often unable to problem-solve effectively and seem incapable of laughing at themselves or their situation. Consequently, they perceive their environment as overwhelmingly serious and stressful. The element of surprise in humor, coupled with its unpremeditated quality, encourages a progressive shift in focus. This shift may then serve to unlock or loosen the rigid, repetitive view that individuals often hold regarding their particular situation.

TECHNIQUE

The creative and spontaneous development of humor by the therapist can capture and crystallize the essence or meaning within the immediate client-therapist interchange. The type of humor under discussion here bears little resemblance to the formal joke, comic routine, or favorite funny story. It is closer to Mindess's (1971) broad definition of humor as an exceptional frame of mind, a way of perceiving and experiencing life. Mindess suggests that humor permits us to gain objectivity and freedom from our own conforming, stabilizing systems of self-control that have distanced us from our authentic, spontaneous selves.

For humor to be appreciated, it is acknowledged in the literature (Hickson, 1977) that the listener must be able to role-play or empathize with the characters depicted in the humorous setting. Nonetheless, psychic distance must also be achieved lest the characters and setting depicted be 'too close to home' or the topic 'too hot to handle.' In psychoanalytic terms, one must be free to release repressed impulses after seeing the point of the story or its cleverness without undue anxiety being aroused to hinder the reception of the humorous intent.

In psychotherapy I have found that verbal picture painting or framing an image, using one of the seven aforementioned humor techniques, helps create the necessary psychic distance. In the process of active listening and attempting to understand what clients are thinking or saying about themselves, the therapist can focus the intervention at a significant point by creating a humorous word picture to frame the essence of the clients' dynamics. The humorous interpretation hopefully serves to shift clients from a fixed view of themselves or their situation, while simultaneously reinforcing the *now* by expanding on what clients are saying about themselves. By focusing the subject matter of the humor onto objects, people, or situations slightly removed from the client, this change of focus can be achieved without being "too close" and raising undue anxiety in the client. Any one or a combination of humor techniques such as exaggeration, implosion, incongruity, and so on can be incorporated or woven into the framed image. Originality, emphasis, and economy are the criteria used to determine whether the figure of speech or original phrasing of words is humorous. The humorous intervention may simply be a metaphor or an interesting word picture.

An incident from psychotherapy illustrates this technique. Lisa (a pseudonym) was becoming aware of the resentment and anger that had built up within her after sacrificing her own ambitions to support husband John's (a pseudonym) lengthy schooling, and now John was considering separation. Lisa articulated her wish to return to school, and her ambivalent feelings of guilt as John was not finished, money was tight, and this decision might alienate him further. She had always felt that John was more important than herself, and his job more vital than hers. In discussing whether her ambitions would necessarily be detrimental to John, she thought not, but said that they do compete with each other all the time. I reminded her of how she had earlier described herself as placing John up on a pedestal from the beginning of their relationship.

Therapist: (*teasing*) Are you trying to climb up on that private pedestal? (*client laughs*) Pretty precarious on that pint-sized platform! (*therapist laughs*) As you were talking, I had an image of you valiantly trying to struggle aboard, with poor John jiggling like crazy and almost tottering off! (*both laugh*)

Using this analogy in a later session, we discussed whether she was ready to stop worrying about hanging on to pedestals and competitions from the past, and instead start establishing her own security. I commented, "Not too many roots on that pedestal!" *(both laugh)*

Another client was talking about his denial of the reality of life.

Therapist: When you established...for example, you told me once that she's got crazy legs...Is it possible that you said to yourself: "Jeezus, I can't marry this woman because she's got crazy legs --what the hell am I doing here?" That would be an example.

Client: Yeah, that's what I thought! (Killinger, 1976, p. 108)

PERTINENT USES

What happens when the therapist through humor paints and projects these verbal images onto the screen of the client's mind? First, this type of humor feeds into a set or a readiness to learn. The client in seeking out therapy is exhibiting intrinsic motivation for self-actualization (Maslow, 1970), or a need for competence or mastery (White, 1959), whichever label one chooses. Such motivation to learn, if satisfied, energizes and patterns new behavior. Second, verbal image humor attracts the client's attention by its use of novelty, surprise, and fresh objectivity. Such new and unexpected ideas help shift typical thinking, which is often within a very narrow frame of reference. Third, the uncertainty, complexity, novelty, and possible ambiguity built into the therapist's humor introduce tension in the listener until the point of the humor can be resolved. When focused energy is released through resolution of the story's punch line, shared laughter often results. Fourth, laughter or enjoyment is contagious, and the pleasure and warmth created from shared amusements and insights can build a rapport or bridge between the two personalities that helps strengthen the therapeutic alliance. The coupling of humor with insight around particular issues under discussion establishes a positive link of association in the mind. Using the previous illustration, the next time Lisa finds herself competing or comparing herself with John, bells may ring in her mind, and the "pedestal" image may emerge to remind her that "there I go again!" Finally, if the therapist through humor successfully models a more expansive, exploratory, and creative approach to viewing life situations from a humorous perspective, the client is also likely to seek out and try such pleasurable patterns or channels or thinking. The client's humor and sense of fun usually emerge and develop in conjunction with his or her ability to shift focus and capture new insights. This in turn allows for a more expansive and exploratory cognitive style.

Spontaneous humor that captures and crystallizes the essence of therapeutic interactions can be facilitative for clients throughout psychotherapy, a view that runs counter to Kubie's (1971) warnings. My study (Killinger, 1976) showed no significant differences in the frequency or effectiveness of humor used by therapists differing in clinical experience in early and later therapy sessions. My clinical experience, however, shows humor to be most effective when the client is close to a major insight or breakthrough. The distance and objectivity that humor creates allow crucial self-perceptions to be challenged in a safe, supportive atmosphere. Direct confrontations, on the other hand, too often are perceived as threatening and are responded to by the client's defense mechanisms.

In the early stages of therapy, clients are often absorbed in issues of trust as they determine whether the therapist is genuinely interested and caring. Clients must therefore decide how to receive a humorous remark, and their confidence in the therapist's motivation ought not be tested too intensely before an acceptance of the therapist's helping role has been established. In addition, the client experiencing emotional turmoil cannot immediately have access to his or her sense of humor. It often lies dormant or takes the form of self-ridicule or sarcasm. At times, the client is too self-absorbed to listen.

Because the therapist does not know how humor has been perceived in the client's past experience, it is best to proceed gradually and carefully. Short humorous comments around the statements clients are making about their situation seem more appropriate in early therapy rather than the more purposive verbal image humor used to build towards major insights. Both humorous approaches require spontaneity and affective warmth from the therapist. Energy, as well, is required in order to create a humorous verbal word picture. When the therapist is tired or straining to follow the client's exploration, he or she may choose not to use this type of humor. I find myself content with metaphoric interpretations with no humorous intent when energy is low for whatever reason.

Who benefits from this type of humor? Most clients seem to benefit and accept the helping nature of the humorous approach as trust develops, and the therapeutic bond is strengthened by the shared laughter and insight. Therapists also benefit from a humorous attitude, especially when involved in intensive therapy with disturbed persons or during discouraging low points when the client seems stuck and not motivated enough to move. Energy invested in seeking fresh insights can help ease one's own discomfort, impatience, or discouragement during a difficult session. Humor can therefore also have "therapist survival" value.

Although the positive aspects of humor are stressed in the literature, humor can also be aggressive, sarcastic, and cutting. The use of the superiority or ridicule technique in particular is often a risk-taking venture. Although the effective therapist does take risks in an effort to urge clients to stretch and grow, one cautionary note is in order. Sarcasm and vindictive ridicule or mimicry that fall within the superiority technique have no place in psychotherapy. This type of negative, black humor is dangerous in that it can lead to misunderstanding and blocking. Perhaps Kubie's (1971) warnings refer to the negative aspects of the superiority technique, rather than to the more positive teasing and joshing or to humor in general. In my study (Killinger, 1976) this type of humor was invariably followed by what was termed a 'recovery statement' by the therapist. When the client reacted with a nervous, anxious laugh in response to superiority humor statements, the concerned therapist would soften his or her approach or defensively rationalize his or her sarcastic behavior. Attention was thus diverted away from the client's stream of thought, and any spontaneity or creative efforts to assist the client were drowned in rhetoric. An example follows:

Therapist: OK. I guess the reality of the situation is you're feeling really attracted to her.
Client: Part of it is I don't like to delude myself. (*in a self-righteous tone*)
Therapist: (*long pause*) You're doing your Hamlet thing though! (*sigh*)
Client: Owww. That was a cat! (*laughing*)
Therapist: That bad?
Client: Owww! (*more laughter*)
Therapist: That's what I call mine. I call it my Hamlet procrastination that keeps me from doing anything. (Therapist goes on to explain his own relevant foibles and feelings around them.) (1976, pp. 111-112)

Such a recovery statement where the therapist softens his approach after the initial sarcastic humor may explain why the superiority or ridicule category means in the study (1976) had only slightly lower ratings for Intent and Outcome evaluations relative to the other two most frequently used techniques--revelation or truth, and repression or release. One might have expected a greater negative difference. The client may have become more positive towards the therapist and have felt freer to explore his problem because of the therapist's sensitivity to his reactions. In any case, beginning therapists might be encouraged to master the recovery statement technique when initially risking the use of humor techniques. By showing sensitivity to any anxious reactions by the client, they can make amends for risking too far by clarifying their intentions. Self-revelation techniques as used in the example may save the day, but the focus of attention will be drawn away from the client's issues. As noted earlier, the superiority or ridicule category was the most frequently used (21.7%) in the study and resulted in laughter on 90.9% of the occasions. This technique was used rarely in the more deliberate planned development of humor where the therapist was often building on a creative idea using originality, emphasis, or brevity.

CLINICAL PRESENTATION

Verbal picture painting using humor techniques creates a situation in which necessary psychic distance can be achieved, while reinforcing the present and keeping clients focused on their own problems. To illustrate, client David (a pseudonym) was beginning to develop insight into the stresses he inflicted on himself by being a busybody. He was overinvolved in people's affairs, saw others as too dependent on him, and consequently felt resentful and put-upon. At the same time, he was anxiously trying to control and be involved in every situation at home, at work, and with his extended family. As David was coming to this realization, I framed a scene and verbally described the picture I had of him. I explained that, in my imagination, I saw him as Charles Atlas, standing tall and firmly planted before us with his huge, bulging, flexed muscles. Perched precariously on top of each biceps sat his worry-wart mom, his complaining but long-suffering wife, his condescending boss, and his "free-advice" seeking buddy-- all pushing and shoving to stay aboard these strong, supportive shoulders. I got up and pretended to stagger across the room under the weight of it all! We both howled, and David said, "That's me!" He then joined in with other things I had forgotten to add to the load. When he told his wife later, they both "laughed themselves silly." David used this image to help tackle the anxiety he experienced while driving his car. The bladder control problems that had brought him into therapy would begin to emerge as worries mounted, and trips were therefore difficult. The mental reappearance of the image apparently served to break him up again. The absurdity of this implosive scene using exaggeration and ridicule techniques shifted his focus from being a "victim" when, in effect, he was controlling others by problem-solving for them. The bladder problem disappeared as he became more relaxed and learned to problem-solve for himself rather than see others' responsibilities as his own. An appreciation of his playful, fun-loving nature developed as he too learned to see the ludicrous side of the situations he created. The aforementioned intervention occurred when the therapeutic relationship was well-established and was used to facilitate insight into key issues that the client was exploring.

In contrast to the more slapstick type of humor used above, a more subtle, brief, and metaphoric humor incident follows that uses the unexpectedness or surprise technique of humor. Karen (a pseudonym), whose bisexual husband had recently left her for a young man, was describing how she and her husband thought alike, and liked the same things. He even bought all her clothes, which apparently was fine with her. Karen seldom disagreed with her husband about most things, and if she did, remained quiet to avoid any confrontations. Thinking about the almost symbiotic relationship that Karen was describing, I asked, "Have you ever thought of yourself as a shadow? *(client laughs)* Shadows are liable to get stepped on, or fade away when the sun goes in!" We went on to talk about her losing herself in the "following" role, and about what this dependency had done to the husband. Karen then remembered that her husband had told her in a recent conversation that he felt close to losing himself and no longer knew who he was. Ego boundaries were obviously very blurred for both of them. The shadow image clarified or highlighted this perception and was referred to by the client in later sessions as her insight broadened.

The last example uses exaggeration and implosion to help the client handle a difficult situation. John (a pseudonym) was deeply depressed and had been oversleeping. He was thus often late and ineffectual at work, and understandably worried about losing his job. He was complaining about his new boss, who was obsessive about neatness, and apparently went around the office at lunch hour to put all the papers and files on people's desk into the center drawers. John was furious at this invasion of privacy, but not in a position to confront his boss. He was beet red in the face, ranting and raving about this man. I interrupted:

Therapist: I've got your man all dressed up!

Client: *(surprised)* I beg your pardon? *(puzzled look on his face)*

Therapist: I've got a sergeant major's outfit on him. Great, old-fashioned tall plumed hat with feather, epaulets on his shoulders, jodhpurs, spurs, sword clanking by his side--the whole deal! I can just see him jump up, go to the coat closet, and climb into his uniform the minute you guys leave for lunch. He straight-

37

ens up full height, clicks to attention, and starts to march around the office until he arrives at *your* desk. He stands towering over it and utters a joyful AHA!, and then proceeds to gather up all your papers and gleefully shoves them into your center drawer! (*client guffaws*) With that picture superimposed in your imagination over reality, you may never be able to see that man or what he does quite the same way again! (*both chuckle*). And thank heavens!

SYNTHESIS

Although personality and maturity may predispose one to a sense of humor, conscious efforts can facilitate this attribute. As therapists, we can model or teach a philosophy of humor when we risk using humor to challenge our conceits and lower our own defenses. Through example, we can invite our clients to laugh at themselves, be more flexible and spontaneous, and gain a more realistic perspective on life.

To talk *about* humor or analyze it too much paradoxically seems to destroy it. *Time* magazine (Byron, 1976), in reporting on the Humour and Laughter Conference in Wales, pictured two fellow panelists who appeared to be sound asleep while listening to papers on humor. The article's writer then quoted Robert Benchley's observation: "There seems to be no length to which humorless people will not go to analyze humor" (p. 44).

To make the transition from analysis and talking about humor to live experience, it is necessary to exercise our humor talents. Energy must be directed on the auditory level towards listening in minute detail to what clients are saying and feeling. On the visual level, imagination must be set free to create interesting and clever verbal pictures depicting the situations and people being described. On the feeling level, our sense of fun and our sensitivity must be combined to guide both our choice of images and the timing of our delivery. The verbal image comes alive through the therapist's skill at storytelling and at painting pictures in imagination.

Humor is a therapeutic tool that demands energy for its creation, yet its rich rewards include a closer therapeutic bond through shared laughter, as well as insights gained and highlighted through fresh images. Clients develop their own humor, which in turn delights and surprises, and both participants share in the magic that is humor!

REFERENCES

Byron, C. (1976, August 2). Killing laughter. *Time Magazine*, p. 44.

Carkhuff, R. R., & Berenson, B. G. (1967). *Beyond Counseling and Therapy*. New York: Holt, Rinehart and Winston.

Freeman, L., & Greenwald, H. (1961). *Emotional Maturity in Love and Marriage*. New York: Harper and Brothers.

Heath, D. (1965). *Exploration of Maturity*. New York: Meredith Publishing Company.

Hickson, J. (1977). Humor as an element in the counseling relationship. *Psychology, 14*, 60-68.

Kaneko, S. (1971). *The Role of Humor in Psychotherapy*. Unpublished manuscript, Smith College School for Social Work, Boston, MA.

Killinger, B. (1976). *The Place of Humour in Adult Psychotherapy*. Unpublished dissertation, York University, Toronto, Ontario.

Killinger, B. (1977). The place of humour in adult psychotherapy. In A. J. Chapman & H. C. Foot (Eds.), *It's a Funny Thing, Humour* (pp. 153-156). Oxford: Pergamon Press.

Koestler, A. (1974). Humour and wit. In *The New Encyclopaedia Britannica* (Vol. 9, pp. 5-11). Chicago: H. H. Benton.

Kubie, L. S. (1971). The destructive potential of humor in psychotherapy. *American Journal of Psychiatry, 127*, 861-866.

Landis, C., & Ross, J. W. (1933). Humor and its relation to other personality traits. *Journal of Social Psychology, 4*, 156-175.

Maslow, A. H. (1970). *Motivation and Personality*. New York: Harper & Row.

Mindess, H. (1971). *Laughter and Liberation*. Los Angeles: Nash Publishing.

O'Connell, W., Rothaus, P., Hanson, P. G., & Moyer, R. (1969). Jest appreciation and interaction in leaderless groups. *International Journal of Group Psychotherapy, 19*, 454-462.

Poland, W. S. (1971). The place of humor in psychotherapy. *American Journal of Psychiatry, 128,* 635-637.
Rogers, C. R. (1961). *On Becoming a Person.* Boston:
Houghton-Mifflin.
Rosenheim, E. (1974). Humour in psychotherapy: An
interactive experience. *American Journal of Psychotherapy, 28,* 584-591.
White, R. W. (1959). Motivation reconsidered: The concept of competence. *Psychological Review, 66,* 297-333.

THE HUMOR DECISION

Harold Greenwald

Dr. Harold Greenwald escapes classification in his professional work. He is keenly aware of absurdity themes and can adroitly highlight the interplay of sense and senselessness in human behavior. He uses humor with natural ease and is able to carve humorous sculptures out of the rocks of therapeutic impasse. His use of humor in psychotherapy shows that absurdity may have therapeutic aspects when patients begin to appreciate the humorous 'flip side' inherent in so many of life's events. This recognition of the absurd limitations of existence may in turn help to immunize patients against interpreting absurdity in negative terms, thus gaining a more realistic life perspective.

Dr. Greenwald is a well-known clinical psychologist and the developer of Direct Decision Therapy (D.D.T.). He is currently President of the Direct Decision Institute in San Diego, California. His publications include <u>Direct Decision Therapy</u> (1973) and <u>The Happy Person</u> (1984).

※　　　※　　　※

THEORETICAL PERSPECTIVE

For me the use of humor is based not only on my theoretical perspective about psychotherapy, but is a fundamental part of my philosophical position. Because I believe the world is an absurd place, I have found that I make peace with that absurdity and even enjoy it by utilizing humor. But it is more than that. It is not just an abstract principle.

When I was very young--around 3 or 4--I found that I could get the approving interest of adults by being funny.

41

But sometimes my humor was misplaced. I remember saying to the principal of the school from which my aunt was graduating, when he pointed his finger at me and told me to keep quiet, "If you do that once again, I'll bite your finger off." Later I realized that whenever they talked about this incident, my parents acted kind of admiring. Even though I had been impolite and had been removed from the graduation, it was obvious to me that humor was a vehicle through which I could win covert approval.

As I grew up in a tough neighborhood, the lower east side of Manhattan, I was smaller than any of the other boys and not quite as tough. My family was a little more middle class in its outlook than the other boys' families. I found that I could escape getting into fights and being beaten up by being funny. In elementary school and high school I was in plays and frequently had a comic part. As I grew up I found that this skill of getting people to laugh was a way of attracting friends and girlfriends. Later on I was delighted to read one of Freud's papers (1928) in which he pointed out that the humorous person has the advantage of taking any situation, no matter how catastrophic it might seem on the outside, and turning it into a source of humor or laughter. All of these factors led me to make a decision early in life in favor of humor.

In my therapy I keep my focus on discovering the decisions people have made early in life and how these decisions are affecting them now, with the perspective of helping them to change those decisions if necessary. My impression is that many of the people I work with would be much better off if they could turn their little catastrophes into sources of humor. In my therapeutic work I focus not on creating a sense of humor, because I am not sure that could be done, but on helping people I work with free themselves of the restraints that adult life has pressed upon them in order to uncover the native sense of humor that is every human being's birthright. A group of small children at play is very funny--they laugh, tell their own kinds of jokes, and frequently get manic. Sometimes when I watch children I feel sad that sooner or later the world and its vicissitudes will train them out of this fortunate way of being.

Also, I have found that if something said is attached to humor, it will be long remembered. Incidents in elementary school, high school, and college that were tied to a joke are still clearly engraved in my mind. For example, in one of my education courses the professor explained that many times children do not understand the vocabulary of the teacher, and this may happen even in such subjects as mathematics. He gave the following example: When a group of students was asked what is an average, a little boy answered, "That's what a chicken lays eggs on," because he had so frequently been given arithmetical examples in which it was stated that "a chicken lays on an average six eggs a week."

In summary, my use of humor in psychotherapy has two major goals: (a) to help the people I work with uncover their sense of humor; and (b) to help them remember some of the things that I have said.

TECHNIQUES

One of the major advantages of humor is that is makes possible nonthreatening interpretations or explanations of behavior. If we can tie something about a person's behavior into a humorous statement, then he or she is much less likely to resist accepting the interpretation or to withdraw from the close relationship, which is a *sine qua non* of effective psychotherapy.

A humorous context can help create a therapeutic atmosphere of freedom and openness. This constructive ambiance in itself can be highly therapeutic. Not too long ago I saw a young man who was unhappy about his work and about the recent loss of a sweetheart with whom he was still working but no longer intimately involved. The first session was conducted in what I try to make my usual informal, rather humorous manner. He came back the next week and said, "I don't know why, but I feel much better. During the week I had fun. I was able to kid my ex-girlfriend. I was able to joke with some of the people I work with, and I don't understand how that happened because you didn't really say anything that would particularly help me." This is an example of how just establishing a humorous context may frequently be helpful.

Specific techniques are hard to describe. I enter each session determined to find something humorous either in the situation between me and the patient or in the situation that the individual I am working with may be facing. This, of course, means suspending the serious, ponderous attitude often suggested in clinical training. Sometimes, when it is appropriate, I will tell stories if they illustrate a point. I will present some particularly useful stories further in this chapter.

PERTINENT USES

Unfortunately it is not possible to use humor with every kind of patient. When individuals are deeply depressed, the most important thing is to first establish essential contact with people who are too unhappy to be interested in communication. Use of humor in the initial phases of treatment could be interpreted as a sign that the therapist is not taking their problems seriously. Humor cannot be introduced in these situations until symptom relief results from the patient's appreciation of the therapist's confidence in his or her ability to improve. Once it becomes clear that the patient has gained some trust in himself or herself and in the therapist, then one can use humor. Humor is also contraindicated when there is a really serious, grim situation in the patient's life such as the death of a loved one or the prospect of surgery. Even in those instances it is sometimes possible to introduce humor once the relationship has been established, but it should not be attempted too early in the relationship.

It is hard to describe in clinical terms the kind of persons for whom humor is indicated. There are particular considerations with each individual and we must be in tune with our patients to know when humor can be used. Otherwise they will feel that they are being ridiculed. It is difficult to use humor effectively if we do not particularly like the person we are working with. It is possible to work efficiently and effectively with somebody we do not like at first, and if we work well, we hope to eventually find the other person likeable. Until this point, however, intended humor may come out as sarcasm and overly heavy irony, which the patient would see as a put down or as the therapist acting superior. Therefore, one important caveat for us as therapists is not to use humor only at the patient's expense, but to be certain that we are willing to use the humor at our own expense as well. This makes the situation more equal. In fact, the use of humor in general and self-directed humor in particular helps to lessen the gap between patient and therapist.

One group of patients with whom I have found humor especially valuable are those who act in the obsessive-compulsive manner. The obsessive-compulsive outlook leads to a very unhumorous, grim way of looking at life. Although these patients are suffering from the grimness, from their compulsions, from their obsessiveness, it often helps for them to see the absurdity of that obsessiveness. As they become aware of the absurdity of their undertakings, their obsessiveness appears to diminish.

One very important piece of advice is not to attempt to be humorous at all times with all patients. A lot of humor grows out of the therapeutic context. The best humor emanates not only from the jokes or stories we tell but from the context of the therapy--what is going on at the moment with a particular patient. Frequently, if humor is used properly, the patient will laugh appreciatively because a chord of truth has been activated. I sometimes define humor as the literal truth presented in an unusual way so that the person finds it very amusing. In many therapeutic situations, patients often value the sense of surprise and the suspension of tension resulting in laughter, which is an excellent release for tension.

CLINICAL PRESENTATION

I will now give some examples related to the use of humor in my clinical work. The first case concerns Ray (not his real name), a 29-year-old student of psychology who was suffering, among other things, from many suspicious feelings. When he came to his first session, he worried that I was taping it. He looked very suspiciously at an electrical plug connected to an empty line that I sometimes used for tape recorders or for a lamp and said, "I think you're taping me." We already had a good relationship because he had been in a class of mine and we had developed a friendship, so I felt comfortable using a humorous intervention with him in the first session. When he started worrying about that plug I said, "I'm glad you noticed it because I want you to know that right now as I talk to you, this microphone concealed here is connected directly with those record shops on Times Square and your session is going out in a dozen different loudspeakers, and people are gathered all over to listen to this crazy guy." This *reductio ad absurdum* approach seemed helpful because it dissolved his suspicion into laughter. Through that humorous exaggeration, I was in a sense interpreting. We know that paranoia has two sides to it, the persecutory and the grandiose. I was at this point transferring to the grandiose the idea that he believed he was so important that his stuff would be secretly transcribed and recorded. By talking about his words being broadcast, we were able to work on dissolving his suspicion about that subject.

At another point he became convinced, on rereading *Catcher in the Rye* by J. D. Salinger, that I was really Salinger. He had all kinds of proof. First, the novel dealt with the west side of Manhattan, and at that time my office was on the west side of Manhattan. Secondly, I had really written this book about him before I even met him. I did not deal with his comments, yet sometime later, when he was talking about feeling anxious and confused, I made an interpretation that seemed to have a remarkable effect on his way of coping with the world. He was telling me how anxious he was, how worried he was, how he felt, as he put it, that the bus was caving in on him when he was coming across the George Washington Bridge. He stated that his "ass hole was dropping out," and that he generally felt just miserable. I said to him "Well, just put on your red hunting hat and everything will be okay." My comment was related to the fact that, in the Salinger novel, very often the hero would put on his red hunting hat and feel good. Strangely enough, all his complaints seemed suddenly forgotten in a deep belly laugh, as he realized what had been occurring in his life. He commented that he was acting like a character in an opera, that he was dramatizing everything in his life almost as if he was the character in the novel, rather than looking at things in a more realistic fashion.

A month later, when he felt so much better that he was able to describe his "cure" in somewhat sad terms, he said, "It's true when I go on the bus now, the walls aren't caving in on me, my ass hole doesn't drop out, but *the opera is missing*." Eventually, of course, the opera came back in the form of constructive creative work. He became a very successful psychologist, and all of his borderline-like experiences were extremely helpful to him in understanding and empathizing with the people he worked with.

In addition to the specific humorous remarks that I have quoted, another helpful element in this case was the whole atmosphere of the treatment sessions. Throughout our interactions, I was able to help him move from looking at everything in a very serious, bitter, grim, suspicious manner to a new perspective from which he could look at things more lightly and begin to reframe them in a humorous and joking way.

In a different case I was dealing with another psychologist, a notorious hypochondriac. He was constantly concerned that he would be taken sick. He was planning a trip from New York to Boston and was very concerned that perhaps he would have a fatal heart attack or appendicitis attack on that trip. I asked him to bring in a map. He asked, "What good would that do?" I said, "Let's bring it in and see." When he brought it in, we looked at the map of the highway from New York to Boston and I asked him to check every major town along the route so he would never be any more than 20 miles from any major town. Because the area was so well-populated, he had to locate in advance a hospital in each of these towns. In this way he would be close to any hospital in case of an attack. Again, being very bright and having underneath all of his hypochondriasis a good sense of humor, he was able to laugh about his worries. Eventually he even commented, "You know, I started once more to worry about having a heart attack, and then I thought of you and then I started to laugh." Transforming fears and anxiety into a source of laughter is one of the most effective uses of humor in the therapeutic situation.

Humor is also a way of making interpretations that the person can accept that would otherwise be rejected. The following example concerns a young man planning to go for a job interview. Before he even went to the first interview, he was already discussing with me all the terrible things that would happen to him if he got the job. First, they would possibly ask him to work overtime. If he worked overtime, he would lose his girlfriend because she would not believe he was working overtime but would think he was running around with other women. Second, there probably was no chance for advancement in that job, so what good would a job like that be? I used the punch line of an old joke that I had told him previously, a joke about a man who is driving on a highway when he has a flat tire. He says to himself, "Well, I have a flat tire, all I have to do is to change the tire." When he goes to open the trunk of his new car, though, he realizes that he has a new tire but no jack. So he says to himself, "I will go to the nearest farmhouse, I'll borrow a jack from the farmer, and come back. Borrow a jack...maybe he won't want to lend me a jack, so I'll pay him something.

How much can he want for a jack, 10 dollars? Who knows? Who am I to set a fee on the cost of the jack? Maybe he'll want 50 dollars for a jack!" At that point he approaches a farmhouse and knocks at the door. The man comes to the door and says, "Can I help you" and our unfortunate motorist says, "You can take that jack and shove it."

Having told that story, which I find useful with obsessives who are always expecting catastrophe, I said to him "You tell them to take that job and shove it. Don't go in there. Don't let them make a fool out of you." He understood what he was doing--that he was catastrophizing without any basis in fact. There was no reason to believe that he would be asked to work some overtime hours. There was no reason to believe that his girlfriend would necessarily leave him if he worked overtime, or to expect the other catastrophes that he had envisaged. Instead of saying, "Your catastrophizing is generally perceived by others as a critical statement," I couched my interpretation in humor by telling him to tell them to take the job and shove it. In this way, he began to see the absurdity of his position. However, it is not enough for patients to see the absurdity of their position. A therapeutic context has to be created in which people can realize that most of life is an absurd project and that therefore they are just being human when they are being absurd.

I have also found that people diagnosed as schizophrenic often have an excellent sense of humor, and that schizophrenia itself is frequently a way of 'putting on' the world. In some instances, a kind of colossal joke begins to unfold when these individuals follow orders literally. You tell a schizophrenic to walk across a field, and he will walk across a field, come to a tree, stand with his nose against the trunk of the tree, and keep going through the motions of walking. In the famous Czech novel *Good Soldier Schweik*, Schweik disorganized the entire Austro-Hungarian army by obeying all orders literally. His captain said, "Stand here," and he stood at the desk. Meanwhile the captain goes out, they have orders to depart for the front, the whole army departs, and he is still standing at the desk. This is similar to what many schizophrenics do. I frequently ask them why they are kidding the whole world, and it is amazing how often they will smile at that remark.

For example, I was in Albuquerque, New Mexico, giving a demonstration for people in the department of psychiatry. They brought in a patient who had just come in the day before. That was fortunate, because frequently when patients are in mental hospitals and particularly when the patient is diagnosed as experiencing a schizophrenic crisis, they get such massive doses of the major tranquilizers that communication is very difficult. This woman had not had any medication. We started to talk, and pretty soon she went off into schizophrenese. When I said something about male or female, she said, "*female, he male, female, my mail*," repeating typical clang associations. "Are you male" she said. I answered, "That depends whether the cudgeon is on the framman part," using double talk. She looked at me, puzzled. She asked, "Cudgeon, what's that?" I said, "I don't know, I just made it up." She nodded her head sagely and said, "I see, you speak a private language," and laughed out loud. I had in a sense unmasked her talking in that way, had accepted it, and had joined in it. She understood my efforts and for the rest of the session spoke relatively rationally about the very real problems she was grappling with. It is interesting that when I can catch the rhythm of schizophrenese and talk back to patients in that same language, they will laugh in appreciation and sort of give it up. Sometimes they will continue, but at least they can start to communicate in the relatively decipherable poetic way that schizophrenics frequently use.

In another case, while I was giving a demonstration in Norway, the patient came in and started screaming at me. I said, "Hey, cut it out. You don't have to talk that way." She stopped screaming and asked, "How do you know?" And I said, "It takes one to know one." Again, she laughed appreciatively and accepted what I was saying.

One more example deals with a woman who had been diagnosed as paranoid schizophrenic and had been on the back ward of a hospital for many years. When she came in to the demonstration, she held her head down, looking very sad, and I asked her what the trouble was. She replied, "I'm being crucified today." I said, "No kidding? So am I." With people who have become stuck in the so-called autistic phase, I find it important to establish a path of communication. In order to communicate, one needs to understand the patient's own way of dealing with the world and to make appropriate use of the element of surprise. When I told her, "I'm being crucified, too," she looked up at me and wanted to know why. I looked heavenward and said, "You know who my father is." At that moment, this woman, who had been considered completely autistic and depressed at all times, looked at me with a broad smile and said, "That's funny, you don't look like Jesus." Her psychiatrist took her back to the ward. Some time later, the psychiatrist came back chuckling and said, "I wonder who is treating who? As I left her at the ward, she turned to me and gave a big, wide wink."

Not being frightened by the symptoms, no matter how extreme, not being frightened by the hallucinations, but entering them in a kind of humorous way, frequently allows us to help the patient make the very difficult transition from acting in this manner to acting more realistically. They may begin to realize that they can deal with reality better if they are not as grim about it.

In yet another case I was dealing with a very bitter, dour man. He had come for sex therapy with the remarkable claim that never in his life had he had an erection. I realized during the first session that he was extremely negative in all of his attitudes. For example, he informed me that he probably would have done better going to the janitor in the building I lived in than to me. I did not argue with this because the janitor at that time was a very intelligent Russian émigré. I told him that it might have been a good idea, but as long as he was with me, we should see what we could accomplish. He was the son of a physician, and had a very unfortunate, bitter, angry relationship with his father. This was carried over into most of his relationships with authority and with other people. For example, his physics professor had told him that under no circumstances should he teach, yet he was now a professor. We talked and I told him that it would not be a good idea for him to have an erection because an erect penis would be a dangerous instrument. He then, of course, set out to prove me wrong.

Little by little, as I continued on my tack of telling him he was not to have an erection, he disobeyed me. For example, he went to a nudist camp and came back and explained that he had had a slight erection, but it was no good. I asked him what the angle was, and he said he did not know. I suggested that in the future if he went to any place like that he should carry a protractor to measure the angle. He snorted, angrily as usual, but underneath it I saw a slight glint of humor in his eyes.

Some time later he reported that he had met a young woman and invited her up to his home. After several glasses of wine, he had persuaded her to go to the bathroom with him, where she showed him hers and he showed her his, like children do. Again he described having an erection, now at a much higher angle. I asked him how hard it was, and he replied, "How do I know? Well, maybe like a hard ink eraser." I replied, "It might be a good idea the next time you have an erection of that kind to apply the Rockwell test." (The Rockwell test is a test of the hardness of metal which is utilized by metallurgists by dropping steel balls of various weights onto surfaces to see how far they penetrate.) Again he snorted, but once more I noticed a minute smile around his lips.

Some time later he said, "Well, it's 2 months and I'm obviously not getting any place." I did not make the mistake I had made previously when I told a patient with similar symptoms that of course he was improving--look at the erections he was beginning to get. Instead I said, "That's too bad, and I know it's my fault." In a sense it was my fault. The implied contract was that he was coming to see me, paying me money, talking, and it was therefore my job to cure him. My statement was also a reflection of what he was thinking. It was almost as if he were saying to me, not directly but covertly, "I defy you to be able to cure me." So I said to him, "No, I haven't been able to do anything for you." He asked, "Then why should I continue to come?" I replied, "You're a scientist; you're such a difficult case; I think it would be valuable to the annals of science for you to continue. In fact, it may be necessary for me to drive you crazy." Again he questioned that and said, "That's not what I came here for." I explained that we could not cure cancer until we knew the cause of cancer and how to create cancer. Therefore because he seemed like such an intelligent and able person, very honestly describing his reactions, then perhaps he would go on with this experiment to see if we could create schizophrenia in him--or if not schizophrenia, at least some degree of paranoia. Incidentally, he was very well read in psychological and psychoanalytic literature. In fact, he accused me of using a "Stekelian technique" on him. At that time I knew very little about Stekel and asked what he meant. He replied that Stekel had said, "Remember, the patient is the enemy." I did not feel that he was the enemy, but obviously he had seen this as an adversarial relationship.

We carried on in this way, and increasingly he began to develop a somewhat sardonic sense of humor. When he made his first attempt to have intercourse and then failed, he was still able to say sardonically something like, "You were worried I would be a Don Juan. You were worried I would be a rapist. I couldn't even make it with this very pleasant, amiable woman who was completely cooperative." I told him I was glad that he was such a good patient and that despite every temptation he still was not having a full erection because I had warned him against it. Finally one day he came in, triumphantly explaining that he had had intercourse three times the day before with his girlfriend. He stated that he felt cured, and then he added, "I suppose you want the credit for that." I said, "Not at all. I did everything in my power to prevent you and you overcame me, and I really want to congratulate you." At that point, for the first time, he laughed out loud. Yet he caught himself in the middle of the laugh and said, "I don't laugh."

SYNTHESIS

I hope these few examples have illustrated the relationship, context, and kinds of things that can be said with humor. From my perspective of psychotherapeutic work, the use of stories is an excellent way of giving interpretations. The brilliant novelist and Nobel laureate, Isaac Bashevis Singer, once told me an interesting story about when the Messiah will arrive. Everybody will get what they want: the blind will be able to see; the deaf will be able to hear; the lame will be able to walk. The only ones who will not get anything will be the fools because they do not know anything is missing. Similarly, many of our most resistant patients do not know that anything is missing--for example, the ones who insist they are well when you can easily observe in an unguarded moment the deep depression that belies such a statement. Also there are the ones who insist they are gentle, and the world is taking advantage of them, although their consuming anger can be quickly detected. All these people in a sense are talking about their wish, not about what really is. To confront such individuals with direct interpretations may be seen by them as offensive and often results in increasing their misery or in their leaving therapy. This is not a therapeutic advance, nor the easiest way to develop a therapeutic relationship. With such patients I find it much easier to create a situation in which they begin to see what they are missing. They are often missing the ability to look at things in a balanced way, must stop making mountains out of molehills, and instead must reverse the process by making their mountains into molehills that can be easily surmounted.

Humor is such a magnificent method of expression. One can accomplish so many things. One of the advantages of humor I discovered in the course of doing psychotherapeutic work is that humor frequently allows us to simultaneously address several layers of functioning. It is possible to tell a story that on the surface just seems like an ordinary joke but really deals with several layers at once. The word "layers" can be understood in terms of the psychoanalytic topography of conscious, preconscious, and unconscious spheres of functioning, including the unconscious resistance against the expression of censored or unacceptable material. From a cognitive point of view, one stops thinking about everything in this world as a catastrophe and begins to see the humor in life's events by looking at the world as the divine comedy that it really is.

REFERENCES

Coleman, J. V. (1962). Banter as psychotherapeutic intervention. *American Journal of Psychoanalysis, 22*, 69-74.

Domash, L. (1975). The use of wit and the comic by a borderline psychotic child in psychotherapy. *American Journal of Psychotherapy, 29*, 261-270.

Ellis, A. (1977). Fun as psychotherapy. *Rational Living, 12*, 2-6.

Freud, S. Humor. (1928). *International Journal of Psychoanalysis, 9*, 1-6.

Fry, W. F. (1963). *Sweet Madness*. Palo Alto, CA: Pacific Books.

Greenwald, H. (1967). Play therapy for children over twenty-one. *Psychotherapy: Theory, Research, and Practice, 4*, 44-46.

Greenwald, H. (1969, Spring). How to keep a patient for a long, long time and make sure nothing happens. *Voices*, pp. 125-129.

Greenwald, H. (1973). *Direct Decision Therapy*. San Diego, CA: EDITS.

Greenwald, H. (1975). Humor in psychotherapy. *Journal of Contemporary Psycho-Therapy, 7*, 113-116.

Greenwald, H. (1984). *The Happy Person.* New York: Stein & Day.

Greenwald, H. (1985). Beyond the paradox. In J. Zeig (Ed.), *Ericksonian Psycho-Therapy, Vol. II. Clinical Applications* (pp. 211-222). New York: Brunner/Mazel.

Grotjahn, M. (1970). Laughter in psychotherapy. In W. M. Mendel (Ed.), *A Celebration of Laughter* (pp. 61-66). Los Angeles: Mara Books.

Kuhlman, T. L. (1984). *Humor and Psychotherapy.* Homewood, IL: Dow Jones-Irwin.

Oring, E. (1984). *The Jokes of Sigmund Freud.* Philadelphia: University of Pennsylvania Press.

NATURAL HIGH THEORY
AND PRACTICE: THE HUMORIST'S
GAME OF GAMES*

Walter E. O'Connell

Dr. O'Connell is in a constant "natural high." His effusive writing style reflects his refusal to accept the constrictions and boundaries imposed upon thought by the written word. His writing tends to appear divergent on the surface, yet eventually converges around two central themes of Adlerian psychology: self-esteem (SE) and social interest (SI). In this chapter, we get a healthy serving of Dr. O'Connell's colorful exposition of Adlerian theory mixed with the author's own theoretical and clinical insights related to Natural High Therapy. Dr. O'Connell draws important distinctions between self-esteem and ego-esteem, and comments upon the pernicious effects of guilt on the development of emotional disturbance. He further offers some guidelines on the role of humor in psychotherapeutic work. In the mosaic of his inner-galactic explorations, some real gems can be found: "If you are passionately pursuing guilt, try feeling guilty about feeling guilty"; "Most of us do not want control over our lives: We merely want control of people and conditions which we allow to control us."

Dr. O'Connell is a leading exponent of the Adlerian school of psychology and the initiator of Natural High Therapy. He is presently a clinical psychologist who has retired from the Veterans Administration Medical Center and maintains a private practice in "Lost Pines" of Bastrop, Texas. His publications include <u>Action Therapy and Adlerian Theory</u> (1975) and <u>Essential Readings in Natural High Actualization</u> (1981b).

*   *   *

*The statements contained in this chapter are entirely the author's and do not reflect the policies of either the Federal Government or the Veteran's Administration.

In the face of paradox and puzzle, mischief and mystery, only a sense of humor allows us to preserve our sanity...Too rigid an insistence on logic must be a symptom of, or produce, insanity. (Bellman, 1970, p. 44)

THEORETICAL PERSPECTIVE

HOW I GOT THERE AND HERE

For as long as I can remember, I have been a keen and puzzled observer of adult behaviors. As a skinny, wide-eyed dwarf, I listened and watched adult tales of hardship and enthusiasm unfold. I noted again and again that the grown-ups who were most happy, productive, and appreciated by others had a peculiar quality often labeled as "good humor." Most of my rare trips by auto those days were to that hideous fortress, the state mental asylum, where I watched the moves of the inmates, two of my mother's siblings included. I arrived at a lasting conclusion. Those grown-ups who did not share laughter with others were not happy, productive, or wanted. They did not understand or appreciate their resultant high nuisance value. These premises were among my first and most incisive clinical judgments.

Thirty years later I had completed my master's thesis and doctoral dissertation on the sense of humor (O'Connell, 1960). Almost a quarter of a century later, as a still puzzled if somewhat less wide-eyed observer, I have created a theory and practice of psychotherapy with the sense of humor as the goal of actualization or individuation. To my knowledge my theory of the natural high, perhaps better named "humorous self-therapy," is an innovative attempt to construct a theory of personality specifically geared to the development of the humorous attitude (O'Connell, 1975, 1976, 1977, 1979a, 1980, 1981a, 1981c, 1981d).

THE THEORY THAT GUIDES ME

Natural high theory follows from the clinical and research observations that those with humorous attitudes are self-oriented but not ego constricted. That is, the humorist knows that self-esteem (SE) is an intuitive process of inner development. Self-esteem carries the well-practiced message that "in spite of my mistakes, incompletions, and chipped edges, I am guilt free." Self-esteem may have positive affects similar to that of ego-esteem, but the process of the latter consists of an addictive leaning upon others as external and fleeting proof of one's worth. Subsequently, ego-esteem becomes a highly dangerous venture, potentially injurious to one's physical and mental well-being.

The humorous perspective requires a sense of purposive belonging in an interacting, expanding universe of positive meanings. This purposive belonging is the *gemeinschaftsgefuehl* of Alfred Adler, badly translated into the social sphere of meaning as "social interest" (O'Connell, 1975, 1981b). Social interest facilitates cooperation-as-equals, in the sense that one does not engage in negative judgments of other persons or of life in general. With self-esteem one does not generate self-guilt. All guilt involves an illogical negative judgment of persons generalized from behaviors (e.g., "That person is forever worthless because of that action"). Projected guilt follows after creating distance from others and then dumping (projecting) guilt-inspired hatred upon the person of others. Lack of social interest (SI) invariably results in problems in living. Adler built his psychology upon this cornerstone. He correctly and consistently focused upon social interest as the only behavior that could not be overdone unto insanity. To Adler, social interest was the behavior that showed the greatest variability between persons. That is, measurements of social interest, if available, would give psychologists their ideal normal distribution curve, one only vaguely approximated by height and intelligence. With social interest, one does not feel "as if" in enemy territory, alienated, and alone. If one refuses to let go of the isolation and negative certainties of guilt, the humorous attitude will simply dissolve.

In addition to SE and SI, a further ingredient necessary for a hearty attitude of humor is the love of the paradox, or the basic mystery of life itself. A humorous paradox is that lived life cannot be perfectly controlled or even described in a world where we all can constantly contribute to human encouragement or discouragement. The most dangerous persons are those who see things as "perfectly clear" instead of "through a glass darkly." Those persons who reach for power (social influence), via the mistaken certainty of perfect omniscience and omnipotence, perceive others who do not share their delusions as hostile, stupid, inferior objects (often to be summarily removed). There is no humor here.

There is no solid separateness of impermeable boundaries in the real universe of the humorist. There are no privileged characters who rule by demands of "divine right" for the humorist. The Newtonian-Cartesian faith in solid separate objects disappears in humorists' smiles. Naming and separating represent the original sin for the humorist. All living creatures are far more than arbitrary labels. Guilt is the culmination of the pernicious belief in boundaries. The laughter of the humorist is directed toward this arbitrary labeling seen as "reality" by the superserious, humorless power seekers. Many theologians with a touch of humor have noted that the devil could tolerate anything but laughter (Hyers, 1969, 1973). In a like manner, our mistaken negative certainties cannot survive humor. Our errors of guilt-creating, distance-provoking, and negative discouragement (seen as "reality" and "human nature") disappear with blameless humor. Blaming persons is a way of creating boundaries and diminishing worth. The humorist intuitively knows this truth, but also realizes that this simplicity is hard to reach in a world that judges persons by standards of "having" and "doing" that are molded by others.

In the present inadequate state of the therapeutic arts, humor is not loved for many interlocking reasons. We are slowly emerging from a pessimistic past, which cherished a "hard" determinism in which the individual was perceived as a passive victim of chemical and/or psychic abnormalities. Experts have been concerned with the negative, especially those conditions and effects that could be easily isolated, replicated, and measured. Inner states of the person have always resisted reliable measurement. The more autocratic the discipline of exploration, the more the tendency to confuse humor with hostile wit and to see it as an ever-present danger to arbitrary authority. There is no doubt that laughter and wit can be seen as potent weapons, especially by those who try to prove their worth as persons by controlling others.

THE HOSTILITY IN HUMOR

Humans of all types and sizes are ambulatory contradictions, having infinite symbolic minds combined with finite physical bodies (Weber, 1970). The Christian Savior, Jesus Christ, was the grand model of the tragicomic combination of God and man (Hyers, 1969, 1973; Weber, 1970). The chronic inability of humankind to tolerate conceptual mixtures of "both," rather than "or," has brought death and destruction to millions. Into this chaotic scene ("comical" when reviewed from a distance) come human psychotherapists bearing their own paradoxical finite-infinite potentialities. Effective psychotherapists function as contradictions. They move with gentle strength and friendly firmness. They help patients relinquish negative certainties and emotions by focusing directly on the psychic pains (Haley, 1963), therefore reconciling that which patients consider irreconcilable.

As Weber (1970) indicates, the very process of psychotherapy is humorous: "The comic hero, with the agility of the clown, can be nimble and quick--and can live with the contradictories...Putting together and accepting the union of what seems to be opposed: that was the work of Jesus. It is also the mystery of psychotherapy" (pp. 124, 131).

Humorous psychotherapy (a synonym for "natural high") is at odds with subtle teachings based on delusional demands for an instant, perfect, painless, and practiceless nirvana. Following quantum physics (Wilber, 1979), humorous psychotherapy plays with boundaries, reconciles opposites, and re-solves apparent paradoxes of solid separateness in time. Everything can be anything else. Life is "both/and" (e.g., life-death, male-female, pleasure-pain) and not "either/or." To the humorous psychotherapist, all phenomena are in a state of flux and process.

Humor means involvement-with-detachment, for one's worth is not in anyway contingent upon perfect competitive performance and goals. To be an ultimate athlete (Leonard, 1975) in the game-of-games of actualization, one performs with gravity-free seriousness. The hostile arena is that of our world, which is usually attempting to judge persons by arbitrary external standards. The humorous psychotherapist accepts the presence of this discouragingly judging world without undue gravity and reactive hostility. However, those whom we label as "sick" tend to identify with these invidious comparisons. Their inner and outer hostilities (depression and paranoia) reflect basic acceptance of external negative judgments of personhood.

The humorous therapist is often alone in institutions that, by their very nature, grasp and cling to the "bad faith" that persons are victims of psychic traumata and defenseless against biological determinism. The therapist cherishing humor is not overwhelmed by (or fighting with) this discouragement of society and its institutions. (Here I am reminded of my aphorism that institutions can collect and classify, but never cure.)

The natural high therapist views the humorous attitude as the criterion of actualization. Following Freud's (1928/1950) conflicting ideas on this subject, wit is a subtle weapon of the unactualized to defend and enhance ego-esteem. In the ego-esteem mode, one's sense of worth resides in external confirmation of the perfection of one's roles, goals, and controls. Wit is therefore used in this mode to create distance from others by putting other heads higher or lower than one's own to promote ego-esteem goals. In this respect, wit techniques have the hidden purpose of putting persons and activities one-down as compensatory maneuvers to feel secure and better-than.

Both wit and humor employ visual and verbal methods of brief, condensed, incongruous, and unexpected situations to bring to awareness sudden switches in meanings. Both wit and humor involve the philosophy that anything can be something else. In effect, what we perceive now has many possible realities. Only madmen hang on to a perfectly clear world of static boundaries (Wilber, 1979). If, as many researchers of wit and humor claim, hostility and aggression are always present in both comical processes (Chapman & Foot, 1976), the object of the sense of humor is quite different. As understood in natural high practice, the aim of humor is to defuse the self-defeating purposes of guilt, seen as the product of one's narrow ego-identity. The weak, unactualized ego wallows in negativity, for it is out of touch with basic sources of purposive significance. Only by an awareness of the subtle operations of the mistaken negative certainties of guilt, without adding further guilt and discouragement, can ego constriction of innate self-esteem (SE) and inherent purposive belonging (SI) evaporate into enlivening humor.

Guilt, discouragement, and ego-constriction lead to all kinds of human craziness. It is tragicomic that we humans cling to and grasp at negativity and use the resulting weakness as "reason" to avoid the encouragement process. It is sadly ludicrous that one fights ego-engendered discouragement through active competition (constantly striving to be "better than" as *persons*). It is humbly hilarious that all of us have early in life lost our enlivening innocence and angrily "sit on a pile of shit, complaining of the smell." It is laughable that it is mainly the grandiose paranoid who believes he or she is god, but allows this honor to no one else. Yet the grandeur of self-actualization and individuation is our unrecognized present and future potential. Natural high states without qualification that humor is the birthright of all humans. It is a constant natural low, a state of non-negative sadness, that the joys of simple being are seldom perceived, hence our perpetual inner and outer warfares. Natural high or humorous psychotherapy accepts the existence of both constant conflicts (the shock of clashes of wills) and natural lows that keep us grounded in the similarities of human pain (see Table 1).

TABLE 1: FIFTEEN AFFIRMATIONS FOR NATURAL HIGH ACTUALIZATION

---

1. Remember you are dying. Give up body and ego attachments, but not involvements.
2. Remember people can give only the love they are capable of at any time.
3. Remember that guilt and attack-thoughts are utterly insane. Witness these sensations, secure in transpersonal meditative space (the nonjudgmental "inner-I-ness").
4. Remember to tell others how much you need their loving feedback.
5. Remember that self-stroking for contribution to growth of others, effort (not perfection), and uniqueness are not motivated by competitive compensatory conceit.
6. Remember you have absolute control of your self-esteem and universal belonging only--but what else do you really need to control?
7. Remember it takes true strength to stay aware of the god-like qualities of persons.
8. Remember your emotional indebtedness to others.
9. Remember to encourage your enemies. They are invaluable for your growth and are in need of your loving kindness.
10. Remember to honor your failure and chipped edges.
11. Remember this universe belongs to God, and not to us, except as we are one with God. Don't damn God's flow.
12. Remember to forgive God and so experience your self/soul, which is infinite and timeless.
13. Remember you will never be able to understand all the details of this mad-sad-glad universe. Honor your intuition as well as your intellect.
14. Remember that life is too serious a game to be taken gravely. You'll never get out of it alive.
15. Remember and accept that there are times when you'll forget all of the above.

Table 2 (p. 63) lists the persistent signs of the weak ego. Table 3 (p. 64) enumerates the self-defeating effects of guilt, part of the weak ego-identity. Humor development follows from a nondefensive awareness of the potentially debilitating innerworkings of ego-constriction. Natural high meditation is practice in becoming aware and letting go of images, words, and tensions that constrict the true freedom of unconditional worth (SE) and belonging (SI). Meditation is a growth exercise for the perpetually-practicing pupil of the natural high. Meditation creates an inner distancing from the ramblings (images, memories, future projections of thought, bodily sensations) of negativity. Meditation is a discipline that introduces persons to their "inner-I-ness" or transpersonal self. This island of relaxed, alert expansiveness has always been with us (Wilber, 1979), yet hidden by humorless ego demands. Experiencing the transpersonal self strengthens the ego and stimulates the development of social interest.

Once one learns the art of meditative one-pointing (mindfully doing only one thing at a time), time can be spent engaged in contemplating symbols of one's unique worth and one's similarity with others. If symbols are allowed to unfold without interpreting, diagnosing, and judging, one will be strengthening inner resources necessary for the appreciation and production of humor. A record of our inner difficulties and experiences gives us knowledge of our inner patterning. Journal-keeping presents an opportunity to help free oneself from the confusion of trying to figure out ego-complexities that are isolated and unverbalized in the head. Journal-keeping can be a companion activity that allows patterns of self-knowledge to emerge and thereby gives direction to humorous change.

THE UNPOPULARITY OF HUMOROUS PSYCHOTHERAPY

The learning of prerequisite skills for humor suffers the same fate as all the neglected positive qualities at the tag end of the 20th century. People demand instant, painless, and practiceless humor. We all would love to change our feelings without a change in inner- and interpersonal behaviors.

Twentieth-century science is no helpmate for learning the secrets of humor. Our lust and idolatry for numbers

TABLE 2: CHARACTERISTICS OF THE WEAK EGO

It is often called the old, incompleted, unactualized, or constricted ego. We need to be aware, share, and laugh at our ways of making ourselves "less than," "better than," "isolated," and "perfect." Do not own, "awfulize," or fight these weaknesses, but honor them as opportunities for growth and expansion (of self-esteem and social interest). Learn to acknowledge and let go of this old ego-identity, and thereby create for yourself (and others) the true freedom of the flow--the fun of the game-of-games. In a word, be humorously involved, but attached to "no-thing."

WATCH FOR CHARACTERISTICS OF THE WEAK EGO

1. Clings and grasps at goals, roles, and controls for meaning.
2. Searches for differences rather than similarities with others.
3. Groups strangers with past negative figures in one's life.
4. Laments the past and catastrophizes the future.
5. Avoids being relaxed and alert, wholly present without judgment in the now.
6. Creates self-guilt--"I am weak, worthless, incompetent for what I did (or did not) do."
7. Projects guilt upon others: "They are worthless, weak, and incompetent because of what they did (or did not) do."
8. Uses "awfulizing," "terribilizing," and discouragement as a litany for life.
9. Labors to create a solid separateness ("I am my ego") and build permanent boundaries around events, persons, and professions. Such boundaries are the ego's declaration of war.
10. Plays in deadly seriousness "the arrows of the weak ego." Self-esteem is diminished by invidious comparisons and ego-esteem is sought by seeming "better than." Ego-esteem is protected by avoiding any activity in which perfection is not guaranteed ("the avoid-dance of perfectionism"). Ego-esteem is protected by a leaning on others (hyperdependent).
11. Seeks power (social influence) at the expense of strength (inner worth and purposive belonging).
12. Crusades for this "perfectly clear" existence and does not smile at the paradoxes of life (humor). Above all, focuses on the childish demands of the weak ego in contrast to the free gift from the timeless inner self.
13. Piteously pursues perfection. Only angels live with perfection; humans who demand perfection from self and others are in a constant state of arousal, and often turn to chemicals and/or cults for immediate relief. Perfectionists never give free strokes.
14. Insists on the use of "futile force." Any influence (inner or outer) seen as force is resisted with an equal or greater force.
15. Resists awareness of all weak ego resistances; therefore denies all of the above.

TABLE 3:   "LETTING GO" OF GUILT

(NEGATIVE JUDGMENTS OF PERSONS)

Guilt feelings are inane, illogical, and injurious to all life.   If actions are mistaken, change them.   <u>Love</u>, not guilt, can strengthen motivation.   We need a war on guilt because guilt feelings:

1. do not lead to a change in behavior, but only continued recrimi-nations against worth and belonging.
2. diminish self-esteem and social interest, thereby causing physi-cal, social, and spiritual destruction.
3. confuse personal worth with behavior.   This act is the worst sin on the institutional mind.   The message of all great spiritual and democratic movements is "Judge not, lest ye be judged." Goals of <u>behavior</u> may be judged; worth of <u>persons</u>, never!
4. are gluttonous and grandiose.   In guilt, I deny all influence of persons and events upon the making of my ego and grab <u>all</u> the blame for past interactions.   In guilt-making, I am grandiose about the future--I lust after perfect prediction of discourage-ment, now-and-forever.   Only God knows the future, and he-she-it is lovingly silent.
5. are weapons that need arms control.   I not only kill myself psychologically, but easily destroy the psyches of the helpless-hapless dependent others.
6. are used to get power (social influence) over others at the expense of SE and SI.   Attention, special service, power strug-gles (active and inactive), revenge, and display of disabilities (real or assumed) are often hidden motives of guilt feelings.
7. can lead to "guilt addiction," because others will dump their guilt on the "victim" who willingly accepts guilt.

---

has overwhelmed the scientific attitude of disinterested observation. We are CWAMAs: count, weigh, and measurement addicts. We suffer the symptoms of withdrawal when we cannot quantify the unquantifiable. We analyze holistic human purposes into mere epiphenomena of early psychic traumata and impersonal psychological or sociobiological forces. We have embraced the "bad faith" of passive victimhood. The humorist realizes that civilization brings with it the discouraging practice of judging persons according to others' standards of having and doing. Such habitual reactions are the basis for ego-identity. The humorous psychotherapist sees the "mentally diseased" not as breaking with reality, but as being too logically attuned to its delusions.

THERAPISTS' ATTITUDES
IN NATURAL HIGH THERAPY

No matter how actualized the advocate of the natural high approach, mindfulness of the following points is paramount:

1. Natural high therapists are aware of their own ego-identities that engender demanding constrictions in times of ego-induced diminishments of worth and belonging. Therefore, natural high therapists are models of their own awareness of loving kindness.
2. Natural high therapists are democratic to the core. This democracy involves encouragement and not pampering. In natural high practice, democratic humor means the patient is free to ridicule, with sudden brief over- and understatements, the tutors' own ego-constrictions. Turnabout is fair play and not hostility.
3. The use of humor is often regarded as hostility by patients who seldom are held accountable for their own discouraged conclusions. It is well to expect, and even anticipate, such ego reactions. "Spitting in the soup" and "take the wind out of the sails" are ways Alfred Adler described his friendly predictions of negativity.
4. Always check immediately the verbal and nonverbal reactions of patients to humorous attacks on ego-pretensions. Knowledge of defensive responses is helpful to gauge the level of dysphoric discouragement.
5. As Willard Beecher, one of the foremost masters of humorous psychotherapy, taught me, "Never get into a pissing contest with a skunk." In other words, therapists who live by the sword (of power) can easily be defeated by the unbridled power techniques of patients.
6. Always give the student-patients credit (strokes) for effort, not perfection. Only angels are perfect and they lead perfectly boring existences.
7. Demand no-thing from patients, except that they will not snore in therapy. The demanding therapist is "the-rapist," subject to the pains of interminable burnout (e.g., discouragement of the professional class).

NATURAL HIGH TECHNIQUES

All natural high techniques are in the service of experiencing one's basic unconscious ways of negating one's worth and that of others. The next awareness to be mastered is awareness of reactions to this guilt by subtle yet pervasive methods of compensating for ego-inflicted damage through shows of having and doing in the external world. Techniques of the natural high are ways of making persons aware of these destructive reactive and compensatory movements, without further negativity.

Later in this game-of-games, techniques become means of practicing the strengthening of the ego. Only the strong ego, in tune with the certainty of one's unconditional personal worth and unqualified purposiveness and belonging, can allow the time and effort to know (experience) the mirthful mystery of being simultaneously unique, similar, and necessary for the evolution of the universe. Most people seldom experience true humor. It is the task of the natural high therapist to explore the essence of guilt, constriction, gloom, and unhappiness. To do so is to take direction without malice against the institutionalized world of boundary-ridden concepts and wasted energies.

Natural high therapy can be threatening to the one-dimensional, unchanging, externalized, and controlling goals of those who cling to and cherish disabling certainties. This threat is very frequently dissipated in the laughter and joy of experiencing self-hood. Natural high therapy is the outcome of a quarter-century project to discover (and invent) an optimistic behavioral-oriented self-training focused on all facets of humankind (inner, interpersonal, and transpersonal). Natural high practice encompasses traditional individual and group therapy. It focuses also on didactic-experiential formats emphasizing psychodrama, instrumented developmental groups (Kurt Lewin), meditation and imagery techniques, and teleodrama (O'Connell, 1975, 1981c). The following are some natural high techniques.

STROKING-FOR-STRENGTH

An exercise of note is the practice of "stroking-for-strength." The ego is made strong enough to turn inward with confidence by practicing (socially with the soliloquy, or alone with journal keeping) stroking for effort, not perfection. Stroking is based upon being a unique survivor of a discouraging world that judges *persons* rather than simply noting the effectiveness of behaviors. Self-esteem can only appear in the company of a strong ego that experiences inner growth. Others can present to us movements, judged by us to be evidence of our tentative worth (ego-esteem), but self-esteem, like humor, is an individual awareness of worth and belonging, not dependent upon the whim of others. Stroking-for-strength is also based upon efforts to encourage self and others. Productive humorists learn to stroke themselves, noncompetitively, simply for existing or "for no reason at all." All techniques of the natural high are centered upon such nonevaluative judgments. For the discouraged, it is essential to stroke for effort and similarity to others. Because the marginal misfits (society's scapegoats) cannot do such acts initially, the natural high tutor acts in loco parentis, reparenting those whose ego-identity has ossified into an inflexible reality. Initial intervention must come from a trusted outsider who has the courage to be noncompetitive (e.g., natural high therapist).

HUMORDRAMA

Humordrama is deeply embedded in the theory and practice of natural high therapy. Humordrama is used in natural high therapy in two senses. Broadly stated, it encompasses the whole thrust of natural high therapy, a theory of personality and psychotherapy specifically developed around the creation of the humorous attitude. In the narrow sense, humordrama is a type of advanced psychodrama (O'Connell, 1975) used after expressions of catharsis and awareness of weak-ego constrictions. Guilt, shared and projected, is the foremost sign of such constriction (habitual decrease of innate worth and inherent belonging). The empty chair soliloquy, and especially the mirror soliloquy, are the main techniques used (O'Connell, 1975). Of greater importance to lifestyle change is the use of humordrama in its broadest sense. In this larger perspective, the happy life entails a mindful awareness of the operation of paradoxes, such as the sad-glad paradox of death (O'Connell, 1981c). The mad misery-makers flatten and fragment life into deadly dualities. Humordrama highlights the constricted, addictive weak ego-identity that does not have to be clung to or fought against, just ridiculed and laughed at as incongruous excessive madness. The combination of psychodrama and humor gave birth to humordrama, which attempts to put into action, through therapeutic structure, a flexible, optimistic, response-able way of life. Clinically the evidence is overwhelming that patients who become involved in humordrama change positively. Humordrama adds a necessary ingredient beyond the preconditions of an encouraging group in a blame-less atmosphere.

In its narrowest sense, humordrama is a group action-technique, employed with a cohesive group that has learned how to cooperate-as-equals. The goal is to become aware of, share, honor, and hang-out with ego-constrictions that prevent enhancement of basic worth and belonging. The next move is to use the technique of humor to laugh at and ridicule the humorless responses of weak-ego identity. Note very carefully that the shared inanities of ego constrictions, not the worth and belonging of the *person*, are the focus of group aggression. Feedback is requested to guard against the possibility of misperceptions that the worth of the person is being assailed (as is the case with wit, not humor).

OTHER GROUP EGO-STRENGTHENING TECHNIQUES

Further group techniques are available, beyond humordrama, that aim at strengthening the weak ego (e.g., stroking-for-strength and contemplation of similarities and worth). The following case example from group psychotherapy may convey the gist of natural high group techniques: A natural high group has been together for 20 sessions. The bulk of the group is composed of American Vietnam veterans loaded with self-guilt and the anger of betrayal against authorities. They have already progressed through lectures and discussions of the skills of the weak ego, and the petty power gains involved, that prevent "letting-go" and give the weak ego its addictive quality.

Part of the generalized anger and projected guilt has already been reframed into growth opportunity in previous sessions by shocking group members with humor. Bill (not his real name), a huge, obese veteran, was the personification of constant overt anger and discouragement. (The names of all group members and patients are fictitious.) His lifestyle theme was to display his combat "dis-ability," seeking constant revenge by verbally idealized murders. Bill perceived lack of authenticity and predicted failure for anyone not "manly" enough to advocate nihilism and violence. As he fumed and frowned deep discouragement, he threatened the democratic change-oriented goals of the group. I smiled, bowed, and accepted the gift of deep discouragement from "the Buddha of Constant Discouragement." We talked about the opportunity given us by Bill as that "Buddha" to practice not being overwhelmed by proferred discouragement nor squandering time fighting it: "Simply acknowledge the presence of the gift and learn to refuse condemning or clinging to it." Bill was profoundly aghast. If he continued his discouraging approach, he was cooperating and giving a gift of love. If he opted for encouragement he was letting go of familiar fixations. He took both options in a spirit of play with the group accepting such games. Bill, itching for a fight and lusting for an autocratic directive to sink his vengeful teeth into, received only strokes (which he was starving for) and was told to go on.

The mirror soliloquy (O'Connell, 1975) would have been used here had Bill not taken the strokes for being helpful. With the mirror soliloquy, Bill would have been guessing at his internalized sentences, moving about in his habitual style. With the mirror soliloquy used in humordrama, one can play both poles of the paradox: the negative certainties of ego-constriction, the deep discouragement of self and projected guilt, and the wily ways of using mistaken negativity to gain subtle social influence (power). The positive pole of the ego-self paradox is the core of humordrama, the overriding jests using brief, sudden, condensed over- and understatements that contrast sharply with deep discouragement. Remember again the democratic spirit of the group--all are apt subjects for the mirror soliloquy. No one is to go away with the bad faith that his basic worth and belonging are being assailed: "If you must choose to be guilty, enjoy it," and "if you are passionately pursuing guilt, try feeling guilty about feeling guilty," are common themes.

Now that Bill was using former negativity in the spirit of self-esteem and social interest, Rex wanted to talk about not feeling angry over losing money. (Rex had been "Mr. Injustice Collector" of this group.) New Vietnam veterans in the group wanted to see reactions in their usual self-defeating style ("Kick the living crap out of....").

However, Bill was silent. Rex did not want to do a soliloquy, preferring not to take the risk of imperfection or "being worse" than others--and not verbalizing this decision. Therefore the moment had arrived for mirroring soliloquies. Eight participants played Rex, moving about in his tempo and disclosing his weak ego-defenses. Rex was not satisfied with the performances, and jumped up to double the mirrors, getting involved inadvertently. When number nine, Harry, did the mirror for Rex, the latter gave an unconscious recognition reflex (a facial "ahhah"). Harry was emitting the tension of change. Rex's depression was changing under the practice of self-stroking (for effort at being a unique survivor of a discouraging world). He was shocked that he was no longer involved in temper tantrums when his demands were not met automatically, immediately, and painlessly. This point marked Rex's gradual change from depression and Bill's "metanoia" (authentic conversion) from paranoia (extreme blame of others).

PERTINENT USES

Natural high practice excludes, no one. Its theory and practice have been used with all classifications of persons from the ages of 5 to 95, from psychotics to "normals," from those just awakening from the sleep of the weak ego to those considered terminal. Limitations on the degree and quality of therapeutic interventions are those imposed by the state of actualization of therapist and client. Discouragement and guilt are universal. Diseases of the weak ego can surface from too much to too little ego-esteem. The strong are the rare persons who experience unlimited self-esteem (SE). The natural high therapist accepts this universality of the weak egos who cling to judgments of persons as "better than/worse than." Natural high knows no victims; there are always alternative responses, even down to the basics of how one relates to one's own death. Everyone contributes to everyone else's world view by what they do or do not do. However, each person is completely response-able for the state of his or her own creative conclusions concerning life.

Natural high practice knows the soul: self-esteem might be called "soul-esteem." Spirituality is thus an important ingredient of humor. Natural high is alert to the many forms of hatred following discouragement.

Natural high contributes to each person's response-ability to let go of discouragement by connecting with the deep Self and an optimistic, interactional universe. Herein lies the essence of the humorous attitude.

CLINICAL PRESENTATIONS

All humans are constricted to some degree, hanging on to ego-induced diminishments of innate worth and belonging. All humans, doctors and patients, can imaginatively and unwittingly provoke or perceive "evidence" to prove their limiting lifestyle fictions. Whether one is grouped into doctor or patient class depends partly upon one's ego-trained reactions to the world, which are based upon judgments of persons. Discouragement is the well-practiced lot that we all share in some form or other, such that discouragement could well be a boon to the development of similarities of social interest!

Case histories of natural high interventions, inherently humorous to both parties of a successful dyadic relationship, are available in prior publications (O'Connell, 1979b, 1981a). The best case study can often be obtained with the help of your own journal keeping and the loving feedback of honest and true friends. However, I include three case history summaries focusing on the change in defeated lifestyles and the ways of maintaining such encouragement in a world lusting after ego-discouragement. I call these persons "patient-teachers" because they continue to be very patient with me and have taught me more than did all the CWAMAs of graduate schools. I will call one case the "OBE-man," (Out-of-Body Experience) another "the patient who survived the psychiatrist," and the third "grandfather of the delayed stress reaction." All are currently functioning very adequately outside of the hospital setting. "OBE-man" managed to get some natural high psychodrama. "The Survivor" touched transformation through natural high psychodrama and natural high meditation. "Grandfather" benefited from natural high art therapy, psychodrama, and meditation.

OBE-man was a Vietnam combat veteran who had been previously hospitalized on two occasions for alcoholism. He was compensated for delayed stress reaction benefits because he had stumbled across a psychiatrist in combat while unsuccessfully searching for a priest. A captive client in one of my conventional group therapy sessions, OBE-man quickly departed when he heard my humorous interactions with a patient who trusted me. This patient was talking about how he had things in control (the weak ego was having its day). "I'll bet I can get you very depressed" was my retort. OBE-man summarily left. All the king's horses and all the king's pharmacopoeia could not get OBE-man back to group again. However, he regarded me ambivalently as a "pompous ass" and a weird kind of guru. He was drawn to natural high, but only to disprove its assumptions. And therein lies the therapeutic rub. He read two of my books, offered free to any interested hospitalized veteran. I was judged to be sufficiently weird to talk with about his early out-of-body experiences. Together we read available literature. Together we found statements saying that one must be grounded before taking off. This was further corroboration of natural high premises. In effect, Jung had experienced a classical OBE later in his career. OBE outread me on Jung and introduced the ward psychiatrist to the wonders of Jung. All three of us taught each other. OBE attended formal courses on out-of-body experiences and was ecstatic at the social interest there. He felt accepted as an equal by professionals, and self-disclosure was rampant with all course participants.

With a ninth-grade education, OBE-man now knows the Jungian road map and can apply it to himself as well as anyone I know. He is making his own way, humorously overcoming the weak-ego ploys of himself and others. For now, OBE-man is able to experience the deep Self and the humor of laughing at his weak-ego ploys.

Survivor was in therapy for 21 years with a psychiatrist in private practice, until the psychiatrist retired. Survivor does not remember talking much, but the psychiatrist did alert him to the ways and values of successfully applying for VA compensation. After his mother's death, Survivor was alone, like OBE-man. Survivor's main activity was to dress in blue (like me) and pace constantly with a worried visage. Survivor *knew* discouragement and held it close to him. Better to be discouraged than nothing at all. Survivor outlasted many group therapists. He just said "I don't know." His superior IQ was in the service of anticipating and provoking discouragement. Survivor did like meditation, but not guided imagery, because he did not want anyone telling him what to do. "Good," I said, "now you'll learn real independence." Survivor said he could not meditate (perfection or utter failure were his only alternatives). Whenever I saw him pacing about, I congratulated him on his ability to one-point discouragement. Whenever I walked past him, he said "I can't do it." I replied, "You are doing it, and can do it better." One day I tried a new group approach. I brought in scores of cartoons ridiculing the assumptions of discouraged patients and pompous therapists. Survivor loved them. Whenever I saw him pacing, I said, "Think of a joke." Each morning thereafter Survivor presented me with a joke. He volunteered for psychodrama and shortly after was tricked (by role reversal) into being a patient. He finally self-disclosed his tragicomic ego pretensions, was able to laugh at these mistakes, and learned to value his deep Self. Survivor eventually left the hospital, found a girlfriend, and even secured a full-time job for the first time in over 16 years. He is risking losing "Social Security" (what a misnomer!) He wears brown and visits often to listen to the state of my ego-pretensions.

"Grandfather" was a successful vice-president for a large clothing chain for many years before it folded. He then collapsed physically and mentally. On the ward he appeared in a catatonic-like stupor, all ego-esteem having evaporated. He is still a medical nightmare, having had operations for cardiovascular, genito-urinal, and visual defects. He suffered through long bouts with nightmares of his unspoken guilt about his atrocities in World War II. Grandfather hated me as "a pompous ass" because I guessed correctly at his constrictions in group before we established a trusting relationship. However, he admired my determination and commitment to stay with the natural high approach. I gave him cartoons, which he still cherishes. Foremost is the drawing of a man in jail, hanging on to only two bars with a dolorous countenance. There are no other bars in the jail. He talked about his constrictions in these terms. In natural high art therapy he drew his dreams and cried in the presence of others for the first time in his life. At the same time he talked to his sons about these experiences, again for the first time. Grandfather still comes to natural high therapy when he returns to the hospital for physical therapy. Open with expressions of his natural highs in the face of real adverse conditions, Grandfather still teaches all his adopted grandsons of the Vietnam era.

SYNTHESIS

Patients who have not learned the natural high rationale and who have not experienced interpersonal trust with me in face-to-face encounters frequently regard me as a "wise-ass," a complete ass hole, "a pompous bastard." The royal road out of this dilemma of distrust is to follow the ways of Alfred Adler, to "spit in the soup," "take the wind out of the sails." I often anticipate these negative reactions to my guessing at weak-ego goals by simply talking about these persistent phenomena before they erupt. Symptoms are encouraged, resistance is reframed as cooperation. Futile force is an ego device that spawns further resistance of patients.

Happily, it is commonplace that those who later cooperate-as-equals and embrace the humorous attitude go through such negative rites of passage. In psychodrama I will often mirror a patient's anger at me in the empty chair technique. I (humorously) show them both how they could be even more angry at me and how they could responsibly and cooperatively resolve the apparent conflict. Because humor capitalizes on the unexpected, changes in the trust level often follow rapidly upon this open encouraging of symptoms.

For years I have been collecting aphorisms, all of which I have said to patients in natural high therapy (O'Connell, 1979a, 1981b). Such epigrams give a flavor of the natural high therapist's output as he struggles mightily and angrily with various ego-constrictions. Such ego-constrictions prevent the development of the individuation experience of unconditional worth and purposive belonging. One cannot reflect too much upon the dictum of "hating the sin, loving the sinner." In this approach even discouragement can be seen as creative (Haley, 1963). Patients readily go into shock at the unexpected when the therapist sees creative encouragement even in the most obviously defensive hostility: "Thank you for helping to give me practice in finding new ways to cope with discouragement. You are helping me to grow in openness, honesty, and humility. Perhaps by hanging out with this stress, I'll also increase my bodily supply of endorphins." Any influence of the therapist perceived by the patient as *force* is resisted with an equal or greater force.

From my collection of thousands of aphorisms, I offer the reader the following selection. They are given in the spirit of flux of Heraclitus rather than that of the flat, expected logic of Aristotle. Such maxims make excellent test materials. I have noted that those who can describe their ego-warfare and that of society by expanding the content of the aphorism can also really understand natural high humor. In Death and Transformation Labs (O'Connell, 1981d) aphorisms dealing with death are given to members of small groups to stimulate self-disclosure and hence enforce group cohesion. By noting your patterns of "likes," "dislikes," and "don't understands" you may be accepting a gift for your own actualization through contemplating the essence of the following maxims:

DISCOURAGENESIS

1. Numbers cannot give meaning.
2. To be alive and human means to have thwarted expectations. The trick lies in not upsetting one-self about being upset.
3. Discouragement is the unpardonable sin.
4. The greatest and most prevalent delusion of mankind is that "Life must be Fair."
5. Pampering is a horrible form of rejection.
6. How short the journey from the helplessness of infants to the hopelessness of adults.
7. See me as a guide, not a stretcher bearer.
8. We are afraid to get too well too quickly, at least in this lifetime.
9. Similarity is not sameness.
10. Hidden beneath the primary lack of social interest and self-esteem of the discouraged person is the abundant grandiosity of being able to predict the future with certainty: the perfection of failure-ship.
11. Despair is a successful defense against hope. With hope, one risks being imperfect.

HUMANISTIC DEPTH PSYCHOLOGY

1. We are all unique persons, but we are courting trouble when we demand "all the rights and privileges thereunto."
2. Think of self-esteem and social interest as your psychic tide. Demands, "drives," and dependencies

75

become very apparent when SE and SI are low. But rocks and snags do not cause the low water.

3. Always in process, we are no-things but never nothing.
4. Allow yourself the luxury of being thoroughly nervous and bored.
5. Your ego might be considered your ego; but yourself is never your Self.
6. Symptoms witnessed gently flow away.
7. Nothing is crazier than the assertion that the well-adjusted Western man is sane.
8. The sayings of saints get inscribed in stone by the same forces that resist their evolutionary implications.
9. If you want to study psychology, do not study psychology.
10. All I give is given to myself.

DRUGS AND OTHER ADDICTIONS

1. Think of all the grant money that would be immediately available for research into natural highs if drug companies could bottle it.
2. The Addict's Prayer: "Dear God, grant me a magic external substance to overcome my weakness for a magic external substance."
3. We become addicted to the reactions of others and suffer "withdrawal" symptoms when we fail to "score."
4. The certainty that the high resides in the external substance is one of the great stupidities of the addict.
5. Ignorance is bad enough, but the combination of ignorance and arrogance together is just too formidable.

INTERPERSONAL RELATIONS

1. Everyone can teach everyone else by example, either good or bad.
2. Any obstacle that I survive will make me strong if I avoid "demandments" and negative nonsense.
3. I can never say "yes" until I can say "NO"--with the whole body, not simply the tongue.

4. We must practice searching for similarities so we can accept differences.
5. Embarrassment is a type of vicious vanity.
6. Most of us do not want control over our lives: We merely want control of people and conditions that we allow to control us.
7. If you lust after the approval of anyone, you are enthralled by the stupidly sinful dis-ease of idolatry (i.e., ego constriction).
8. Demanding strokes from other folks is addictive--and may be injurious to your health.
9. We spend excessive time and energy demanding that the devil reward us for our virtues.
10. We can fake experience to others, but never to ourselves.
11. Social interest means being aware of the deficiency of it in all persons.
12. We have sufficient problems trusting ourselves without obsessing about the trustworthiness of others.
13. Any relationship that you cannot risk losing through honest self-disclosure and feedback is idolatrous and may be injurious to your health.
14. I am not my brother's keeper, but I am his contributor.
15. Don't drop bombs to kill flies--or send canoes to contest battleships.

LOVE AND ENCOURAGEMENT

1. If you say you can love only one person, you are confusing love with possession.
2. We will stamp out mental illness when we stamp in encouragement.
3. Never diagnose unless you treat.
4. Don't cry over spilt shit: Make it into fertilizer.
5. Stroke yourself for effort (not perfection) and someday you may be able to stroke yourself for just existing.
6. Everyone is responsible, but no one is to blame.
7. Accept what you get at this moment: It is right for you as you are.
8. I know of no drastic psychiatric therapy that does not work. The question is, "When it works, what does it do to the patient's premises about life?"

RELIGIONS: INSTRUMENTAL VERSUS INSTITUTIONAL

1. The unpardonable sin is to believe in one.
2. Life is full of miracles if you don't demand any.
3. Life is simple but our lies are complex.
4. Blessed are the soul makers, for they accept and even celebrate their tensions, without recourse to the psychic numbings of pills, drugs, booze, and violence.
5. One should be grateful for, and grow with, the grace of God rather than passively pray for it.
6. If you are searching for a quiet, simple, and safe spot, support your local insane asylum.
7. All successful psychotherapists are faith healers. They teach clients faith in self, others, and faith in a loving God.

REFERENCES

Bellman, R. (1970). Humor and paradox. In W. Mendel (Ed.)., *A Celebration of Laughter* (p. 44). Los Angeles: Mara Books.

Chapman, A., & Foot, H. (Eds.). (1976). *Humor and Laughter: Theory, Research, Applications*. London: Wiley.

Freud, S. (1950). Humor In *Collected Papers* (Vol. 5, pp. 215-222). London: Hogarth. (Original work published 1928)

Haley, J. (1963). *The Strategies of Psychotherapy*. New York: Grune & Stratton.

Hyers, C. (Ed.). (1969). *Holy Laughter: Essays on Religion in the Comic Perspective*. New York: Seabury.

Hyers, C. (1973). *Zen and the Comic Spirit*. Philadelphia: Westminster.

Leonard, G. (1975). *The Ultimate Athlete: Re-Visioning Spirits, Physical Education, and the Body*. New York: Viking.

O'Connell, W. (1960). The adaptive functions of wit and humor. *Journal of Abnormal and Social Psychology, 61*, 263-270.

O'Connell, W. (1975). *Action Therapy and Adlerian Theory*. Chicago: Alfred Adler Institute.

O'Connell, W. (1976). Freudian humour: The eupsychia of everyday life. In A. Chapman & H. Foot (Eds.),

Humor and Laughter: Theory, Research, Applications (pp. 313-329). London: Wiley.

O'Connell, W. (1977). The sense of humor: Actualizer of persons and theories. In A. Chapman & H. Foot (Eds.), *It's A Funny Thing, Humour* (pp. 143-147). Oxford: Pergamon.

O'Connell, W. (1979a). *Super-Natural Highs.* Chicago: North American Graphics.

O'Connell, W. (1979b). The demystification of Sister Saint Nobody. *Journal of Individual Psychology, 35,* 79-94.

O'Connell, W. (1980). Natural high therapy. In R. Herink (Ed.), *The Psychotherapy Handbook* (pp. 416-420). New York: New American Library.

O'Connell, W. (1981a). Natural high therapy. In R. Corsini (Ed.), *Handbook of Innovative Psychotherapies* (pp. 554-568). New York: Wiley.

O'Connell, W. (1981b). *Essential Readings in Natural High Actualization.* Chicago: North American Graphics.

O'Connell, W. (1981c). The natural high therapist: God's favorite monkey. *Voices: The Art and Science of Psychotherapy, 16, 4,* 37-44.

O'Connell, W. (1981d). Spirits in thanatology. *Death Education, 4,* 397-409.

Watzlawick, P. (1978). *The Language of Change: Elements of Therapeutic Communication.* New York: Basic Books.

Weber, C. (1970). A God who laughs. In W. Mendel (Ed.), *A Celebration of Laughter* (pp. 119-133). Los Angeles: Mara Books.

Wilber, K. (1979). *No Boundary: Eastern and Western Approaches to Personal Growth.* Boulder: Shambhala Publications.

HUMOR IN
PROVOCATIVE THERAPY

Frank Farrelly and Michael Lynch

Frank Farrelly is a provocative man! His resolve to facilitate human change has taken him beyond the bounds of traditional approaches to psychotherapy. The new techniques he has developed are certain to stir up strong reactions from both patients and clinicians. It is evident that Farrelly's approach works very well for him. It is also evident that this approach requires a continuously "provocative" therapeutic stance. The question posed to the reader is to assess how much of Farrelly's approach can be adapted to everyday clinical work with different patient populations. Can Farrelly's techniques be used by other therapists without being subject to patient misinterpretation? Can the therapist's empathy still come through despite the provocative style? Which patients would benefit most from such techniques? Which therapists would benefit most from including such techniques in their work? Would Farrelly's approach be as beneficial for the well-motivated patient as it would be for recalcitrant or emotionally entrenched patients?

The chapter outlines the basic assumptions upon which Farrelly's approach is founded, and illustrates provocative therapy techniques with numerous clinical examples from Farrelly's therapy sessions.

Frank Farrelly is a social worker in private practice in Madison, Wisconsin, and is the founder of Provocative Therapy. He has conducted many workshops on provocative therapy in the United States and Europe, Australia, and New Zealand. His publications include <u>Provocative Therapy</u> (1974), co-authored with Jeffrey Brandsma, which has been translated into Italian and German and will soon be released in French.

The second author, Michael Lynch, PhD, is a mental health professional and a sagacious student of the provocative therapy approach. He is presently located in Charlotte, North Carolina.

* * *

81

THEORETICAL PERSPECTIVE

Provocative Therapy grew out of the experiences of Frank Farrelly, the senior author, in working with hospitalized psychotic patients in the 1960's. It was a product of experimentation with different modes of relating to patients and inadvertent discoveries along the way. Over the past 2 decades it has been used with outpatients and inpatients with a broad spectrum of presenting problems, diagnostic categories, different social classes, and widely varying age ranges. The theoretical base of provocative therapy consists of 10 assumptions and 2 hypotheses regarding the change process.

ASSUMPTIONS

The first assumption is that "people change and grow in response to a challenge." Many therapies emphasize the safe aspects of the therapeutic relationship. The provocative therapist does not perceive therapist acceptance alone as a sufficient condition for client change. Although the client may feel better in talking to the therapist, "feeling better" is not invariably synonymous with "getting better." We believe that if the organism is offered a safe environment it may either grow and evolve or stagnate and continue its nonproductive habits. Although the human organism needs safety so that it can live in a relatively predictable world, it also needs stimulation. Productive therapy assumes that change is more likely to occur when individuals are presented with nonoverwhelming challenges they cannot avoid and with which they must somehow learn to cope. Moreover, one of the therapist's objectives is to assist the person through an experience of "constructive anger" at himself or herself or at the image the therapist is painting of him or her. The term "constructive anger" as used here refers to a state of self-annoyance coupled with a desire to be different. It is important to note that although the experience of constructive anger is unlikely to be generated in an overly safe environment, it is as unlikely to occur in a "dangerous" environment, one in which the client perceives the therapist as hostile and primarily critical. Consequently, the provocative therapist's role in this regard is twofold--to support clients at one level and simultaneously challenge them at another level. By carefully blending indirect support and direct provocations, the therapist is able to help clients transform self-defeating behaviors into self-enhancing ones.

The second assumption of provocative therapy is that "clients can change if they choose." One of Farrelly's early and significant experiences at Mendota Mental Health Institute came one day when he "threw therapy out the window" and expressed his rage at a psychotic patient for writing obscene and terrifying letters to a young secretary. When the patient angrily replied that he could not be held responsible because he was "mentally ill," Farrelly was stunned. This experience and later ones convinced him that choice plays a major role in the development of "crazy" thoughts and behaviors as well as in the onset of mental disease.

The assumption that clients can change if they choose is vital if therapeutic change is to occur. In provocative therapy it is acknowledged that many unfortunate experiences do happen to people that they do not deserve. It is acknowledged that there are many socio-cultural and other factors that exert influence over the individual. Yet if people are to change, the focus of therapy must be upon their responsibility for their lives and their responsibility in the maintenance of self-defeating beliefs and behaviors. The task of the provocative therapist is to move clients out of the powerless position of "cannot" and into the perception that their dysfunctional patterns frequently (albeit not invariably) result from their choices.

Some well-intentioned therapists today, operationally believing in clients' deficits and fragility, inadvertently reinforce their clients' inadequate self-images. They perceive their clients as victims of life's circumstances who will shatter rather easily if confronted. Although it is undeniable that human beings have "breaking points" or that victims exist (witness the genocide of the German Jews in World War II, the Biafran tragedy in the 1960's, molested children today, and many other painful current examples), we still hold a third assumption regarding psychotherapeutic work: "the psychological fragility of clients is vastly overrated both by themselves and others." Provocative Therapy maintains that it is ultimately nontherapeutic to offer large amounts of positive regard while withholding genuine feelings of occasional doubt, irritation, or anger so as not to "harm" the client. The provocative therapist believes in the adaptability and resiliency of humankind. Instead of shielding clients from reality, the provocative therapist helps them become aware that they can handle their problems better than they or others think.

The fourth assumption is that "clients have far more potential for achieving adaptive, productive, and social-ized modes of living than they and most clinicians assume." Some therapists may inadvertently convey the idea that the client is inherently incapable of change. On the other hand, the provocative therapist seeks to provoke clients into giving expression to their inner resources so that they can get in touch with their personal power and actively participate in the healing process.

The fifth assumption is that "clients' maladaptive, unproductive, antisocial attitudes and behaviors can be drastically altered whatever the degree of severity or chronicity." The provocative therapist perceives *all* clients as capable of change, even those who have severe or chronic disturbances. Far from being overwhelmed by clients' psychopathology or chronicity, the provocative therapist enters clients' inner worlds and utilizes the energy in these to help them bring about constructive change.

The sixth assumption is that "adult or current experi-ences are at least if not more significant than childhood or previous experiences in shaping clients' values, operational attitudes, and behaviors." Inherent in this assumption is the idea that "the peer group, mass media, or pluralistic societal value and reward system, and the individual's own choices shape adult personality at least as much as Momma and Daddy" (Farrelly & Brandsma, 1974, p. 74). (All subsequent citations in this chapter, unless otherwise noted, are to Farrelly & Brandsma [1974]). The therapist engages clients indirectly in humorous and bantering behavior to help them gain a wider perspective on their problems. However, the main thrust in therapy is to provoke affective-perceptual experi-ences that are as real and significant to the inner life of clients as their past life experiences have been. In this sense, provocative therapy is not an excursion into the past based on the belief that the significant causes of human behavior are *past* causes. Rather, provocative therapy attempts a "living theater" production with the spotlight on current causality and corrective experiences.

Consequent upon our belief in the importance of cur-rent experiences, we adopt the seventh assumption that clients' behaviors with the therapist are relatively accu-rate reflections of their habitual patterns of social and interpersonal relationships. Thus, the therapy session is a microcosm of clients' psychosocial lives. The provocative therapist observes client behaviors while becoming actively and spontaneously involved with clients to provoke them into displaying an even wider array of their behavioral repertoires. Once a therapist sees first-hand the behavioral tools, tactics, and strategies that clients have, the therapist can then proceed to help them alter or discard dysfunctional patterns. This is accom-plished in one of three ways: (a) by presenting clients with evaluations of how significant others will very likely perceive and react to those attitudes and behaviors, (b) by humorously modeling (with highly probable "future scenarios") the negative social consequences that result from such attitudes and behaviors, and (c) by making clients aware of the feedback available to them from their own social relationship matrix.

The eighth assumption is that people make sense. The human animal is exquisitely logical and understandable. With Horace, the Latin poet, we believe that *nihil humani alienum est* (nothing human is foreign to me). Even those fellow human beings who suffer from severe psychologi-cal difficulties are not alien to us. We firmly believe that what is most personal is most universal. Although voice print analysis and fingerprinting experts can attest to our individual uniqueness, it is also clear to any observer of the human condition that human similarities outweigh human differences. The basic experiences of love, hate, hope, joy, fear, ecstasy, and agony are universally shared through the ages and are central to human existence.

The ninth assumption of provocative therapy is that the expression of the therapist's genuine noncontradictory negative feelings toward the client can markedly benefit the client. Provocative therapy incorporates what has been called "tough love." In this eminently human way of relating, there can exist warmth and confrontation, caring and annoyance, compassion and limits. It is a fully hu-man existential encounter that at times can be perceived as the psychological equivalent of a Pier Six brawl or conversely, as making love.

The tenth assumption of provocative therapy is that "the most important messages between people are nonver-bal," and occur simultaneously on different levels. The most relevant messages between people are believed to be implicit, covert, indirect, and at times telepathic. This implies that the most effective way for the therapist to experience the client is to observe not only by "listening with the third ear" but also by "seeing with the third eye."

HYPOTHESES

In addition to the 10 assumptions, provocative therapy is based on two hypotheses. The first hypothesis concerns clients' self-concept and intrapsychic well-being (increased self-confidence, alleviation of depression and anxiety, etc.). The second pertains to adequacy in reality testing and meeting the reasonable expectations and needs of others (in interpersonal relationships and task performance areas with employer, spouse, and family, etc.). The two hypotheses are as follows:

1. If provoked by the therapist (humorously, perceptively, and within the client's own internal frame of reference), the client will tend to move in the opposite direction from the therapist's definition of the client as a person.
2. If urged provocatively (humorously and perceptively) by the therapist to continue his or her self-defeating, deviant behaviors, the client will tend to engage in self-and-other-enhancing behaviors that more closely approximate the societal norm.

RATIONALE FOR USING HUMOR

Humor is an essential ingredient in provocative therapy. Far from being utilized haphazardly, it is a tactical and strategic tool that serves specific functions. Clients are often more likely to accept therapist messages when such messages are communicated humorously (whether directly or indirectly). One message more likely to be received if it is communicated humorously is therapist acceptance and positive regard toward clients. The provocative therapist typically does not convey caring or liking for clients explicitly. Warmth is communicated implicitly by humor, physical touch, affectionate banter, and twinkle in the eye. In the following case example a private client is leaving a therapist's office at the end of an interview in which he discussed his homosexuality. The therapist claps his hand on the client's shoulder:

Farrelly: *(sighing dejectedly)* Well, see ya next week, Hopeless. *(suddenly "noticing" his hand on client's shoulder, pointing with other hand at it)* Do you see that hand? Now that is *trained* acceptance! *(therapist leans forward, placing his forehead close to client's forehead, grimaces disgustedly, in a tone of "revulsion")* Actually I can't *stand* you tutti-frutti, closet queen pansies, but....

Client: *(laughingly, snorts, shakes his head, punches therapist gently in ribs)* Boy, you just don't quit, do you, Frank? OK, next week. *(leaves waving, shaking his head, and laughing)* (Farrelly & Brandsma, 1974, pp. 63-64)

Many therapists believe in the "growth through pain" school of thought. While agreeing that some discomfort seems an inevitable concomitant of certain tasks (cleaning the oven, engaging in psychotherapeutic change, or learning the piano), provocative therapists believe in growth through gladness, not just sadness. We agree with Father Francis MacNutt, O.P., in his book *Healing* (1974) that the majority of sickness or pain is nonredemptive.

As therapists we naturally realize we are dealing with human pain and suffering, and we are not insensitive clowns jesting at others' scars, never having felt a wound ourselves. Rather, we maintain that we can convey the humorous aspects of even painful life situations for clients, thereby challenging them to a new, broader perspective and energy release that can lead to healing. A spoonful of sugar really *does* help the medicine go down:

Farrelly: *(tapping her on the knee)* What's the problem, Connie *(fictitious name)*?

Client: *(hands tightly clenched, tears brimming in eyes, speaking haltingly in a tremulous voice)* I...just learned that...my 27-year old daughter...is a...homosexual. *(she stops, unable to speak, puts a hand to her throat, swallowing painfully)*

Farrelly: *(leaning forward, places his hand on her forearm, maintains eye contact steadily; in a quiet, solemn measured, tone of voice)* I'm glad

Client: you've told me her *core...salient...*personality
characteristic.
*(begins to nod, stops abruptly, looks astounded,
and bursts out laughing while tears stream down
her face)* God! This is *ridiculous!* And all
day, scared to come up here and get inter-
viewed at this workshop, I was thinking
angrily, "He can't make fun of *this!*" *(the audience of 150 therapists join her in laughter)*
(Farrelly, 1979)

A common cognitive process involves gathering sen-
sory data from the self and the world and then interpreting or organizing it into perceptions. These perceptions
determine what humans see and what they do not see, and
tend to delimit human experience and behavior. One of
the functions of humor is to provide a means for the
therapist to move clients from fixed, narrow, and
dysfunctional perceptions into more flexible, broader, and
more usable ones.

Humor is compelling and influential. It has
impact. It changes people's minds. We suspect its
compelling quality comes from the deeply paradoxical nature of our existence; people are more
suggestible and compliant during the orgasm of
laughter. We suspect that a humorous statement is
just as likely to be remembered as a serious
statement. Humor continues to influence us over
time. (Farrelly & Brandsma, 1974, p. 99)

TECHNIQUE

The goal in provocative therapy is to provoke an
affective and perceptual experience within clients that
will result in five different types of behavior:

1. Affirming their self-worth, verbally and behaviorally;
2. Asserting themselves appropriately both in task
performances and relationships;
3. Defending themselves realistically and authenti-
cally against the excessively negative assessments
others make of them;
4. Engaging in psychosocial reality testing and learning the necessary discriminations to respond

adaptively: Global perceptions lead to global reactions; differentiated perceptions lead to adaptive reactions;

5. Engaging in risk-taking behaviors in personal relationships, especially communicating affection and vulnerability to significant others. (Farrelly & Brandsma, 1974, p. 56)

In order for the client to reach these goals, the techniques used by the therapist must provoke clients into experiencing themselves in a spontaneous and genuine manner. Such techniques must also allow the therapist a vast range of responses in order to outmaneuver client attempts to thwart or contain the therapist. Humor enables the provocative therapist to "float like a butterfly and sting like a bee." And, we would add, "hug like a teddy bear." The following example illustrates how humor can be utilized to go "one step beyond" and contain client behavior:

Client:	*(seductive, whining, demanding)* Are you out of sugar?
Therapist:	Huh? Am I out of what?
Client:	*(arrogantly)* I drink coffee with sugar.
Therapist:	Sug---
Client:	Yeah, if you don't have any sugar, forget it!
Therapist:	*(acting hypnotized)* Who needs sugar when we got *(therapist staring at client's naked knees)* uh....
Client:	*(noticing therapist's reaction, disgustedly)* Oh, brother! *(client leans back, pulls skirt down over her knees)*
Therapist:	*(looks pointedly at client's knees, gently pulls client's skirt hem down even further, with raised eyebrows and an "innocent" voice tone)* Well, don't worry about it, my weakness is liquor.
Client:	*(bursts out laughing)* (Farrelly, 1980e)

Bandler (1978), a co-founder of Neuro-Linguistic Programming, modeled Farrelly's work and concluded that Farrelly induces a trance state within the client. Indeed the provocative therapeutic experience for the client can be compared to a journey into a real life comedic theatre created by the therapist's colorful blending of imagery and humor. Learning to think in "three-dimensional, colored holograms" can rapidly facilitate the healing process.

Farrelly and Brandsma (1974) stress that "if the client is not laughing during at least part of the therapeutic encounter, the therapist is not doing provocative therapy and what he is doing may at times turn out to be destructive" (p. 95). Unfortunately, some newcomers to provocative therapy often perceive only the confrontive and humorous aspects of the system and erroneously assume that provocative therapists simply try to irritate the client into mental health via sarcasm, banter, or ridicule. It is important that this notion be dispelled. For provocative therapy to be successful, the client must experience the therapist as warmly caring and fundamentally supportive. The 95% rate of return for second interviews in Farrelly's clientele attests to this fact. Metaphorically speaking, the provocative therapist is not across the room shooting barbs of humor at the client. Rather, the therapist is *with* the client (within the client's internal frame of reference), using humor to push out from the inside the imprisoning walls of the client's habitually dysfunctional thought patterns. Thus the therapist can demonstrate that the client's mental prison has more exits than it has walls and that laughter, like Joshua's trumpet at Jericho, can bring these walls tumbling down.

Although humor is a major tool of provocative therapy, it is not the goal of treatment. In provoking the affective and perceptual experience of change, humor can be placed aside as therapist and client experience together the client's feelings or while the therapist offers support through shared silence, touch, or softly whispered tender statements such as "those little baby women can just get their little dirty grubby hands around your heart strings sometimes...can't they Tommie?" (Farrelly, 1980f).

A number of humorous techniques are utilized in provocative therapy: (a) expressing unverbalized or implicit client thoughts; (b) accentuating the negative; (c) emphasizing the dreaded aspects of change and the positive aspects of the status quo; (d) supplying immediate feedback; (e) listing and (f) using the four languages of provocative therapy. Let us now look at each of these techniques in detail.

One of the humorous techniques utilized in provocative therapy is that of expressing the client's unverbalized or implicit thoughts and feelings. The provocative therapist makes a habit of bringing the client's doubts, fears, and socially "unacceptable" feelings into the open where they can be dealt with. The provocative therapist is willing to think the unthinkable, feel the unfeelable, and say the unutterable in order to bring "that which is hidden into the light." Humor is often simultaneously the cause and effect of this process. One reason why this technique proves humorous is that some of the subsidiary rationales we use to guide our behaviors are often quite ridiculous and nonsensical. Whereas we may not grasp their absurdity simply by thinking them, we become intensely aware of their irrationality when we hear them spoken aloud and perceive the reactions from others.

Seeing the world through the eyes of the client and then relaying that perception to the client through reflective techniques connects the therapist to the client's system and establishes a trust or bonding between therapist and client. The client feels understood. The provocative therapy technique of expressing what the client thinks and feels but is reluctant to *say* can be construed as an extension of the reflection technique; that is, the therapist reflects the unsaid as well as the said. The client often responds with astonishment, replying with such statements as "you're reading my mind," or "you must have talked to my family." Although the swiftness of the therapist's empathy can be alarming for the client, the client fundamentally feels his or her phenomenological world is deeply and accurately understood. In this way, trust is established much more quickly than it would be had the therapist waited for the client to divulge the "unutterable."

The benefit of expressing the client's thoughts and feelings is that client "secrets" are then less likely to become obstacles separating therapist and client. For example, if an obese client comes in for therapy with a presenting problem other than weight, both therapist and client are more likely to feel comfortable with each other and work better together if the weight problem is acknowledged than if it is "politely" ignored. Once laid out in the open, client thoughts, doubts, and fears can become grist for the therapeutic mill, to be processed and resolved. The plot thickens, so to speak, and the pace quickens. An example of expressing a client's perceptions and attitudes follows in an excerpt from a provocative therapy workshop in front of a large audience of psychotherapists. The client is a therapist who recently has lost two of her own clients through suicide.

Therapist: *(touching her knee, in a loud, nonchalant tone of voice)* OK, Frieda *(fictitious name)*, what's the problem?

Client: *(in a trembling voice)* Uhm...I've had...*(catches her breath)* two suicides within the last 3 weeks and I've been primary therapist...responsible.

Therapist: *(flatly)* Yeah.

Client: Uhm, and they both did it after they left *(sic)* the hospital.

Therapist: *(flatly)* Yeah.

Client: *(struggles on painfully)* And I've had this lump in my throat for the past *(her voice breaks)* 2 days. *(quickly hurrying on)* Friday I went to the second--*(she stops abruptly, struggles for emotional control; audible intake of breath)*, and, uh, *(pauses, sharp intake of breath)* I haven't...I told the mother *(her voice breaks piteously)* that I was sorry...*(long pause; on the verge of tears, she smiles fleetingly, raises her hands, palms upward, and lets them fall helplessly in her lap, continues in a choking but perky and jaunty tone of voice)* That's it.

Therapist: *(maintaining eye contact steadily; abruptly, in a flat tone of voice)* So you killed them.

Client: *(astounded, nonplussed, bursting out laughing in a choked tone of voice)* Oh, shit! *(gasping and laughing; several in audience laugh uneasily)* Give me a break! *(half crying, half laughing)* I mean, damn! *(gasping with lump-in-the-throat laughter)*

Therapist *(interjecting laconically, slowly)* Well, "Give me a *break*"?? I mean, Frieda, for God's sake....

Client: *(gasping with astonishment and laughter)* Oh! Shi---

Therapist: *(continuing blandly)* Sounds like your therapy is like *cyanide.*

Client: *(doubling over with laughter)* Ohhh!....

Therapist: *(finishing nonchalantly)* For God's sake.

Client: *(continuing to gasp with laughter)*

Therapist: *("innocently")* Huh? (Farrelly, 1980b)

Humor in Provocative Therapy

Because much of human behavior is related to how people perceive their bodies, many of the implicit thoughts the provocative therapist verbalizes have to do with body image. Because body image tends to be the most intimately personal dimension of our self-concept, it would seem important to bring to the fore the gestalt of attitudes, feelings, and values that each of us harbors (consciously and unconsciously) about our body. In order to provoke unrehearsed, spontaneous reactions from clients about themselves in concrete and specific ways rather than in diffused and generalized terms, the provocative therapist frequently talks in detail about their body images.

For example, a 30-year-old woman with an identical twin married sister could not believe that men would date her for any reason other than sex because she was "ugly." A very pleasant, kind person, she was definitely attractive both physically and personally, although she did not realize this.

Therapist: *("disgustedly")* Well, I see what you're talking about. My God! Nobody but a sex maniac could go out with a gal like you, with big feet, thick ankles, bulging calves, bowlegged....

Client: *(nervously laughing)* No, I'm knock-kneed.

Therapist: *(in an "annoyed, disgusted" tone)* Okay, okay, you're knock-kneed, you've got fat thighs, sagging buttocks, a protruding abdomen, thick waist, flat chest, broad shoulders, a lantern jaw, jug ears, bulbous nose, furry eyebrows, two little pig-eyes, and hair that looks like an abandoned rat's nest. But I'll say one thing for you, your teeth sure look good.

Client: *(laughing explosively)* They're false! *(therapist and client dissolve in laughter)*

With relative quickness she changed her 30-year-old personal myth about her attractiveness (Farrelly & Brandsma, 1974, pp. 177-178).

Perhaps the most recognized of the provocative therapy techniques is that of overemphasizing the negative. Whereas therapists of other orientations may directly or subtly attempt to persuade the client to give up dysfunctional and excessively gloomy images of self or of the world, the provocative therapist subscribes plausibly to the client's negative perceptions even more than does the client. The therapist acts out the negative half of the client's ambivalence and even marshals idiotic evidence to support the client's irrational contentions. A related technique is that of proposing reasons and offering excuses for the client *not* to change. In doing this, the therapist attempts to persuade the client with inane and absurd arguments that change is too difficult, or that the status quo is more desirable or natural. An example illustrates these satirical techniques in action:

Client: *(weary tone)* I've tried to get all my good strokes out of performance and, you know, being in control and doing things.

Therapist: *(flatly)* Yeah?

Client: *(in a flat, tired tone)* And here lately I've just realized that...that, uh, I'm not really getting...mmm, I'm not really getting what I want out of that, the self-esteem and everything, it seems like....

Therapist: *(interrupting forcibly)* You gotta do *more*!

Client: *(startled, raising her voice, speaking more quickly)* It seems like, that I need how... somehow to learn how to let go more, and just flow with things....

Therapist: *(remonstrating)* Let *go*?! You gotta tighten....

Client: *(finishing)* And get some self-esteem from that.

Therapist: *(shaking his head, flabbergasted at her "stupidity")* No, no *no*! You got it...180 degrees *wrong*, you got it all backasswards. Now you got...you're sort of a performer and achiever?

Client: *(tiredly)* Mhm.

Therapist: *(enthusiastically cheer-leading)* You gotta bear *down*!

Client: *(flatly)* I've been programmed that way.

Therapist: *(firmly)* Well, that's good, that's alright, somebody did it right, because I *tell* ya, if you're just gonna get strokes in relationships, forget it: they'll hurt you every time, disappoint ya...The only thing ya got really *stable* in life...is *achievement*!

Client: *(quickly, energetically)* That's what it *seemed* like.

Therapist: *(nodding agreement)* Well, that's just what it....

Client: *(finishing)* For a long time.

Therapist *(forcibly)* What *seems, is!*...What you *feel*, you *are!*

Client: *(protesting)* But it hasn't been *working* lately!

Therapist: *(assuredly)* Well, that's 'cause you probably been slackin' off!

Client: *(nodding)* Uhm, could be, yeah.

Therapist: *(loudly)* You got to tough--tighten it up and do some *more!*

Client: *(laughs ruefully)* Yeahhh....

Therapist: See what I mean?

Client: *(grinning)* Uh huh.

Therapist: *(explaining)* You *ARE* your achievements.

Client: *(quickly)* I...somehow I rebel against that, too.

Therapist: *(arrogantly assured)* Well, that's...you're getting a snotty attitude, Mathilda *(fictitious name)*, and that's not gonna help ya....

Client: *(laughs)*

Therapist: *(firmly)* See? Now snotty achievers don't get good str....

Client: *(quickly)* You know, like being liked for who you are and not for what you can do, kinda business.

Therapist: *("disgustedly")* Ohhh, "who ya are," my God in heaven, there are a lot of people going around and telling folks that, and I tell ya, it just makes me *cringe!* *(in a loud pulpit tone)* "YOU ARE WORTH WHILE, BECAUSE YOU *ARE*." Now, *I* say, God! you try to go sell *that* in the open market, and there aren't going to be many buyers! (Farrelly, 1980c)

One of the variations of believably overemphasizing the negative used by the therapist to assist the client in reality testing is that of *reductio ad absurdum*. Here the therapist exaggerates the client's negative statements and carries them to their "logical" extremes until the client rejects them as preposterous. Another similar variation is that of accepting without question the client's claims of worthlessness or hopelessness. (For example, therapist to client, "Now I don't try to cure anybody anymore. I just try to help you accept your limitations. You have within you, they say, the total power to cure yourself, but obviously they weren't considering people of your ilk.") In using these techniques, the provocative therapist relates to clients simultaneously on two levels. On one hand, by not arguing against the client's self-defeating claims and taking the client's perceptions as literally true, the therapist in effect enters the client's phenomenological world and gains rapport. On the other hand, the therapist is indirectly lampooning the client's negative perceptions by energetically overemphasizing and exaggerating them.

Another way of encouraging change in this system consists in helping clients internalize important personality functions they have abdicated and projected onto others. More specifically, clients often collapse into helpless, irresponsible, or socially deviant postures that force others in their immediate families or in society to take over their responsibility functions (keeping their behavior in check, pressuring them to act rationally, etc.). As long as others, including well-intentioned therapists, fulfill the responsibility aspects of their personalities, clients remain mired in irresponsible and helpless modes of functioning. However, by overemphasizing negative deviances, the provocative therapist strengthens clients' inhibitions and resistances to their own dysfunctional behaviors and moves them into more rewarding ways of being.

Habitually, the provocative therapist tends to drag his or her feet while the client progresses toward healthier and satisfying ways of being. Changing from an old way of being to a new way is a crucial period in a person's life, and the transition is scary. In order to facilitate the client's letting go of the negative aspects of self so that he or she can focus on emerging positive aspects, the provocative therapist (a) focuses on the dreaded aspects of the changes, provoking the client to talk about the positive aspects, and (b) talks longingly and nostalgically about what the client is leaving behind, provoking the client into making such comments as, "Well, that's a lot of shit; that job wasn't *that* good," or "No, that relationship really wasn't what I wanted." Some typical provocative therapist responses to client changes are: "That's OK, dear. You can always retrace your steps and go back to the you that you and I (therapists places hand warmly and gently on client's arm, simultaneously grimacing disgustedly) know." Or, "Don't worry about it, fella; it's probably just something you ate. It'll pass."

As mentioned earlier, a central focus in provocative therapy is helping clients get in touch with their power. By playing the interminably reluctant Messiah (dragging his or her heels and endlessly procrastinating while professing enthusiasm for rescuing clients), the provocative therapist leads clients into flexing their psychological muscles. Clients are provoked to actively seek knowledge and feedback from their relationships and environments and to develop maze smartness. Moreover, clients are provoked into mobilizing their power and becoming increasingly self-confident, thereby becoming active participants in caring for others rather than remaining in the passive and powerless modality of wanting, wishing, and waiting for love from others. In the following example, the therapist uses humor to facilitate a client's "owning" his power:

Client: *(seriously and sincerely)* Boy, you have really helped me.

Therapist: That's a fact!

Client: I'll never forget you.

Therapist: *(laconically)* You ought not to. Of course I'll forget *you*, but then I'm *much* more memorable than you are and you're just another client. Yeah, I've definitely done an incredible job considering *(therapist gestures toward the client)* the poor material I've had to work with. Ninety-five percent of the credit goes to me.

Client: *(taken aback, protesting)* Well, Frank, I think *I* did 95% and you did 5.

Therapist: That's the trouble in this clinical field. You just work and slave with people and *give, give, give*! That's the kind of thing...they're just a bunch of glory hoggers, these clients. *(Therapist suddenly covers his face with his hands, and "sobs uncontrollably.")* (Farrelly, 1965)

One of the most important techniques of provocative therapy is supplying clients with immediate feedback. In order to function optimally, the human organism requires frequent feedback from its psychosocial, cultural, and familial environments. Whereas many therapists seem to withhold feedback from clients (perhaps because of their belief in client fragility), the provocative therapist believes that clients have a right to the therapist's perceptions about them and to feedback from other sources to which the therapist has access. In a sense, the provocative therapist helps clients become aware of the

impact they are having on other people and then asks, "Is
this the impact you want to create?" In this respect,
offering feedback does not always have to occur within a
somber, confrontive, tense context. In provocative
therapy, feedback is often communicated to clients in a
humorous and sometimes indirect manner. The following
example deals with a bright, young male client in a
provocative therapy workshop before a large audience:

Therapist: Now, anybody else kind of...know you pretty
good?
Client: *(brief pause)* Yes.
Therapist: *(abruptly)* Who?
Client: *(pauses)* Ah.
Therapist: *(interjecting)* Your mommy, yeah.
Client: *(explaining)* A good *friend*....
Therapist: *(flatly)* Yeah.
Client: He's here today.
Therapist: Yeah. Does he know ya?
Client: Yes.
Therapist: *(quickly)* Yeah. How...what's he think about
your *(sighs)* droopy-drawers, lead-ass, you
know *(client, audience laugh)*, existentially
profound *(audience laughs louder)*, wet-
blanket, raining-on-his-*parade*-attitude?
Client: *(laughing; therapist laughs with him)* Uhm...I
don't know what he thinks about....
Therapist:) Well, so he prob...Okay, ya didn't *ask* him.
Client: Noooo.
Therapist: *(Continuing)* Because ya don't want to get an
earful. That's *good!* *(audience laughs)* That's
smart! *(audience laughs louder)* Yeah!
Client: *(remonstrating)* No he will...he listens real
good to my, uh....
Therapist: Yeah?
Client: Complaining and....
Therapist: *(quickly)* Whining.
Client: *(nodding agreement)* Whining.
Therapist: *(flatly)* Whining. We don't call it "whining,"
OK? We call it...*(in a deep, solemn voice tone)*
"lamenting the existential inanities of life,"
you know. *(client and audience burst into
laughter; therapist protests loudly)* Solomon did
it! *Listen*, some of the most profound people--
really!
Client: *(Pauses; vacant expression)* Really?

Therapist: Yes. They have...*(leaning forward, eyeing client intently, placing hand on client's forearm; speaks more slowly)* You're in a *classical, profound* tradition.

Client: *(pauses)* I get the feeling that, uh *(pauses)*, you think I'm too existential.

Therapist: *(raising his chin, eyelids at half-mast, looking at client; flatly)* Not at all. *(audience bursts out laughing) Not* at *all! (definitely) No,* you can *never* be too existential. *(audience continues laughing)* Look, it's one of those things that you just can't get enough *of! (audience laughs loudly)* (Farrelly, 1980a)

Another technique of the provocative therapist is that of listing. This technique is used in two ways. First, the therapist uses listing to compile ludicrous arguments supporting clients' self-defeating ideas or to paint a negative picture of clients. The purpose of this tactic is to help clients take a good look at themselves and consequently experience a desire to move in an opposite direction. The following is an example of the listing method:

Therapist: *(with mock reasonableness)* Well, okay. We gotta lay out the picture here, alright? So here you are: dumb, ineffective, pushy broad, trying to *shove* everybody around, just *intimidate* the hell out of 'em, *bulldoze* them with a Niagara of verbalizations. Shit--small wonder it's not workin' too good. (Farrelly, 1980d)

A second use of listing is that of challenging clients to prove or substantiate their self-affirmatory and assertive statements. By using listing in this manner, the therapist can guide them into focusing on their good aspects and qualities. For example:

Client: *(patiently)* Mr. Farrelly, you *know* there are good things about me too, and you know...

Therapist: *(interrupting flatly)* Well, name three.

Client: *(pausing reflectively)* I'm young.

Therapist: *(laconically)* Well, at 30 you'll never see 29 again. Go ahead.

Client: *(bursts out laughing)* Well, you...why must you joke *(laughs)* all the time?

99

Therapist: *(in a "reasonable," persuasive tone)* Well, you felt that too. When I first saw you, you said, "Oh God, I'm 30!"

Client: *(nodding agreement with a grin)* Yeah, am I older or not...*(then dismissing this idea)*...and I *am* a good worker.

Therapist: *(with mild incredulity)* You *are*?

Client: *(with assurance)* Yes. (Farrelly, 1977)

The four languages of provocative therapy provide another cluster of techniques the therapist uses in building a theatrical, larger-than life reflection of the client's world. By selecting and blending the four languages throughout therapeutic work, the therapist paints pictures and relates feedback for the client's consideration. The four languages of provocative therapy are (a) religious-moral language, (b) locker room language, (c) professional jargon, and (d) body language. The following example illustrates the therapist's combining professional jargon with religious-moral language. The patient is a chronic schizophrenic who has spent half her life in mental hospitals and has had multiple behavioral problems including extensive and indiscriminate sexual acting-out, poor job history, and so on:

Therapist: *(puzzled)* I can't figure out whether you are *immoral* or whether you have learned self-defeating acting-out, anti-social behavioral patterns of promiscuity; or whether you are *weak* or whether you have a highly impaired ego functioning related to your significant early emotional deprivation; or whether you are *lazy* or simply are chronically dependent and overwhelmed by feelings of inadequacy in task performance areas.

Client: *(pauses, somewhat embarrassed)* I think I'm immoral, weak, and lazy. (Farrelly & Brandsma, 1974, p. 74)

An example of locker room language is illustrated below in an excerpt from an interview during which the therapist worked with a man who complained about not being "turned on" to his wife:

Therapist: *(disgustedly)* Well, maybe she's just, you know, a bag, and she just couldn't, uh, you know, turn on a sex maniac.

Client: *(laughing)* It's *possible....*

Therapist: *(triumphantly)* Well, *OK!...(inquisitively)* What's she look like?

Client: *(smiling)* She's very attractive.

Therapist: *(flatly)* Very attractive. Who says so? You got widespread confirmation of that, or what?

Client: *(nodding)* Yahhh.

Therapist: Other people tell...say she is? Your *mother* says she is.

Client: *(forcibly)* No, no.

Therapist: *(pursuing)* Got any buddies who say, "Hey, hey, *hey*! I know....

Client: *(remonstrating)* She doesn't elicit that kind of response from others.

Therapist: *(ironically)* Oh, she just...like, she has a beautiful *soul.*

Client: *(explaining)* Nooo, she's *physically* attractive.

Therapist: *(flatly)* Physically attractive, but you just, just don't feel the old *zing*, huh?

Client: *(brief pause, meditatively)* Yes.

Therapist: *(looking at the client's crotch and nodding his head toward it)* What? Is it just sort of hanging there like yesterday's overcooked noodle or what?

Client: No, that's...uh, the....

Therapist: C'mon, whattaya mean? "No, it's not that." What is it then?

Client: *(thoughtfully)* It's not that I don't get an erection, that's not the issue, I *want* more....

Therapist: *(interrupting)* But it's just like your *soul* doesn't get erected.

Client: *(looking up, thoughtfully)* Uhm....

Therapist: *(continuing)* You just don't get the glazed eyes and dribbling out of the left corner of your mouth....

Client: *(interrupting)* Well, look....

Therapist: And pawing the ground, and going *(mimics a bull)* "Moo-oooooo!" That kinda thing? (Farrelly, 1978)

The fourth language of this system is a bodily kinesthetic language. The provocative therapist typically sits close to clients. Sitting close tends to intensify the you-me here-and-now quality of the relationship between therapist and client. The provocative therapist uses body language (gestures, body posture, voice tone, inflection, and physical touch) to capture the client's attention, to facilitate reception of therapist messages, as well as to communicate warmth, acceptance, and positive regard. Physical touch may vary from a tap on the knee, a hand on the shoulder or forearm, or a gentle pat on a client's cheek à la "The Godfather." Touching conveys intimacy, and represents a powerful mode of encoding messages from one human being to another. Touching can also be abused, as in the instance of sexual exploitation of clients by therapists. We strongly feel that a word of caution is in order here: any therapist who uses touching must be clear that he or she is not serving his or her own needs at the expense of the client.

PERTINENT USES

While one benefit of provocative therapy is its ability to produce rapid client change, another benefit is its applicability to widely disparate client types. It can be used successfully with virtually any client who walks into the office. (Therapist in waiting room, pointing at a sulky adolescent boy with closed eyes, says, "Bring in the body; as long as it's warm we can do therapy.") Over the past several decades provocative therapy has been used with clients in every diagnostic category from chronic schizophrenic patients to manic depressives to character disorders and neurotics. It has been utilized with clients who act-out and those in acute psychotic episodes as well as with autistic children and the deaf. Age is no barrier; provocative therapy has been used with clients from age 2 to those in their 80s. It has been used with clients whose IQs range from the mentally retarded at the educable level to genius. Moreover, provocative therapy has been used with both inpatient and outpatient populations within the context of individual, marital, family, and group therapy. A cautionary observation may be in order here:

However, it should be emphasized that therapy systems do not directly help clients. Instead therapy systems help therapists organize the kaleidoscopic ideational, affective, and behavioral phenomena that individuals bring to therapists to treat. Again therapy systems do not help people; people help people. (Farrelly & Brandsma, 1974, p. 85)

Finally, it should be emphasized that provocative therapy does not consist in the therapist pushing the client into change with a psychological bulldozer. Rather, the provocative therapist is beside the client, humorously walking hand in hand through the client's world. Thus, the provocative therapist embodies the dictum that gaiety is wiser than wisdom, always attempting to be aware of where the client is at *this* moment. Again, rather than bulldozing, the therapist is frequently finessing the client and bypassing his or her subliminal assumptive sets. Like a cat burglar's second-story caper, provocative therapy is an inside job.

SYNTHESIS

A different mode of experiencing provocative therapy is to enter into the process from inside the client. Over the past 2 decades thousands of clients have given voice to the fluid mandala of their multiple reactions and internal processes after the first interview with the senior author. Their composite experiences might be summarized as follows:

I, the client, walk into the therapist's office with my anxiety, embarrassment, hurt, anger, and depression; and somehow while I give my symptomatology and life history in a mature and proper way, I feel something is awry. The story of my existence suddenly becomes a three-dimensional movie and spins rapidly ahead, sideways, and back in time in a crazy Alice-in-Wonderland type of logic. I find myself intrigued, annoyed, and then chewing on my lip to keep from laughing at the sheer incongruity of it all. A lump appears in my throat, my eyes become misty, and yet I find myself laughing. I strive to maintain emotional and intellectual control of this crazy conversation, a conversation about some of the most important aspects of my life. And sitting beside me is this clown who somehow seems to know *exactly* what I think and feel, and how I live and move. He sounds as if he were *there* when I had that fight with my parent, my lover, my spouse, or my child. God! It's eerie and frightening; I feel completely naked, that my life is a totally open book for this stranger to peruse at his whim.

And yet his scary depth of accurate understanding shatters my isolation; I feel deeply and centrally comforted, and realize that I am not alone. This person, this fellow human being is knowing me at a level that few others ever have, and yet he was a total stranger only minutes ago. I listen as he talks and those old feelings I've had now begin to make *sense*. Then I begin to think: maybe I could be understood by others, and maybe even *I* could understand those people who are important to me but who puzzle me so. Yet he talks so crazy at times and he's so embarrassingly intimate that I want to slow down, wave my hands, and protest, "Now just a minute! This isn't funny; this is serious!" Yet a laugh gurgles up within me, through the lump in my throat and, in spite of myself, I burst into a guffaw--feeling puzzlement, embarrassment, astonishment, and annoyance while tears of laughter trickle down my cheeks. "Serious?" he says. "Hell, *I* know it's serious; *you're* the one laughing inappropriately at this stuff!" Whatever happened to my composure and the things I had organized to say? This isn't anything like interviews I've had with other therapists. I can't tell what *he's* going to say next; worse yet, I don't even know what *I'm* going to say next. The three-dimensional movie of my life, technicolor, with sounds and smells and flavors and feelings, suddenly speeds into the future when I'm taking that exam, or am in the argument with my spouse-lover-family. And this guy, this crazy court jester, brings alive in a wildly funny but serious way how part of my life could be in shards and pieces if I keep thinking or sulking or feeling sorry for myself and acting the way I do. How vivid it all is! And what if he's right?! All the effort spent trying to ignore it, trying to ignore myself: it all strikes me now-- there's no escape. As I bounce about in this Alice-in-Wonderland world of my agonies, my ecstasies, my emotions, my idiotic ideas and zany solutions, the movie reel wildly careens off the projector, unraveling its contents into the air and it hits me: *this is my life!* And this is provocative therapy. And I've never heard anybody talk like this before, or understand me this way before, or make my life as real before.

As the color fades and the sounds diminish I sink down into the chair and an almost post-orgasmic lassitude seems to fill me. I got through the first interview. I'm aware now that there's a lot more to talk about and I've gotta come back. Now I walk down the hall, and as I pull my car keys from my raincoat pocket I burst into laughter again. A couple passes me on the steps; they would never believe me if I told them.

REFERENCES

PUBLICATIONS

Bandler, R. (1978, March). *Analyzing the Analyst.* Presentation at Temple University Psychiatry Department, Philadelphia, PA.

Farrelly, F., & Brandsma, J. (1974). *Provocative Therapy.* Cupertino, CA: Meta Publications.

Farrelly, F., & Matthews, S. (1981). Provocative therapy. In R. J. Corsini (Ed.), *Handbook of Innovative Psychotherapies* (pp. 678-693). New York: Wiley.

Ludwig, A. M., & Farrelly, F. (1966). The code of chronicity. *Archives of General Psychiatry, 15,* 562-568.

MacNutt, F. (1974). *Healing.* Notre Dame, IN: Ave Maria Press.

NOTES AND AUDIOTAPES

Farrelly, F. (1965). *Private Practice Interview.* Madison, WI: Author's notes.

Farrelly, F. (1977). *Provocative Therapy Cassette Series* (Audiotape, Tape 4, Side 1). Chicago, IL: Instructional Dynamics Institute.

Farrelly, F. (1978). Analyzing the analyst--identifying effective interventions [Audiotape]. *Audio Digest Foundation, Psychiatry,* Vol. 7, No. 15.

Farrelly, F. (1979, May). *Provocative Therapy Workshop.* Minneapolis, MN: Author's notes.

Farrelly, F. (1980a). *Kansas City Provocative Therapy Workshop* (Audiotape, Tape 2, Side A). Lawrence, KS: Audio House.

Farrelly, F. (1980b). *Kansas City Provocative Therapy Workshop* (Audiotape, Tape 2, Side B). Lawrence, KS: Audio House.

Farrelly, F. (1980c). *Kansas City Provocative Therapy Workshop* (Audiotape, Tape 4, Side B). Lawrence, KS: Audio House.

Farrelly, F. (1980d). *Kansas City Provocative Therapy Workshop* (Audiotape, Tape 5, Side A). Lawrence, KS: Audio House.

Farrelly, F. (1980e). *Kansas City Provocative Therapy Workshop* (Audiotape, Tape 9, Side B). Lawrence, KS: Audio House.

Farrelly, F. (1980f). *Kansas City Provocative Therapy Workshop* (Audiotape, Tape 10, Side A). Lawrence, KS: Audio House.

THERAPEUTIC STRATEGIES
WITH THE COMIC CHILD

Rhoda Lee Fisher and Seymour Fisher

How does a therapist deal with a nonconforming, comic child? What lies behind the comic routines? How do children become nonconforming in the first place? Drs. Rhoda Lee Fisher and Seymour Fisher tackle these questions in their attempt to shed some light on the family scenarios, as well as the dilemmas and fortunes of the misunderstood child. They take a closer look at the children who make others laugh on the outside while feeling lonely and conflicted on the inside. In this chapter, we learn that comic children are involuntary participants in the strident tragicomedy of parental distress. Their absurd antics may be understood as a form of self-inoculation against the frightening absurdity of parental parameters. In effect, the comic child may be unconsciously telling the parents, "I can't fight your absurdity, so I'll join you in it." On the flip side of the same coin, the child's humorous repartee to the parents' absurd behavior may be giving his or her parents the message, "I'll play your unfair game, but don't expect me to take it as seriously as you do." In this respect, the child's humor may represent a buoy to emotional adjustment that can be judiciously channeled to facilitate and activate the therapeutic process. The Fishers present specific therapeutic guidelines on approaching both the comic child and his or her parents, including when and how to use humor in such interventions. It is quickly apparent that the scope of their findings is not limited to therapy with comic children. Their insights provide a logical clinical framework for psychotherapeutic work with children of any diagnostic group, making this chapter of particular interest to child and family therapists.

Drs. Rhoda Lee Fisher and Seymour Fisher are talented research scientists and skilled clinicians. They are affiliated with the Department of Psychiatry at the State University of New York-- Upstate Medical Center in Syracuse and maintain a private practice in clinical psychology. Their publications include <u>Pretend the World Is Funny and Forever: A Psychological Analysis of Comedians, Clowns, and Actors</u> (1981).

❋   ❋   ❋

THEORETICAL PERSPECTIVE

For some time we observed that a significant proportion of children referred to us for psychotherapy and/or psychological evaluation were funny. Approximately 10% of our referrals fell into this "funny" group. Though their presenting symptoms seemed to logically fit into one or another of the usual diagnostic categories, their own personal embellishments of conventional symptomatology had a humorous tone. Their presenting problems had a distinctive comedic flavor that drew our attention, and not infrequently we found ourselves laughing, as if we were watching a TV situation comedy.

In describing the classroom behavior of one of the "funny" children, an exasperated teacher depicted him as periodically seeming to be moved by a force beyond his control. One day, she recounted, he stood up next to his desk, held a sheet of thick crisp paper above his head, and crumpled it. "He seemed almost to be in a trance," she continued. The teacher called his name and he responded in an apparently dazed fashion, as though she had awakened him from a dream. "Sit down," she demanded. "Oh, thank you," he replied humbly and reseated himself. The class was more amused than alarmed with his outlandish behavior, and there was a good deal of snickering. His teacher was puzzled and angry with his lack of control and yet frustrated that there seemed so little she could do about it. Her embarrassment and irritation typify the reactions of most adults to these funny children. We began to realize that the funny ones were often more frustrating and annoying than other disturbed youngsters. They seemed to stir up less pity and compassion about their plight. We became curious about them. Why did they behave so absurdly? We began to observe them more closely. We inquired about their school behavior and their relationships with their parents and others.

We were struck with the humor and the absurd elements in their behavior. They seemed to be set to turn the world topsy-turvy and would not exercise the usual restraints, whether it be in school, at home, or during the therapy hour. This irrepressible quality seems, in some contexts, to endear them to their peers, but they often go "too far." Eventually, they end up antagonizing most of the major adults in their lives. Funny children are difficult to deal with in the conventional mode. They resist being tamed. They have a knack for causing chaos wherever they go and whatever they do. Nothing is sacred, and that includes psychotherapy. Working therapeutically with them taught us not to expect any of the usual responses to conventional interpretations, nor could we expect them to reveal much concerning their actual feelings. Their behavior in the therapy situation was difficult to follow as a logical sequence. We learned not to predict outcome, even in the short run. It became obvious that some new formulations were in order if we were to deal with the funny ones successfully. This chapter will describe some of the procedures we have found successful in the treatment of the comic personality. We will review some of our research findings, as described in our book, *Pretend the World Is Funny and Forever: A Psychological Analysis of Comedians, Clowns, and Actors* (1981), that are pertinent and relate directly to the psychotherapeutic approaches we have developed. Incidentally, although there are a number of papers concerned with the use of humor in treating adults (e.g., Bloomfield, 1980; Kubie, 1971; Poland, 1971; Rose, 1969; Rosenheim, 1974), we have not found any publications that even tangentially concern therapy with comic children. Let us begin by presenting some typical accounts of comic children in order to convey the flavor of their antics. Consider the following:

A 4-year-old boy was referred because he was phobic. He had developed a sudden and intense fear of dandelions. Never before had he had such a fear. He would absolutely not walk on any grassy patch that he suspected might contain a dandelion. He cried, screamed, carried on, but would not set foot on the grass with the potential culprits. A kindergarten child was referred as emotionally disturbed. His teacher described him as "hyperactive" and unmanageable in the classroom. His unpredictable behavior kept her in a state of upset. He might fall off his chair. He might eat his crayons. Once he dropped his pants in front of the class. In Harpo Marx fashion he would pilfer the possessions of his classmates, tuck them under his overcoat, and as he left the classroom his teacher would spot the obvious bulges in his coat. Another child was referred because he was enuretic. He had been enuretic for some time. His parents had used every available method of curing the enuresis and yet they continued to be unsuccessful. Finally, after much effort, they were able to train their 7-year-old to get himself out of bed when he needed to use the bathroom, but he would simply stop at the foot of his bed and saturate a small throw rug. He never urinated anywhere else at night. Yet no one in his family saw his behavior as funny. No one questioned his ability to restrain himself only until he got to the little rug. If he could be trained to the rug, why could he not get to the commode? We jokingly wondered whether this was the patient's fantasied commode. Or perhaps it was his request for a room with an attached bath? We were obviously struck with the humor in the situation. The boy's parents certainly were not. They were angry about the burdensome persistence of his problem.

We were so intrigued with such comedic behavior that we decided to study it with a two-pronged approach. We would not only probe the dynamics of the "little comedians" but also the grown-up variety. We thought that we could learn a great deal by studying adults who were comedians, who had committed their lives to being the funny ones. This actually led us into a program of research involving professional comics. We intensively appraised 45 professional comics and clowns and also two control groups (viz., actors and entertainers). Subjects were evaluated with an identical series of tasks. We began with a semi-structured interview covering early background, family life, perception of parents, importance of religion and other moral values, relationships between the parents, and the role of humor in family communications. In addition, the Rorschach Inkblot Test and the Thematic Apperception Test were administered. Further, a series of early memories were systematically obtained. An analysis of the materials obtained enabled us to develop a number of quantitative scoring systems for both the interview and projective data. The scores expressed the concerns and unique fantasies of the comics. A comparison of the scores obtained by the comic group and the actor and entertainer controls demonstrated a variety of significant differences.

Let us first consider a particularly important difference that emerged with reference to the theme of good versus evil. To an unusual degree, we found professional funny people preoccupied with this theme. Goodness and badness fascinated them. The professional comics seemed obsessed with how good or bad they were and how good or bad others were. The focus on good versus bad emerged not only in interview material but also in projective fantasies. We developed a Rorschach good-bad score, basically counting precepts focused on good-bad images (e.g., church, Mephisto, cross, saint, hell, judge, sinner). Similarly, for the Thematic Apperception Test we counted characters assigned particularly unworthy roles. Both the Rorschach and Thematic Apperception good-bad scores were found to be significantly elevated in the comics. Related to the comics' concern with denying badness was a unique kind of "nice monster" imagery that appeared in their Rorschach responses. This imagery emphasized the goodness of objects usually considered bad or evil (e.g., "Tiger. He's lovable." "Monster...wants to be friends...Waiting for someone to come along. Lonely."). In several other normal samples these "nice monster" responses proved to be rare, appearing only about 20 times in every 100 protocols.

The comics' preoccupation with the good-bad polarity proved to be a prototype of their concern with many other polarities. They were, for example, inclined to see their parents at opposite poles. They usually talked about father in positive, even glowing terms. They put him on a pedestal of goodness and elevated him to a special position. Father was someone who was a "good." On the other hand, mother was seen as the punisher. She was an aggressive critic who enforced the rules. The comics see mother as unusually tough, as lacking the soft maternal qualities that mothers presumably usually possess. She is, in many ways, a "bad." In the clinical context in which we studied comic children, the intake procedure also included gathering measures on the parents. The parents responded to the Rorschach blots and filled out the Parental Attitude Research Inventory, the Vernon-Allport Study of Values, and a Family History Form. We undertook an analysis of such data from 15 sets of parents of comic children and utilized suitable noncomic children as controls. The findings upheld the results obtained from the professional comics. We found the mothers of the child comics to be detached and relatively distant from their kids. They felt weighted down by motherhood and wanted to find a way out. Motherhood made them feel martyred and irritable. We discovered too that the inkblot imagery obtained from the fathers had a passive quality. Overall, the data indicated that the parents of the comic children loaded them down with demands that they not ask for the prerogatives of childhood and insisted they take unusual responsibility for themselves.

TECHNIQUE

Working with comic children is a difficult process. These kids have set themselves in opposition to convention. They dig their heels in against social expectations. A dramatic representation of their resistance is usually seen in their school deportment. School somehow becomes associated in their minds with the pressures of society. It provides a major interface for their resistance. One of their favorite phrases is "school sucks." Comics are so very determined to defend themselves against the demands that school makes that they are willing to go to any extreme. The extremeness of their position adds to their troubles. They get adults angry and thereby create a spiraling series wherein their provocation and the adults' angry responses increasingly and alternately intensify each other. It is often as important to reduce the intensity of the teachers' and the school's reactions as it is to reduce the intensity of the parents' reactions, so that these children can at least survive in the school environment. The aims of therapy with comic children are not to change their character structure, but rather to reduce the extremeness of their responses. We have found that the comic defense is a good, meaningful way to deal with the world and should not be stripped away.

As a consequence of our work with comic children, we have been able to establish some guidelines for treating them. They have all the characteristics that predict a good therapeutic outcome. They are bright, sensitive to the motives of others, and articulate. Yet they are among the more difficult to treat. They miss therapy hours, drop out of therapy without reason, and are erratically unpredictable in the way they relate to their therapist. They can, in addition, become the therapist's source of entertainment and therefore distract the therapy from its basic goal. Their knack for paradox introduces still other difficulties. They work at not thinking in terms of straight-line relationships or cause and effect. They look for the flaw, for the exception, and are alerted to contradictory alternatives. The therapist usually depends on logic and insight for results, but when working with comedic personalities it may be necessary to go with the illogical to an unusual degree. Note too that comic children find it necessary to test in the most extreme fashion whether the therapy situation is a safe one. They continually create temptations for the therapist to reject and attack them. They are alternatively aggressively provocative and seductively self-deprecatory. They tease, drop topics of conversation without warning, and change directions (verbally or physically) without apparent reason. Their unpredictable behavior certainly helps to avoid involvement and to maintain distance.

ESTABLISHING THE RELATIONSHIP

Being the comic children's friend involves convincing them that the relationship will not burden them with a new set of expectations. They are unusually sensitive to being weighted down. Joking and stirring up chaos are insurance against being further overloaded. Initially then, the therapist gives the message that *NOTHING IS NECESSARY*. Therapy hours are devoted to nonsense, joking, eating, going for a walk, a car ride to nowhere in particular, and so forth. An interesting paradox is that while comic children may begin by filling the therapy hour with nonsense to avoid involvement, they may gradually see the creation of such nonsense, with its funny implications, as an obligation. They may begin to feel responsible for fostering a funny ambiance and devote themselves to filling the hour with fun for their therapist. When this happens, they will react by disengaging themselves from the treatment. They are not going to remain in a situation where they are further burdened. Signs of anger and rejection will surface. They will find ways to wiggle out of treatment like they wiggle out of homework.

DEALING WITH DEPRIVATION
AND OVERLOAD FEELINGS

As we have indicated, comics feel deprived and un-
loved. Their sense of unworthiness is tied to their sense
of being undeserving. Overt succorance communications
are unusual for them and they find it difficult to accept
offerings directly. "Filling them up" in the therapy
context generally has to be accomplished via some
amusing and often complicated disguise. Note a few
examples of the comic child's concealed succorance tactics. One child did tricks with animal crackers. A jar of
animal crackers was always open on the office table and
each time he came in he would demonstrate how he could
flip the crackers in the air and catch them in his open
mouth. He would flip them up and into his mouth, in as
quick succession as he could. This occurred regularly at
the start of each therapy hour and lasted for about 20
minutes, during which time he consumed a large number
of cookies. Another child always arranged his appointments near the lunch hour. He generally brought his
lunch along. He consistently complained about what a
rotten cook his mother was and routinely proceeded to
throw the brown bag in the wastebasket. This was the
therapist's signal to invite him out for a sandwich and a
shake, which he always accepted. It was a ritual that
meant: "My mother is non-nurturant and I am hungry.
Will you give me something to eat? Do you care whether
I go hungry or not?"

Comic children are obviously hungry, both literally
and figuratively. They long for nurturance and maternal
kindness. They have been socialized to help others and
not to expect anything for themselves. Food is an unusually important medium for them. They often complain
about food at home. Relatedly, they feel that they are
treated unfairly and that more is expected of them than
of their siblings. Therapy with comic children must deal
with their intense feelings of deprivation. Providing food
can be one vehicle through which the therapist can
express nurturance. The nurturant approach also includes
touching, sometimes in jest, sometimes by way of emphasis. Interest in various personal feats and achievements is
another possible area for nurturant support. Encouraging
comic children to perform their gymnastic routines (at

which they are often quite skilled) or some special trick they have perfected helps to convey support.

WORKING WITH PARENTS

It is essential to work with the comic children's parents. The parents are extremely angered by their trouble-making children. The children have so endlessly made life difficult for these parents that they often have little compassion for their children's discomforts. The parents want to punish and control them. The parents' anger seems so justified that it is difficult for them to appreciate how their comic offspring perceive them. It will help if the parents can understand how deprived of their support the children feel. Reducing the open expression of the parents' hostility is in itself helpful in quieting the extremeness of the comics' responses. Therapeutic discussions with the parents oftentimes focus on why they feel so overloaded themselves and what, in fact, is causing them to overload their comic children. A supportive therapeutic relationship helps to relieve the parents, which in turn reduces the stress they place on their offspring. One particularly helpful technique in allaying the parents' anxiety is to make them aware of the humor in their children's antics. They can often learn to laugh at what, up to that point, has seemed to be tragic. We have also found that providing a humorous perspective can, at times, soften the bitterness of teachers and principals, who have been under siege by some determined comic child.

The comic children's mothers, in particular, operate at a high level of tension. These mothers are inclined to feel that they alone carry the family burden. They complain that they are not understood and that their families do not consider their needs. They describe other family members as self-oriented and too busy or preoccupied with their own interests. Often, they are angry that their husbands do not shoulder a sufficient amount of responsibility for things that go on at home. During therapeutic contacts with the mothers considerable time is devoted to strategies that will help them feel less martyred. This may variously involve providing catharsis for grievances, encouraging more direct communication with other family members, and suggesting possible alternatives for obtaining self-gratification. Helping the mothers to feel less imposed upon helps defuse the tension experienced by all family members.

CONTRADICTION

As noted earlier, comic children have been exposed to unusual amounts of contradiction in their lives. Contradiction becomes a *cause celebre* for them. They make jokes about it and are attracted by polarized alternatives. They are determined to be contradictory, since they see themselves dealt with in contradictory terms. Despite their apparent ease with contradiction, the truth is that they are distressed by the agonizing contradictions within their own lives. These contradictions typically involve such themes as how to be a good and bad object at the same time; how to satisfy parents who often have starkly opposed expectations; and how to simultaneously accept the obligation of caring for others and playing the role of the ridiculous one who refuses to take any responsibilities. Comic children need to feel that the contradictions they juggle are understood, even though they seem to be making light of such contradictions.

One 6-year-old girl almost always opened her therapy hour by offering the therapist two choices: two different games to play, two different foods she might want, two different places she either had been to or to which she might want to go. The therapist and she would then follow each other around in a circle and deliberate between the alternatives. Unexpectedly one or the other would change directions or speed, and then they would continue. Whenever the child would sense something contradictory, she would begin to pace back and forth or circle in a special lighthearted fashion and debate between the alternatives. The message shared by the child and the therapist was clear: "This dilemma is frustrating but also tolerable if reduced to the absurd." The child understood that the therapist shared her appreciation of humor as a way of coping with polarizations. She also grasped that the therapist recognized the impossible polarizations in her personal world.

PERTINENT USES

The techniques for the treatment of comic children have been developed to deal with their special problems. As noted, we generally have been able to alleviate the extremeness of their symptoms. We have been able to make them more comfortable and more reasonably able to fit back into their environment. They do not, as the result of therapy, lose their sense of humor, but they have less need to create chaos. Reducing their stress and also the discomfort felt by the authority figures who surround them contributes importantly to stabilizing their lives. In fact, the mechanisms and symptoms seen in these children are also seen in other children in less extreme forms. Thus, we have observed that a fair percentage of the children referred for treatment with problems other than the comic configuration are also suffering from feelings of being overburdened to some degree.

Obviously, overload derives from many different sources. Some children may feel they must bridge the emotional gaps between their parents. Others may feel obligated to fail in order to make their parents seem more successful by comparison. Still others may feel they must stay home from school to watch and protect their anxious mothers. Our work with comic children has shown that an important means in lifting the load is providing a humorous perspective. If the adults and/or children can catch the humor in the situation, the size of the psychological burden is reduced. If one can laugh, then what is happening is less toxic.

An example is provided by a phobic girl who would not go to school. She was an unusually attractive 15-year-old who had always gone to school, done her homework, and in general held up her own end of things. However, she gradually developed difficulty in leaving home to go to school. She would become quite ill. If made to attend school, she was quickly referred to the nurse's office. Her parents were angry, puzzled, frightened. They punished her refusal to go to school by forbidding her to leave home after school hours. By the time they brought her for treatment she was at home 24 hours a day. An analysis of the underlying dynamics revealed that the girl was extremely symbiotic with her mother and was unconsciously driven to stay home to protect and care for her. She had essentially arrived at the conclusion that she had to be her mother's nursemaid. It was important to demonstrate to the parents the humorously ridiculous nature of what was occurring. Note the following:

Therapist: Well, your daughter is indeed a very responsible girl and she is worried about you and,

117

	would you believe it, she's staying home to care for you! *(the therapist smiled in amusement)*
Mother:	She doesn't have to do that. She makes a mess of the kitchen. She doesn't have to do that. That's silly. She's only making trouble for me. She's no help at home!

As the image of their "helping" daughter began to register, the parents were able to conjure up a variety of corroborative incidents. They began to laugh and a series of examples poured out about her burning pancakes and setting the toaster on fire, as she frantically tried to be "helpful." When the father excitedly added the story about her grabbing the fire extinguisher and spraying foam all over the kitchen, there was a crescendo of amusement that placed the whole issue in its proper perspective. The therapist summarized it all by saying, "But that's what it's all about. She is worried about you guys and she is more and more hanging around to take care of you."

In order to highlight the latent humor in such situations it is often suggested to parents or teachers, "Imagine that you are watching this on TV. You'd think it was *VERY* funny. It's a lot different when you are part of the action. It is hard to see how funny it really is." We refer to the parents' position as that of the straightman for the joke. "The straightman never laughs. What is so funny about having a bucket of water dumped on your head? But if you stand on the sidelines and watch the action, you can appreciate the fun."

Relatedly, our therapeutic approach in such cases consists in helping the parents of comic children gain the perspective that their children's absurd behaviors are a direct response to the inherent absurdity in parental behavior. A similar approach has been helpful in therapy with noncomic children who display circumscribed absurd symptoms. By way of illustration we would mention: (a) a 4-year-old boy who repeatedly urinated in his mother's solid brass antique cuspidor, and (b) an anorexic girl who would only eat one brand of crackers that she and her mother pretended did not exist, but which mother secretly replenished as soon as they were consumed. Such behaviors sound absurd but were treated by the respective families with utmost gravity. We not only pointed out the humor inherent in these ridiculous behaviors, but perhaps more importantly made it clear to the parents that the children's ridiculous acts must somehow be mirroring the absurdities in parental conduct.

In both of the cases just cited, we eventually learned that the parents' absurdity resided in their persisting to lure their offspring into a "secret" pact that required denial of one's own sexual identity and instead called for becoming an asexual entity. They had systematically laid down rules that asserted, "You cannot act in ways that are normally accepted to be typical of children of your biological sex. We have our own special reasons for wanting you to be asexual and you will have to fit our mold if you want to survive in this family." Such a dictate is obviously absurd and the children in question developed "symptoms" that conveyed the message, "If you treat me in odd, crazy ways, I have the right to be just as odd." Our cumulative observations of the link between absurdity in comic children and the ridiculous demands of their parents have given us the confidence to look for equivalent links whenever we encounter patently ridiculous behavior in a child. We are now much quicker to spot specific absurdities in parental behavior that are setting the children off.

CLINICAL PRESENTATION

This section will be devoted to putting skin and bones on some of the general notions we have been discussing. At this point we will look hard at one case. Consider the following instance revolving around an 11-year-old boy, Sam (not his real name). Sam lives in a tract house with his mother and father and 8-year-old sister. They seem to be a conventional middle-class family. Both parents are employed. Father is a salesman. Mother is in sales at a "better" dress shop. The parents have had serious ups and downs in their relationship. Whatever their disagreements, they do agree that their son has had an awful school career. His relationships with his teachers have been impossible. He does not get his work in and seems to misunderstand assignments. There is always some frustrating problem preventing him from doing what he is supposed to do. Whichever way the chips fall, Sam usually ends up as the outstanding nonfunctional member of his class. With the hope that a fresh start would help, his parents moved him to a new school, but within a few short weeks he had reinstated himself in his special position as the "pain-in-the-neck" student. Sam's parents had been given all kinds of suggestions for improving his school work, and they had experimented with such alternatives as grounding him for poor grades, assiduously helping him with his homework, and asking his teacher to send home weekly status reports about his progress. But nothing had worked, and it was impossible to sustain him as an actively participating student.

A psychological diagnostic evaluation of Sam clearly demonstrated that he psychodynamically matched the comic prototype. Based on these findings, we immediately began to treat him and his parents. One of the first strategies in dealing with Sam was to get into issues of overload and nurturance. Sam needed to be comforted and filled up. He needed to feel that he was not an evil person for wanting to take instead of give. He needed to learn that there were occasions when there were no strings attached. He required assurance that he could accept nurturance without anything accusatory happening. There was plenty of cocoa when he came for a treatment hour, and the cocoa offer always included, "Can I fix it for you?" Cookies were available on a convenient table and placed so they were within easy reach. Because Sam felt so overburdened, it was helpful for him to perceive the therapy hour as not just one more burdensome occasion. His progress psychotherapeutically depended on his knowing that (a) he would not be burdened with new demands, (b) no one would make him do anything, and (c) he would not be put down. Subsequently, the therapist adopted the stance of a tolerant friend. Thus, Sam's therapy sessions did not have a set topic of conversation. Some hours were spent playing dominoes or cards and hardly exchanging a word. Some were spent discussing a series of ridiculous topics that were in no way sequentially related. There was no need to set standards or to demand logic or the completion of anything.

After a while Sam began to talk about topics pertinent to the comic dynamics. One of the first issues he brought up had to do with the prime comic theme: "Am I good or am I bad?"

Sam: About smoking, I feel good and I feel bad at the same time. I'm just gonna try to quit so I don't have to feel good and bad at the same time.

Therapist: Somewhere there is a balance between good and bad.

Sam: I don't want to smoke too much. Sometimes I don't want the rest of the cigarette. I give the rest of the cigarette to my friends. I like smoking but I'm cutting down because I don't like it. I like it because I like the taste. And I hate it because I have asthma. So I'm cutting down and still smoking at the same time.

Therapist: You have to find a balance between good and bad.

Sam: Like a boat when it rocks back and forth.

Therapist: It keeps tipping back and forth.

Sam: So I don't feel either good or bad. I feel good about smoking but I feel bad at the same time. If I feel bad about smoking I feel good at the same time. I'm gonna try to quit so I don't have to feel good and bad at the same time; or bad and good at the same time!

Therapist: That would end the conflict. Are there other things that make you feel good and bad at the same time?

Sam: Sometimes the kids. They get rowdy. I get rowdy with them. I'm having a good time but I'm afraid I'll get caught and get in trouble.

Therapist: What does rowdy mean?

Sam: We go down to MacDonald's and spit on the mirrors. It's fun but I think, "Gee, I'm gonna get in *SO* much trouble!" I'll turn around, go back and have a good time with them.

Therapist: All the time you know it's both good and bad. It must make you feel funny.

Sam: Yes. Strange. I don't want to get in trouble. It's not my main thing in life to get in trouble....

Working with Sam's parents also focused on issues pertinent to good versus evil. The parents were everlastingly preoccupied with whether Sam was a good or a bad boy. Here is an excerpt that illustrates their preoccupation:

Father: Sam's been good. Nothing too earthshaking.

Mother:	Except that he is on school parole. One more thing and he will be kicked off the school bus. He hit a kid.
Father:	The boy hit him first.
Mother:	No. The boy behind him was kicking him. The boy next to him got it. Sam couldn't reach the kid behind him so he hit the kid next to him. The bus driver said, "Sit down and behave." But what did Sam say? His own bit of charm! What did he do?
Father:	He said, "Send me to the goddamn principal. I don't care."
Mother:	So the driver did. *(therapist registers amusement)*
Mother:	How could he do this? He missed all of his morning classes. He was only at school for 2 hours! How could he get in trouble? And he answers me, "I was good in school." Well, let me tell you, he's been a beast at home.

These parents were completely fed up with their offspring. They could not say anything about him without being critical. He was their special scapegoat. They wanted him to be compliant and to do exactly as they told him. Actually, there was a good deal of data indicating that unconsciously they wanted him to devote himself to servicing them and to making their lives more tolerable. Sam was obviously in rebellion against being the scapegoat. His resistiveness kept his parents stirred up. His mother was generally dissatisfied and acutely so with him. She often tried to upset him and to keep him off balance. He tried to stand up to her accusations and did a fairly good job. But his holding his own was in itself an overburden. A child his age should not find himself in such an oppositional and defensive position relative to his mother. Her toughness and anger were frequently pointed out to her by the therapist.

Sam's father was inclined to take a less severe attitude toward him than mother did. This difference in parental severity toward the child was also observed in our studies of professional comics. Note the father's attitude toward Sam in the following:

Father:	Sam is doing well. But he did have his first temper tantrum in a long time. It was violent. Bad. He said he hated his mother. That he

                hated me too. He found out that he wouldn't get his own way. He came out from talking to his mother. He lost his temper. He hit the wall. His hand went through the wallboard.

Therapist: Do you know you are laughing while you describe it?

Father: I don't see any great tragedy in it. It is there and there is a lesson to learn. Either you hurt your hand or break the wall. You just cause yourself more problems. Hitting it doesn't do anything for you.

Sam's mother felt that the father was not sufficiently strong in his responses to Sam's misbehaviors. She said that he just did not seem to care. She felt she had to bear the entire load of Sam's behavior, and saw her husband's forgiving attitude toward Sam as an indication of his irresponsibility and lack of investment in the family. During the course of therapy she became more and more openly angry at her husband. She described a long series of failings on his part (e.g., he did not pay bills on time and he had promised long ago to remodel their kitchen and the room was still in an incomplete state). Sam's mother eventually announced, in the course of the therapy, that she would be better off without her husband and that she wanted him to move out. He did so. However, he really did not want to lose his home and his family, and after a number of conjoint therapy sessions with his wife he agreed to devote more attention to the family's needs.

His demonstration that he was willing to assume more family responsibilities had a positive effect on his wife. She felt that the burden for the survival of the family was less squarely on her shoulders. In turn, she was able to relieve some of the burden she usually put on her son. The father moved back into the house. Sam began to improve as his mother relieved the pressure on him and as his parents were able to confront each other directly and to work out a redistribution of responsibilities. He increasingly showed a better capacity to cope with the demands that one normally places on an 11-year-old boy. This was especially evident in his improved ability to survive at school without getting into major clashes with his teachers. He was able to sustain his adaptation even after therapy was terminated and has continued to do so during several years of follow-up.

SYNTHESIS

We have sketched a therapeutic approach to comic children that calls for a grasp of their unique world view. To win the confidence of comic children, therapists must register an awareness of these children's absurdly oriented perspectives. This means participating behaviorally in some of their funny strategies. Actually, therapists need to demonstrate that they simultaneously approve of the comic style and yet understand that it involves a difficult chronic commitment to soothe others. Therapists in contact with comedic children often walk a tightrope that requires therapeutic balancing. On one hand, it would seem essential that the therapist accept the child's right to be ridiculous or funny. On the other hand, the child cannot be expected to shoulder the unreasonable responsibilities that have been implicitly linked with, and have largely instigated, his or her absurd role in the family. Once they are comfortable in the therapy situation, comic children tend to focus on their central conflict, which revolves around the issue of whether they are good or evil. They zestfully invite deprecation and condemnation as evil children, and a major aim of the therapy is to moderate the extremeness of such self-immolation. Therapists can do so by refusing to deprecate the child, by calling attention to his or her intent to elicit attack, and by approving comedy as a substitute to putting oneself down. Furthermore, therapists can communicate their willingness to be supportive and nurturant without blaming and issuing accusations of evil. An important adjunct in moderating comic children's behavior is to give their parents insight into the degree to which they have unreasonable expectations. Such parental expectations overload the child and convey the absurd message, "You are bad because you make us suffer by expecting us to nurture you and care for you as if you were a child." The mothers often take the lead in transmitting this message, and their traumatic impact may sometimes be dramatically reduced by tracing and alleviating the causes of the mother's own sense of overload. This would be exemplified by restoring a more balanced distribution of responsibilities between a comic child's mother and her spouse who has been passively retreating from participation in family events. In general, we have found that treatment of the comic child is anfractuous, that it calls for being comfortable with the absurd, and that it must enlist rather than attack the comic style of defense.

REFERENCES

Bloomfield, I. (1980). Humour in psychotherapy and analysis. *International Journal of Social Psychiatry, 26,* 135-141.

Fisher, S., & Fisher, R. L. (1981). *Pretend the World Is Funny and Forever: A Psychological Analysis of Comedians, Clowns, and Actors.* Hillsdale, NJ: Lawrence Erlbaum.

Kubie, L. (1971). The destructive potential of humor in psychotherapy. *American Journal of Psychiatry, 127,* 861-866.

Poland, W. S. (1971). The place of humor in psychotherapy. *American Journal of Psychiatry, 128,* 127-129.

Rose, G. J. (1969). King Lear and the use of humor in treatment. *Journal of the American Psychoanalytic Association, 17,* 927-940.

Rosenheim, E. (1974). Humor in psychotherapy. An interactive experience. *American Journal of Psychotherapy, 28,* 584-591.

HUMOR IN
PRAGMATIC PSYCHOTHERAPY*

Richard Driscoll

Dr. Richard Driscoll is a practically-minded clinician. A major aim of his professional efforts is to codify therapeutic interventions within a recognizable, easy-to-follow frame of reference. His chapter asks clear-eyed questions and provides sensible answers related to the clinical uses of humor. Dr. Driscoll specifies how the use of humor can be connected to the overall objectives of the therapeutic enterprise, thus situating the distinct coordinates of humor on the therapeutic map. Some of his humorous imagery manifests his surrealistic vehemence: frogs with wings, chilly birds warming up in fresh cow dung. He "calls 'em like they is, see, and he sees 'em like he calls 'em."

Dr. Driscoll is a clinical psychologist in private practice in Knoxville, Tennessee, and the elaborator of Pragmatic Psychotherapy (1984).

*   *   *

A major challenge facing counselors and psychotherapists today is how to select, from the various therapy orientations, the interventions best suited to the problems of particular clients. The effectiveness of humor or of any other intervention depends not only on the theoretical orientation with which it is associated, but on its appropriateness to the problems of the case at hand. An adequate organizing framework can be a real benefit in our efforts to apply relevant aspects of competing

*I wish to express my appreciation to Peter Ossorio and Howard Pollio for their helpful contributions and comments.

orientations to particular cases. In this chapter, a pragmatic approach is introduced for organizing psychotherapy across theoretical orientations, and humor is shown to be useful to attain several of the integrated guideline objectives.

THEORETICAL PERSPECTIVE

Pragmatic psychotherapy organizes and integrates aspects of various orientations and provides a way of selecting from among them to suit the needs of each particular client. The approach uses ordinary language concepts to structure observations and method selection guidelines for organizing interventions. The basic principles are found in Driscoll (1984) and related material (Bergner, 1983; Driscoll, 1985, in press; Farber, 1981; Ossorio, 1976). The cover term "pragmatic" refers, in language analysis, to the social influence of statements, and also means emphasizing practical considerations over ideology.

ORDINARY LANGUAGE

Ordinary language concepts access the wealth of distinctions needed in everyday social relationships, and are already familiar and easily understood by all. Ordinary language concepts are used here to clarify clinical material and to integrate formulations from competing theoretical orientations. Ordinary language thus provides a welcome answer to the problem of incompatible languages among theoretical orientations. Many of the formulations presented appear commonsensical, in that they clarify and build upon our experience and judgment.

INTERVENTION GUIDELINES

The objective of psychotherapy is to alleviate major restrictions in the client's ability to participate in meaningful and satisfying ways of life. Interventions are made in order to influence the client to change, and are understood and organized here according to the objectives to be accomplished by using such interventions. A set of procedural guidelines are used to specify the objectives that we find important in session after session with a broad range of clients. Compiled from the apparent objectives of numerous current interventions, they provide a way of organizing the useful techniques from various orientations.

Guideline objectives can be identified as pertinent in particular clinical circumstances, and interventions are selected to accomplish those objectives. In this way the guidelines can assist us in selecting interventions appropriate to the problems of particular clients. The guidelines thus specify the *clinical strategies* or *principles of change* suggested by Goldfried (1980) as heuristic connections between the broad goals of therapy and the specific techniques chosen at any given moment.

There are 26 guidelines, which are briefly outlined here and referred to in parentheses in the text.

I. The Therapeutic Relationship

1. *Be on the client's side.* Be committed, and protect against or resolve interfering attitudes.
2. *Maintain an alliance.* Be active, and correct misunderstandings clients have of the relationship.
3. *Maintain credibility.* Show the sense of what you are doing.
4. *Communicate an understanding of the client's position.* Actively listen.
5. *Share responsibility.* Take responsibility in ways that enable the client to take responsibility.

II. Accreditation (Affirm and build upon existing strengths)

1. *Legitimize.* Show the client the sense he or she makes.
2. *Make it acceptable.* Create a comfortable atmosphere. Interpret clients' characteristics in ways they can accept. Introduce norms. Use humor.
3. *Confirm the client's control.* Legitimize the ways the client controls things already.
4. *Don't buy victim acts.* Legitimize the reasons for the acts.
5. *If it works, don't fix it.* Avoid introducing unnecessary uncertainties into areas of appropriate functioning.

129

III. Assessment

1. *Assess what matters.* Look for what is pertinent to your interventions.
2. *Use ordinary language concepts.* Take advantage of the richness of our existing language.
3. *Collaborate.* Two heads are better than one.
4. *Weave together assessment and intervention.* Intervene early, and learn from your interventions.
5. *Don't expect the client to be somebody else.* When clients do not comply, alter intervention tactics.

IV. Clarifications

1. *Clarify situations.* Address misperceptions.
2. *Clarify concepts.* Introduce and apply appropriate distinctions.
3. *Adjust reactivity.* Deal with perceptions of things as bad, wrong, intolerable, or catastrophic.
4. *Deal with the reality basis of emotions.* Clarify and challenge the circumstances that evoke the emotions.
5. *Clarify operating premises.* Clarify the perhaps invalid means clients use to attain their ends.
6. *Present alternatives.* Suggest more practical ways to get what clients want.

V. Instilling New Patterns

1. *Use illustrations and images.* Images imprint and hold concepts in clients' minds.
2. *Familiarize.* Bring it home. Reiterate important ideas. Include practice activities.
3. *Structure carry-over.* Make notes for clients. Assign homework tasks.

VI. Motivations

1. *Appeal to what matters.* Present suggestions as means to get what clients really want.
2. *Avoid generating resistance.* Coercion elicits resistance, so avoid or alter interventions that clients perceive as coercive. (Resistance can sometimes be used paradoxically to motivate constructive reactions.)

A FORMULATION OF HUMOR

Much humor plays on that which is serious or conventional as a stage for an alternative perspective that is whimsical, absurd, or otherwise not serious. Littmann (1983) emphasizes this serious-nonserious contrast in her paradigm case formulations of humor. The typical joke may be presented in a way that asks us initially to take it seriously or at face value, and then it is twisted so that we must take the same material nonseriously. The first impression does not simply vanish, but remains as the background for the alternative. In other cases, the casual or whimsical alternative may precede the more serious alternative, or the two may be introduced together. However constructed, the offhandedness and the seriousness stay together in our minds, and it is the pitting of one against the background of the other that is the basis of our amusement.

Playing casually with degradation, sex, and other areas of vulnerability and squeamishness, the joke can juggle our most serious concerns. Some go to greater lengths to set the stage, but even the simplest joke plays off against our ordinary awareness of the seriousness of life's events. Spoofing our profession, one popular joke asks, "How many psychiatrists does it take to change a light bulb?" The answer is, "Only one, but it takes a long time and the light bulb has to really want to change." The opening line invites us to take it somewhat at face value, and we do so knowing we will be fooled and only because we cannot think of any other way to formulate it. The second line builds upon the first, introduces a whimsical metaphor for the serious concerns of length and impact of treatment, and thereby alters the nature of the question. This placement of the whimsical against the serious is the basis of our amusement.

Humor functions in psychotherapy in much the same way. Many of the issues and concerns are truly serious ones. Through humor, we invite our clients to see their concerns as both serious and nonserious at the same time, and to be amused by the serious-nonserious configuration. The effect is to liberate the clients from their overinvolvement with the seriousness of the matter, without having them lose the sense that it is serious.

In therapy, as in the joke, an attempt at humor can fail, and in many of the same ways. The pertinent concerns may be simply too serious for someone to be willing to make the transition to a lighter viewpoint. The concerns may not be of real interest to begin with, or the twist may not be compelling. Presentations vary in timing and charm, and a great deal rides on the relationship with the person presenting the humor. Perhaps most importantly, humor in psychotherapy must play properly on the seriousness of the issues while offering a nonsolemn alternative. Out clients must trust that we are taking their concerns seriously before they will allow us to take them light-heartedly as well.

Humor in therapy takes many forms including wisecracks, anecdotes, parables and tales, jokes, incongruities, clowning and playfulness in voice modulation, pretend naïveté, burlesques, exaggerations, and other colorful portrayals of attitudes and positions. Good humor in our interventions adds amusement and a change in perspective. While laughter may follow, it need not be taken as the standard for good humor.

TECHNIQUES

Humor usually arises spontaneously from the dynamics of the moment and can be easily forgotten by the end of the session. That is probably how it should be, for humor is often fragile, whimsical, and tightly related to the immediate focus of concerns. In other instances we can bring humor in from other contexts or generate it in a session and then remember and use it again and again in similar situations with other clients. Such humor thereby becomes *stock* humor or standard humor, and is available to us even when we are tired or not particularly original. Although our stock humor generally changes over time as we see new possibilities or grow tired of the old lines, it is good to have some to rely on and to measure other humor against. Several of the illustrations used here involve stock humor that can be easily applied by others in appropriately similar situations.

The approach here is to be clear about what we are trying to accomplish in our sessions and to draw upon specific forms and uses of humor as they contribute to our intelligible aims. Humor can be used to accomplish several of the guideline objectives of pragmatic psychotherapy. Humor can make material more acceptable to clients (II-2), strengthen the illustrations and images we use to portray principles (V-1), avoid generating resistances (VI-2), and maintain our own balance with our clients (I-1). Although these are taken here in turn, humor can often accomplish several of these aims at once.

Humor usually arises intuitively and spontaneously from our involvement with the serious concerns at hand. We must appreciate the incongruities, and any application of humor that is merely mechanical could be counterproductive. Familiarity and ease with the uses of humor and its related aims and outcomes should augment our intuitive understanding of when and how to blend it into our clinical interventions.

HUMOR TO MAKE THINGS ACCEPTABLE (II-2)

Constructing the appropriate atmosphere in therapy sessions is essential. Clients are usually troubled people who find too much of their lives painful already; yet many of the issues and concerns they must wrestle with to get better can be especially painful as well. While some pain during therapeutic work may be unavoidable, it would not seem congruous to advocate a program of suffering through session after session as a general method for learning to overcome suffering. We would do well to find ways to allay the pain and to make the issues and the sessions themselves more comfortable for our clients.

The use of appropriate humor is one way of making material more acceptable. Humor can break the tensions when things get too serious, and the amusement and enjoyment are a welcome alternative to the uneasiness or pain clients too often experience. Clients may come to see their concerns as more tolerable, and the toughest material can be better managed in a lighter atmosphere. Laughter can go a long way towards easing the anguish. By accepting or even enjoying the material in the sessions, clients begin to accept themselves better and to improve their outlook on life. Clients who laugh in their sessions tend to reveal information more readily, making our job of assessment easier and speeding the therapeutic process.

There are parallels in other contexts where humor is used to convey serious messages. The humor in good social and political commentary both conveys the message and also protects it against the wrath of those whose foibles are being exposed. Some are still offended but find it awkward to object too publicly to something that is asking to be taken in fun. As in standard satire, humor in therapy can allow us to get away with interpretations that clients might otherwise find too objectionable.

In challenging a client's various insidious positions, we portray and may want to dramatize, burlesque, spoof, tease, or even ridicule the position. In a marital session the husband becomes offended by something his wife says and, relying on his usual *modus operandi*, he sulks. Normally protective of him, the wife tries to make amends, but to no avail. His moodiness could control and sour the session, and I must challenge it. Sulking involves seeing oneself as provoked or mistreated, and maintaining an angry silence in order to show the provocateur that he or she cannot get away with such mistreatment. I can legitimize and show the husband the sense he makes, to allow him to see his position in a more acceptable manner, as follows: "It must seem really insensitive of her to say that she is so frustrated by you. So you have reason to let her know that it is unfair to you, and that she had better change and take it back and not say that sort of thing anymore."

Interpreting sulking is always touchy, because the man who is sulking is already offended and is asking others to tread lightly and to give in to him lest they might offend him more. The sulker is presenting himself as someone who cannot take it, and inviting everyone to treat him accordingly. Sulking can be powerful, but it is also the tactic of a child against a parent or other individuals perceived to be in authority. I decided to introduce humor into our intervention by acting out the husband's position playfully but in a childishly pouty manner and with childish modulation and intonation: "You are not being fair to me. So I am not going to even talk to you, and that will show you so that you learn to treat me better. And besides, after what you did to me, you deserve it."

My intervention is on several levels at once, and therein lies both the punch and the safety. I am understanding and legitimizing his position and apparently arguing it for him, but by merely saying it aloud I am thereby exposing the immaturity and manipulativeness it involves. I am also being playful in acting with the pretend innocence of a child, yet conveying an interpretation that might otherwise be read as antagonistic. The humor in the intervention allays the objections long enough for the client to recognize himself in it, and from there it spoils the justification so that it becomes awkward to continue sulking. As in other social commentary, the humor both conveys the message and also protects it against the force of the objection.

By introducing our clients to the practice of humor, we are presenting a constructive response and inviting them to assimilate it as they are willing and able in their own lives. Clients who improve tend to acquire some of the characteristics of their therapists, so in using humor we are modeling a way of being for our clients. Showing how humor can get us through the tensions and impasses in therapy, we are suggesting to our clients an alternative to their own sometimes inflexible and too serious ways of managing tensions. We are introducing them to what may be an essential ingredient of a lighter and more joyful way of life. Generating alternative ways of acting is a component of most active psychotherapy approaches and is one of the guidelines of pragmatic psychotherapy (IV-6).

Each psychotherapy orientation has its own favored methods to make things acceptable. Analytic approaches emphasize the timing of the interpretations. Client-centered therapy accepts whatever clients say, whereas other orientations suggest ways to challenge the self-rejection (Driscoll, 1981, 1982). Many of the "games" or interpretations suggested by transactional analysis have a humorous twist that allays the seriousness and makes the message easier to swallow. Humor is but one of a broad range of methods we might use to make things more acceptable to clients.

HUMOR IN ILLUSTRATIONS AND IMAGES (V-1)

Ordinary conversation can become bland and too easily forgotten, and we look for ways to intrigue our clients and to imprint important concepts and principles in their minds. Livening up the conversation, the use of illustrations and images, aphorisms, and parables can portray critical principles in ways that are more readily remembered and utilized. Images and illustrations that have humorous aspects can be especially appealing and intriguing, and are thus more apt to imprint and sustain the message.

Standard images can be used to portray and retain concepts for ourselves and our clients. The status concepts below are useful but slippery enough that they would be hard to grasp without an accompanying image

135

or illustration. Some persons contribute heavily to the assignment of status or social position, and can by their judgments place other people in arbitrary or unfair positions otherwise unrelated to personal qualities and worth. We can use the following *Three Umpires* image (original source unknown) to introduce status and status assignment, and then draw the appropriate parallels.

> A sportswriter interviews three umpires:
> "And you, sir," he asks the first umpire, "what is the nature of your job?"
> "Some is balls and some is strikes," replies the first umpire, "and I calls 'em like they is."
> "I see. And you, sir," he asks the second umpire, "what is the nature of your job?"
> "Some is balls and some is strikes," replies the second, "and I calls 'em like I sees 'em."
> "I see. And you, sir," he asks the third umpire, "what is the nature of your job?"
> "Some is balls and some is strikes," replies the third, "and what I calls 'em, see, that's what they is."

Here, the third umpire is a status assigner, for what he calls 'em, see, that's what they is.

It is often therapeutic to focus on those who are acting as status assigners for our clients. The wife who argues with her husband but allows him to be the judge of when she is or is not making sense is thereby allowing him to assign a value to her arguments and to her as well. So she loses every argument and comes close to losing her mind as well, not because she does not make sense but because she cannot convince him that she makes sense. I suggest that the husband maintains control by judging the worth of the arguments, and present the principles in the *Three Umpires* image. I portray the husband as the third umpire whose opinion counts not because it is fair and accurate but because the participants have agreed to go along with it. Adapted to this situation, the punch line becomes "Some wives make sense and some is nonsense, and what I calls you, see, that's what you is." The image legitimizes her sense of confusion, for it shows her the sense it makes for her to feel that she makes no sense at all. The important next step is to challenge her acceptance of him as the arbiter of her sanity.

Three Umpires provides a nice introduction to some of these situations. The image explains the predicament and at the same time it takes out some of the sting. Most clients are intrigued by the presentation and enjoy the fun. Although some cannot remember the sequencing, they do come to understand the status assignment factors and so have a start in working on those issues. Illustrations and images are used in Adlerian, transactional analysis, hypnotherapeutic, humanistic, and guided fantasies approaches, among others. Humor contributes here to the strength of an already established method.

HUMOR TO AVOID GENERATING RESISTANCE (VI-2)

Clients overly committed to repetitive patterns can challenge our capacities for finding versatile methods to gain sufficient therapeutic leverage. Although we must clarify and challenge the concerns that impede change, too much repetition or force of argument can make us appear coercive and thus evoke resistance in these clients. Humor can break the pressure and recast us as allies to our clients, and in some cases even capture their imaginations.

One client listens to anything I say, but always returns to her favored position. "If only he would stop drinking," she persists, "then I'm sure we could work everything out between us." She has proven herself impervious to any indications that he is not going to stop, and something new is needed: "And if only frogs had wings, they wouldn't bump their asses." The comment conveys her entanglement and gives a moment's break from the monotony.

In working with clients who lash out in tight situations when they would do better to stay quiet, we need to turn their attention to their own contributions to the tensions. These clients focus on the provocations others are handing them and consider themselves justified in lashing back, but they remain blind to the problems that they cause by their reactions. We can use the following "Keep Your Mouth Shut" story to break set and focus them on getting out of the troublesome pattern:

A bird falls out of its nest, lands in the cold snow, and is about to freeze to death. A Saint

Bernard comes along, and gently takes the bird in his mouth and carries him over to a large and very fresh patty of cow dung, and drops him off there. The bird warms up in the dung, so he is going to be all right. But he notices the smell, and he begins to chirp loudly. And a fox in the area hears the bird squawk, and comes over and eats him.

It is a terrible story. But there is a moral, as you might well expect: "It's not always your enemies that get you there, and it's not always your friends that get you out. But when you're in the shit, keep your mouth shut."

In a typical application, I am trying to persuade a teenage girl that she would do better being somewhat civil to her mother. We have confirmed that the mother is indeed overly critical and otherwise impossible, and we have explored her belief that being nice would be a lie and a violation of her integrity because it is not how she feels. She sees that her sharp remarks aggravate and intensify the animosities, and that some conventional pleasantries might help her mother ease off a bit. But the provocations she faces are real, and her inclinations are to continue to fight back. My advice to stay pleasant is becoming repetitious and a bit wearisome to both of us, and I do not want to appear to be siding with her adversary. The "Keep Your Mouth Shut" tale provides a welcome change of pace. Initially startled and intrigued, she appreciates this particular presentation and can see the advice as valuable.

The story takes the long way around and goes in through the back door, taking one's mind off the immediate problem and intriguing the client with an entirely new problem. The complexity of the reversal commands attention, and sets one up for the final line. One wants to remember the twist, so the punch line stays with the client well. In this case, the moral gives a rebellious teenager a new perspective on the mundanities of required compliance. Resistance was suggested in psychoanalysis as a major impediment to treatment, and avoiding or minimizing resistance is important in a wide variety of orientations. Humor makes a nice contribution to an old task.

HUMOR TO FORTIFY OUR OWN ATTITUDES (I-1)

For those of us who spend 20 or more hours a week with the woes of others, humor can be a lifeline to sanity. Woven into the serious concerns we work with, it can release our own tensions and lift our spirits.

Although perhaps we ought to like everyone we work with, we actually tend to like most those clients who are easy to converse with and who make us feel useful and those clients whom we find interesting and fun. We are inclined to tire and have to work on our attitudes with clients whom we find mundane and boring. Seeing humor in our clients and in their triumphs and foibles means that we are seeing them as more interesting persons. The humor makes it easier to genuinely appreciate the person in spite of the tensions, and contradictions, and confusions, or perhaps even because of them. By casting lights of various shades and colors on our clients, humor makes it easier for us to be genuinely interested in them. Consequently, humor may help us maintain the proper interest and balanced attitudes toward our clients. The more balanced attitudes are important to those on both sides of the therapeutic relationship.

Good humor requires attention, personal connection, and sensitivity to the ongoing concerns, and in that sense it is not easy. Perhaps some of the best therapeutic humor arises out of a vital tension between our expectations and plans for our clients and the sometimes unpleasant reality of what we see them actually doing. But the energy level plays both ways, for using humor requires more from us and at the same time it gives more back. The good use of humor requires our full attention and commitment and takes our energy, and at the same time humorous sessions can be more satisfying for us and perhaps even re-energizing. When we are fully involved, we are more likely to wind up with the good feeling of tiredness that comes from honest hard work.

The right attitude is in turn an essential ingredient in therapeutic humor. Warmth and compassion are critical. Any annoyance or bitterness we might have can be too readily conveyed in the humor we use, turning it into hostile humor and upending the trust that must be there for the clients to accept humorous comments. When we are feeling annoyed at a client it might be a good idea to avoid humor altogether, unless we can point the humor directly at ourselves and at our troublesome attitudes.

When we consider the benefits of humor in therapy, it is the friendly variety of humor we are referring to, and most obviously not humor motivated by hostility toward the clients.

The attitude of the therapist toward the client is held to be important in a variety of orientations. Client-centered therapy exhorts us to love our clients, whereas the psychodynamic orientation interprets our tendency to dislike them. Humor can add a new angle to the vital requirement of maintaining a positive stance toward our clients.

PERTINENT USES

Most of my training emphasized the seriousness of the therapeutic process in the very serious context of the graduate training experience; but I have always been attracted to those few instructors and colleagues, and to clinical methods, that showed a sense of humor, and have learned much from them. I believe that the use of humor is something we can assimilate from the right training experiences and augment and improve upon ourselves. Although psychotherapy sessions are usually thought of as serious business, I have experienced at least some laughter in most of my sessions and a lot of laughter in many of them. An associate in the office next to mine was able to confirm my impression and expressed some interest in upgrading the soundproofing.

APPROPRIATE CLIENTS

There are some reasonable limitations regarding with whom and where we can use humor. For instance, we cannot use humor with those who would consider that we are not taking them seriously enough, who would feel we are laughing at them rather than with them, or who would be otherwise offended. Obviously we must watch our step with paranoids or other clients who manifest an edgy disposition and do not tend to stay long in therapy anyway. Also, using humor can be a frustrating and thankless task indeed with those who listen but simply do not get it.

The use of humor should not jeopardize our therapeutic relationship with our clients. Specifically, it is important to maintain an alliance with our clients (I-2) and to maintain credibility in ourselves and our methods

(I-3). Humor that is not appropriate to certain situations and clients might easily undermine these relationship factors. An intervention to obtain any objective may go wrong if it inadvertently undermines another aspect of the process, and we should be careful that attempts to lighten things up do not sacrifice critical aspects of the therapeutic relationship.

Clients are ready for humor when the relationship we have with them will allow humor. Personality and other factors are important in that they contribute to the relationship. Clients who are overly suspicious or touchy may not be able to establish stable enough relationships to allow much humor. Some clients seem relatively comfortable with us from the beginning, and others come to trust us over time. All must feel we are taking them seriously before they allow us to be lighthearted as well. We might do well to gauge the opportunities for humor not so much by general personality factors as by the nature of the relationship we have established with clients.

Some clients are not so edgy but merely serious minded and stuck in their ruts. Persons who are used to a grimly serious approach to life usually expect that therapy should be similarly hard and joyless. Any humor we might try to use in therapy seems frivolous to them and in violation of solid professional practice. We may be able to establish some credibility for our more playful methods by clarifying and challenging their too serious attitudes about life. We can note that they expect this and other aspects of their lives to be strictly serious, and then question whether they are limited in their capacities to let loose and enjoy things, or suggest that they are so limited. We can ask if they want to learn to enjoy things more, and promote our lighter approach in the therapy sessions as a good introduction to balancing stressful lives. This position, if accepted, allows us to use humor but still remain credible.

SUGGESTIONS FOR BEGINNERS

How would I advise trainees or recent converts to begin using humor in psychotherapy? Obviously, it is best to start with your already existing sense of humor and style of relating. Begin by paying some attention to the ways you express humor and the ways others respond. Look at the humor you might be already using in your therapy sessions and in everyday social relationships, and puzzle a bit about what it is and what makes it work.

Those who have been trained in the tradition that holds psychotherapy to be a solemn and strictly reverent activity need to take a closer look at the injunctions, and to break free from them. What are the assumptions that make it so strictly serious, and what is so threatening about laughter? There is a continuum from seriousness to playfulness and amusement and from there to laughter. I believe you can try to be a bit more playful with your clients, and more entertaining, offhanded, and light-hearted. Although laughter may follow, it is not good to reach too far for it. Pay attention to how your clients are responding, and go with what works for you.

Observing others who use humor well can be invaluable. So much rides on relationship, context, and timing, which are hard to portray properly in written form. The playfulness in voice intonations--which is one of my favorites--is a good way to begin with new clients and is not particularly risky, but it is much better conveyed by example than by words. Some of the stock humor suggested here may be applied in the appropriate situations. Moreover, the therapist's skills in the clinical uses of humor can be significantly enhanced through supervision and clinical workshop training on appropriate contexts and proper pacing. Some trial and error may be necessary to find out how humor will work for you.

CLINICAL PRESENTATION

I recently reviewed a complete transcript of a first marital therapy session, and can offer here some observations on how humor played in with this particular case. The husband has just found out about an affair his wife had had some years ago. He is tormented by it and angry at her but wants to maintain the marriage.

Our initial task in the beginning session is to make clients comfortable with us and to establish an alliance, so we do better to play things relatively straight until they have some trust in us and we get to know them. With this couple the first laugh is from me about 20 minutes into the session, and probably a bit too soon.

The wife contends that he tries to control everything, and feels she does not get to be a real person around him. He contends that he has to be responsible for everything:

Husband:	The husband has to be the head of the household.
Driscoll:	Does she get a real say in things?
Husband:	But somebody has to make the decision.
Driscoll:	And that has always got to be you.
Husband:	Somebody has to be responsible.
Driscoll:	Somebody, but not her (*laughs*). You mention that you always get put in the position of responsibility....

This is shaping up as a confrontation between us. I am trying to convey some playfulness in my comments and my laughter here is an attempt to break the tension and invite him to see the imbalance between them as a bit humorous. But he does not seem to be going along with it, and my comment feels awkward to me. So I continue more straightforwardly, trying to make it more comfortable between us. I return to being more playful a few minutes later and continue that way for much of the session.

By 40 minutes into the session we have established a lighter and more playful mood, so that several of the comments are fun ones. At 60 minutes some of my humor meets with somewhat better reception. The focus is on the sexual problems:

Wife:	I get affectionate with him. And he says "I'm sorry, you've waited too late," or "I'm too old." Or something like that.
Husband:	When I've been asleep for an hour and you come in and you get all lovey dovey, I'm just not in the mood without a little foreplay. (*they both laugh*)
Driscoll:	I remember a scene in a movie where two teenagers who are real inexperienced are trying to get it on. And she says, "I'm going to need some foreplay." So he reaches over and kisses her, and says, "Is that enough?" And she says, "Yeah, I guess so." (*all laugh*)

Here I am bringing in something that I have used before as stock humor. It takes their attention off the

143

seriousness of their problems for a moment and gets a laugh, and they continue.

Toward the end of the 90-minute first session he is talking about turning away from her sexually (because of his hurt and anger over the affair):

Husband: I recognize that this is not normal. I love the woman. But I want her and we get in bed and start the foreplay, and I don't even want to look at her.

Wife: How can you make love to somebody you won't look at? (*she laughs*)

Driscoll: A woman can do it backwards, but a man can't. (*she laughs; he smiles, and seems to enjoy the joke*)

Wife: He turns his head (*away*).

Husband: I do not want to see her. It's painful to look at her.

The humor goes over here and makes a small contribution to breaking the tension and producing some fun out of the trouble and pain. They continue on the same issue:

Husband: I wanted her free to enjoy (sex). And then when she started getting free (of her inhibition), it seemed like I got it.

Driscoll: That happens sometimes. You can't get the problem all the way out the window. It just jumps from one side of the bed to the other.

Toward the last of the session both of them are apparently more comfortable with the situation, and she is laughing at several comments that would not strike anyone as particularly funny from the transcript:

Husband: I wondered what it would take for you to open up (and enjoy sex).

Wife: I do enjoy sex.

Husband: You show no emotion. You just lie there like a rubber doll.

Driscoll (*to husband*): Did you hear her say that she does enjoy it?

Husband: I heard what she said.

Driscoll (*to wife*): What would it take to convince him?

Wife: (*laughs*) Well, I've been trying.

The laughter here comes out of the tensions of the session and from the atmosphere of playfulness that I am striving to create. Playfulness and amusement alternate with seriousness or with hurt and anger through the remaining therapy sessions with this couple.

It seems on reflection that much of the laughter in therapy comes not from anything particularly clever or witty, but from the high tensions in combination with some playfulness and a sense of letting go and making the best of it. Laughter can be contagious, so once we get it going it can continue somewhat on its own. Some humor in therapy may be easier than writings on the subject might suggest, for the things that people laugh at in sessions can be a lot more ordinary than the things writers on humor must present to convey amusement to the readers.

SYNTHESIS

Laughter, it has been said, is the universal language. Although not always interpreted in the same way, it does convey something similar and understandable across a wide variety of cultures and peoples. So it is perhaps especially fitting in writings on humor that we use ordinary language concepts that can be readily understood by all of us, rather than concepts with more narrow uses from particular theoretical orientations.

In introducing humor into our therapy sessions, we should be aware of our goals. Humor contributes to several of the guideline objectives of pragmatic psychotherapy. Similar objectives are common to a number of orientations, and familiarity with these guideline objectives may help us identify when some humor might be appropriate and beneficial.

The current interest in humor may be a sign that something is afoot in a field that has taken itself too seriously for far too long. The social sciences have been concerned with appearing properly scientific at the expense of clear communication and honest recognition of the mystery behind the inquiry. Many journal articles are tedious at best and can be obscure or irrelevant, relying on thick literature reviews with respectful references to other authorities to provide credibility. A tabulation by Armstrong (1980) found a striking .70 correlation between the prestige of academic psychology journals and the difficulty and obtuseness of the writing, suggesting little appreciation or even tolerance for lively and to-the-point presentations. But clinical practitioners are demanding clearer and more practical material. Communications between academicians and practitioners are often strained, but were the two to go their separate ways, it would be at the expense of both.

The introduction of some playfulness and humor into the arena may indicate awareness of the existing contradictions. There is a growing movement toward rapprochement and integration between separate therapy orientations, but progress is slow. Whereas idealists believe that things can change, only romanticists believe that things change easily. Perhaps things will change in our fields and perhaps in the right directions, but I believe that they will not change easily or without considerable effort. In the meantime, it is best to keep our sense of humor.

REFERENCES

Armstrong, J. S. (1980). Unintelligible management research and academic prestige. *Interfaces, 10,* 80-86.

Bergner, R. (1983). Emotions: A conceptual formulation and its clinical implications. In K. E. Davis & R. Bergner (Eds.), *Advances in Descriptive Psychology* (Vol. 3, pp. 209-227). Greenwich, CT: JAI Press.

Driscoll, R. (1981). Self-criticism: Analysis and treatment. In K. E. Davis (Ed.), *Advances in Descriptive Psychology* (Vol. 1, pp. 321-355). Greenwich, CT: JAI Press.

Driscoll, R. (1982). Their own worst enemies. *Psychology Today, 16,* 45-49.

Driscoll, R. (1984). *Pragmatic Psychotherapy.* New York: Van Nostrand Reinhold.

Driscoll, R. (1985). Commonsense objectives in paradoxical interventions. *Psychotherapy, 22,* 774-778.

Driscoll, R. (in press). The teenage prosecutor: A case in pragmatic family therapy. In J. Norcross (Ed.), *Casebook of Eclectic Psychotherapy.* New York: Brunner/Mazel.

Farber, A. (1981). Castaneda's Don Juan as psychotherapist. In K. E. Davis (Ed.), *Advances in Descriptive Psychology* (Vol. 1, pp. 274-304). Greenwich, CT: JAI Press.

Goldfried, M. (1980). Toward the delineation of therapeutic change principles. *American Psychologist,* *35,* 991-999.

Littmann, J. (1983). A new formulation of humor. In K. E. Davis & R. Bergner (Eds.), *Advances in Descriptive Psychology* (Vol. 3, pp. 183-207). Greenwich, CT: JAI Press.

Ossorio, P. G. (1976). *Clinical Topics* (LRI Report #11). Boulder, CO: Linguistic Research Institute.

HUMOR AND LAUGHTER
IN BEHAVIOR THERAPY

W. Larry Ventis

In this chapter, Dr. Ventis presents a refreshing view of how humor can productively complement behavior therapy techniques without substantially deviating from the conventional behavioral paradigm. First, Dr. Ventis explores the promising challenge of incorporating a complex cognitive phenomenon like humor into behavior therapy work. Second, he artfully demonstrates how humor can be blended with the classical behavioral procedures of systematic desensitization, assertive training, modeling, and reinforcement.

Dr. Ventis's work corresponds with recent trends within the behavioral school seeking to take into account the cognitive aspects of functioning in designing behavior therapy interventions, as illustrated in the work of Michael Mahoney, Aaron Beck, and Albert Ellis. The utilization of humor is in accordance with the cognitive trend in behavior therapy, and brings the tension-reducing properties of humor to assist in the process of behavioral change.

Dr. Larry Ventis is a clinical psychologist and Professor at the Psychology Department of the College of William and Mary in Williamsburg, Virginia.

❋　　❋　　❋

Reports on the purposeful use of humor and laughter in behavior therapy have been rare. Rimm and Masters (1979), in their general text on behavior therapy, cite only two case studies, one referring to the use of humor in behavioral treatment, the other referring to the use of laughter. Similarly, Kuhlman (1984) includes only these same two behavioral case studies in his review of existing studies on humor and psychotherapy.

Such a scarcity of references to humor in the behavior therapy literature might suggest that behavior thera-

149

pists are a grim and humorless lot; however there is evidence that refutes this. For instance, the *Journal of Behavioral Analysis* includes an article by Dennis Upper (1974) entitled, "The Unsuccessful Self-Treatment of a Case of Writer's Block." It consists of the author's credits, and a blank page, with a reviewer's comment in a footnote that he could find nothing wrong with the manuscript. Further, Kazrin and Durac (1983) have a brief report in *Behavior Therapy* presenting a device for group penile plethysmography that looks suspiciously like an electric milking machine with several attached hoses. Clearly at least a few behavior therapists can both create and enjoy a good joke.

Although formal reference to humor or laughter is rare in behavior therapy literature, one does occasionally find case reports and treatment procedures in which the apparently inadvertent use of humor or laughter seems to have clinical significance. Consider, for example, the stimulus satiation treatment by Ayllon (1963) of a hospital patient who hoarded towels. The patient was given regular deliveries of from 7 to 60 towels over a period of weeks until there were 650 towels stacked in her room. Indeed, 650 towels were sufficient to satiate her, and she not only stopped hoarding but also started returning the extras herself. Clearly the therapist had a humorous perspective in implementing this successful treatment, and audiences consistently respond to the description as humorous. There is, however, no explicit mention of humor in the title of the article itself.

Laughter, too, has sometimes been reported, though not as an intended ingredient in therapy. For instance, Wolpe and Lazarus (1966) reported on the use of a flooding technique with an agoraphobic woman. The woman's problem began when she fainted on a public street while pregnant. She subsequently developed an intense fear of being in public places that was maintained for several years, sharply restricting her ability to function normally. The flooding procedure essentially consists of describing the feared stimuli in vivid detail while the phobic person imagines the scene as realistically as possible. The therapeutic rationale is that if the person repeatedly experiences his or her fear in the phobic situation in the absence of any objective harm, then the fear will eventually extinguish. In this particular case there was a lengthy and grueling description of the client's fainting alone in the street while passers-by ogled her exposed thighs and made crude remarks. The client showed considerable anxiety, and then became quite hostile toward the therapist. The description was resumed and, by Lazarus's report,

> Approximately 10 minutes later the patient grew strangely quiet, as though a state of protective inhibition had supervened. She then burst into hysterical laughter which subsided after a few minutes. "This whole thing is so damned absurd," she remarked. (p. 139)

The client then refused to continue with the flooding procedure, though she did continue treatment to a successful conclusion. Kuhlman (1982) describes a similar occurrence in which unexpected uncontrolled laughter was associated with a crucial insight experience during systematic desensitization. Thus, in both of these cases, client laughter is noted, but it was not purposely included or elicited in either case.

From the brief examples presented, it is apparent that the occasional presence of humor and laughter in behavioral therapy approaches has been previously acknowledged, although the purposeful use of either of these ingredients in behavior therapy has not been actively pursued. In this chapter I shall be primarily concerned with humor and laughter as central and purposeful ingredients in behavior therapy.

THEORETICAL PERSPECTIVE

The neglect of humor in behavior therapy may lie in the difficulty of integrating a complex cognitive phenomenon like humor into a behavioral paradigm. But for some time now there has been a prominent and growing interest in integrating cognitive psychological concepts into behavior therapy (e.g., Mahoney, 1974; Meichenbaum, 1977). The use of humor offers one specific opportunity for this integration.

Humor and laughter may also have been neglected because behavior therapists and researchers have done quite well at empirically demonstrating the effectiveness of behavior therapy procedures in the absence of much formal attention to humor and laughter. Thus, it has not been necessary to consider them. I believe, however, that humor and laughter may be shown to highly facilitate many treatment processes.

The theoretical perspective that I have found most helpful in attempting to use humor in behavior therapy is based on the work of Arthur Koestler (1964), an author of decidedly non- or even antibehavioral orientation. Koestler's work offers a provocative rationale for the inclusion of humor in behavior therapy. His ideas also imply that humor and laughter, though frequently occurring together, may serve rather different therapeutic functions in a behavioral context. Despite being sharply critical of behavioral psychology, Koestler's language and perspective actually show considerable compatibility with behavioral views. Consider the following statement:

> Humor is the only domain of creative activity where a stimulus on a high level of complexity produces a massive and sharply defined response on the level of physiological reflexes. (p. 31)

The two concepts are here clearly delineated, humor being a complex cognitive stimulus and laughter a physiological reflex-like response.

To better understand this complex stimulus, humor, let us consider two hypotheses in Koestler's work. The central concept in Koestler's analysis of humor is bisociation, a term that he coined in purposeful contrast with association. Bisociation consists of

> the perceiving of a situation or idea, in two self-consistent but habitually incompatible frames of reference, M1, and M2. The event L, in which the two intersect, is made to vibrate simultaneously on two different wavelengths, as it were. While this unusual situation lasts, L is not merely linked to one associative context, but bisociated with two. (p. 35)

The concept of bisociation is perhaps best clarified in the following joke:

> Each of two Indian braves, Running Water and Falling Rocks, approached their chief and asked to marry his daughter. Having no established method for deciding between the two, the chief proposed a trial by ordeal. The two would go into

the wilderness wearing only loin cloths and return in 30 days. The brave who returned in the best physical condition on this day would win the chief's daughter. The two agreed and departed.

The weeks passed quickly, and the entire tribe eagerly awaited the results. Finally, on the thirtieth day Running Water came crawling into the village at sunset having barely survived the ordeal. The chief declared him the winner, but then began to worry about the missing brave. The chief had, after all, designed the trial. A search party was sent out but had no luck. Then the chief had a tower built from which he kept a vigil for the young man. Weeks passed, then months, and still no trace of the missing brave.

The brave was never seen again, but you can still see signs on the highway saying, "Watch for Falling Rocks."

The term "Falling Rocks" belongs in two distinct and typically independent associative contexts, as a proper name in the story (M1), and as part of a warning sign in contemporary experience (M2). The joke purposely cultivates the former and unexpectedly, but logically (if somewhat oddly), joins the two contexts at the punch line, via their one common term, "Falling Rocks" (L). Koestler's analysis lends itself to a behavioral perspective. Humor as a cognitive stimulus is analyzed in terms of associations and associative context, a fairly standard way for behaviorists to approach cognition.

The second hypothesis offered by Koestler on the nature of humor concerns an emotional ingredient.

The more sophisticated forms of humor evoke mixed and contradictory feelings; but whatever the mixture, it must contain one ingredient whose presence is indisputable: an impulse, however faint, of aggression or apprehension. (p. 52)

In this perspective, aggression and apprehension are both posited to be part of the humor experience, because Koestler assumed them to have similar physiological bases. For instance, in the example above, the narrative raises at least mild apprehension over the fate of the missing brave. If there is any aggressive impulse present, it probably consists merely in the audience having been briefly misled or fooled.

Briefly then, for Koestler, humor is a complex cognitive stimulus based on a process of *bisociation*, the joining of otherwise disparate associative contexts via some common element. It is further assumed always to involve an aggressive or apprehensive impulse, an ingredient that he called an "*aggressive-defensive* or *self-asserting* tendency." As to laughter, in addition to characterizing it as a reflex-like response to a complex stimulus, Koestler also hypothesized that it serves to eliminate excess emotional tension: "In a word, laughter is aggression (or apprehension) robbed of its logical *raison d'être*, the puffing away of emotion discarded by thought" (p. 56).

If we apply this claim to the joke above, any apprehension elicited by concern for the missing brave in the story is suddenly rendered superfluous at the punch line due to the complete change in the reader's conception of the situation. Of course, only the reader knows if laughter occurred. However, Koestler's hypothesis that laughter serves to release emotion is a controversial contention.

The proposed interrelationship between humor and laughter is summarized in the following overview statement:

> The sudden bisociation of a mental event with two habitually incompatible matrices results in an abrupt transfer of the train of thought from one associative context to another. The emotive charge which the narrative carried cannot be so transferred owing to its greater inertia and persistence; discarded by reason, the tension finds its outlet in laughter. (Koestler, 1964, p. 59)

From these several hypotheses one has a theoretical rationale for the inclusion of humor and laughter in behavior therapy, and the implications for the significance of the two are somewhat different. First, consider humor. If a therapist tactfully introduces humor into the context of situations that may be fear or anger laden for the client, then this could help the client see the stimulus situation in a new, more constructive, less fearful, or less hostile perspective. If the client can create humor, that is, make a joke, in a situation to which he or she has responded almost exclusively with intense negative emotion, then the client's humorous reaction may reflect a significant and useful change in the associative context within which he or she views the situation. For example, instead of viewing a situation as simply fearful, the person may think of the same situation as partially fearful, partially humorous, or even predominantly humorous. It may be that self-efficacy cognitions, that is, the anticipation of personal mastery of a difficult problem, may constitute a critical associative context here (Bandura, 1977). The ability to see humor in a context previously viewed as more exclusively fearful or aversive may denote an increment in self-efficacy. Self-efficacy expectancies, in turn, have been demonstrated to show close agreement with behavioral change (Bandura, Adams, & Beyer, 1977). In attempting to fit this more directly into Koestler's perspective, it may be that on the one hand perceptions of failure, helplessness, or weakness and on the other hand, self-efficacy, are two associative contexts that can profitably be bisociated in therapy.

Shifting our attention to laughter, it may be viewed in two ways: (a) it may serve as overt evidence that a change in the client's cognitive construction of a problem is occurring so that the previous negative emotion is no longer implied or dominant, or (b) the laughter itself may physiologically relieve the fear or anger associated with the situation. To the extent that the latter point is true, the therapist might sometimes find it desirable to elicit laughter in situations where tension reduction is a goal.

The differentiation between humor and laughter may sometimes prove superfluous because the two often occur jointly and because we cannot really exert very good control over the occurrence of laughter. I still think it is important to differentiate their functions, however, because it provides a therapeutic rationale for the use of humor even in the absence of overt laughter. Consequently, the disputed cathartic effects of laughter are not critical for possible therapeutic effects of humor.

Finally, I realize that more rigorous behaviorists may object to basing therapy methods on theoretical speculations about the nature of humor or laughter, but a simpler rationale is available. If humor can be paired with a previously fearful or angering stimulus situation, however one views humor theoretically, it is usually more constructive or adaptive than fear or anger. Whichever of these rationales one prefers, the basic implication for treatment is still the same: introduce humor into a previously discomforting situation and perhaps also elicit laughter.

TECHNIQUES

The following techniques are standard behavior therapy procedures with some modification for the inclusion of humor. As needed, I will try to distinguish between the standard procedure and any changes made to accommodate the use of humor.

SYSTEMATIC DESENSITIZATION

Systematic desensitization is a treatment for irrational fear or excessive anxiety. The original rationale for its effectiveness is based on counterconditioning, or substituting one conditioned response for another via the classical conditioning process (Wolpe, 1969). Usually in desensitization, relaxation is substituted for fear or anxiety. Some have argued that the basic change occurring in desensitization is in the way the client thinks about the feared situation (e.g., Goldfried, 1971). At any rate, the typical systematic desensitization process is as follows:

1. The client is trained in systematic relaxation (e.g., Jacobson, 1938) and is instructed to practice regularly at home until he or she can voluntarily relax.
2. The therapist determines whether the fear is irrational to insure that the treatment is appropriate and that the client will be motivated.
3. The therapist and client then jointly establish a hierarchy of scenes and events associated with the feared stimulus situation, the hierarchy being ordered in a gradual sequence from the least to the most anxiety arousing.
4. Beginning with the least anxiety arousing item, the therapist verbally presents the hierarchy scenes to the client one at a time. The client attempts to imagine the scenes as vividly and realistically as possible while remaining relaxed.
5. If the client begins to experience anxiety during the presentation of any hierarchy item, he or she is instructed to signal the therapist, at which point they terminate the scene, return to a lower level

item, and work their way back up through the sequence to the difficult item and beyond.

6. The process is continued in this fashion until the hierarchy is successfully completed. Usually, the successful completion of the imagined hierarchy greatly facilitates the client's comfort when encountering similar situations in actuality.

Humor may be used in desensitization in two ways. Both may be functionally characterized as *comic relief*. When the client has excessive difficulty learning to relax or when there is insufficient time for the proper training of relaxation, humor may be included in the hierarchy scenes in an attempt to compensate for the inadequate relaxation. Thus (a) the client may be requested to relax as much as possible, and then (b) either consistently, or on an unpredictable schedule, humorous content can be included in the otherwise standard hierarchy scenes. If the client finds the material humorous but does not actually laugh (in my own experience smiling is more common than open laughter), then a possible mechanism for any therapeutic effects would consist in cognitive changes in the client due to viewing the feared stimulus situations in a humorous way rather than in a predominantly fearful perspective. As suggested earlier, a humorous perspective may serve to enhance self-efficacy cognitions, and the therapist may purposely try to facilitate this goal by pointing out and reinforcing the client's ability to tolerate or even smile through previously difficult stimulus situations. If the client laughs at the scenes, then there is the additional possibility that some of the fear may be physiologically relieved via the laughter.

A second, less extensive use of humor in desensitization represents comic relief as an aid in getting through a difficult item in a hierarchy during an otherwise standard desensitization process. Thus, instead of going through step 5 as described above, the therapist may stop and, without advance explanation, represent the same difficult item but with added humorous content. This often greatly facilitates progressing through the hierarchy. In a recent dissertation, Shocket (1985) found some support for this use of humor in that subjects who were presented with humorous hierarchies in desensitization required significantly fewer scene presentations to complete their hierarchies than did subjects given standard desensitization. However, the therapist needs to guard against using this procedure if the difficulty is due to an excessively large jump in anxiety arousal in a poorly constructed hierarchy that does not represent a gradual sequence.

ASSERTIVE TRAINING

Unlike systematic desensitization, there is little consensus on exactly what constitutes assertive behavior or assertive training. Wolpe and Lazarus's (1966) definition of assertive behavior as "all socially acceptable expressions of personal rights and feelings" (p. 39) probably represents a position that could be accepted by most. Assertive training then consists of procedures aimed at facilitating assertive behavior. The reader desiring a more thorough overview could refer to Rimm and Masters (1979). Some of the procedures associated with assertive training include the following:

1. Identify deficits in assertiveness via one of the available assertiveness scales, or by interview, or typically both, specifying situations and/or individuals with which the client may experience difficulty.
2. Convince the client that assertion is justified, has value, and is not harmful to others.
3. Engage in behavioral rehearsal in which client and therapist act out interpersonal problem situations with the therapist modeling appropriate assertive behavior, coaching the client to facilitate the effectiveness of his or her attempts, and reinforcing successful assertive behavior or even good approximations.
4. Behavior rehearsal and subsequent attempts at assertive behavior in the natural environment are often implemented using a hierarchy of situations arranged in order of difficulty level, beginning with the least difficult items first. The behavioral rehearsal situation itself can be viewed as an approximation of *in vivo* interactions and generally less difficult than the latter.

Because we have already seen that humor is assumed to contain a "self-assertive" tendency, assertive training presents some obvious opportunities for the inclusion of humor. One application of humor in assertive training is roughly equivalent to its use in systematic desensitization. Most individuals who are not sufficiently assertive experience excessive fear about the consequences of being assertive. Consequently, creating or emphasizing humorous aspects of assertive role play often appears to help reduce the client's fear.

One such technique consists primarily of *exaggeration.* Nonassertive individuals often have mistaken expectations of how others will react if they express their feelings. During behavioral rehearsal, if the therapist unexpectedly exaggerates the other person's reaction, for instance acting ludicrously and childishly outraged or rejecting, the client can then see such a reaction as exaggerated to a ridiculous degree. This process can help clients focus, in turn, on how their own expectations may be exaggerated relative to any reaction that is likely to occur. For example, a submissive client objected to her roommates' criticism of a friend's singing and guitar playing, but was hesitant to raise her objections with her friends. In rehearsing this interaction the client said, "I don't think his singing is too bad." The therapist (representing the roommates) replied, "What ?! You like that interminable cat-like yowling?" The client smiled and, in discussing it, acknowledged that the roommates' responses were probably very mild and that her fantasy of their response was probably much exaggerated, as manifested in the therapist's reply.

Another technique is pertinent to social skills training, a subcategory of assertive training. In social skills training the client learns specific social skills he or she may lack. One application of humor in social skills training can be characterized as *situation comedy.* In this instance, the therapist suggests and models humorous or playful lines or interactions that the client may try in actual life situations if desired. For example, many clients in a college setting feel awkward and inhibited in getting acquainted with someone they have just begun to date. The greater the inhibitions about assertion, the more awkward one may feel in this circumstance. For this particular problem I often suggest that the client try playing a sentence completion game with his or her date. In this game the two people agree to take turns beginning a sentence for the other to complete. The created sentence stems may be anything from ludicrous ("Warts are excellent for...."), to inquisitive ("My favorite type of exercise is...."), to personal ("My initial reaction to you was...."). Similarly, the person responding may be candid or humorous just so long as the sentence is finished. The therapist usually needs to model some types of sentence stems and responses in the behavioral rehearsal to be sure that the process is understood. It almost invariably happens, when this is attempted, that the two people drift in and out of the game or away from it as interesting responses generate quite ample conversation and comfortable mutual self-disclosure.

Although this procedure may seem somewhat distant from the theoretical rationale offered earlier, I believe it is directly derived from it. By structuring what is an otherwise awkward and tense situation for the client into a playful perspective highly conducive to humor (bisociating the two via the game, perhaps), the client is enabled to enjoy, rather than endure, this getting-acquainted period in a comfortable structure. Accordingly, such a comfortable structure promotes spontaneity and facilitates the exercise of humor if desired. I find it important that the game impose no obligation to be humorous at any particular point. Thus, although the game may promote humor and joking, the client is not in the position of worrying about whether a rehearsed joke will be funny.

Finally, in the context of assertive training, teaching appropriate expression of feelings via humor can help excessively aggressive individuals verbalize their feelings rather than engage in violent behavior. A provocative technique for treating this type of problem establishes a hierarchy of situations where anger or aggression may be inappropriately elicited and presents the entire sequence in ludicrous, slapstick fashion. Such a case has been reported (Smith, 1973) and will be described in some detail in the Clinical Presentation section of this chapter.

MODELING

Modeling is used extensively in behavior therapy, both explicitly as a purposeful process (e.g., the therapist models assertive behaviors in assertion training) and implicitly, in that the therapist conveys a sense of competence, some optimism, and so on, during the course of therapy. In all of the techniques described above, by using humor, the therapist is at least implicitly modeling for the client that humor has specific constructive uses. To the extent that the therapist values humor, he or she can also model its constructive use in the way that a clinical problem is conceptualized. As a brief example, in the college setting where I work, student procrastination is a frequent problem. In discussing procrastination with clients I have sometimes found it helpful to characterize our joint efforts as a battle with the "Big Behind." While this sort of application of humor does not produce any dramatic transformations in behavior, it does help to convey that a problem can simultaneously be taken seriously and be described humorously. Moreover, this type of feedback can give clients the message that the therapist sees value in enjoying humor even while addressing difficult personal problems.

REINFORCEMENT

This section describes a slightly different emphasis in applying one of the most widely known behavioral procedures--reinforcement. The preceding techniques have consisted of therapist-initiated procedures that mainly include the therapist's humor. A final category at least as important as any of those previously mentioned, if not more so, is that of client-initiated humor. When clients are able to joke about personal issues that had previously been painful or embarrassing, their humorous reactions usually represent a significant turning point in their view of themselves. Almost always the ability to find the humor in a human problem is an advantageous skill. Although therapists have little control over the occurrence of client-initiated humor, we do have an opportunity to reinforce it once it occurs, sometimes by directly complimenting the person's sense of humor, but more typically by an honest laugh at a good joke. Thus, in this instance the therapist mainly needs to serve as an *appreciative audience*.

The therapist's attention to humor encourages the further exercise of potential humor skills that clients have neglected due either to inhibition or to having seen little value in humor.

PERTINENT USES

The approach I have described attempts to integrate humor and laughter into existing behavior therapy procedures. Due to its complex cognitive nature, humor may also contribute to existing efforts to make greater use of cognition in behavior therapy. Clients for whom humor seems most appropriate include those whose faulty beliefs imply or amplify excessive negative emotion (e.g., fear, anxiety, depression, anger), or those for whom an unnecessarily negative emotional response has become conditioned to particular stimulus situations, though the two are not mutually exclusive.

Before trying any of these procedures I would urge a beginning therapist to learn behavior therapy thoroughly through training and practice. Because behavior therapists have furnished clearer operational definitions of their treatment procedures than many other schools, readers or mental health professionals sometimes erroneously assume that these procedures can be easily implemented after having just read about them. In actuality, extensive practice is necessary for therapeutic success. Further, those who are being supervised in therapy may choose to discuss any of these procedures with their supervisors prior to implementing them. Otherwise, you might be surprised by a super-serious supervisor.

A further precaution for therapists at any level of experience is to remember that the use of humor and laughter in therapy is not a goal in itself but one option for facilitating therapy. The effective use of humor in behavior therapy will not necessarily leave the client thinking that the therapist is a "wild and crazy guy," though the client might have that impression on occasion. Moreover, the inclusion of humor in behavior therapy does not imply that humor will be used with a high frequency (i.e., the therapist is always joking) or that the therapist does not take the whole process seriously. Rather the therapist remains vigilant for the appropriate inclusion of humor when the need and opportunity arise, as with other specific therapeutic interventions.

A further caution is that humor not be used erroneously to distort or deny feelings that actually remain unchanged. Even the realm of popular songs describes the joker as always laughing on the outside but crying on the inside. This is not a result therapists of any school should promote.

Another type of humor that can be detrimental, though perhaps not in all cases, is self-deprecating humor. Although humor has great constructive potential, it can also serve self-defeating, destructive, or defensive ends.

162

CLINICAL PRESENTATION

Although a few examples of humor and laughter in behavior therapy have already been presented, this section presents case studies in which humor was a featured part of treatment. First let us consider the two case studies alluded to earlier. The first was a case in which I used humor to accomplish systematic desensitization (Ventis, 1973), and also illustrates a therapeutic instance of *comic relief.*

SYSTEMATIC DESENSITIZATION

A 20-year-old co-ed complained of anxiety about attending a sorority banquet later the same day. She had had only one serious dating relationship with another college student. They had dated each other exclusively for 2 years but had recently ended their relationship at his insistence, and he had begun dating one of her sorority sisters. She now was required to attend a banquet where she was certain to see them together. She was afraid he might embarrass her or that she might humiliate herself by showing that she still cared for him.

Systematic desensitization was attempted, but because there was so little time, it was not feasible to train her in relaxation. Therefore a brief five-item hierarchy was constructed, beginning with the young woman dressing for the banquet and ending with her in the banquet room. For the last item, which involved waiting in the banquet hall for the boyfriend and his date to arrive, the end of the item was created to appear ludicrous, without previously informing the client. Thus the girl imagined herself in the banquet room, sitting, waiting, watching for new arrivals until the young man entered--dressed in leotards. At this point the girl smiled and continued to imagine the scene, eyes closed. The scene was repeated, and this time the young man entered doing the hokey pokey, which took a little while for the banquet crowd to identify. The scene was repeated a third time, and the young man came in juggling a head of cabbage, a tennis shoe, and an electric razor whose cord kept getting tangled around his wrist. In the final presentation, the scene was described in matter-of-fact fashion with no purposeful humor. The ex-boyfriend entered the hall with his date, spoke quietly to the client, and was unobtrusively present for the duration of the scene presentation.

The client completed the scene without signaling tension, and this lack of tension was pointed out to her in a discussion session afterwards. She subsequently made it through the banquet with only mild apprehension. She later reported spontaneously reimagining some of the humorous scenes during the banquet and feeling amused.

ASSERTIVE TRAINING

A second case study, originally presented as an instance of desensitization, is functionally quite similar to assertive training. As reported by Smith (1973), the case dealt with a young mother's excessive anger in response to both her 3-year-old son and her husband. Acquaintances described her as having had a violent temper since childhood. When upset, she would react to either the child or husband with extreme rage, screaming, and physical assault. The description sounds compatible with a diagnosis of explosive personality.

After unsuccessfully attempting seven desensitization sessions with relaxation in two hierarchies involving interactions with both child and husband, the therapist attempted to make humorous the items in the two 10-item hierarchies, using what he described as slapstick comedy:

> As you're driving to the supermarket, little Pascal the Rascal begins to get restless. Suddenly he drops from his position on the ceiling and trampolines off the rear seat onto the rear view mirror...As you begin to turn into the supermarket parking lot..., your main concern is the two elderly and matronly women that you're bearing down upon...One, who is clutching a prayer book in her hand, turns and, upon seeing your car approaching at 70 mph, utters a string of profanities...and lays a strip of Neolite as she sprints out of the way and does a swan dive into a nearby manhole. (Smith, 1973, p. 578)

The author reported relatively quick results. The client completed both hierarchies in the first session in which humor was used, without reporting anger. After three sessions, relatives commented on improvements in her temper.

Nine treatment sessions were conducted during which humorous scenes were presented. Pre- and post-treatment sessions of MMPI profile were taken, as were changes in skin conductance and heart rate. The latter two were measured just prior to scene presentation and during hierarchy scene presentation. All measures supported the conclusion that the patient had undergone considerable improvement. Finally, as the control of her anger improved, the woman was able to apply several other behavior modification procedures and control her child more appropriately. Although the author approached the case from a counterconditioning perspective, in discussing the successful results he suggests a slightly different paradigm: "...it is probable that the humor exerted its effects at least partly by modifying cognitive mediational processes" (Smith, 1973, p. 580).

We thus have two case studies, one dealing with excessive anxiety, the other with excessive anger, in which humor was substituted for voluntary relaxation in the systematic desensitization paradigm and resulted in therapeutic success. As suggested earlier, I have chosen to present the case involving the treatment of anger as an instance of assertive training insofar as the woman was learning via humor to substitute more appropriate expression of feeling in place of inappropriate anger and aggression.

REINFORCEMENT

A third case provides an example of the therapist reinforcing the client's spontaneous use of humor. The client was a male college student who had been sexually impotent for over 2 years. Formerly he had had a satisfying sexual relationship, but after this relationship ended he found himself impotent with a new partner. He had been completely unnerved by the occurrence. Subsequently he experienced such intense anxiety over the possibility of a recurrence that continuing impotence was pretty well assured. He felt so embarrassed and pained by the experience that he had for some time avoided even sexual fantasy and was reluctantly concluding that sex was only for other people. One approach we decided to use was systematic desensitization for a range of heterosocial and heterosexual behaviors and situations.

While attempting to establish a hierarchy of situations associated with differing degrees of anxiety, he had become clearly uncomfortable in describing situations, and I in turn felt awkward at not being able to help him feel more at ease. Nonetheless, we had managed to establish a basic hierarchy. Continuing, I asked if there were any specific anxiety arousing sexual situations we had neglected to include. Instantly he replied, "Well yes, if a date were to lay on her back and yell, 'Screw me!', I could get right uneasy." We both had a good laugh, the client enjoyed himself, and finishing the task at hand seemed noticeably easier.

In the next session I commented directly on the client's previous joke, noting that I considered it very valuable both that he had such a keen sense of humor and that he felt comfortable enough in therapy to joke about what was obviously a difficult problem. In subsequent sessions, while implementing desensitization, I also occasionally referred to his joke during the scenes we had included in the hierarchy. For example, a description of foreplay would be followed by the comment, "...assuming she does not suddenly lay back and yell, 'Screw me!'" My intention was both to ease his discomfort in getting through scene presentations and to show that I had enjoyed his joke.

As therapy continued we both did a moderate amount of joking that I considered to be modeling and reinforcing the use of humor, though it was always spontaneous. When we terminated at the end of the academic year he was dating again and seemed pleased with the gains he had made in self-confidence and heterosocial skills. He had not established sexual intimacy with anyone, but he did seem confident and comfortable with this possibility, should an appropriate opportunity arise. The basic treatment in this case was systematic desensitization for excessive anxiety about heterosocial and heterosexual interactions. The reinforcement of the client's use of humor, however, seemed to facilitate both completion of the desensitization and the development of his self-confidence.

The three cases described above show possible applications of humor in the behavioral treatment of irrational fear, explosive personality, and secondary impotence. The first two cases are of particular interest because in the first case there was no time for standard desensitization; in the second, standard desensitization had already been tried and judged ineffective. Thus these two cases illustrate the feasibility of including humor in behavior therapy with the possibility of producing quicker results than could be reached by standard procedures, as well as producing positive results where standard procedures prove inadequate.

SYNTHESIS

Humor and laughter have been advanced as possible contributors to therapy. Seeing humor in that which has previously been viewed as a personal problem may enhance a sense of self-efficacy in the situation and therefore constitute a significant change in one's thinking. In addition, laughter, characterized by Koestler (1964) as "the puffing away of emotion discarded by thought" (p. 56), may help to relieve emotional arousal that has become superfluous due to the client's new humorous perspective. Either or both of these functions may be therapeutic. The general implication is to facilitate the client's seeing humor and maybe even laughing in dealing with issues previously viewed as problems.

The inclusion of humor in hierarchy items in systematic desensitization may serve the purpose of *comic relief*, either when used extensively as an alternative to relaxation or when used to get past difficult items in standard desensitization. The relief may be accomplished either conceptually or physically, depending on whether laughter is elicited.

The use of *slapstick comedy* is relevant to both systematic desensitization and assertive training. Fear- or anger-arousing situations are consistently paired with ludicrous or exaggerated imagery in an attempt to change the client's interpretation of the situations and their consequent feelings.

An additional application of humor in assertive training may be characterized as *situation comedy*. In these cases the therapist helps the client to structure a problem situation in a way that is conducive to comfortable spontaneous humor while actually interacting in the live situation.

In all of the above procedures as well as in the way the therapist conceptualizes clinical problems, modeling of the value and uses of humor may be therapeutic.

Finally, just as a good audience elicits the best performance from a professional comic, when the client shows spontaneous constructive humor, the therapist may act as an appreciative and *reinforcing audience.*

REFERENCES

Ayllon, T. (1963). Intensive treatment of psychotic behavior by stimulus satiation and food reinforcement. *Behaviour Research and Therapy, 1,* 53-62.

Bandura, A. (1977). Self-efficacy: Toward a unifying theory of behavioral change. *Psychological Review, 84,* 191-215.

Bandura, A., Adams, N. E., & Beyer, J. (1977). Cognitive processes mediating behavior change. *Journal of Personality and Social Psychology, 35,* 125-139.

Goldfried, M. R. (1971). Systematic desensitization as training in self-control. *Journal of Consulting and Clinical Psychology, 37,* 228-234.

Goldstein, J. H., McGhee, P. E., Smith, J. R., Chapman, A. J., & Foot, H. C. (1977). Humor, laughter, and comedy: A bibliography of empirical and nonempirical analyses in the English language. In A. J. Chapman & H. C. Foot (Eds.), *It's a Funny Thing, Humour* (pp. 469-504). New York: Pergamon.

Jacobson, E. (1938). *Progressive Relaxation.* Chicago: University of Chicago Press.

Kazrin, A., & Durac, J. (1983). Group penile plethysmography: An apparatus for clinical research. *Behavior Therapy, 14,* 714-717.

Koestler, A. (1964). *The Act of Creation.* London: Hutchinson.

Kuhlman, T. L. (1982). Symptom relief through insight during systematic desensitization: A case study. *Psychotherapy: Theory, Research, & Practice, 19,* 88-94.

Kuhlman, T. L. (1984). *Humor and Psychotherapy.* Homewood, IL: Dow Jones-Irwin.

Mahoney, M. (1974). *Cognition and Behavior Modification.* Cambridge, MA: Ballinger.

Meichenbaum, D. (1977). *Cognitive-Behavior Modification.* New York: Plenum.

Rimm, D. C., & Masters, J. D. (1979). *Behavior Therapy* (2nd ed.). New York: Academic Press.

Shocket, S. (1985). *The Use of Humor in the Treatment of an Anger Response.* Unpublished doctoral dissertation, Virginia Consortium for Professional Psychology, Norfolk, VA.

Smith, R. E. (1973). The use of humor in counterconditioning of anger responses: A case study. *Behavior Therapy, 4,* 576-580.

Upper, D. (1974). The unsuccessful self-treatment of a case of writer's block. *Journal of Applied Behavioral Analysis, 7,* 497.

Ventis, W. L. (1973). Case history: The use of laughter as an alternative response in systematic desensitization. *Behavior Therapy, 4,* 120-122.

Wolpe, J. (1969). *The Practice of Behavior Therapy.* New York: Pergamon.

Wolpe, J., & Lazarus, A. A. (1966). *Behavior Therapy Techniques: A Guide to the Treatment of Neuroses.* Oxford: Pergamon.

HUMOR IN
GROUP THERAPY

Sidney Bloch

In this chapter, Dr. Sidney Bloch presents a refreshing Continental perspective elucidating recent clinical insights within the European schools of group psychotherapy. Using the work of Irvin Yalom and the interactional school of group therapy as a theoretical foundation, Dr. Bloch asks judicious questions about the function of humor in group psychotherapy. He examines both the benefits and potential liabilities of utilizing humor in group work, focusing on therapist-related, patient-related, and group-related dimensions of humor use. His conclusion suggests that the advantages of using humor in group therapy abundantly outweigh its avoidable disadvantages when the therapist is willing to maintain objectivity about his or her own attitudes while showing sensitivity to the patient's concerns.

From this we would infer that, whenever three or more people are gathered in the name of group therapy, good humor can certainly blossom in their midst.

Dr. Bloch is a consultant psychiatrist at Warnerford Hospital in Oxford, England, and a clinical lecturer at Oxford University. His recent publications include Therapeutic Factors in Group Psychotherapy (1985) and An Introduction to the Psychotherapies (1986).

*   *   *

THEORETICAL PERSPECTIVE

When Lawrence Kubie (1971) argued,

that humour has a high potential destructiveness, that it is a dangerous weapon, and that the mere fact that it amuses and entertains the therapist

and gives him a pleasant feeling is not evidence
that it is a valuable experience for the patient or
that it exerts on the patient an influence towards
healing changes (p. 861),

I concurred with him completely. Although Kubie did
concede that humor had a very limited role in the therapeutic encounter, his catalog of risks was so unnerving as
to convince me that any potential benefits were heavily
outweighed by the hazards.

Committing myself to a "humor-free" psychotherapy
with the *individual* patient at that time seemed reasonable
enough. Such a stance was in accord with the psychoanalytic principle, to which I then adhered, of the
therapist maintaining a particular incognito--the classical
blank screen--and thus facilitating the development of a
patient's transference reactions. But when I began to
practice small group therapy this commitment was radical-
ly undermined. In applying this therapeutic mode, it was
virtually impossible to keep humor at bay. I soon realized
that humor is inescapable in individual as well as in other
modes of therapy. This change might have been linked to
the particular school of group therapy I opted to study,
namely the interactional school (see Yalom, 1985 for a
comprehensive account of this school). In this approach,
the therapist adopts a relatively "transparent" position and
encourages interactions between all group members rather
than focusing exclusively on patient-to-therapist transfer-
ences. This relative transparency inevitably entails the
therapist's expression of a wide assortment of feelings and
attitudes, humor certainly among them.

Apart from these particular features of the theoretical
approach facilitating the incorporation of humor into the
group, the inherent properties of the group itself can
facilitate humorous expression. The continuing chronicle
of eight people meeting with a therapist or pair of co-
therapists week after week for a couple of years or more,
and developing as a result an atmosphere of trust and
solidarity, can encourage group members to manifest the
whole range of emotional experience at one point or
another, from the outpouring of deep sorrow to the joyous
celebration of some achievement. The expression of
humor in these circumstances is inevitable. My experience in leading groups of this kind paved the way for the
following assumption: because humor appears to be an
intrinsic feature of the therapy group, the question is not,

as Kubie had formulated it, whether it should have a place or not but rather how it can be optimally built into the group's culture.

I shall return to this matter after addressing another pivotal factor that indicates the importance of humor to human experience, and therefore to treatment, as well. Kubie's (1971) argument seemed ill-conceived. By stressing the hazards of humor he had lost sight of its potential benefits. The source of this other perspective is that towering figure in psychology, Gordon W. Allport. In his seminal volume on the human personality, Allport (1937) highlighted the role of humor in promoting "self-objectification." A clumsy bit of jargon perhaps but still a useful short-hand term to cover a central aspect of all forms of psychotherapy (I exclude the behavioral approach in this context), namely the goal of attaining knowledge of oneself as a prerequisite for personality change. For Allport, the "most striking correlate of insight is the sense of humour" (p. 222). Humor has the special quality of bringing a new perspective. The ordinary events of life as well as its problems and misfortunes can be seen afresh through their reformulation via humor. Routine and customary frames of reference are dislodged and are replaced by novel frames of reference. Furthermore, a sense of proportion is achieved when the person able to use humor learns to appreciate the absurdity and even ludicrousness of his situation. Allport also links this appreciation to the concept of self-acceptance by quoting the novelist George Meredith, who defined true humor as the capacity to laugh at the things one loves, including oneself and, notwithstanding, to continue that love. Because the toppling of self-deception and the development of appropriate self-regard are two basic objectives of all forms of insight-oriented psychotherapy, including the diverse schools of group therapy, Allport's notions about the salience of humor in the process of self-objectification are noteworthy.

Equally noteworthy in determining a rationale for the application of humor in group treatment is the work of George Vaillant (1977). Setting out from the premise that mental health is in large measure bound up with the development and application of mature styles of adaptation, Vaillant has elaborated a classification of defenses or coping mechanisms. These defenses can be categorized into four groups according to their degree of sophistication. Level 4, comprising the most "mature" mechanisms, is used by adolescents and adults who have succeeded at integrating reality, their interpersonal relationships, and their private feelings. Humor is an example of a mature mechanism insofar as it enables one both to tolerate and to face the unbearable. Vaillant's conceptualization resembles that of Allport when he avers that "Humour can never be applied without some element of an 'observing ego'" (p. 386). If we assume that mature adaptation to the problems and challenges of living is a major aspect of mental health and that humor is one important means of accomplishing such adaptation, it makes sense to utilize the therapy group as a forum in which group members can learn to value this function of humor as well as to enhance their own sense of humor.

So, what do we now have in the way of a rationale for introducing humor into the therapy group? First, we make an assumption, derived chiefly from clinical observation, that an intrinsic feature of the group--at least the long-term group whose members develop a sense of belonging and loyalty and create what Yalom (1985) has conveniently called a social microcosm--is the shared experiencing of a broad array of emotions including humor. Second, we note that humor is one of the closest associations of self-knowledge, a prerequisite for change, because it offers a novel frame of reference for personal exploration. Third, humor promotes self-acceptance as patients learn not to take themselves and their situation too seriously. Finally, a group can emphasize humor as one of a repertoire of mature defense mechanisms that contributes to effective adaptation.

These were the chief factors leading me to conclude that humor deserved a place in the group process. But still nagging were Kubie's (1971) cautionary words, in particular his reference to the therapist's use of humor to satisfy his own needs rather than to recognize how his patients might benefit. Thus, on those occasions when I felt amused by circumstances occurring in my group therapy practice, I also questioned whether the group members were profiting from such episodes, or even possibly being harmed in some way.

This concern ultimately found expression in my attempt to study systematically the potential uses and risks of humor. In carrying out this exercise I became considerably more confident that humor could be applied effectively. I also became reassured that possible hazards could be delineated and thereby prevented. The results of this work form the body of this chapter.

TECHNIQUE

With a rationale available for the inclusion of humor in the therapy group, the inevitable question follows: How should the therapist set about doing this? One option is to identify in more detail the specific purposes to which humor can be put, and then to devise a set of techniques to achieve those purposes. The snag in using this approach is that the application of humor may come to assume the qualities of a mechanical procedure. Humor becomes little more than a contrived therapeutic tool for manipulation by the therapist. An alternative option is to regard the use of humor as a creative process with spontaneity as its key ingredient. The therapist is then left to his or her own devices concerning how to pursue and apply humor. The disadvantages of this approach are its relative vagueness and its vulnerability to misapplication.

A third option exploits the positive features of the previous two but without the snags. In this approach the therapist has awareness of the functions and benefits of humor yet allows it to occur spontaneously. The first premise to be considered at this point, then, concerns how to identify and differentiate a number of specific roles for humor. Some colleagues and I have conducted a methodical observation of a number of long-term outpatient groups and canvassed the views of over a dozen group therapists in order to formulate a classification of the uses of humor (Bloch, Browning, & McGrath, 1983). The results are presented below.

The second premise concerns the nature of a sense of humor. The assumption is made that every therapist is endowed with the capacity to appreciate humor, albeit in greater or lesser measure. As Jonathan Swift has put it, "Tis never by invention got, men have it when they know it not."

With these two premises in mind we can state that humor is an appropriate feature of group therapy when the therapist appreciates its various purposes and encourages its free and spontaneous expression in relation to those purposes. Because the use of humor also entails risks, we need to add another requirement, namely that these potential risks are identified and the therapist remains aware of them. To this end, we have also proposed a classification of risks (see below).

THE USES OF HUMOR

The following classification of the uses of humor is not applicable to all forms of group treatment or to all patients participating in groups. It is derived from the study of closed, long-term outpatient groups, run weekly for periods ranging from 18 to 24 months, and led by therapists adopting an interactional model in which change is conceived as stemming chiefly from the relationships formed between members rather than from the relationship between each patient and the therapist (Bloch, 1986). Because such a group has time to evolve into a cohesive and mature working system, humor can be readily incorporated. Whether this classification can be applied to short-term groups or groups with a regular turnover of members is questionable. Considerable care would be needed when introducing humor in any group that could not establish a climate of trust and cohesion because of its open door policy.

The related question of which patients are best served by humor cannot be fully answered yet. Clinical experience suggests that the typical member of a long-term, insight-oriented group is a potential beneficiary. He or she is of at least average intelligence, is psychologically-minded and shows a capacity for the acquisition of insight, has sufficient ego-strength to withstand the challenge of self-exploration and change (Lake, 1985), and is motivated to work for that change. Patients unable to profit include the actively psychotic, the paranoid personality, the severely schizoid, and the markedly depressed--the first three because of the risk of their misconstruing the purposes of the humor, and the last because they are too enveloped by gloom.

In developing the classification of the uses of humor we considered it heuristically advantageous to categorize in terms of the therapist, the patient, and the group as a whole. We have identified 10 ways in which humor can be therapeutically useful, either by promoting a desirable group dynamic or by increasing the benefit that a particular member may obtain from a specific group process. The therapist's three uses of humor enable him or her to be seen in a way that has therapeutic import, and to offer interpretations that might otherwise be difficult to convey. The four uses of humor that are patient-related facilitate novel modes of self-expression and self-observation. The three categories applicable to the group as a whole cover the functions of humor as a releaser of tension, as a promoter of cohesiveness, and as a means of appreciating dynamic processes occurring in the group. Let us now consider each of these categories in detail together with brief clinical illustrations where appropriate.

Therapist-Related Uses

Modeling. The therapist serves as a model for group members, mostly in an implicit way, exerting considerable influence through shared attitudes and behavior. If we assume that a main goal of therapy is to dislodge obstacles to a patient's more spontaneous self-expression, then the role of humor in this context becomes obvious: the therapist acts in a spontaneous, good-humored fashion, when appropriate, thereby serving as an immediately accessible model for patients. This reinforces the point made earlier regarding humor as a creative phenomenon, not a contrived clinical tool. Modeling is not a calculated strategy but depends instead on a personal quality of genuineness and authenticity, reminiscent of Carl Rogers's (1961) concept of congruence as a necessary ingredient in the therapeutic encounter.

The "juicy pear" incident serves to illustrate. In an extended "marathon" group session the members took a dinner break. The patients ate in a rather uncomfortable way with self-consciousness predominating. Quite unexpectedly the therapist bit into an over-ripe pear, scattering juice all about him. Instead of greater self-consciousness, the therapist's successful handling of this potentially embarrassing situation in a lighthearted and amusing way allowed the patients to laugh along with him and to feel more relaxed during the rest of the meal.

Transparency. Although various theoretical schools differ in their evaluation of how much self-disclosure on the part of the therapist is optimal, the interactional model used here regards "transparency" as advantageous because it enhances the therapeutic relationship and demystifies the clinical process (Weiner, 1978). Thus, the therapist's thoughtful disclosure of such universal qualities as vulnerability, compassion, uncertainty, fallibility, and warmth is considered desirable. The therapist's capacity to laugh at himself or herself without showing embarrassment is relevant here and is illustrated in the case of a homosexual patient who divulged to the group how he frequently felt ridiculed and stigmatized as the butt of jokes about "gays." Fellow patients immediately rallied to his support, citing their own experiences of being labeled as psychiatric patients and suffering the effects of derision as a consequence. The therapist then revealed amusingly that he had long been the target of unflattering wisecracks about "shrinks." Out of the ensuing laughter arose a productive exchange about the nature of sarcasm and a consensus that it might reflect anxiety in the joker about the recipient of his ridicule.

Interpretation. Among the several functions of interpretation is the promotion of a patient's curiosity about himself or herself so that the self can be seen afresh from a new angle. The typical patient in group therapy has become bogged down, unable to approach his or her problems in other than stereotyped, entrenched ways. The effect is one of stagnation and secondary demoralization with the feeling of being stuck, even trapped. Humor, especially in the form of metaphor, can effectively grapple with this pattern through the juxtaposition of images, constructs, feelings, and thoughts not usually linked with one another (Koestler, 1975). This permits the adoption of an unexpected perspective of the world, with the added bonus of being amusing. In considering this novel perspective, Shiryon (personal communication, June 11, 1984) wittily refers to a two-step process: first, humor is an "eye-opener," then it becomes an "I-opener." For Viktor Frankl (1969), the creation of a new perspective through humor also enables the individual to achieve a sense of detachment and thereby to gain "the fullest possible control over himself."

The case of Adam illustrates spicing an interpretation with humor. A long-complaining group member, his contribution replete with moans and groans, Adam remained quite blind to how he brought most of his problems upon himself. Following an episode during which this pattern was more than obvious in the group, the therapist told the following joke. "A worker had grumbled daily about the contents of his sandwiches. When his colleagues suggested that he ask his wife to prepare something different, the worker retorted: 'Wife?

I make these sandwiches myself.'" Everyone chuckled, Adam included. The joke's relevance was immediately appreciated, paving the way for an illuminating discussion about Adam's behavior. This new look not only triggers a process of self-examination, but the vivid imagery involved (one can easily picture Adam preparing his lunch to an accompanying symphony of grunts and snorts) can be adopted as a shorthand code in any subsequent appraisal of the problem being tackled. Thus, for example, any mention in subsequent meetings of Adam's "sandwiches" was completely meaningful to the group, and at the same time potentially amusing.

The effectiveness of a humorous code is well demonstrated in the case of Paul, who had been labeled the group's "pillar of misery" in recognition of his immutable dolefulness. Following a trip he had made to a Greek island, Paul was coaxed into describing the experience. Reluctantly he took up the invitation, and gradually painted a verbal picture of a cove at sunset. The image he conjured up of tranquility and peacefulness became progressively more palpable until the group, including Paul, spontaneously began to twitter and then to laugh openly. There had been a universal recognition of the complete incongruity between Paul's apparent incapacity to feel pleasure and his emotionally-laden description of the cove. Not only was it obvious that he was indeed able to experience joy, but thereafter this discovery could be simply and humorously referred to as "Paul's cove."

Patient-Related Uses

Sense of Proportion. It was Gordon Allport (1956) who commented so aptly that, the neurotic who learns to laugh about himself may be on the way to self-management, even to cure. Cure may seem unduly ambitious, but the basic point has widespread support. Thus, H. S. Sullivan (1970) suggested that humor bestows "the capacity for maintaining a sense of proportion as to one's importance in the life situations in which one finds oneself" (p. 172), and Mindess (1976) proposed that humor may constitute a form of acceptance whereby despair is tempered and hope instilled. Mintz (1984) has advanced the interesting idea that humor enables one to confront the serious without treating it seriously (which does not imply that the serious should be treated trivially). All these comments imply that a person cannot afford to take his life too seriously: it is more adaptive to appreciate the absurdity or even ludicrousness of one's situation. For the typical patient in therapy whose everyday problems have assumed overwhelmingly grave proportions, humor can exert a counteractive influence and lead to a more balanced perspective, wonderfully reflected in the verse from Ecclesiastes: "A time to weep, and a time to laugh; a time to mourn, and a time to dance" (Chapter 3, verse 4). Moreover, the therapist using humor is attempting to promote in the patient what Vaillant (1977) has described as "one of the truly elegant defenses in the human repertoire" (p. 116).

In the following case humor helped Mary gain a sense of proportion vis-à-vis her deeply felt anxiety about her femininity and relations with men. Deeply embarrassed by any mention of sex in the group, Mary wriggled out of any such discussion until on one occasion, after summoning up pluck, she described the visit of a man to her apartment, his adoption of the role of "counselor," and his effort to convince her to talk about her sexual problems. A flurry of suggestions from group members ensued accompanied by a complete avoidance of the more fundamental issues involved. As details of the embarrassing encounter between Mary and the self-appointed counselor emerged, its "soap opera" quality became evident and with it a shift of mood in the group from serious and practical to good-humored and lighthearted. Mary, suspended between morbid introspection and budding amusement, began to recognize the ludicrousness of both the awkward evening she had described with such gravity and the group's clumsy effort to help her through naïve advice. Through her amusement she was then better placed to delve into her ambivalence about her sexuality.

Overcoming Earnestness. Related to the previous category is humor's role in reducing undue earnestness. So often in the patient with longstanding neurosis or personality disorder--especially of the depressive, schizoid or obsessive type--a tone of gravity and even grimness characterizes his or her every thought and utterance. We are not referring here to depressed affect that has a distinctive quality and where the use of humor may well be counterproductive. Earnestness is best conceptualized in terms of the incapacity or unwillingness to indulge in play, release inhibition, and permit the childlike spirit of creative fun to express itself. Thus the judicious introduction of a humorous, playful tone into the ethos of the group, coupled with establishing this humorous tone as a sanctioned norm, can help to penetrate the wall of earnestness a patient has erected around himself. This image can be taken further by quoting Grotjahn (1971) who commented, "Therapy is not a laughing matter but neither is it a wailing wall." Along the same lines, Rosenheim (1976) suggested, "A smile here and a laugh there might be the keys to the heavy gates that confine these (overly serious) people and deny them spontaneity and occasional carefree experiences."

Promotion of Social Skills. The group format lends itself well to the inculcation or enhancement of a patient's social skills because he or she has repeated opportunities over an extended period to relate to fellow group members in diverse ways. Because the ability both to appreciate and to create humor is an omnipresent feature of social discourse and contributes importantly to personal interaction, the group can provide a relatively safe environment for members to practice and learn to obtain the beneficial social effects of humor.

Self-Disclosure and Catharsis. Divulging highly personal information is commonly a distressing or embarrassing experience. Yet such an experience has therapeutic effects in that it enables the discloser to unburden himself or herself of long-held "secrets" and paves the way for greater self-awareness (Bloch & Crouch, 1985). Jourard's (1971) dictum is most appropriate in this context: "Make thyself known, and thou shall then know thyself" (p. 7). Catharsis--the release of potent emotions such as grief, guilt, shame and anger that brings a sense of relief--is closely associated with self-disclosure, and the two processes often occur together.

Self-disclosure and any associated emotional discharge is often a demanding task for a patient in group therapy. He or she is most ambivalent: on the one hand there is a sense of need to unburden oneself and share with fellow patients personal information long held to be unsharable. On the other hand the patient is exceedingly anxious because of the unforeseeable effects of the self-revelation. The use of humor, whether intentional or not, can facilitate the act (Hankins-McNary, 1979). If the humor is then sensitively perceived and recognized as a vehicle and not as an end in itself, the patient can be encouraged to alter the tone of his or her communication and deal more directly with what he or she is struggling to unfold.

A discussion about the consequences of parental death and Tony's humorous participation therein illustrates the above. Several members spoke of their fears and concerns, but Tony remained on the periphery. When urged to share his feelings, he talked animatedly about contemporary funeral rites. The lampooning quality of his commentary was reminiscent for fellow patients of Evelyn Waugh's *The Loved One*--both had the same trademark of biting satire. It soon became clear, notwithstanding the group's amusement, that Tony was in fact displaying a deeply felt anxiety about how he would cope with the deaths of his aging parents. With the group's support, he was able to face this anxiety squarely and adopt a serious attitude. Thus, Tony's more authentic disclosures seem to have required the vehicle of satire and might not have taken place without it.

Group-Related Uses

Cohesiveness. Clinical observation repeatedly suggests that a group will exert more therapeutic effect if its members have a sense of belonging and acceptance and are mutually supportive and caring (Yalom, 1985). A substantial body of research buttresses this observation (Bloch & Crouch, 1985). Humor is one of the many factors that can contribute to cohesiveness: shared laughter and good humoredness, provided they are not at a patient's expense, help to promote an atmosphere of cordiality and friendliness. However, two caveats apply. First, a therapist's attempt from the outset to introduce a lighthearted tone in order to speed up the creation of a cohesive group is likely to fail because it will seem contrived. Second, the excessive use of humor may generate the quality of cohesiveness but in such abundant amount that the members come to relish the coziness that follows to the exclusion of the hard work underlying the process of change.

Insight into Group Dynamics. In the interactional model of group therapy, the focus is predominantly on the here-and-now, that is, on what actually takes place in the group--in particular between patients and to a lesser extent between each patient and the therapist and between each patient and the group as a whole. The mature group is typified by its members' shared ability to discern and appreciate the relevance of various processes such as undue dependency on the therapist, avoidance of distressing topics, scapegoating, and rivalry. An amusing episode, an outburst of laughter, the cracking of a joke, bantering, and satire, are some forms of humor that may have significance for the whole group. Dealing with the humor enables members to understand what it represents in terms of group dynamics.

The following example involved the use of banter. Two men in an established group indulged in jolly banter to an extent that it was readily perceived by their co-members and labeled as the "Woody Allen act." Thereafter, the group was amused by mere reference to this label. During the course of a particularly hilarious Woody Allen "performance" the therapist interrupted the proceedings to query why the group was having so much fun. Caught in the act, as either performers or audience, the patients reflected on what had transpired and realized that they had collusively participated in a strategy to maintain a *modus vivendi* between the two Woody Allens. The pair had been arch-rivals for several weeks in a struggle to achieve power in the group. The occurrence of banter, its identification, and then subsequent appraisal constituted a sequence in the attainment of insight into the underlying interpersonal dynamics.

Reduction of Tension. Finally we turn to the use of humor to lessen undue tension. Tension is an inevitable feature of every therapy group, or at least of every group that faces up to the problems of its members. Its value lies in motivating patients to closely examine the issues that account for the tension. When tension exceeds an optimal level, however, it may become counterproductive. Because tension is not easily tolerated, efforts are made to retreat from the challenge of wrestling with the work at hand. The therapist, or a sophisticated patient, may try to reduce such a dislocating level of tension. Humor can be particularly effective here.

This is demonstrated in the case of a group whose tension had reached an unbearable level because of a conflict between two members. Maggie and Hilary had established close ties as a result of shared problems regarding their ambivalent sexual feelings. However, their constant competition for the group's attention often led to discomfort in the rest of the membership. At one meeting their rivalry reached an acrimonious crescendo, the atmosphere was charged, and the group was reduced to a paralyzed silence. Then, quite unexpectedly, Hilary (who regularly gave Maggie a ride home after each session) commented jokingly, "The fact, Maggie, that I cannot give you a ride home tonight has nothing to do with our fight." The remark had the desired effect--the tension was broken in an instant through the shared laughter that ensued.

THE RISKS OF HUMOR

A discussion of the value of humor would be incomplete if we failed to consider the risks involved in the use of humor. Except for Kubie's (1971) oft-cited paper, the topic has been bypassed or barely mentioned. Kubie's emphasis on the potential destructiveness that could result from the introduction of humor into individual therapy could be as readily applied to group therapy. Particularly in the hands of the inexperienced, Kubie argued, humor could protect the therapist against his or her own anxiety and also camouflage any hostile feelings he or she harbored against patients. Ridicule, satire, mockery, and sarcasm are examples of how the use of humor may go awry.

With Kubie's warning ringing loudly in our ears, my colleagues and I turned our attention to the possible risks of applying humor in a therapy group and attempted to classify these by adopting the same procedure as for the classification of uses, namely, by systematically observing several outpatient groups and by seeking the views of several group therapists.

We have identified eight potential risks. Of the four applicable to the therapist, three are intimately bound up with countertransference and the therapist's unwitting resort to humor in order to cope with anxiety, to disguise aggressive feelings towards a particular patient, or to win the group's affection or admiration. A therapist's excessive use of humor may create confusion in his or her patients about the actual purpose of the group. Included in the patient-related category of humor risks are the member who acts the clown in order to ingratiate himself or herself, scapegoating with an ostensibly humorous quality, and an avoidance of distressing self-examination by means of self-mockery. In the group-related category of humor risks, the group members can misuse humor to avoid addressing significant issues, with frivolous preoccupation as the sole result of such an avoidance. Because the therapists we consulted were far less able to recall examples of humor causing harm than of humor having a beneficial effect, clinical illustrations are scarce. In fact, several of the risks listed were regarded as theoretically possible, based on experience where these risks were anticipated but avoided.

Therapist-Related Risks

Defense. Therapists incapable of handling their own anxiety in the face of a demanding group episode may unwittingly wriggle out of this ordeal by using humor as a defensive maneuver. They may succeed in reducing their own discomfort, but their patients will have lost an opportunity to wrestle with an important issue. If this becomes an established pattern, not only may the group lose its therapeutic thrust, but the therapist's avoidance tactics may serve as an undesirable model for patients.

Joking as a Veil for Aggression. The sense of frustration and anger that a therapist may experience towards a patient can illuminate for the therapist the nature of the patient's psychopathology. The pattern of demandingness, dependency, and seductiveness in the hysterical personality springs readily to mind. The therapist may, however, fail to perceive the real nature of his or her aggressive feelings. Because psychotherapy is a caring profession, the therapist may encounter difficulty in acknowledging that he or she has feelings that seem to contradict this caring. William Blake's incisive remark that "Opposition is true friendship" may be helpful here. If the therapist unconsciously resorts to humor to deal with his or her aggression, manifested as belittlement, ridicule, sarcasm, or innuendo, the patient is deprived of any opportunity to respond appropriately or to learn.

Self-Display and Ingratiation. A therapist's need to be admired, to attain popularity, or simply to be liked by patients can be associated with his or her misuse of humor. In a group, he or she may act good-humoredly and display a keen wit and charm in an unconsciously determined effort to achieve these ends. The therapist's own needs may be fulfilled, but the group will suffer from insensitive and inept leadership.

Confusion. Excessive use of humor by a therapist can generate a sense of bewilderment in patients. Probably having been led to expect that psychotherapy is fundamentally a serious enterprise, the patient then encounters a therapist who acts in contrary fashion. The patient now wonders, What is the real purpose of treatment? How much fun am I supposed to have? Will I be regarded as a wet-blanket if I do not participate in the good-humoredness? There are further complications. Because the patient is left in doubt about the serious basis of therapy, he or she may become puzzled as to when the therapist is genuinely serious or only joking. The ensuing frustration then undermines the potential effect of any substantial intervention made by the therapist, and the group's work is thus severely hampered.

Patient-Related Risks

Clowning. Just as the therapist may use humor to win the group's affection, a patient may act the "clown" to achieve the same ends. Commonly, the adoption of the role of clown perpetuates a longstanding pattern of interpersonal behavior. Initially fellow patients may warm to the clown, unaware that this will be his or her sole style of relating. However, a growing recognition that clowning represents the individual's only way of relating to others leads inevitably to group irritation and frustration and to a sense that the clown disrupts the serious work of the group. The result is predictable--from a position of providing the group with amusement the clown is pushed to the periphery and later even ostracized.

Scapegoating. The unjust selection by the group of a member as the target of aggressive feelings in order to deal with a demanding problem quite unrelated to him or her can take many forms of especially punitive humor. Because the scapegoat is the butt of ostensibly "harmless" jokes--the hostile quality of the interaction being well disguised by the humor--he or she is under pressure to respond in similar fashion lest he or she be labeled as ill-humored. The effect of such scapegoating is thus magnified--picked out unjustifiably in the first place, then criticized for a lack of good humor.

Avoidance through Self-Mockery. The final humor risk in the patient-related category is the use of self-derisive humor (akin to clowning yet distinctive). Self-mockery is one of its forms: the patient jokes at his or her own expense in an effort to diminish the significance of his or her own contribution. For example, he or she may immediately follow the disclosure of some highly personal information with a self-critical "crack." In essence the message is, "Please don't take me seriously; I was only kidding a moment ago. I don't deserve your attention anyway."

Group-Related Risks

Frivolous Avoidance. Even the most dedicated, conscientious group needs periodic digression from its endeavor. No group could tolerate a continually high level of emotional intensity without pausing to "catch its breath." A temporary flight into carefree lightheartedness is especially helpful and will be appreciated by all participants for what it is--a playful interlude. This appreciation will be entirely missing in a group whose members indulge repeatedly in frivolous occupation with the object of avoiding any serious work at all. In this case the interlude is replaced by continuous play, the original task of the group ignored.

CLINICAL PRESENTATION

In the previous section I provided clinical illustrations of the various uses of humor in group psychotherapy. In those cases, humor contributed in a specific way to the progress of a patient or to the welfare of a group. My purpose in this section is to complement those accounts by describing how humor played a pivotal role in the treatment of a patient in the course of a particular session. I hope that this more detailed illustration will convey a flavor of the type of humor I am proposing as relevant to group therapy; I have also referred, in parentheses, to relevant categories of the use of humor dealt with earlier in the chapter.

Leslie, a 19-year-old student, was referred for psychotherapy by her general practitioner after she had sought his help for a longstanding feeling of social isolation and difficulty in developing close relationships. During the assessment interview, it emerged that she had felt very much alone since the death of a brother from leukemia 8 years earlier. Leslie had been especially close to him-- they were only a year apart in age--and much more so than to her other two siblings who were several years younger than her. Paul's death came as a shattering blow to Leslie: she withdrew socially, her school work suffered. No word was uttered by any member of the family about the tragic loss in the years that followed and it was as if Paul had never lived. Leslie continued to be socially withdrawn, to the extent of becoming quite friendless during her teens. She also enjoyed only limited emotional engagement with her family.

A new clinical development--feigned bereavement--occurred soon after she left home at the age of 18, to start a college course. Then she began to share with fellow students her sense of grievous loss of both her parents through a motor car accident. It had the desired effect. Her confidants displayed appropriate sympathy and offered her the emotional support she had so obviously craved from her own family in the wake of her real loss 8 years earlier. This extraordinary process of deriving comfort from virtual strangers endured for several months, until it accidentally emerged that Leslie's parents were not only far from dead but also anxious about her relative isolation. At the same time it also became common knowledge that she had indeed suffered a tragic loss.

By this time she had been a member of a weekly outpatient group for several months. Although her attendance record had been impeccable, she had remained on the group's periphery. She retreated even further when her feigned bereavement became known to the group. But the pattern of her nonverbal communications was obvious, reflecting a mixture of despair, guilt, and shame. Leslie hesitantly divulged how wretched she felt at having lied about her parents' deaths. Her shame was so pronounced that she could barely face them or her siblings when she visited home. The group felt immobilized. How could they possibly help Leslie in her forlorn plight? Their sense of "stuckness" was magnified by Leslie's apparent resistance to receive comfort by the group.

Humor, paradoxically, provided the means of surmounting the impasse. During an especially tense session, again stemming from the group's incapacity to soothe Leslie in her despair, the topic of binge-eating as a source of comfort was aired. One group member described in humorous fashion how she had consoled herself in the past by consuming all manner of sugary things, from "sticky toffee to the humble prune." Two other members then regaled the group by cataloging their favorite sweet foods. The atmosphere soon lightened (see Group-Related Uses; Reduction of Tension).

Then, quite unexpectedly, Leslie divulged her own idiosyncratic habit of comforting herself with a particular brand of white milky chocolate. Unlike the others, however, she did not gobble the chocolate down but broke the bar into a "hundred pieces" and then, like a mouse, nibbled away at them. Her description was vivid and her tone lighthearted. The group was delighted to witness this previously concealed sense of vitality. Apparently encouraged by this reaction, Leslie continued: "The only snag is that for every one bit of chocolate I nibble, ten get scattered about whether on my bed, on the settee in the lounge, or on the piano!" Messy bits of chocolate encountered by the family in their favorite chairs had not exactly made her popular at home (see Patient-Related Uses; Self-Disclosure and Catharsis).

Up to this point, Leslie's mood was still perceptibly cheerful but I sensed that she would soon veer away from exploring further what seemed to be the important "chocolate" theme. How could we keep her on course without provoking resistance? By maintaining the humor perhaps? It was thus that I proceeded to the use of pun and to a humor-spiced interpretation.

Therapist: "Leslie, I have an idea for you to munch on, to get your teeth into! (*Leslie twitters, as does the rest of the group*) You leave a trail of sticky chocolate around the house, right? Your folks, your brother, your sister, go into the lounge room intent on relaxing on the settee. Suddenly they encounter this sticky stuff and exclaim-- 'Drat, it's Leslie again with her chocolate bars.' They are irritated but they recognize your presence; it's inescapable, you are a member of the family household whether they like it or not" (see Therapist-Related Uses; Interpretation).

A pause ensues. Leslie is pensive and the group attentive. She soon embarks on an intensely personal disclosure about how lonely she has felt at home since Paul's death. She has never been able to share her profound sense of grief with either her parents or her siblings. It's as if there has always been a conspiracy of silence surrounding Paul's death. She recalls that all efforts on her part to ventilate her feelings in the weeks following the funeral were deflected. It was then that she felt she had no option other than to withdraw into her own private world of sorrow.

The group is engrossed. They begin to acknowledge Leslie's sense of loneliness through her adolescence and how desperate she must be to obtain emotional support from her family. Leslie's engagement with her fellow group members has never been more intense than on this occasion. Towards the end of the meeting, she has undoubtedly gained from the experience. She has shared the most painful episode of her life and has begun to appreciate how the dynamics of the family have led her to adopt extraordinary procedures, to wit, feigning bereavement to the outside world and leaving her personal "sticky stamp" at home (she can use puns too!). One result is her attainment of a sense of perspective and proportion: the chocolate story has demonstrated how in the midst of her woes, there is also an element of the ludicrous.

Leslie manifests this sense of proportion in her reply to a question about how she is feeling as she leaves the session:

> Chewing gum would have been a better bet; I could have planted bits in strategic places in the house and made my family captive. Then they would have had to listen to me, and to learn how much I have needed them (see Patient-Related Uses; Sense of Proportion).

The group express their pleasure at Leslie's imaginativeness and there is a generally felt sense of a considerable breakthrough.

Breakthrough indeed it proved to be. In subsequent sessions, Leslie acquired progressively deeper insight into the nature of her problems and continued to exercise, most appropriately, her delightful sense of humor. Moreover, she and the group could readily be reminded of her progress by reference to "that sticky chocolate." She also developed sufficient confidence to broach with her family the subject of her feeling isolated from them.

This step marked the onset of a process of emotional reattachment that effectively ended her many years of loneliness, allowing her to feel that she was once again a full member of her family.

SYNTHESIS

I will now attempt to summarize the central tenets of my approach to humor in group therapy. Salameh (1983) has distinguished between therapists who use humor "naturally and implicitly without seeking further elaborations or theoretical justification for their humorous interventions" (p. 62), and other therapists who have made humor an "explicitly important cornerstone of their therapeutic work and have developed theories of psychotherapy in which humour plays a major role both structurally and operationally" (p. 62).

My position lies midway between these two approaches: humor warrants an important place in the culture of the group but it is only part of a more comprehensive process and therefore does not constitute a cornerstone; neither is it based on a comprehensive theoretical model. Although it is tempting to try to devise an all-encompassing theory to explain the benefits of humor, the disadvantage lies in the constraints this may impose on the many and diverse ways in which humor finds expression in the group. In this respect Goethe may be correct when he asserts that, "All theory, dear friend is gray, but the golden tree of actual life springs ever green." Thus, the group therapist values the "golden tree," that is, the varied functions humor can have in the life of the group.

The therapist's appreciation of humor is not merely "natural" or "implicit"; rather he or she is aware of how it can be applied in particular ways, each intended to achieve certain effects. This awareness does not call for a set of humorous interventions as if they were technical operations; this would be tantamount to a mechanical exercise, quite contrary to the essential character of humor--its creativity and spontaneity. Instead, its effective application rests on an attitudinal quality in the therapist whereby he or she values humor as part of human experience and is cognizant of its beneficial effects in the clinical sphere; the therapist thus encourages its free expression both personally and in patients. At the same time, however, he or she does not neglect the

191

potential risks and shoulders the responsibility to insure that humor is not misapplied.

Given the importance of these attitudinal qualities, it is doubtful whether therapists can be formally trained to deploy humor. But, as Rosenheim (1976) has suggested, they can be encouraged "to actualize the humorous potential they do have," by being shown that they have a sense of humor and that it can be enhanced. The therapist also needs encouragement to indulge in play, a phenomenon closely related to humor. D. W. Winnicott (1971) has suggested that psychotherapy is in part about two people playing together. When playing is not possible because the patient lacks or has lost the capacity to do so, it is the therapist's task to nurture or to revive the sense of play. The group therapist has a similar job. He creates a social forum in which patients may learn how to play, either afresh or perhaps for the first time. Playing arouses those very qualities that are desirable in the quest for change--curiosity, spontaneity, and eagerness.

Martin Buber was once asked what he thought about Freud's comment that the ability to work and to love were central in providing a sense of meaning. He replied that Freud's notion was incomplete. Faith and humor were the missing ingredients. In referring to humor he remarked: "The real philosopher has to have a sense of humour, an awareness of the comic, not only about the world we live in but also about himself" (cited in Hodes, 1972, p. 151). The patient in group therapy is akin to this philosopher as he or she strives to obtain a novel view of himself or herself in order to live more creatively. Humor is unquestionably a significant contribution to this process of change.

REFERENCES

Allport, G. W. (1937). *Personality: A Psychological Interpretation.* London: Constable.

Allport, G. W. (1956). *The Individual and His Religion.* New York: Macmillan.

Bloch, S. (1986). Group therapy. In S. Bloch (Ed.), *An Introduction to the Psychotherapies* (2nd ed., pp. 80-112). Oxford: Oxford University Press.

Bloch, S., Browning, S., & McGrath, G. (1983). Humor in group psychotherapy. *British Journal of Medical Psychology, 56,* 89-97.

Bloch, S., & Crouch, E. (1985). *Therapeutic Factors in Group Psychotherapy.* Oxford: Oxford University Press.

Frankl, V. (1969). *The Will to Meaning.* New York: New American Library.

Grotjahn, M. (1971). Laughter in group psychotherapy. *International Journal of Group Psychotherapy, 21,* 234-238.

Hankins-McNary, L. (1979). The use of humor in group therapy. *Perspectives in Psychiatric Care, 17,* 228-231.

Hodes, A. (1972). *Encounter with Martin Buber.* Harmondsworth: Penguin.

Jourard, S. (1971). *The Transparent Self.* New York: Von Nostrand.

Koestler, A. (1975). *The Act of Creation.* London: Picador.

Kubie, L. (1971). The destructive potential of humor in psychotherapy. *American Journal of Psychiatry, 127,* 861-866.

Lake, B. (1985). Concept of ego strength in psychotherapy. *British Journal of Psychiatry, 147,* 471-478.

Mindess, H. (1976). The use and abuse of humor in psychotherapy. In T. Chapman & H. Foot (Eds.), *Humor and Laughter: Theory, Research and Application.* (pp. 331-341). Chichester: Wiley.

Mintz, L. (1984, June). *Misconceptions in Humor Research.* Paper delivered at the Fourth International Congress on Humor, Tel Aviv, Israel.

Rogers, C. (1961). *On Becoming a Person.* Boston: Houghton Mifflin.

Rosenheim, E. (1976). Humor in psychotherapy. *Current Psychiatric Therapies, 16,* 59-65.

Salameh, W. (1983). Humor in psychotherapy: Past outlooks, present status, and future frontiers. In P. McGhee & J. Goldstein (Eds.), *Handbook of Humor Research: Applied Studies* (pp. 62-88). New York: Springer-Verlag.

Sullivan, H. S. (1970). *The Psychiatric Interview.* New York: Norton.

Vaillant, G. (1977). *Adaptation to Life.* Boston: Little, Brown.

Weiner, M. F. (1978). *Therapist Disclosure: The Use of Self in Psychotherapy.* Boston: Butterworths.

Winnicott, D. W. (1971). *Playing and Reality.* New York: Basic Books.

Yalom, I. D. (1985). *The Theory and Practice of Group Psychotherapy.* New York: Basic Books.

HUMOR IN
INTEGRATIVE SHORT-TERM
PSYCHOTHERAPY (ISTP)

Waleed A. Salameh

With good humor and wisdom, Dr. Salameh explains in this chapter his therapeutic system of Integrative Short-Term Psychotherapy (ISTP). This explanation is replete with illustrative metaphors and clinical examples, and ends by clarifying both the general value of ISTP and the various contributions which can be made with the uses of humor in the ISTP approach. In each discussion of his techniques, Salameh gives a detailed and carefully organized description of the particular aspects being considered. His general attitude is one of considerate helpfulness for the reader in achieving a working acquaintanceship with ISTP. The humor uses are illustrated in detail, with vivid clinical examples.

In his schema, Dr. Salameh regards humor as a remarkably effective tool, which is not only technically useful but will also tend to exert a powerful influence both on the nature of the specific therapeutic context and on the overall complexion of patient-therapist relationships. His rationale for this model is extensively explained in his presentation.

Dr. Salameh is a clinical psychologist in private practice and Director of the San Diego Institute for Integrative Short-Term Psychotherapy. As a consultant to various clinical settings, he has conducted numerous workshops in the ISTP approach and in Humor Immersion Training, a training system he has elaborated to facilitate humor development skills. His recent publications include the book chapters "Humor in Psychotherapy: Past Outlooks, Present Status, and Future Frontiers" (1983), "The Effective Use of Humor in Psychotherapy" (1986), and "Humor As A Form Of Indirect Hypnotic Communication" (in press-a).

*   *   *

> Nine-year-old Johnny asked his father: "Dad, where do I come from?" The father, who had never before discussed the sexual facts of life with his child, decided to seize this golden opportunity and tell Johnny all about the birds and the bees. So he embarked on a long-winded explanation about men's and women's sexuality, how babies are born, and so forth. Johnny listened patiently to his father's explanation. When the father was finished, Johnny said nonchalantly: "But Dad, I know all that. What I meant was, where did I come from? Like my friend Rodney, he came from Cincinnati."

The above joke unveils the fact that different human beings can come from different places. In this chapter, I would like to introduce Integrative Short-Term Psychotherapy (or ISTP), the approach I developed to understand where the individuals I do therapeutic work with are coming from. I will also discuss how humor enters into ISTP to help illuminate where patients are coming from, and to facilitate their going somewhere else if they so choose. Lastly, I hope to convey a sense of when and how to use humor in psychotherapy, depending not only on where patients are coming from but also on where they happen to be at the moment that a humorous intervention is contemplated. I will make extensive use of clinical vignettes and case examples throughout the chapter to clarify specific techniques and unravel theoretical precepts.

THEORETICAL PERSPECTIVE

Humor does not represent a theory of psychotherapeutic work. It is rather a way of being, an attitude, and a technical tool which needs to be incorporated within the therapist's theoretical frame of reference. Since I find it difficult to dissociate my use of humor in psychotherapy from my overall treatment approach, the purpose of this section is to briefly present the major tenets of ISTP.

Integrative short-term psychotherapy (ISTP) is a time-limited approach to the treatment of emotional illness. It is designed to quickly and effectively modify self-destructive behaviors, emphasizing the uncovering of inner conflicts and repetitive patterns that have crippled the patient's functioning. It is short-term because the treatment is completed within a determined number of sessions which is estimated by the therapist during the initial evaluation interview. It is integrative because it aims to help the patient integrate therapeutic learnings in a way that prompts constructive action resulting in durable emotional and behavioral change, with concomitant cognitive restructuring. The therapist proceeds systematically, addressing the patient's psychological stumbling blocks early on in treatment and continually focusing on the significant areas of disturbance. In terms of age groups, ISTP is pertinent for treating the problems of young and mid-adulthood. Senior citizens also tend to be good candidates for ISTP treatment. With respect to patient populations, ISTP is specifically appropriate for the treatment of personality disorders, sexually-related dysfunctions, depression, stress-response syndromes, the treatment of both perpetrators and victims of sexual or physical abuse, adjustment disorders, success anxiety and other anxiety reactions, developmentally-related transitional crises, and relationship failure. ISTP cannot be used to treat infancy or childhood disorders, manic-depressive illness, or schizophrenic and psychotic disorders. However, it can provide the therapist with a structured approach for understanding the psychological development of these mental disorders, the therapeutic use of such structure being proportionate to the degree of patient availability for psychotherapeutic work. The principles and techniques learned in ISTP can be adapted to individual, group, family, and couple therapy.

ISTP was developed through the amalgamation of five processes: (a) culling the most elegantly relevant principles and incisive moments from the author's repertoire of training experiences, both academic and clinical; (b) integrating these principles with insights that emerged from everyday therapeutic work with patients and from thinking about the process of psychotherapy; (c) searching for a sound yet simple model of psychotherapy that can be clearly communicated and adapted without unnecessary abstractions. As a result of working against patient legacies of confusion and misunderstanding and being exposed to mastodonic manifestations of high priest psycho-babble, one comes to value the clarity, vigor, and economy that simplicity can bring to human communication. Humor appeals to the human need to communicate simply and economically; (d) adopting a short-term rather than a long-term treatment paradigm; and (e) wanting to include the beneficial properties of humor within a systematic approach to psychotherapeutic work.

The ISTP treatment approach rests upon the productive integration of four important foundations of a successful psychotherapeutic intervention: (a) a process model to implement a specific method of treatment; (b) working propositions to aid in understanding the development of emotional difficulties; (c) facilitative therapist traits to fully place the therapist on the patient's side in the quest for personal change; and (d) an intervention strategy to guide the course of treatment.

Let us now examine each of these four factors in detail:

THE ISTP PROCESS MODEL

The ISTP process model is the cornerstone of therapeutic movement in ISTP. Figure 1 (p. 199) depicts the model. Essentially, the process model encapsulates a universal chronology retracing the seasons of being that individuals automatically bring with them into psychotherapy, as well as the progressive stages that the therapist works through with patients in ISTP. The process model consists of six elements:

1. *The Archaeological Stage.* The identification of past influences and learnings in a person's life including parental constellation, significant others, family upbringing, childhood and adolescence, early traumatic or positive episodes, educational or military experiences when applicable, and other formative patterns of early development.
2. *The Contemporary Stage.* The "presenting problem," a person's present situation and that which has prompted him or her to seek help at a given point in time.
3. *The Immediacy Stage.* The exploration of the "here and now" relationship between therapist and patient, including the patient's feelings toward the therapist as well as the therapist's feelings toward the patient. It can be safely assumed that the same major patterns learned by an individual at the archaeological stage and carried into the contem-

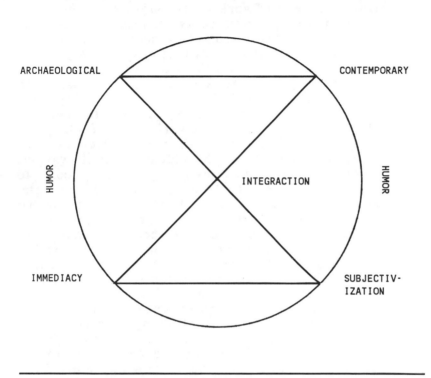

Figure 1.   ISTP Process Model

porary stage will be replayed at the immediacy
stage with the therapist, that is, the patient's
interaction with the therapist will tend to represent a microcosm of his or her interactions with
others. The therapeutic relationship then becomes
a laboratory for the patient to risk interpersonal
openness, try out new modes of interaction, and
undergo a *corrective emotional experience*. The
therapist's task at this juncture is to make clear
connections between Archaeological-Contemporary-
Immediacy (or ACI) material for the patient such
that the common threads underlying thought and
behavior can become apparent.
4. *The Subjectivization Stage*. This stage reflects a
   critical turning point in psychotherapy and in-

cludes two phases: (a) The patient, having objectively or cognitively understood the ACI connections, moves to "working through" the emotional implications of such an awareness. An integral part of the re-educational process at this stage is the recognition that one's feelings do not go away just because one wants them to. Subsequently, the patient can learn to accept and even welcome feelings instead of fighting them or treating them as explosives; if one attaches danger to feelings, then one will deny one's right to feel. The subjectivization of personal experiences and understandings allows individuals to settle various emotional scores, do grieving if necessary, come to grips with their feelings about their parents, acknowledge the validity of their emotions, let go of lingering doubts, own their needs, and finish unfinished business; (b) The second fundamental element in subjectivization work is a progressive bridging and harmonization between the cognitive and unconscious aspects of the self. As patients begin to explore their subjective world, they can develop an appreciation of unconscious insights and resources, gradually allowing these resources to be utilized to effect productive change. If the different parts of the self can be likened to the voices in a choir, then the acknowledgment of the different voices of subjectivity can enable each voice to take its appropriate place and make its particular contribution. In this sense, giving proper voice to different parts of the self allows the individual to deliver a fuller rendition of the choir of personhood. In a choir each voice is important, but all voices agree to cooperate in order to create the harmonious sound that expresses the choir's distinctive identity. For example, the voice of the unconscious can contribute important raw materials, historical learnings, and early constructive resources. The voice of cognition can contribute analytical machinery, structure, and focus. Accordingly, the patient may come to realize that cognitive and unconscious voices can work synergistically, rather than counteractively, along with the other voices of subjectivity within the choir of personhood.

5. *The Integraction Stage.* As coined by this author, the term *integraction* refers to a harmonious blend of integration and action whereby patients are able to integrate their learnings in psychotherapy to reach new personal configurations involving constructive behaviors toward self and others. A change in self-concept usually includes a change in one's perceptions of reality and concomitant actions that would naturally derive from such a perceptual-emotional shift. At this stage, patients typically test out new behaviors, take *healthy risks*, initiate a more mature relationship with the therapist based on realistic perceptions and mutual appreciation, seek corroboration rather than validation for their actions, and can eventually conclude treatment.

6. *The Humor Stage.* This stage encompasses the continuous use of humor throughout psychotherapy to lubricate the machinery and infuse liveliness into the therapeutic process--what tastes bland to the unconscious does not sink in, whereas flavorful and crisply succinct forms of communication tend to be easily assimilated. The therapist who uses humor and encourages a healthy humorous perspective on the patient's part is indirectly inculcating a mechanism of attitudinal healing, a back-up (or back-off) system that can be expected to kick in during periods of distress to provide perspective, self-nurturance, and courage.

Throughout the therapeutic work in ISTP, the therapist sticks to the above model, moving with the patient through each stage and encouraging movement to the next stage. It is not necessary to begin with the archaeological stage, but it is vital that connections be made among the various stages during psychotherapy with the goal of leading up to integraction.

FIVE WORKING PROPOSITIONS

Proposition 1: The School of Personal History

Everyone comes from a place called childhood. Childhood is a place of learning and assimilation. Children go to school in the family just as they go to school in the traditional educational system. Over time a child learns certain emotional and behavioral patterns (both maladaptive and constructive) from either or both parents in terms of personality style, self-perception, and how to approach relationships with others. These parental patterns are then reincarnated within the individual and acted out without conscious awareness in youth and adult life. The repetition of such patterns perpetuates a personal history that gets replayed in similar ways through various personal and interpersonal life events. Typically, individuals seek psychotherapy when they consciously or unconsciously acknowledge that they have reached their level of incompetence regarding the repetition of maladaptive personal history patterns that they feel unable to stop and that they will usually replay with the therapist. Subsequently, a major goal of ISTP is to make visible for the patient the invisible part of personal history that may be causing dysfunctional behavior, so that new nonrepetitive behavior can emerge.

Proposition 2: Mirror Love

Human beings are naturally inclined to seek love and recognition from others. When children seek healthy love from their parents and do not receive it, they engage in a distortional project: they begin to imitate or mirror undesirable parental traits as the only alternative for *getting close* to a rebuffing parent. Mirror love thus provides the only possible form of identification with the parent(s) that neutralizes the risk of rejection. This distorted form of identification usually takes place when healthy identification with a mature and caring parent is not available to the child. Through the experience of psychotherapy, the patient can learn to replace mirror love with emotionally mature forms of identification and appropriate expressions of love toward others that are not crippled by the fear of rejection.

Proposition 3: The Heroic Project

As Becker (1973) pointed out, most individuals (even the most humble, angry, or self-deprecating) tend to think of themselves in their inner sanctum as unsung heroes. The challenge of therapy is to properly acknowledge, channel, prune, balance, and help synchronize the human

bent for heroism so that it can lead to constructive outcomes.

Proposition 4: Native Endowments

It is quasi-impossible to have a life that is completely
devoid of constructive or happy experiences. Most individuals already possess within their psychological repertoire many of the resources they need to change.
However, these constructive resources can sometimes elude
the person's cognitive reach. In ISTP, individuals are
assisted at recomposing past successes, positive memories,
and early rewarding interactions. If these resources are
experienced in a revivified way, they can then be enlisted
to recharge and help reconstruct present capacities. The
effective use of reframing strategies (i.e., guided imagery,
role-playing, hypnosis, humor, task assignments, use of
indirect metaphorical communication, etc.) in therapeutic
work can help facilitate such a revivification.

Proposition 5: Self-Determination

The quest for personal change ultimately converges
around the theme of self-determination and how individuals choose to create their own worlds. Although a person
cannot be held responsible for being thrown into a certain
family and having certain parents (i.e., unconditional
situations), it is important for patients to realize that the
perpetuation of dysfunctional patterns in adult life or the
negation of authorship regarding essential decisions (i.e.,
conditional situations) constitute a denial of personal
responsibility that will block the way to further growth.
Accordingly, the resources for personal change can be
positively mobilized when one realizes that one is the
maker of reality and not just its witness. ISTP focuses on
this point of confluence between unconditional and
conditional situations, on the interplay between bounded-
ness and freedom in human experience. Patients are
encouraged to own their choices as to their self-concept,
and the way they have chosen to envisage their own
world and the world of others. Once choices are owned,
they can then either be maintained or altered depending
on the direction one intends to take. Furthermore,

individuals are helped to make their available options explicit so they can develop informed decisions.

ELEVEN THERAPIST FACTORS

The personal characteristics that therapists bring into the consulting room can exert an important influence on the course and nature of psychotherapy. The research conducted by Carkhuff and his associates (Carkhuff, 1969; Carkhuff & Berenson, 1967) has identified important therapist traits that were found to differentiate effective therapists and their distinct style of therapeutic intervention. Together with other facilitative characteristics identified by this author, these traits form a group of helpful therapist factors that constitute an integral part of the ISTP approach to treatment. These traits are defined as follows:

1. *Respect.* Respect involves a recognition of the patient's personal worth, of the patient's right to make his or her own choices, and of the patient's ability to constructively change his or her knowledge, affect, beliefs and behaviors in identified problem areas.
2. *Empathy.* Empathy is the ability to accurately perceive both verbal and nonverbal expressions of the patient's feelings or cognitions and to communicate this understanding to the patient.
3. *Concreteness.* Concrete communication corresponds with zeroing in on specific (how, what, when, where, who) feelings, experiences, and behaviors that are personally relevant to the patient. The opposite of concreteness is vagueness, which is indicated by boredom and aimlessness on the part of either therapist or patient. When the therapist is focusing on appropriate material, there is usually no feeling of vacuum in the therapeutic interaction.
4. *Confrontation.* The therapist uses confrontation to point out discrepancies wherever they may occur. Discrepancies commonly exist between verbal versus nonverbal behavior, insight versus action, stated versus actual knowledge, beliefs versus behavior, ideal versus real self, illusion versus reality, patient's verbalization of failure and

inadequacy in situations where actual strength and adaptation were shown, and patient's verbalization of successful coping in situations where actual dysfunction and maladaptation were shown. Confrontation is optimally helpful when it is simultaneously coupled with statements of affirmation (the therapist's verbal recognition of the patient's constructive aspects). In this way, individuals can digest and productively react to relevant confrontation of maladaptive patterns without feeling devastated in their personal worth. Furthermore, confrontation should not be confused with rudeness, explosiveness, personal attacks, or the expression of dogmatic views. When used appropriately by the therapist, confrontation can provide a model of assertive communication for patients.

5. *Genuineness.* Genuineness refers to being authentic beyond role or technique in interaction with the patient and expressing accurate information regarding feelings and reactions toward him or her. Genuineness also means that the therapist shows commitment to the patient's treatment, with the readiness to examine and monitor the factors that may hamper such a commitment.

6. *Warmth.* Showing appreciation, encouragement, and concern for the patient can be manifested in verbal and nonverbal therapist behavior. Warmth is also expressed by helping patients feel comfortable in working with the therapist.

7. *Self-Disclosure.* Self-disclosure, when appropriate, consists in relating relevant examples or incidents from the therapist's own history that are directly pertinent to the patient's issues. Such information is communicated for the purpose of denoting common human reactions to universal developmental and social experiences, thus illustrating specific items to be learned and facilitating patient self-exploration. The therapist's transparency makes him or her more human and underscores the value of reducing hidden agendas in interpersonal communication as patients learn to unburden themselves of "hidden" emotional material. Nonetheless, self-disclosure does not provide a license for therapist testimonials or deviations away from patient issues.

8. *Interpersonal Patience.* Ideally, the therapist carefully and patiently listens, allowing patients time to convey their concerns and alternatives on their own, in their own words. In addition, the therapist avoids discrediting patient expressions, or offering immediate solutions that may run the risk of seemingly oversimplifying the patient's problems.

9. *Articulate Use of Language.* A solid vocabulary permits the therapist to use concise as well as allegorical forms of language without stumbling in search of appropriate words. Because language is a major tool of psychotherapy, inadequate verbal skills can lead to confusion or lack of clarity resulting from inarticulate verbalizations, misnomers, unfortunate connotations, use of "loaded" terms, and other linguistic misconstructions. Articulate use of language also includes the therapist's ability to adapt his or her language to the patient's language style.

10. *Ethical/Legal Responsibilities.* The effective therapist possesses a thorough knowledge of the ethical and legal aspects of conducting psychotherapy and can translate this knowledge into practice in interactions with patients.

11. *Humor.* Both the existing evidence regarding the therapeutic uses of humor (Chapman & Foot, 1976, 1977; Goldstein & McGhee, 1972; McGhee & Goldstein, 1983; Salameh, 1983) and clinical experience allow us to postulate that humor is another core facilitative trait of effective therapists. The therapist uses nonsarcastic humor to devitalize patients' maladaptive patterns, convey insight in economical formats, encourage creative problem-solving, and establish successful rapport with clients. Table 1 (pp. 207-209) presents a five-point *Humor Rating Scale* constructed by the author (Salameh, 1983) to help rate therapists' use of humor in psychotherapy. Level 1 on the *Humor Rating Scale* refers to destructive humor, Level 2 to harmful humor, Level 3 to minimally helpful humor responses, Level 4 to very helpful humor responses, and Level 5 to outstandingly helpful humor responses. An illustrative clinical vignette is included for each of the five levels of therapist humor.

TABLE 1: HUMOR RATING SCALE*

Level of Therapist Humor	Clinical Vignette

Level 1 - Destructive Humor

Therapist humor is sarcastic and vindictive, eliciting patient feelings of hurt and distrust. Therapist abuses humor to callously vent his or her own anger toward patients or the world and is consequently insensitive to and unconcerned with the impact of his or her humor on patients. Therapist humor may judge or stereotype patients; its caustic quality denigrates patients' sense of personal worth, leaving them with a typical "bitter aftertaste" reaction. Since the therapist's use of humor is destructive and retaliatory in nature, it tends to significantly impede patient self-exploration and divert the therapeutic process.

Therapist to patient who reports feelings of inadequacy related to a negative self-image: "Well, you obviously have much to be modest about; your face could sink a fleet, and on top of it you have the IQ of a tree. On the other hand, being stupid could help you qualify for disability payments."

Level 2 - Harmful Humor

Therapist humor does not manifest the blatant patient disrespect found at Level 1, but is still not attuned to patients' needs. Therapist mixes the irrelevant use of humor with its abuse, at times introducing humor when it is not applicable to the issues at hand. The therapist may follow-up his or her abuse of humor with a "redemptive communication" that essentially acknowledges the inappropriateness of the previous abusive comment and attempts to make verbal or nonverbal amends for it. Overall, therapist humor is harmful and incapable of facilitating therapeutic process because it is indiscriminate and invalidated either by missed timing or the attempt to redeem derisive comments.

Patient states that he is confused about his goals in life and unable to understand himself. Therapist replies, "Here you go off on a fishing pole again! It's almost like your mind is full of wallpaper." Patient, with a nervous titter: "So I guess I should be perfect! Asking confusing questions can lead me astray, right!" Therapist, now self-conscious: "Well, uh, I'm like that too sometimes. Sometimes I can't think straight." Therapist goes on to explain about his own periods of confusion, indirectly apologizing. Attention is gradually shifted away from the patient's experiencing.

Level of Therapist Humor	Clinical Vignette

Level 3 - Minimally Helpful
Humor Response

Therapist humor <u>does not</u> question the essential worth of individuals and is adequately attuned to patients' needs. Therapist uses humor for and not against patients as a means of reflecting their dilemmas in a concerned yet humorous manner. Therapist humor promotes a positive therapist-patient interaction, yet remains mostly a reaction to the patients' communication rather than an active or preferred therapist-initiated mode of communication.

A married couple is reporting to the therapist that their sexual contacts have gradually decreased in frequency and are presently relegated to rare "special occasions" instead of being a continuous element of the relationship. Therapist: "So I guess it's (sexuality) now like the good old Christmas tree. It's a hassle to get it from the attic and set it up. It's nice while it lasts, but it only gets turned on once a year!"

Level 4 - Very Helpful
Humor Response

Therapist humor is substantially attuned to patients' needs and to helping them identify new options. Therapist humor may expose or amplify specific maladaptive behaviors yet simultaneously conveys a respect for patients' personhood. It facilitates patients' self-exploration while inciting them to recognize and alter dysfunctional patterns. The educational, comfortable, and enjoyable nature of therapist humor stimulates a positive and candid patient-therapist relationship. Nevertheless, therapist humor still lacks some of the intensity, timing, and graphic language characteristic of Level 5 humor responses.

Obsessive patient constantly rejects interpretations with the statement, "No, that's not my bag." Therapist: "So what is your bag, or rather, what's your briefcase?"

Level 5 - Outstandingly Helpful
Humor Response

Therapist humor conveys a profound understanding of patients, is characterized by spontaneity and excellent timing, and challenges patients to live to their fullest

During a group therapy session, a manipulative patient is recounting to the group his repeated failings at achieving honest nonmanipulative commun-

208

Level of Therapist Humor	Clinical Vignette

Level 5 (Cont'd)

potential. Therapist humor reflects his or her emotional and cognitive freedom used to facilitate patients' emotional responsiveness and cognitive restructuring. It generates significant self-exploration and accelerates the process of patient change by defining problems, condensing and symbolizing therapeutic process material, identifying new goals, and promoting constructive alternatives. The creative nature of therapist humor can elicit decisive existential insights and encourages patients to develop their own humor along with other attitudinal changes.

ication with others. Although he tries, others don't seem to believe or respond to his "authentic" self-revelations. Therapist: "You know, your situation reminds me of a corrida scene with the bull and toreador. We don't know whether you're the bull for whose slaughter we should feel sorry or the toreador whose courage we ought to admire." Another group member: "But he's really not the bull; he sets other people up as being bulls." Patient, laughing: "So I end up being the toreador. I give my coup de grace and demand my Olé!" Group members, in unison: "Olé!"

Note: This author's observational data indicate that physical responses to Levels 1 and 2 humor are usually characterized by a preponderance of giggling, tittering, forced laughter, or short anxious laughs. Level 3, 4, and 5 humor usually elicits predominantly diaphragmatic or abdominal gut-level laughter.

*From "Humor in Psychotherapy: Past Outlooks, Present Status, and Future Frontiers" by W. A. Salameh in Handbook of Humor Research: Applied Studies (Vol. 2, pp. 72-74) P. E. McGhee & J. H. Goldstein (Eds.), 1983, New York: Springer-Verlag. Reprinted by permission of Springer-Verlag.

TWELVE INTERVENTION RECOMMENDATIONS

The last component of the ISTP system to be summarized in this section is the therapist's intervention strategy. At the foreground of the intervention strategy is the initial evaluation interview which sets the tone for the rest of the treatment. The initial evaluation usually lasts 100 minutes and proceeds as follows: (a) The patient is asked to identify his or her goals in seeking treatment. The therapist verifies that he or she clearly understands the patient's goals. (b) The therapist specifies how the patient strikes him or her and proposes additional therapeutic goals to be addressed during the course of therapy. The therapist also assesses at this time whether the patient is a good candidate for ISTP. (c) Patient and therapist then reach a mutual agreement on the therapeutic goals. (d) The therapist determines (and communicates to the patient) an estimated number of sessions needed to achieve the agreed-upon therapeutic goals. The number of sessions would vary according to each patient's individual needs. (e) The therapist explains the ISTP perspective in simple terms, including the need for active patient participation. Office policies are also explained at this time, and any patient questions or concerns are duly answered. (f) The patient is asked whether he or she feels comfortable with the therapist and can make a commitment to treatment for the estimated number of sessions. After completion of the initial evaluation process, the following 12 intervention recommendations will convey the thrust of the therapist's intervention strategy in ISTP:

1. Maintain therapeutic focus throughout treatment. Stick to the therapeutic foci identified in the initial evaluation session until therapeutic goals have been achieved and the patient has formulated new foci of interest leading to increased personal fulfillment.
2. Establish as quickly as possible a positive working alliance with the patient. Communicate commitment and convey support for the patient's active participation in the therapeutic process.
3. Attend to immediacy/process issues in the initial phase of treatment for indications of important patient behavior patterns, resistances, conflict areas, communication style, reactions to the therapist, as well as personal limitations and strengths. It is particularly important at the outset of therapy not to import knowledge into the session but to use session-generated material in order to develop working hypotheses or bring important patterns into the patient's awareness. Psychological process is not unlike the human pulse: It is always there; it can be taken at various arteries; if it is missed at one point it can always be accurately detected at another; and it reflects the person's overall health condition.

4. Make Archaeological-Contemporary-Immediacy (ACI) connections once historical data have been gathered, relating past patterns to present functioning. Depending on the patient's needs, resistance level, and defensive formations, ACI connections can be conveyed both directly and indirectly at different junctures in therapeutic work. ACI connections can be made directly by pointing out recurring themes and the general structure of patient defenses and coping mechanisms around these themes. Indirectly, ACI themes can be expressed by using anecdotes, humor, and other modes of metaphoric communication.

5. Encourage Subjectivization by helping the patient express the unexpressed emotional correspondents attached to specific experiences in the ACI constellation. In addition, help the patient acknowledge and constructively utilize the voices of subjectivity, including both unconscious resources and cognitive insights.

6. Move to Integraction with proper consideration given to the patient's pace and personal absorption levels. Assist the patient at detecting alternatives, developing autonomy, and shortening the distance between insight and action. Keep in mind that the acid test of therapy is whether the patient effects actual changes in everyday behavior toward self and others. Assign homework when indicated, such as practical readings related to the patient's issues, expressing feelings to significant others by way of unaddressed letters, and other specific activities that provide a propitious context within which the patient can discover pertinent alternatives.

7. Help the patient differentiate between primary and secondary goals and realign his or her actions accordingly.

8. Provide continuous support throughout treatment to give the patient a *corrective emotional experience*, thus conveying a successful (but by no means exclusive) model of mature relationships with others.

9. Enlist the help of the patient's resources. Identify and highlight previous constructive experiences, positive interactions, and past or current successful coping mechanisms. Use guided imagery, rehears-

als, and related approaches to help the patient recuperate and reactivate personal resources in addressing present or future challenges.

10. Use humor when applicable, encouraging the patient's development of a personal sense of humor. Underscore the use of humor as an attitudinal healing system.

11. Take time for an evaluation session at midpoint in treatment to review progress and specifically discuss what has been accomplished so far as well as what work remains to be done.

12. At termination, ask the patient to review the overall progress made, therapeutic gains, and future direction. Emphasize preventive aspects and continuing self-help activities. Arrange for follow-up, and leave the door open for the patient to reestablish contact should it be desired.

TECHNIQUE

Given the above psychotherapeutic matrix, we can now examine two technical applications of humor in psychotherapy, to be differentiated according to classification and thematic context.

CLASSIFICATION

The classification of therapeutic humor techniques provides a structural core that the therapist can utilize to construct humorous interventions. Table 2 (pp. 213-216) (Salameh, 1983) defines 12 humor techniques and illustrates each with a clinical vignette. The written version of these vignettes may not completely reflect their full "live" impact as they occurred during psychotherapeutic work and within the context of patient statements, yet it is hoped that the essential flavor of each interaction can still be conveyed.

THEMATIC CONTEXT

Beyond the above techniques, humor may have particular clinical relevance in the process of working through certain therapeutic themes. The following thematic contexts reflect typical uses of humor in ISTP:

TABLE 2: THERAPEUTIC HUMOR TECHNIQUES*

Therapeutic Humor Technique	Definition	Clinical Vignette
Surprise	Using unexpected occurrences to transmit therapeutic messages.	Drilling noise outside office. Patient is talking about his domineering wife. Therapist: "Your wife is talking to you now!"
Exaggeration	Obvious overstatements or understatements regarding size, proportions, numbers, feelings, facts, actions.	To patient who romanticizes his depression while refusing to consider alternatives: "I could help you, but I guess that wouldn't do any good anyway. You know we all die eventually."
Absurdity	That which is foolish, nonsensical, insane, irrationally disordered. That which is without having any logical reason to be.	A young businessman is spending inordinately long hours at the office and on business trips. He reports that his wife has complained about his increasing lack of interest in their sexual relationship. Therapist responds: "It sounds like the best way for you to get more invested in your sex life is to make it tax deductible!"
The Human Condition	Refers to problems of living that most human beings encounter, viewed from a humorous perspective to stress their commonality.	Therapist to a perfectionist patient who worries that he is not being "totally honest" in communicating all his feelings to others: "As the holy books have indicated, it is difficult for mankind to be honest at all times. But if you want to be a phony, you should be honest about it."
Incongruity	Linking two or more usually incompatible ideas, feelings, situations, objects.	Oppositional female patient reacts to therapist interpretation by stating that she "has already entertained that possibility." Therapist responds: "You've entertained it, but you didn't go to bed with it."

Therapeutic Humor Technique	Definition	Clinical Vignette
Confrontation/ Affirmation Humor	Confronts patients' maladaptive and self-defeating behaviors while affirming their personal worth as individuals. Assumes that patient confrontation is best digested by patients when coupled with affirmation.	A patient in group therapy is confronted by other group members regarding his compulsive nose-blowing behavior. He passionately defends his need to "breathe clearly." Therapist responds: "You know, we can all see that you've got a lot of intensity, but you don't have to blow it out your nose!"
Word Play	Using puns, double entendres, bons mots, song lines, and well-known quotes or sayings from popular culture to convey therapeutic messages.	Therapist to patient who keeps depriving himself of what he really wants: "You know what Oscar (Wilde) said, 'I can resist anything but temptation.'" To another man who prevents himself from enjoying life or other people because he refuses to take small acceptable risks: "Mae West did say, 'When I choose between two evils, I always like to take the one I've never tried before.'"
Metaphorical Mirth	The use of metaphorical constructions, analogies, fairy tales, and allegories for therapeutic storytelling to help patients assimilate new insights or understand old patterns.	Patient is talking about how his interpersonal communication is becoming less confused as he really listens to others and gives relevant feedback. Therapist: "It's like that lion you see at the zoo who always growls at you but you don't know what he means. And one day you go to the zoo and he smiles and says, 'Hi, there, I've been fixin' to talk to you.' And you talk to each other and become pen pals."
Impersonation	Humorously imitating the typical verbal response or maladaptive style of patients and of significant	Patient repeats a characteristic "Fssss" sound with his tongue whenever he experiences sadness or other "vulnerable" emotions, so as to block the

Don't make mistakes ⟶

214

Therapeutic Humor Technique	Definition	Clinical Vignette
Impersonation (Cont'd)	others they may bring up in therapy.	expression of such feelings. Therapist imitates this "Fssss" sound when patient displays it. Patient gradually shifts from suppression to acknowledgment of his feelings.
Relativizing	Contextualizing events within a larger perspective such that they lose their halo of absoluteness. Relativizing gives the message that: "Nothing is as serious as we fear it to be, nor as futile as we hope it to be" (Jankelevitch, 1964).	Patient recounts his painful struggle with his "weight problem," even though his physician informed him that he is only 3-5 pounds overweight. Therapist: "Well, I notice you've lost some weight behind the ears since last week."
The Tragi-Comic Twist	A delicate humor technique requiring almost surgical precision that consists of a transformation of patients' detrimental tragic energies into constructive comical energies. It begins with a well-timed implicit or explicit juxtaposition of the tragic and comic poles of a given phenomenon followed by a reconciliation of the two poles in a humoristic synthesis that triggers laughter.	Patient who has chosen depression and crying as a behavioral mode of response to any environmental stressor is crying in session about feeling rejected and tense. Therapist responds: "I guess you're trying to relax now." Patient's crying turns into frantic laughter as he replies: "That's one thing I do really well, I know how to cry." Therapist: "Maybe you can relax about crying." More laughter. Therapist asks patient why he is laughing. Patient: "I suppose there are other ways of releasing tension besides crying." The entire session then focuses on the above issue.
Bodily Humor	Using the entire body or specific muscle groups in physical activity aimed at imitating or creating nonverbal reflections	Patient exhibits a typical rotational hand movement to express disillusionment with others' behavior when it does not meet his "requirements." Therapist uses this same hand

215

Therapeutic Humor Technique	Definition	Clinical Vignette
Bodily Humor (Cont'd)	of typical maladaptive mannerisms in order to encourage their extinction.	movement in therapy whenever patient is expressing disillusionment with therapist's behavior not meeting his expectations.

*From "Humor in Psychotherapy: Past Outlooks,   Present Status,   and Future Frontiers" by W. A. Salameh in Handbook of Humor Research: Applied Studies (Vol. 2, pp. 76-78) P. E. McGhee & J. H. Goldstein (Eds.), 1983, New York: Springer-Verlag. Reprinted by permission of Springer-Verlag.

1. *Humor may be used to expose the sanctimoniousness of inflexible, uncompromising attitudes.* Humor can help deflate rigid defenses so that patients may examine their real needs and wishes. In the following example a patient was explaining the sharp contrasts between his mother's and father's personal styles. The mother was a rigid woman who would not allow any "swear words" in her house. The father, although passive and self-effacing, seemed to be able to express himself humorously. The patient was describing a Thanksgiving dinner when his father had actually succeeded at making his mother laugh.

Patient: My father recited this limerick:

"Of all the fishes in the sea
I'd like to be a bass
I'd climb up the seaweed trees
And fall down on my...."

and he stopped. My mother laughed, looked at my father reproachingly, and said, "Oh, Clark!" (*fictitious name*). My father smiled and continued, "and fall down *on my hands and knees.*" See, Mom thought that Dad was going to say, "and fall down *on my ass.*" She was starting to reprimand him for

	using a profane term. But Dad caught her at her own game.
Therapist:	Your father was trying to show your mother how her rigid expectations can prevent openness to other points of view.
Patient:	Yes (*laughing*), he wanted to show her that she couldn't figure things out because she thought she already had everything figured out.

The interaction then focused on how the patient's own rigid filters prevented him (as they did his mother) from enjoying life due to his frequent urge to make judgments about what was occurring at the moment.

2. *Humor may be used to point out ACI connections.* In using the ISTP process model, humor can make it easier for patients to see the connections between past and present patterns. In the next example a 30-year-old carpenter had sought treatment to clarify his emotions regarding an impending divorce. The patient was a reformed alcoholic and had reported that his overly zealous "condemning" attitude at Alcoholics Anonymous meetings had elicited negative criticism from other A.A. members. Throughout treatment, it had become apparent that the patient was highly self-critical. It was also evident that his mother was hyper-critical and that he was quite talented at initiating relationships with women who were overly critical of him, such as his first wife and now his soon-to-be-divorced second wife. Yet he seemed adamant about taking himself too seriously and was refusing to see how his own solemnity prevented him from finding alternatives. I had pointed out to him that his severity was preventing him from developing his sense of humor, and he perceived my comment as a criticism.

Patient:	Well, for me, that's just another thing to criticize myself for, to beat myself with, that I don't have a sense of humor.
Therapist:	You'll never be a perfect comic.

217

Patient: (*laughs*) That's funny! I'll never be a perfect comic!

Therapist: You'll never be a perfect comic! I suppose that's one more thing to be unhappy about for the rest of your life. Just like you could never be a perfect child for your mother, a perfect alcoholic, a perfect Alcoholics Anonymous member, a perfect husband. Now you'll never be a perfect comic!

Patient: (*laughing intensely*) I can never be perfect at anything!

Therapist: You're perfectly imperfect. Even a suggestion about something that's supposed to be spontaneous like humor gets processed through your critical channels and becomes another *duty*.

This interchange marked a turning point in the patient's attitude, and he gradually became less rigid with himself and others. "The Perfect Comic" theme was productively used as a reference point in later sessions to point out unnecessarily critical attitudes toward oneself or others.

3. *Humor can lower the "fog index."* The publishing industry uses the expression "high fog index" to describe cluttered or vague writing that needs to be simplified. Relatedly, humor is used in ISTP to break down seemingly complex concepts into bite-sized explanations that patients can easily assimilate. The following example involves an impulsive patient who complained about being misunderstood by others in her personal and work situations. She insisted that these misunderstandings were totally due to other people's problems, and that her communication problems would automatically dissolve if others could change the way they dealt with her. It was becoming increasingly clear that she did not recognize the part she played in the perpetuation of her difficulties.

Therapist: It seems like you don't want to control yourself. You want to go on doing what you do. You just want to control

the people who control you so that
they can control you better.

Patient: (*laughs*) I want to orchestrate the
world. Such a big orchestra!

Therapist: Yes, and it would be so interesting if
you could just orchestrate yourself.

Subsequent to this interpretation, the patient was
able to discern more readily how she created a
large part of her communication problems. She
began to shift the focus of her energies from
complaining about how others were treating her to
examining how she could change her own behavior.

4. *Humor may be used to "freeze" maladaptive
behaviors for the patient's consideration.* Humor can
provide a refreshing tool for illustrating maladaptive behaviors "on the spot" when patients exhibit
them. This process is similar to "freezing" a scene
in a television football game or replaying it in
slow motion so that the viewer can see exactly
what each player did. In this example an anxious
patient in group psychotherapy had a habit of
interrupting others and seldom listening to
feedback. Whenever other group members attempted to communicate with him, he would
curtail the interaction and interject with his own
irrelevant remarks before others had the opportunity to explain their viewpoint. In one group session
he was carrying on with his rambling, aimless
commentary. Other group members had expressed
their irritation with his style.

Therapist: Okay, you win. You get the Olympic
gold medal for verbal diarrhea.

Patient: (*laughs intensely*) Verbal diarrhea!
(*group members join in laughter*) But
how come I feel constipated on the
inside?

Therapist: I guess diarrhea is not the cure for
constipation.

Patient: (*continues to laugh*) I need to even the
flow both on the inside and on the
outside.

The group session then focused on the patient's
"constipated" upbringing with a father who taught

him not to express any feelings ("men never cry"), and how his "verbal diarrhea" represented a form of emotional protest aimed at countering subjectively-felt restrictions, an awkward way of balancing the restrictive scale.

5. *Finally, humor can facilitate acknowledgment of unspoken emotions, unwritten interpersonal scenarios, or hidden agendas.* Humor can help to introduce awareness of unconscious motivations and give patients permission to express hitherto unacknowledged needs or emotions. This example concerns a 25-year-old woman who consulted because of "problems at home." Although she had a college degree and a well-paying job, she was still living at home and calling her mother from work at least twice a day. The patient stated that the family's problems were caused by the father, an edgy, irritable man. Yet it was also apparent that the patient did not want to acknowledge her mother's contributions to the family's dilemmas. In essence, the mother seemed to be a manipulative, passive-aggressive woman who had encouraged the daughter's dependency. In one session, I was pointing out how the mother maneuvers to get the patient to align with her against father.

Patient: Ooh! I didn't realize this about Mother. I thought my father was the odd one in the family.

Therapist: He certainly carries the flag!

Patient: (*laughs*) He'd be the first to join the posse.

Therapist: He'd even volunteer to precede the cavalry and go scouting in enemy territory.

Patient: (*laughing intensely*) Oh yeah!

Therapist: Your father is out there with the flag while you and your mother are having a telephone conversation behind enemy lines.

Patient: (*continues laughing, now more intensely*) We're such a glorious threesome!

The session then focused on the family's hidden agendas, including the parents' competition for the daughter's affection, and how the patient herself contributes to the conflict scenario.

PERTINENT USES

This section addresses six guidelines concerning the appropriate use of humor in psychotherapy.

INTRODUCING HUMOR

It makes sense to start a gourmet meal with appetizers before bringing in the *pièce de résistance*. Because humor is a largely indirect form of communication that may be subject to misinterpretation, it is usually helpful to preface the use of any form of humorous intervention by relating the following to the patient during the first therapy session:

> It is important for you to know that I am your ally, *totally* on your side, and that we're *cooperating*, working together to tackle your problems. My orientation is not to judge you or tell you what to do but to help you *clarify* your available choices, where you are now, and where you can go from here if you so decide. I respect the *courage* you have shown today by seeking treatment for intimate issues that are usually hard to talk about. I will do my best to *support* you and help you feel comfortable throughout our working together. I may sometimes use humor in working with you, not to make light of your problems but to point out recurring patterns or help identify new options. I also encourage you to use humor because positive forms of humor can help us see things in new, refreshing ways. When I use humor at a certain point, I may ask you what I meant by using a joke or story and you might want to ask me what I meant as well, so that things can *make sense* as we go along.

This type of introduction can allay patient apprehensions about humor and create a cognitive framework within which humorous interventions will not only be welcomed but will also receive favorable consideration. In this respect, it is important for patients to feel that humor is not at their expense and that they own the solutions embedded in the humorous metaphor. Accordingly, I sometimes encourage patients' anchoring of solutions by asking, "Why are you laughing?" A patient's explanation of why he or she found what I said to be humorous can help to "lock in" an interpretive cycle that has been fermenting throughout the therapeutic work.

CREATING A HUMOROUS ENVIRONMENT

The second important guideline for encouraging humorous expression in psychotherapy is the inclusion of humorous objects in the therapeutic environment. For instance, some of the humorous objects in my consulting office include a concave mirror that deforms the body in unexpected and often hilarious ways (which patients are invited to use), a statuette of a laughing Zen monk, and humorous books on the bookcase shelves. Such objects help communicate an unwritten message to patients that humor is healthy and welcome, in the proper measure, within the context of psychotherapeutic work. Once patients sense that their humor is acceptable in psychotherapy, they may feel free to try new humorous responses or bring forward their own humorous style. The therapist can then support healthy humor and discourage sarcasm or other harmful abuses of humor as indicated in each patient's specific situation.

USING HUMOR WITH DIFFERENT PATIENTS

Humor is best received by most patients when the therapist has developed a good level of trust and a constructive working alliance with the patient. Once an adequate rapport has been established, humor can be utilized with patients experiencing a variety of emotional problems. For example, humor is particularly effective with obsessives to highlight their absurd worries and to illustrate how they count the minutes instead of living them. Humor can also be used with depressives to help them explore a more cheerful outlook on life, and with character disorders to accentuate recurring manipulations. Moreover, for those patients who equate emotional honesty with pain, humor can convey the message that it is liberating and enjoyable to express honest emotion. For those patients who function in the "should" mode, humor can encourage an acceptance of their real, as opposed to ideal, needs.

On the other hand, special care needs to be taken in using humorous interventions with severely disturbed psychotics or with paranoid and manic-depressive patients who may sometimes misinterpret or deform the therapist's humor. However, a serene and cheerful approach in working with these patients can still impart a feeling of hope and human warmth while allowing them to freely bring forth their own sense of humor. In addition, therapists may need to exercise cautious judgment in using humor with individuals who have been victims of a recent trauma or who are hypersensitive because of an impending disconcerting event such as divorce, severe physical illness, or other major life transition.

I suggest the following sequence in using therapeutic humor with any patient: (a) Take a brief history of the patient's past and present experiences with humor. Are such experiences negatively tainted, or are they constructive in scope? What are the patient's feelings surrounding these humor experiences? (b) Ask the patient for his or her favorite joke or about a recent enjoyable or humorous experience. (c) Move on to situational humor (humor about current events, the weather, humorous news items). (d) Use self-directed humor by communicating to the patient some personal humorous experiences that may be of relevance to the patient's own issues. (e) Once a sense of mutual trust has been established, allowing for more relaxed interactions, one can proceed to unobtrusive patient-directed humor (humor related to the patient's own dilemmas, paradoxes, absurd patterns, or maladaptive behaviors). Of course, patients can also be encouraged throughout treatment to unburden themselves of unnecessary solemnity and to develop their own humorous perspective.

THE THERAPIST'S ATTITUDE TOWARD HUMOR

The therapist's attitude regarding humor is of the essence because an inflexible and solemn therapist would probably be unable to convey a humorous attitude to his or her patients. Furthermore, as Greben (1981, 1984) indicates, the therapist's unresponsiveness and detachment can impede productive patient change on any significant therapeutic dimension. We cannot prescribe humor for our patients unless we can accept it in our own lives. It often seems difficult for therapists to enter into the world of humor for many reasons. Some therapists may reject humor because they associate it with overt aggression or due to past negative experiences in being the victim of sarcasm. Others may feel that using humor discredits patients or may even discredit the therapist's own "professional" stance. Moreover, conventional clinical training does not usually encourage a humorous perspective since one must often work against the backdrop of the grim view of life presented by many patients who harbor a pessimistic outlook. Although it may be understandable why patients are pessimistic, it is often *not* understandable why we cannot raise our "humor quotient" as we struggle with the stress of working with distressed individuals. Milton Erickson is reported to have once stated to a collaborator, "Man does not live by protein alone" (Zeig, 1985). In this sense, humor is at times the best gift we can offer both our patients and ourselves in order to move from a negative view to a constructive one where problems are solvable.

Beyond the attitudinal factors, the therapist's use of humor can bring electricity to therapy sessions and helps to sharpen therapeutic sensitivity that may get dulled by stress or burnout. In other instances, humor represents a form of constructive therapist self-disclosure that reveals the therapist's human side to his or her patients. Moreover, timing is a major factor in the therapeutic humor equation. Therapeutic humor is well-timed, taking into account the patient's sensitivities and specific needs at the moment when a humorous intervention is considered. The judicious therapist is also aware of when *not* to use humor, depending on the therapeutic material under discussion and the patient's level of absorption. Interns and therapists in training may want to consult with their supervisors about how and when humor may be appropriate with different patients.

HUMOR IMMERSION TRAINING*

How do individuals develop a sense of humor? Does one's sense of humor evolve naturally or can it be stimulated by exposure to and specific training in humor creation techniques? What are the emotional and cognitive attitudes that can boost humor, and the attitudinal blocks that inhibit it? Can one learn to replace sarcasm and destructive humor with more constructive forms

*Humor Immersion Training is trademarked by the author.

of humorous expression? My work in the area of humor (Salameh, 1981, 1982, 1983, 1984a, 1984b, 1984c, 1985a, 1985b, 1986, in press-a, in press-b) has allowed me to ponder these questions at length. Simply put, my impression is that although certain family constellations may predispose some individuals to be more humorous than others, most individuals can still learn to create humor through a specific training program. Like biofeedback, psychodrama, hypnosis, or any other therapeutic technique, humor is a skill that can be taught, learned, and practiced. Subsequently, I developed Humor Immersion Training (HIT) as a workshop training experience for therapists and other individuals interested in exercising their "humor muscles." In essence, HIT provides a specific new technology for humor development. Table 3 (pp. 226-227) summarizes the 12 facets covered in HIT workshops.

LIMITATIONS AND ETHICAL CONSIDERATIONS IN USING HUMOROUS APPROACHES

It is crucial to differentiate between therapeutic and destructive humor. What is discussed in this chapter is a wholesome, therapeutic form of humor that covers a wide range of psychological states: joy, happiness, lightheartedness, serenity, cheerfulness, *joie de vivre*, gusto, zest, contentment, gaiety, bliss, conviviality, celebration, and other associated experiences. Such forms of humor would by definition exclude sarcasm, scorn, mockery, and other abuses of humor commonly known as "put-downs," which can usually be detected by the "bitter aftertaste" reaction they trigger when used toward self or others. Table 4 (p. 228) summarizes some of the differences between therapeutic and harmful humor.

Accordingly, Facet 7 (in Table 3) of HIT consists in training participants--through various role-play situations and exercises depicting nontherapeutic versus therapeutic humorous interventions--to distinguish the therapeutic use of humor from its harmful abuse. In this respect, it is important to indicate that therapeutic humor works best in conjunction with the other facilitative therapist traits identified in the theoretical perspective section. Humor can effectively mobilize patients when it is empathic, genuine, and respectful, even as it confronts patients' defenses. It is not fueled by anger but rather by joy and

TABLE 3: HUMOR IMMERSION TRAINING PROGRAM FACETS

Facet	Name	Material Covered
Facet 1	Benefits of humor	Emotional, cognitive, physiological, economic, communication, and anti-stress benefits of humor. Exercises.
Facet 2	Attitudinal blocks to humor	Eleven major attitudinal blocks that stop us from exploring our humorous side. Exercises.
Facet 3	Entering Humorland: Humor creation techniques	The holy trilogy of humor-making, timing, attitudes that foster a humorous outlook, the anatomy of jokes, increasing humorous exposure, 20 specific humor-making techniques with an exercise to practice each technique.
Facet 4	The narrative laugh: Telling humorous stories	Ten techniques for constructing humorour stories. Humorous stories in contemporary culture. Sufi and Zen stories.
Facet 5	Diamonds in your own back yard	Unearthing personal humor experiences through guided imagery techniques. Exercises.
Facet 6	Humorous instruments	Humorous Sentence Completion Blank, Humor Questionnaire, Objective Humor Test. Test-taking exercises.
Facét 7	Therapeutic versus harmful humor	Differentiating therapeutic from harmful humor by using the Humor Rating Scale (Salameh, 1983). Exercises.
Facet 8	Beating your conceptual rut: Humor and creativity	Relationship between humor and creativity. Using humor to stimulate creative thinking. Techniques of toying with ideas, challenging assumptions, seasoning thoughts, changing contexts, breaking off the perceptual blues, and increasing creative manifestations.
Facet 9	Thoughts on happy people	The place of humor in mature adjustment. Distinctive personality traits of happy individuals.
Facet 10	Doing it	Translating workshop learnings into action. Where and how to begin.

Facet	Name	Material Covered
Facet 11	Post-workshop follow-up	Humor Immersion Training Manual (Sala-meh, in press-b), audiotapes, refer-ences, and detailed list of resources.
Facet 12	Laughers Anonymous	Workshop participants can maintain their humorous involvements by joining Laughers Anonymous, a membership or-ganization founded by the author. Laughers Anonymous (L.A.) is dedicated to the promotion of laughter and hu-mor, and to the identification of con-structive approaches to happiness. The organization publishes Laughers Anonymous Newsletter two times a year, and serves as a resource for audio-tapes, videotapes, instructional media, references, and other humor-related materials.

by an authentic commitment to help patients change in healthy ways. The *Humor Rating Scale* (Table 1) can provide a useful reference point to help discriminate between destructive and helpful forms of humor. The scale makes clear that humor, like any other powerful communication tool, can be abused to convey nontherapeutic messages at Levels 1 and 2. By using the *Humor Rating Scale* to rate role-played, live, or video-taped therapeutic interactions, therapists can (a) have a reference point by which to assess whether their present level of humorous intervention is harmful or helpful, and (b) rate their improvement in using humor therapeutically following HIT workshops.

CLINICAL PRESENTATION
THE CASE OF THE APPEASER

In this clinical presentation, I will first present the patient's background, then my psychotherapeutic strategy using the ISTP process model, followed by vignettes from three pivotal sessions.

PATIENT'S BACKGROUND

A 35-year-old chemist sought treatment because of "relationship problems" with his girlfriend. The patient

TABLE 4: THERAPEUTIC VERSUS HARMFUL HUMOR*

Therapeutic Humor	Harmful Humor
Concerned with impact of humorous feedback on others.	Unconcerned with impact of comments on others.
Has an educational, corrective message.	May exacerbate existing problems.
Promotes the onset of a cognitive-emotional equilibrium.	Prevents the onset of a cognitive-emotional equilibrium.
May question or amplify specific maladaptive <u>behaviors</u> but does not question the essential worth of all human beings.	Questions sense of personal worth, such as in racist jokes.
Implies self- and other-awareness.	Implies self- and other-blindness.
Has a gentle, healing, constructive quality.	Has a callous, "bitter aftertaste," detrimental quality.
Acts as an interpersonal lubricant; constitutes an interpersonal asset.	Tends to retard and confound interpersonal communication; constitutes an interpersonal liability.
Based on acceptance.	Based on rejection.
Takes into account others' needs and welfare.	Reflects the perpetuation of personal dysfunctional patterns.
Strengthens, brightens, and alleviates.	Restricts, stigmatizes, and retaliates.
Aims to reveal and unblock alternatives.	Aims to obscure and block alternatives.

*From "Humor in Psychotherapy: Past Outlooks, Present Status, and Future Frontiers" by W. A. Salameh in <u>Handbook of Humor Research: Applied Studies</u> (Vol. 2, p. 84) P. E. McGhee & J. H. Goldstein (Eds.), 1983, New York: Springer-Verlag. Reprinted by permission of Springer-Verlag.

held a prestigious position in a large corporation, for which he was selected from a pool of 110 applicants. During his first session he reported that, when he was notified of having been chosen for the position, his response was that the search committee had made a mistake--he strongly felt that he did not deserve to be the successful candidate. The patient was depressed and dissatisfied, especially in his relationship with his girlfriend. He described his girlfriend as an unhappy, explosive woman prone to experiencing prolonged fits of rage during which she would insult and denigrate him. The patient's typical response in those situations was to keep silent and eventually appease his girlfriend without resolving the situation.

The patient came from a middle-class New York family. He depicted his mother (a fifth-grade teacher) as a caring woman who dedicated much of her time to raising her two children (the patient had only one brother, 4 years older than him). However, he characterized his father (an engineer) as an impatient, explosive man, short-tempered in his interactions with his family. The patient saw his father as rigid, emotionally restricted, and unwilling to express affection or warmth toward his wife and children. The patient's parents had traversed numerous periods of marital conflict, triggered by the father's angry outbursts, which would typically end in limbo with the mother backing off and taking a passive stance while the father's behavior invariably escalated to another crescendo of explosiveness. At the point he entered treatment, the patient had moved from New York City to California. He saw his major problems as depression, loneliness, dissatisfaction, boredom with his everyday life, and relationship problems with his girlfriend.

PSYCHOTHERAPEUTIC STRATEGY

Table 5 (pp. 230-232) presents the major clinical issues, therapeutic strategies, and therapeutic goals for each of the six stages in the ISTP process model (Figure 1):

THREE PIVOTAL SESSIONS

The following vignettes from three sessions with The Appeaser illustrate the tactical use of the ISTP process model and how humor enters into ISTP work.

TABLE 5: THERAPEUTIC STRATEGY USING THE ISTP PROCESS MODEL

STAGE	SIGNIFICANT OTHERS	CLINICAL USE	THERAPEUTIC STRATEGY	THERAPEUTIC GOAL
Archaeological	Father	Patient is angry at father for being explosive toward him and depressed about father's rejection of him. Patient represses his playful aspects due to fear of punishment. He repeats his father's patterns in passive-aggressive behavior, rejection of his own feelings, low self-esteem, and rare bouts of anger when he feels extremely despondent.	Point out anger, make ACI connections. Examine patient's perceptions of therapist as similar to father.	Change perception of authority as punitive. Encourage assertive expression of emotions including anger, sadness, and joy.
	Mother	Patient has experienced a positive nurturing relationship with his mother who accepted and cared about him. Patient has also incorporated some of his mother's appeasing passive aspects.	Show gentleness in approaching patient while adopting an active treatment approach. Point out passivity when manifested.	Energize nurturing and caring aspects. Facilitate expressions of gentleness and other soft emotions. Help replace appeasement style with authentic responsiveness and ability to express needs, likes, and dislikes.
Contemporary	Girlfriend	Patient is replaying passive role with explosive girlfriend who rejects his emotional needs and punishes him for disagreeing with her.	Point out similarities between father's and girlfriend's personality styles.	Encourage mature relationships with nonexplosive individuals who are able to acknowledge patient's emo-

STAGE	SIGNIFICANT OTHERS	CLINICAL USE	THERAPEUTIC STRATEGY	THERAPEUTIC GOAL
Contemporary (Cont'd)	Project Supervisor	Patient replays passive pattern with pushy project supervisor at work.	Same strategy as with girlfriend: father/supervisor similarities.	tions instead of rejecting them.
Immediacy	Therapist	Patient will tend to see therapist as punishing authority figure who will criticize him and reject his emotional needs.	Introduce reality into patient's perceptions of authority by accepting patient's emotions. Make ACI connections between father/girlfriend/project supervisor/and expected versus actual reactions of therapist.	Help bring patient fully into the present when relating to others, such that he can be aware of his emotions and verbalize them instead of appeasing others and retrenching into his negative inner projections of how others may be perceiving him. Enhance self-respect and patient's sense of emotional freedom.
Subjectivization	Father, mother, girlfriend, project supervisor, therapist	Patient has built up an unexpressed emotional reservoir of anger, depression, fear, and hurts about past and present experiences of rejection that he needs to work through and discharge.	Make ample room for patient's expression of his emotions about decisive past and present life events.	Help patient achieve a sense of reconcilement and completion about his personal history while accepting and harmonizing the different aspects of the self in order to productively address the conditions of his present reality.

STAGE	SIGNIFICANT OTHERS	CLINICAL USE	THERAPEUTIC STRATEGY	THERAPEUTIC GOAL
Integrac- tion	All indi- viduals mentioned above and new rela- tionships	Patient needs to integrate his new therapeutic learnings and try out novel ways of relating to himself and others.	Show respect for the positive changes in patient's self-concept and encourage pa- tient's actions to anchor these changes in everyday life.	Support patient's initia- tion of constructive ac- tions aimed at restructur- ing his personal and inter- personal situation. Cor- roborate the concrete changes in patient's be- havior.
Humor	Therapist and new relation- ships	As a child and college student, pa- tient manifested a spontaneous sense of humor and playfulness that he now sees as an unacceptable part of him.	Accept patient's hu- morous expressions. Use humor throughout treatment at all five stages above as indi- cated to make ACI connections, further emotional rapport with the patient, allow the patient to express the full range of his emotional reactions, and draw him into the here-and-now process of treatment.	Encourage patient to reviv- ify his sense of humor with the ability to show play- fulness and flexibility toward himself and in his relationships.

Session A

The first session to be discussed took place during the first third of the patient's treatment. His appeasing style and "neutral" emotional screen had been pointed out for his consideration. His placating maneuvers had also been identified, including how he uses appeasement to block off emotional involvement. The patient's appeasing emotional style would unfold in the following manner: Whenever others expressed emotional material to him (or whenever he felt any strong emotions asking for expression within himself), he would typically choose not to respond to the emotional messages and would "neutralize" the situation by diluting the emotional aspect, by making a long-drawn intellectual commentary about the matter at hand, by withdrawing and not verbalizing any response whatsoever, or by getting very angry on rare occasions under rising emotional pressures. The clinical assumption here was that the patient's emotional reluctance was connected to a double-edged fear. On one hand, he wanted to appease others so that they would not get angry at him like his father did. On the other hand, he subjectively experienced an inner rage at his father that he feared would surface if he let his emotions show. Session A was preceded by an angry letter from the patient to our office complaining that the format of his billing statements was "inconvenient." The timing of the patient's letter coincided with a major clash with his girlfriend during which he had gotten infuriated with her and had told her that she "did not know who he was." The session started with a discussion of his letter to the office.

Therapist: Your letter expressed some strong emotions.
Patient: I was angry that I wasn't being taken seriously as someone who deserves good receipts.
Therapist: Yes, and yet it seems like there was much more to your letter than just asking for elegant-looking receipts. You did not want me to dismiss your concerns like your father did.
Patient: Somehow I expect these things to happen to me.
Therapist: In other words, you expect that I would treat you the same way that your father treated

you, that I would also neglect what is important to you.

Patient: I don't like being neglected.

Therapist: Your anger is a way of you unconsciously asking for your emotions to be acknowledged, like saying, "I'm sick of people in authority not taking my feelings seriously; I want you to respect my emotions."

Patient: I don't get no respect!

Therapist: Yet even you don't acknowledge your own emotions. You either appease your girlfriend and therefore deaden you feelings *or* you get angry like your father and still hide your other emotions under the anger blanket.

Patient: (*smiles*) I need a dimmer switch instead of an on/off switch.

Therapist: Exactly!

Patient: I'm beginning to understand what my anger is about, how it's just the other extreme of the appeasement.

Therapist: (*laughs*) The dimmer switch can work so much better, gives you a wider range of lighting.

Patient: (*laughs*) It really does.

Therapist: (*after silent pause*) And I wonder what your feelings are towards me right now.

Patient: I'm not angry at you, and I don't feel like you're angry at me. You listen.

Session B

The patient started to show more emotional differentiation after Session A, with increased ability to voice his feelings in different situations. Session B occurred during the second half of treatment. The session began with an exploration of the current lack of liveliness in the patient's life as opposed to his earlier humorous experiences.

Patient: I remember I used to have fun when I was a kid. We used to live next door to a mean, cranky old man. He would do things like call the police to complain about us if our football inadvertently fell in his backyard when we were playing. So this one time I really fixed

	him up. I poured gasoline on his plants and put noisy firecrackers on his windows! (*laughs*)
Therapist:	(*laughing*) A Fourth of July bash.
Patient:	And I also remember telling a pompous teacher to get stuffed (*laughing more intensely*).
Therapist:	(*laughs*)
Patient:	These things also went on during my college years, funny things I did with my fraternity brothers like wearing strange costumes at parties, staying up all night telling jokes, things like that (*patient's face begins to light up as he talks, his eyes begin to sparkle, his cheeks become red; his overall facial expression conveys vigor, buoyancy, and èlan*).
Therapist:	What is happening within you right now? It seems like something clicked; you suddenly seem full of zing.
Patient:	(*laughs*) I just feel happy when I remember the fun things I did as a kid and in college. It's a part of me that I've shut off lately, but I really enjoy being this way. The things I did back then were a lot of fun but somehow I now associate all these episodes with me being a bad person.
Therapist:	You don't look like a bad person at this moment. You seem full of ebullience, like you've recaptured a part of you that is very important. It doesn't sound like you were bad in doing these things. Sounds like you were playing and having fun, and not allowing others to cramp your style. Yet now you rarely show your colors.
Patient:	Now I see doing fun things as bad.
Therapist:	At some point you may have decided that the vivacious, playful part of you was bad and proceeded to repress it. And just this instant something changed when you allowed yourself to regain the lively, joyful part of you. I feel privileged for being able to witness you in this way with all your energy and spontaneity.
Patient:	(*laughs*) Thank you. I enjoy being this way. It makes me feel alive.
Therapist:	You decided to repress this lively part of you and you can decide to bring it back.

Patient: I need to be around people who appreciate the fun part of me instead of those who ignore my humor or put me down for being funny.

Following this session, the patient became more spontaneous and began expressing his excellent sense of humor in appropriate ways. He also manifested a greater degree of emotional maturity in his relationships. He had broken off the arid relationship with his explosive girlfriend, had gone back to New York on vacation and initiated a long, honest conversation with his father about his anger and his need for the father's recognition, and had vocalized his dissatisfaction towards a pushy project manager at work.

Session C

This final excerpt is from the patient's last treatment session. The session began with a review of his progress throughout the course of treatment and the constructive changes he had made in his life.

Patient: I feel that I now can deal with whatever comes up more constructively, more humorously. I don't feel as heavily burdened by the unpleasant events that can occur.

Therapist: The purpose of therapy is not to sanitize life so that people won't catch emotional viruses. It just gives you a structure for dealing with the problems more constructively.

Patient: (*laughs*) Things don't need to be cast in stone, I have room to move.

Therapist: You don't have to live in an emotional museum.

Patient: My therapy helped me get back in touch with some feelings which I thought I had lost, and I am more confident listening to those feelings. Things were real confused, almost out of focus. I think I'm back in focus now.

At the end of this session the patient was given a Treatment Evaluation Form to fill out and mail back to our office. The completed form was returned to the office a week later. At the bottom of the last page the patient had jotted, "This is a terrible form!", thus humorously expressing his understanding of the dynamics underlying his initial complaint about the "inconvenient format" of his billing statements.

It would be appropriate at this juncture to examine how humor was used to accomplish therapeutic goals in the case presented above. It is clear that humor fulfilled four specific functions in the patient's treatment:

1. Humor was used in making ACI connections for the patient's consideration (Session A).
2. Humor helped bring back the full range of the patient's emotional responsiveness, including those emotions that he had come to see as unacceptable (Session B).
3. Humor was helpful in extricating the patient from his aimless inner preoccupations and drawing him into the here-and-now process of treatment where his current preferences and emotions could come into play (Sessions A, B, and C).
4. The introduction of humor contributed to energizing the therapeutic relationship and furthering emotional rapport between patient and therapist. The humorous interchanges also provided the patient with the corrective emotional experience of establishing a successful relationship with a nonjudgmental representative of authority who could show emotion as well as give permission for the patient's appropriate expression of emotional material without fear of disparagement.

SYNTHESIS

This chapter has explored the functions, limitations, and potential of humor as a therapeutic tool within the author's Integrative Short-Term Psychotherapy treatment model. Nonetheless, humor can find relevant use within any treatment orientation when therapists are able to coordinate it with their overall theoretical perspective, attune it to their emotional style, and synchronize it in accordance with each patient's needs.

With this in mind we can now ask: What are some of the factors that therapists need to ponder when considering the use of humor in their interventions? First, it is important to find out where one is coming from regarding humor. If one is a spontaneously humor-

237

ous individual, then one can begin to introduce humor into therapeutic work with the appropriate patients and at the appropriate time. If one is a solemn or "neutral" therapist, one can question the assumptions held behind the solemnity and neutrality to see if such a stance is valid or even necessary. Both the humorously endowed therapist and the solemn or neutral therapist can benefit markedly from systematic training in the therapeutic functions of humor to fine-tune their skills in this aspect of clinical work.

It is time for humor to take its legitimate place as an important therapeutic tool. It is time to change the traditional image of the therapist as a neutral screen or as an unresponsive figure. The therapist's transparency and his or her appropriate expression of patient-related emotional reactions, including humor, can bring a sense of realism and warmth to the therapeutic process. Solemnity is not synonymous with either effectiveness or seriousness about one's work. Humor helps us do our work more seriously, more energetically, and more effectively.

Ultimately, humor represents a choice--a choice for fluidity over staticity, for hope over diffidence, for a finger in the pie.

REFERENCES

Becker, E. (1973). *The Denial of Death.* New York: Macmillan.

Carkhuff, R. R. (1969). *Helping and Human Relations: A Primer for Lay and Professional Helpers* (Vols. 1 & 2). New York: Holt, Rinehart & Winston.

Carkhuff, R. R., & Berenson, B. G. (1967). *Beyond Counseling and Psychotherapy.* New York: Holt, Rinehart & Winston.

Chapman, A. J., & Foot, H. C. (Eds.). (1976). *Humour and Laughter: Theory, Research, and Applications.* London: Wiley.

Chapman, A. J., & Foot, H. C. (Eds.). (1977). *It's a Funny Thing, Humour.* Oxford: Pergamon Press.

Greben, S. F. (1981). Unresponsiveness: The demon artefact of psychotherapy. *American Journal of Psychotherapy, 35,* 244-250.

Greben, S. F. (1984). *Love's Labor.* New York: Schoken Books.

Goldstein, J. H., & McGhee, P. E. (Eds.). (1972). *The Psychology of Humor.* New York: Academic Press.

McGhee, P. E., & Goldstein, J. H. (Eds.). (1983). *Handbook of Humor Research* (Vols. 1 & 2). New York: Springer-Verlag.

Salameh, W. A. (1981). *Personality of the Comedian: The Theory of Tragi-Comic Reconciliation.* Unpublished doctoral dissertation, University of Montreal.

Salameh, W. A. (1982, August). *From Discordant Childhood to Creative Adulthood: The Making of Stand-Up Comedians.* Paper presented at The Third International Conference on Humor, Washington, DC.

Salameh, W. A. (1983). Humor in psychotherapy: Past outlooks, present status, and future frontiers. In P. McGhee & J. Goldstein (Eds.) *Handbook of Humor Research. Applied Studies* (Vol. II, pp. 61-88). New York: Springer-Verlag.

Salameh, W. A. (1984a, April). Inviting Alice (and Allen) to humorland: On bringing humor into psychotherapy for fun and profit--Part I. *Academy of San Diego Psychologists Newsletter,* 1-8.

Salameh, W. A. (1984b, May). Inviting Alice (and Allen) to humorland: On bringing humor into psychotherapy for fun and profit--Part II. *Academy of San Diego Psychologists Newsletter,* 1-9.

Salameh, W. A. (1984c, August). *Humor as a Facilitative Therapist Trait in Psychotherapeutic Work.* Paper presented at the 92nd Annual Convention of the American Psychological Association, Toronto, Canada.

Salameh, W. A. (1985a, June). *Humor Immersion Training*^{TM}*--A New Technology for Humor Development.* Paper presented at The Fifth International Conference on Humor, Cork, Ireland.

Salameh, W. A. (1985b, August). *Integrative Short-Term Psychotherapy (ISTP)--A New Clinical Approach.* Paper presented at the 93rd Annual Convention of the American Psychological Convention, Los Angeles, California.

Salameh, W. A. (1986). The effective use of humor in psychotherapy. In P. A. Keller & L. G. Ritt (Eds.), *Innovations in Clinical Practice: A Source Book* (Vol. 5, pp. 157-175). Sarasota, FL: Professional Resource Exchange, Inc.

Salameh, W. A. (in press-a). Humor as a form of indirect hypnotic communication. In M. Yapko (Ed.), *Hypnotic*

and Strategic Interventions: Principles and Practice.
New York: Irvington.

Salameh, W. A. (in press-b). *Humor Immersion Training*™
*Manual: The Definitive Workout Manual for Exercising
Your Humor Muscles.*

Zeig, J. K. (1985, February). *Special Techniques of Ericksonian Therapy.* Paper presented at The First San
Diego Conference on Hypnotic and Strategic Interventions, San Diego, California.

HUMOR IMMERSION TRAINING™

Humor Immersion Training™ Workshops are conducted
by the author on a regular basis in San Diego, California,
and nationally. For more information on registering for a
HIT Workshop or arranging for a workshop to address
specific organizational needs, please contact: Waleed A.
Salameh, PhD, Director, San Diego Institute for
Integrative Short-Term Psychotherapy, 1335 Hotel Circle
South, Suite 207, San Diego, CA 92108. Telephone: (619)
260-1014. The following materials are used in the HIT
training workshops:

Salameh, W. A. *Humor and Your Mental Health.* Cassette
tape #HA01. (Ordered at above address.)
Salameh, W. A. *Relaxation Through Humorous Suggestions.*
Cassette tape #HA02. (Ordered at above address.)
Salameh, W. A. *Humor Immersion Training*™ *Manual.*

HUMOR IN
STRATEGIC FAMILY THERAPY*

Cloé Madanes

In this chapter, Cloé Madanes tackles the issue of using humor in strategic family therapy as she examines some of the interesting reverberations within families that can present the therapist with absurdly humorous configurations. Faced with exponential manifestations of absurdity by members of a given family system, the therapist can use humor to (a) penetrate the family system, (b) deflate the constrictive hold of a family's unwritten dysfunctional code of conduct, and (c) offer new alternatives that are formulated in the same symbolic language as that implicitly used by family members. Madanes uses humor in strategic family interventions by redefining problems in an unexpectedly humorous fashion and by organizing tasks that alter the patterns of interaction among family members. As illustrated in the chapter, the constructive denouements of such interventions are both surprising and exquisitely humorous.

Madanes's work belongs in the "paradoxical" tradition of therapeutic work advocated by Milton Erickson, Jay Haley, and Paul Watzlawick. The stuff of paradox is the stuff of unconscious motivations and needs, of unconscious wishes and fantasies. In the paradoxical perspective, interventions are switched to a different order of interpretation whereby therapeutic prescriptions may seem to run counter to the patient's rational expectations while simultaneously making excellent sense at the level of unconscious processes. Such work validates the proposition that some shuffling of patients' mental and emotional matrices may be a necessary part of psychotherapeutic work to help patients discover new alternatives and subsequently settle into an adaptive psychological equilibrium of their own choosing.

---

*This chapter is adapted from an earlier chapter by the author. Reprinted by permission from Cloé Madanes, "Finding the Humorous Alternative," in Behind the One-Way Mirror: Advances in the Practice of Strategic Therapy (San Francisco: Jossey-Bass, 1984, pp. 115-138).

241

Cloe Madanes is Co-Director of the Family Therapy Institute of
Washington, DC. Her recent publications include Behind the One-
Way Mirror: Advances in the Practice of Strategic Therapy (1984).

*   *   *

THEORETICAL PERSPECTIVE

Humor, like all man's efforts to make sense of the
world, involves the issue of classification. That is, an
event can be classified as sad or amusing, boring or
exciting, trivial or important, depending on the context
that defines it. In therapy, this context develops from the
interaction between the therapist and his or her clients.
A therapist can create a humorous context to lessen his or
her own power or authority, to help a client feel at ease,
or as part of the strategy to solve the presenting problem.
A situation can be defined in various ways, just as the
same story can be told as a comedy, a drama, a satire, a
romance, or a mystery. Therapy often can be seen as an
effort to change the genre--from drama to comedy of
errors, from tragic romance to adventure story, and so on.
Victor Frankl (1960) and Milton Erickson (1954) were
probably the first to introduce the idea of humor as a
legitimate aspect of therapy. Frankl's technique of paradoxical intention involved asking a patient wishing to get
over a symptom to deliberately try to have the symptom
right there in the therapist's office. For example, if a
patient were afraid of passing out, Frankl would ask him
or her to try to pass out right there in the office. Frankl
explained that a patient is usually perplexed by a request
to deliberately suffer the symptom that he or she has
come to therapy to resolve and laughs at the absurdity of
the situation. This laughter is what Frankl was after.
Frankl might not have been the first therapist to use
paradox, but he appears to have been the first to suggest
that change is related to finding humor in the situation.
Humor often is found by an observer but not by the
participants at that time. In his paper "Indirect Hypnotic
Therapy of an Enuretic Couple," Erickson (1954) describes
a young couple who consulted him because, shortly after
their wedding, they discovered that they were both lifelong enuretics. Erickson instructed them to deliberately
and simultaneously wet the bed every night for a period
of 2 weeks and then to sleep on the wet bed. As a result
of this directive, the involuntary bed wetting disappeared

after the 2 week period. It is doubtful that this instruction appeared humorous to the couple at the time it was given, but Erickson writes that they were amused when they came back to report the results.

Humorous interventions often do not appear humorous to family members and clients. It is only in retrospect, after the problem has been solved and people have a more optimistic view of life, that the humor becomes apparent. The uniquely human characteristic of being able to laugh at one's own predicament seems to disappear during serious conflicts and be recovered as these conflicts are resolved.

Probably humor was being used by therapists for decades, but it was Frankl and Erickson who brought it out of the closet in professional publications. Today there are numerous publications that deal with the subject, and it is accepted in a variety of therapeutic modalities.

TECHNIQUE

A therapist can follow either of two broad approaches in using humor to change the context of a person or the drama of a family. One is based primarily on the use of language to redefine situations. The other relies on organizing actions that change a course of events and modify sequences of interaction. Some therapists prefer one or the other approach, but some, like Milton Erickson, are masters of both. (The therapists in the examples presented in this chapter are: Richard Whiteside, MSW; Joe Pastore, MSW; Lyn Stycinski, PhD; Bette Marcus, PhD; Heidi Hsia, PhD; June Kaufman, PhD; Neil Schiff, PhD; Frank Schindler, PhD; Galen Alessi, PhD; Judith Mazza, PhD; and Patricia Davidge, MSW.)

TALK

Strategic therapy often involves changing the genre and can begin with a redefinition of the problem through the use of humor. For example, a 30-year-old alcoholic who refused to hold a job lived with his parents, who were retired and ill. The parents were preoccupied with the young man and spent their time bickering about him. They described him as a bum, without either a goal in life or a career. The therapist said that the young man was not a bum and that he did have a career, but that his career was not recognized or socially acceptable in our culture. His career was to entertain his parents, to keep them busy and focused on him rather than picking on each other. Was he on an alcoholic binge? Had he gotten in trouble with the law? Had he found a job and then lost it? All these concerns kept the parents entertained and kept him involved with them. He was like the recreation director on a cruise ship, keeping the old people amused, and he really should be making a salary at his job instead of receiving only criticism. Perhaps if he were appreciated instead of only criticized, he would develop more interesting ways of entertaining his parents than getting drunk and raising hell. Maybe he would take them to a movie, on a picnic, or even to a museum and provide a wider variety of recreation for them.

The therapist, who was close in age to the young man, said that he, in fact, respected and admired the son for having chosen a career that goes against the cultural values of our time, does not lead to a good income or to a contribution in some area of endeavor, and is not conducive to marriage and children, the things most men want to have. The therapist added that he himself had chosen a career as a therapist (against the wishes of his father, who wanted him to be a banker) and that he was not nearly as devoted to his own parents as the young man was to his, for he saw them only occasionally. This was because he, the therapist, had other interests; but, he remarked, because we are all different from one another, who is to say that one person's way is better than another's? Although the therapist's view was taken by the family as being more sarcastic than humorous, the young man improved and the parents went away on vacation for the first time in years. They said that if their son would not leave them, they would move to another state and leave *him*.

Language can be manipulated in infinite ways to be humorous and therapeutic. A middle-aged alcoholic was in therapy with an eager young man who was determined to cure him. The alcoholic was an expert at asking for help and then refusing to be helped, and he constantly complained about his problems while refusing to do anything to change his situation. He appeared to enjoy frustrating the young therapist, who responded to every rebuke with increased interest. The therapist was instructed to begin every statement he made during a session with the words, "I am not going to tell you," so that he would be negating what he would immediately say. The therapist said, for example: "I am not going to tell you that a man should not beat his wife," "I am not going to tell you that a man in your situation should be looking for a job," "I am not going to tell you that you should take care of your children." As the session progressed, the man became more and more irritated with the therapist, until finally the irritation turned to laughter and he began to ask, "What else are you not going to tell me?" By disqualifying his own statements in this way, the therapist was able to disengage from his intense involvement with the alcoholic and become more effective in influencing him.

Often the wisdom of popular humor lies in forcing us to realize that the unit is the system. For example, a favorite story about drivers is the one about the woman stalled in the middle of traffic. As she starts her car 20 times in a row only to have the engine die before she can move, a man behind her keeps blaring his horn even though he can see her predicament. Finally, the woman gets out of her car, goes to the driver behind her, and says, "I'm awfully sorry, but I don't seem to be able to start my car. If you'll go up there and start it for me, I'll stay here and lean on your horn." (This story, as well as several others in this chapter, were taken from Ralph Marquard, *Jokes and Anecdotes for All Occasions*, 1977.) The humor in this story is similar to that in an intervention in which the therapist promises a wife that he will criticize her husband himself if the wife is nice to the husband. Because it is necessary for someone always to be critical of the man, the therapist will take on the job and free the wife for a more pleasant interaction. In this case, as well as in the story about the drivers, the unit is a dyadic pair that is working together to maintain the status quo. Many techniques of therapy are similar to the punch line of a joke, as the punch line is so often the truth about interpersonal relationships. Wife and therapist can change positions, just as the two drivers can change positions, leading to humor.

Another approach that involves changing positions has to do with changing the perspective of a person in a family. A young couple consulted for divorce counseling when their divorce was about to become final. The husband was 22 years old and had an unstable job history. The wife was 26 and had married him when she accidentally became pregnant. At the time of her marriage, the wife's father had recently died, and she was living with her mother, who was trying to overcome her depression. The two women had decided that it would be nice to have a baby. The grandmother went to work to support her daughter and grandchild. Both women excluded the young man, who alternated between brave attempts to become a responsible breadwinner and aimless wanderings across the country. The wife sued for divorce, which was about to become final when the baby was 2 years old.

The couple came for divorce counseling to negotiate visitation and to improve communication so they could deal better with the child. However, the husband had the secret agenda of getting back together with his wife. In the second session, the husband's wishes were made explicit, and the wife made it very clear that she would not go back with him. Before the third session, the divorce became final. During that week, the husband unexpectedly appeared at the wife's house and demanded to be driven somewhere. The wife refused, and the husband took a knife and slit his arms longitudinally, shouting, "This will give you pleasure!" Then he grabbed the baby and ran down the street. The wife caught up with him and took him to the emergency room, where he got some stitches.

After this crisis, all available family members were invited to the next session. The young man, the wife, the baby, an uncle of the young man, and the young man's father, who came from another state, were present. The grandmother did not arrive until the session was over. The young man appeared depressed and humiliated. The therapist asked each person how he or she thought this kind of dangerous act by the young man could be prevented in the future. The wife and the young man said that surely he must be mentally ill. The father and the uncle said that the young couple had made a mistake in continuing to see each other when they were separated, that there should have been a cooling-off period with more distance between them. It sounded to the supervisor as if the two older men were right and the therapeutic error had been not to arrange for this distance. A strategy was planned to correct the mistake.

The therapist asked the young wife to leave the room with the baby because the therapist wanted to speak to the men alone. She then told the father and uncle that what the young husband needed was an attractive, strong young woman on his side to counteract the power of the ex-wife and her mother. He needed a woman with whom he could enjoy having sex and who would be jealous about and possessive of him. It was the duty of the father and uncle to help the young man find such a woman, because he obviously was not willing to do it by himself; otherwise, such a handsome young man as he would be involved with a woman already. In fact, he was probably occupied in fighting them off. Therefore, right after the session the father and uncle had to take the young man out on the town to pick up a girl, or at least to meet women.

The three men laughed, and the atmosphere of the session turned to something similar to that of a bachelor party. The young man said that he did not need help and could pick up a girl by himself quite well. The therapist would not hear of it. The father and uncle said that they both were married and their wives would not look favorably on this idea. The therapist said that she understood that this was a sacrifice she was asking of them and of their wives, and they would have to explain to their spouses that this had been a therapeutic recommendation. In fact, the therapist would be happy to write letters to the wives explaining the situation. Stroking their moustaches, father and uncle said that they would just have to sacrifice themselves and go out looking for girls. There was a great deal of joking and laughter as they planned where they would go. The young man forgot his depression and participated actively in the discussion, suggesting which would be the better places. The therapist said that that night would be just the beginning. From then on, father and uncle had to collaborate in finding women for the young man until he was involved in a sexual relationship with a strong, beautiful woman who would protect him from his ex-wife and her mother. There was more laughter, and the uncle suggested that attractive women could be found in places other than night spots--for example, in church. The idea was accepted, and further plans were made. The session ended with the three men taking off for a night on the town.

From then on, the sessions involved only the three men and had the same focus: the father and uncle were to advise the young man and help him find women. The father was put in charge of all decisions with regard to his son's life, and it was decided that there would be no visits to the ex-wife until he was involved with another woman. Arranging for this involvement was not an easy task. There were ups and downs, and it took more than 2 months for the young man to begin to have sexual relations with other women. Other issues were dealt with in various ways, and the ex-wife and grandmother were seen separately. The mood, however, remained changed. The humorous directive of asking the father and uncle to sacrifice themselves by helping the young man find women changed the focus of the therapy. Instead of dealing with mental illness, depression, loss, and separation, the theme of the therapy was fun and sex.

The humor in a story often consists of some kind of reframing or relabeling of a situation. For example, in the midst of a heated argument, a wife began beating her diminutive husband. In terror he ran into the bedroom and crawled under the bed. "Come out!" she cried. "No!" he shouted back from under the bed. "I'll show you who's boss in this house!"

In therapy, it is often useful to relabel the weak as powerful and the powerful as weak, and the truth is always a matter of interpretation. A young, beautiful wife was always cutting down and rejecting her husband while complaining that he was inhibited and did not express himself or communicate his feelings as she expected. The husband kept apologizing but defending his need to spend long hours at his office involved with his promising career. The therapist told the wife that, in fact, her criticism and rejection of the husband were extremely kindly to him, because he probably could not tolerate having a loving wife. He had not received enough love and caring from his father during his childhood (the husband had talked about this in therapy), and therefore he was not prepared to receive the love which he had been so badly deprived from anyone--particularly not from a beautiful wife whom he loved. If she was not critical and rejecting, if she were loving and devoted to him, he would be overwhelmed, might not be able to tolerate her affection, and might even leave her. Her rejection was really a manifestation of love that the husband should appreciate, because it was a way of staying close to him in a fashion that he could tolerate. The therapist said that she would work to improve the couple's relationship but that the wife must always maintain a certain level of rejection so that the husband would not get upset; the therapist did not want to improve the relationship to the point that the husband would leave the wife. For several weeks, the couple discussed in therapy what they could do to have more fun with each other and to have a better marriage, but always the therapist reminded the wife to be rejecting; and every session began with the therapist asking the couple whether the wife had been sufficiently rejecting since the last session. As a result, the wife became considerably less rejecting and the husband much more tolerant of having a loving wife.

A young man who was struggling to become an opera singer was referred to therapy by his voice teacher, who thought he could not reach certain notes because of emotional difficulties. The young man was in his mid-twenties, lived with his parents, held a menial job even though he had a college degree, and struggled to improve his singing. He spent a great deal of time keeping his mother company and was distant from his father, an engineer who was not sympathetic to the son's artistic vocation. The young man's difficulty in singing was solved in two sessions by asking him to deliberately make two mistakes: one that his teacher would notice and one that she would have trouble perceiving. As the young man struggled to make these mistakes, his skill improved, and he reached the notes that had presented difficulties. He said to the therapist, however, that his main reasons for coming to therapy were that he wanted to improve his relationship with his father and that he wanted his father to appreciate him. The therapist, a young, attractive, exotic-looking woman, said that she found his concern about his relationship with his father extremely interesting because it was so unusual. The young man asked why it was unusual, and the therapist answered that most young men in therapy these days are concerned with other things, so she had not had the chance to work with one who was mainly concerned about his father. She found this very moving and, although she did not know whether she could help him, she was certainly interested in the therapy because it would be a new learning experience for her.

The young man asked what things other young men were concerned about, and the therapist answered, "Oh, mainly having more sex and making more money. That is mainly what they want, and it is not half as interesting as your problem of improving your relationship with your father and getting him to appreciate you." The young man said that he, too, wanted to have more sex and make more money; in fact, he would like to spend some time talking about that. The therapist said she knew that that was not so and that he was mainly concerned about his father; what was so fascinating to her was that this was such an old-fashioned problem. Young men many years ago had brought that problem to therapy quite frequently, but nobody at the Family Therapy Institute had heard of a young man having that problem in recent years. The problem was so old-fashioned that it could not have even been the subject of an Italian opera--only of a German opera, because they were more boring. In fact, what the young man should do was write a German opera about a young man who wants to be appreciated by his father. There was a discussion of how such a story could go, the vicissitudes of such a young man, and how he would finally be appreciated by his father after a long life of suffering. (This approach was suggested in personal communication by Claudio Madanes, 1983.) The young man agreed to write the German opera, then actually wrote it and read it to the therapist. As he was working on it, his interest in his father diminished and his interest in sex and money increased.

In relation to these new interests, it became apparent that there were no women in his life at all. He talked about his difficulty in finding a girl he liked and in approaching such a young woman. The therapist said that that was not his difficulty at all. His difficulty had to do with tolerating rejection. Because it was so difficult for him to tolerate rejection, he could not approach women for fear of being rejected. Therefore, what he had to do was practice feeling rejected. For this purpose, he had to stand at a certain corner in front of a certain boutique and spend several hours during two weekends inviting women to have a cup of coffee with him. They would refuse and he would have the experience of being rejected and tolerating it. Surprisingly, so many women accepted the invitation that the young man did not really have the chance to experience rejection.

As he began to feel more comfortable with women, the young man explained that one of his fears had always been that he would be taken for a homosexual. Because of his work in the theater, he thought that he had certain mannerisms that could be thought of as effeminate. The therapist told him that that presented a wonderful opportunity and that he should practice leading a woman to believe that he was gay and then unexpectedly seduce

250

her. The young man said that, in fact, he had already had that experience. Once he and a friend, after unsuccessfully trying to find girls at a beach resort, had pretended to be homosexual and had been very successful at convincing two girls to go out with them. The therapist said that she had not realized that he had such a range and that it would be difficult to arrange for experiences of rejection for him.

The therapy ended when the young man became involved with a girl who was very interested in sex. He then had to find a better job so he could move out of his parents' house and have some privacy with her. By this time, he had lost interest in whether his father really appreciated him. His concern about his father, his difficulties with women, and his fear of homosexuality had all been reframed in humorous ways that led to change.

Not only in therapeutic interventions but also in interviewing technique, there is a parallel between popular humor and therapy. Take the story of the young man who is going on his first blind date and is nervous about not having anything to say. His brother advises him, giving him a formula that never fails: talk about family, food, or philosophy. Any of those topics is guaranteed to get a girl talking. So the young man goes to meet the girl, who is pretty and shy. Eager to make a good impression, he follows his brother's advice and begins to talk about the family. "Tell me, do you have a brother?" he says. "No," she answers. So he moves to the topic of food. "Do you like noodles?" "No," she says again. So the young man remembers his brother's advice. He'll talk philosophy. "Tell me," he says, "if you had a brother, would he like noodles?"

As in this story, in therapy it is often necessary to ask questions about apparently unrelated subjects in order to obtain information on which to base a hypothesis for change. When these questions are combined with a request to one family member to comment upon the relationship of two others (Selvini Palazzoli et al., 1978), the effect is often humorous: "If your mother and your wife were to talk about your job, would they agree that you should strive for a better position?" "If your husband and your son were to talk about you, what would they say?" "If you daughter were worried about you, what would she be worried about?" "Would your wife be worried about the same thing as your daughter, or would she worry about something else?" Such hypothetical questions, which address issues between two or three people that might not have been addressed explicitly before, are the kinds of questions that lead to information about metaphor, planning, and hierarchy. The more guarded and reserved the family, the more humorous and off-the-wall the questions appear. However, as soon as an important issue is addressed, the questions no longer seem absurd or humorous.

ACTION

Slapstick is a form of humor that involves actions often mocking violence. It is sometimes used in therapy as a way of redefining a situation through actions rather than through verbal statements. A couple in their sixties consulted because of marital unhappiness. One of their problems was the wife's complaint that the husband became irritated by what she considered to be her idiosyncrasies, which he should accept benevolently. One such idiosyncrasy was her habit of doing things quickly and walking fast so that he could not catch up with her. For example, she would hand him a cup of coffee and drop it on the floor before he could grab it. They would get out of the car to go to a movie, and she would rush ahead of him in a way that he considered rude. She was asked to show how she walked fast in the session, and she jumped out of her chair and sprinted toward the door. She was asked to do this once more, and this time the husband was to run after her, grab her, and give her a big Rudolf Valentino-style kiss. The couple did this with much laughter. They were asked to practice this scene during the next week. The wife was to purposefully run away from the husband, and the husband was to grab her and kiss her dramatically, whether they were with friends, in the middle of the street, in a restaurant, or whatever. The slapstick routine counteracted the irritation and resentment of the couple's interaction, and the humor freed them to try new ways of relating.

It is not uncommon, when humor is used in therapy, for a family member to attempt to establish a secret coalition with the therapist. This is usually conveyed by nonverbal means, through a certain look out of the corner of the eye and a certain smile, twisted to one side, implying that the therapist and that person are together in pulling the leg of another family member. In the previous example, when the husband was asked to act like

Rudolf Valentino, he said with a wink and a smile that he did not know who Rudolf Valentino was and had never seen that type of kiss, implying that he was too young to know. The implication was that the therapist and he would humorously coax the wife out of her bad habit, while, in fact, the therapist's plan was to change both their behaviors.

It has been said that in all humor there is an element of defiance, be it of authority, socially accepted norms, or rules. Defiance can be used in ways that are not only humorous but therapeutic, as antagonism is changed into playful challenge. Penn (1982) describes a technique to be used with young couples who may present marital, sexual, or communication difficulties and whose situation can be understood as resulting from the couple's difficulty in establishing a boundary around their relationship and protecting it from intrusions by and overinvolvement with in-laws. The couple is asked to visit both sets of in-laws; during these visits, the wife is to be overtly and exaggeratedly affectionate to the husband, holding his hand, whispering in his ear, kissing him, giggling, sitting on his lap. The husband is to respond by showing that he is pleased but shy and not rejecting. The couple is then to go home and make notes of the behavior they observed in the older couple as they performed their parts. Usually the in-laws send the couple home early, since it becomes clear that they have something going on between them from which the older couple is excluded. The young couple can separate more easily from their parents through playful defiance than through unfortunate confrontations. The same approach can be used when one of the spouses is involved in conflictual ways with siblings, friends, or other relatives.

Not only defiance but also violence can be turned to a humorous encounter in a variety of ways. One young couple consulted because of the fighting and violence in their marriage. They described a sequence in which the wife would criticize the husband, he would withdraw, she would pursue him, and, eventually, in frustration at his silence, she would start hitting him; to her shock, he would hit her back, sometimes quite painfully. They were both attractive, intelligent, and successful, but they could not change this interaction, which made them unhappy, horrified them, and prevented them from deciding to have children. The therapist conducted a long session exploring the consequences a happy relationship would have for both their extended families and asked them to think further about those issues. Then he suggested that, in the next 2 weeks, every time the wife provoked the husband's anger, and particularly when she hit him, the husband, instead of hitting her back, should put his hand up her skirt or under her blouse and fondle her. Some of their fights had been in public, so this behavior would also take place even if it had to be in public. The couple laughed and agreed to do this. The directive was repeated for 6 weeks, and the violence and fighting disappeared. However, the husband said that, although they had not had the opportunity to follow the directive because there had been no fights or provocations, he had had opportunity to fondle his wife in different circumstances. Therapy was terminated after 2 months; the couple had decided to have a baby and the wife thought she was already pregnant.

Often a story is humorous due to an incongruity between a situation and the framework in which it takes place. Woody Allen, for example, a masterful humorist, depends in many of his characterizations on the incongruity between two factors: his alleged prowess as a lover and his mousy physical appearance. As a writer, he also works on the humorous aspects of incongruities. In *The Stolen Gem*, a satire on detective fiction, a character says, "The sapphire was originally owned by a sultan who died under mysterious circumstances when a hand reached out of a bowl of soup he was eating and strangled him" (Allen, 1981, p. 21).

The element of incongruity is common both to humor and to paradoxical directives. A couple consulted about their 12-year-old son, who had been setting fires for 7 years. This activity endangered the father's job, because he worked for the government in situations in which he and his family repeatedly needed to obtain security clearance; this clearance was in jeopardy because of the child's firesetting. In fact, at an army party, the boy had set fire to explosives, an event that had driven the father to distraction. The mother could not leave the child alone in the house for 5 minutes for fear that he would burn it down. The father worked long hours and had little contact with the son. In the first session, the therapist had the boy demonstrate how he set a fire to see if he could do it properly. For this purpose a coffee can, papers, matches, and water were brought into the room. When the boy set the fire and put it out, the therapist criticized him severely, saying that he did not know the first thing about fires. He had not closed the match box; he had set the fire too close to the edge of the can so that a paper could have floated out and burned him; after pouring water in the can, he had put one hand inside too soon while touching the hot can with his other hand, and either hand could have been burned. All this, said the therapist, proved that the boy was completely incompetent about fires, and the irony was that he claimed to be an expert, judging from all the fires he had set. When the therapist left the room for a moment to empty the coffee can, the boy, who had listened to the therapist's harangue incredulously, said to his parents, "This guy is crazy."

The therapist came back and asked the father to demonstrate for the son how to set and put out a fire correctly. Then he told the father that he needed to spend more time with his son in a fatherly way--and what better way than to spend time teaching the boy about fires as he had done in the session? He was directed to supervise the boy in this endeavor, setting a variety of fires with different materials in different places and putting them out. Father and son were to do this six times a day every day. The mother was to keep notes on their activities. The parents complied and carried out the task for several weeks. Sometimes the father, because of his long working hours and difficult schedule, had to awaken the son in the middle of the night to set a fire. On several occasions, the indignant child said that the therapist was crazy, and on occasion the parents seemed to think the same. The spontaneous firesetting, however, stopped immediately, and soon the boy asked whether he and his father could spend the time in more constructive ways than setting fires. Eventually, the therapist consented to this suggestion, and father and son discovered common interests and enjoyed each other. The directive to set fires was incongruous in the context of a therapy designed to end the firesetting. The father was asked to encourage the son to set supervised fires rather than not to set fires at all. (This approach was inspired by Braulio Montalvo, who used a similar intervention to bring a mother and daughter closer together. For other cases of firesetters, see Montalvo, 1973 and Madanes, 1981b). The ordeal of setting fires, first in the session and then several times a day to the point of having to get out of bed to set a fire in the middle of the night, the therapist's criticism of the boy as an inadequate firesetter, and the child's indignation at the therapist were humorous. In fact, the child was so provoked that he set out to demonstrate to the therapist that he was competent in all areas, and his grades in school improved remarkably. There was a quality of the absurd in the therapist's directives. This element of ridicule is common to humor and to paradoxical directives.

An element of incongruity often is also useful in training therapists. Haley (personal communication, 1983) tells about his approach to a very shy student, who was terrified of Haley's supervision behind the one-way mirror. He instructed her to go into the therapy room to interview a family and to be sure to properly make three mistakes. Two of these mistakes would be obvious, and one mistake would be one that would not be evident to Haley. The student conducted the interview and after a while came out of the room to discuss the problem with Haley. He asked, "Did you make the three mistakes correctly?" She answered, "Screw you!" and was no longer overconcerned about his opinion. It is incongruous to ask a therapist to make mistakes properly in the context of teaching how to do therapy properly.

A therapist under supervision was a professor of behavior modification and was very concerned with telling people just what they should be doing. He had a difficult case of a little girl referred by her school for a variety of problems. She had been adopted by her grandparents after being abandoned by her mother. The therapist was instructed to deal with all problems by only saying to the grandparents, "I am curious to see how you will resolve that." This made sense in terms of increasing the grandparents' confidence as parents, but it was not the kind of directive approach the therapist was expecting to learn. However, he struggled to follow the supervisor's instructions, and the problems of lying, failing in school, and thumb sucking were dealt with only by saying, "I am curious to see how you will resolve that." The grandparents benevolently resolved all problems in a couple of months, and both the school and the therapist were impressed. Asking a student to make mistakes deliberately or to refrain from giving any directives is incongruous in the context of a directive therapy, in which the student is interested in learning how to give directives properly. However, just as with clients, it is usually only later that the student sees the humor in the situation.

An understatement of a problem can lead to humorous directives. A compulsive vomiter came to therapy after 17 years of bulimarexia, which had resulted in the loss of all her teeth, various somatic problems, and years of unsuccessful therapy. The therapist told her and her family that what she was doing was simply throwing away food by mushing it up in her stomach first and then throwing it into the toilet. Why not mush up the food with her hands instead and place it in the toilet directly? This would be less harmful to her body than having the stomach do the work. The family was to provide the food and supervise the process. Saying that 17 years of compulsive vomiting was simply throwing away food by passing it through the stomach first was an understatement of a severe self-destructive compulsion. The instructions were followed, however, and the vomiting disappeared eventually as a result of this and other paradoxical interventions.

A common element in popular humor and in strategic therapy is an ordeal designed to solve a problem, as in the cases of the firesetter and the compulsive vomiter. Take the story of the man who complains to the doctor about his uncontrollable cough. The doctor gives him a bottle of castor oil and tells him to go home, drink the whole bottle, and come back the next day. When he comes back, the doctor asks, "Did you drink the castor oil?" "Yes," says the man. "Do you still cough?" "Yes." The doctor gives him a second bottle of castor oil and tells him to drink it and come back the next day. The man follows the instructions and reports the next day that he is still coughing regularly. The doctor gives him yet another bottle and repeats the instructions. When the patient returns, the doctor asks, "Do you cough now?" The patient answers quiveringly, "I don't cough anymore. I'm afraid to."

This story is reminiscent of the ordeals often prescribed by Erickson to his patients (Haley, 1963). An old man complained that he could not sleep at night. He said that he only slept 2 hours even if he took sleeping pills and that his physician was worried about the amount of medication he was taking. Erickson found that the man, who lived alone with his son, felt he should do more housework, particularly waxing the floors, but he hated the smell of the wax. Erickson said to him, "I can cure you of your insomnia if you are willing to give up 8 hours sleep." The man said that he was willing to make that sacrifice. Erickson told him that he should get ready for bed that night and put on his pajamas at his usual time, 8:00; but instead of going to bed, he was to wax the floor all night. At 7:00 the next morning, he was to get dressed, have breakfast, and go to work as usual. The next night he was to repeat the procedure and polish the floors all night. He was to do this for four consecutive nights. Because he only slept 2 hours a night anyway, this only meant giving up 8 hours of sleep. The man went home and polished the floors for three nights. The fourth night he decided to lie down and rest his eyes for just half an hour. He awakened at seven the following morning. The next night he decided to go to bed at 8:00, and, if he could read the clock 15 minutes later, he would get up and polish the floors all night. A year later he was still sleeping soundly every night; he did not dare suffer insomnia for fear of having to spend the night polishing floors. Erickson says, "You know the old gentleman would do anything to get out of polishing the floors--even sleep" (Haley, 1963, p. 49).

PERTINENT USES

Humorous interventions in therapy include an element of surprise, of the unexpected. A humorous redefinition, explanation, or directive takes the family by surprise in a way that gives strength, drama, and impact to the intervention. Humor often allows the therapist's creativity to match the creativity of the symptom. To have impact a therapist must have the ability to tolerate ridicule, to appear absurd, to risk loss of face, since sometimes the laughs turn on the therapist in unexpected ways. Humor should not be confused with sarcasm, however. It is therapeutic to laugh with the client, not at the client. It is better for a therapist to ridicule himself or herself than a patient or a family.

What makes change possible is the therapist's ability to be optimistic and to see what is funny or appealing in a grim situation. Humor involves the ability to think at multiple levels and in this way is similar to metaphorical communication. When a therapist talks about a meal or a game of tennis in ways that are metaphorical of a sexual relationship, the humorous aspect of the communication becomes apparent as soon as the connection is made between the two levels. Thinking at multiple levels also involves the ability to be inconsistent, to be illogical, and to communicate in non sequiturs, jumping from one subject to another, associating what seems to be unrelated in ways that appear humorous and are therapeutic. In order to use humor in therapy, the therapist must have a sense of humor, whether or not the client does.

CLINICAL PRESENTATION

The author used a similar approach in the case of a woman who was a compulsive cleaner. She lived with her second husband and her daughter from a first marriage. The symptom had developed when she remarried and quit her job. She cleaned the house and everything in it constantly and compulsively. It took her hours to clean the kitchen after each meal and, to avoid the cleaning, her cooking was simple and uninteresting. Often her husband would bring home take-out food to prevent her from having to wash and clean the kitchen for hours after cooking a meal. Frequently, she had to get up in the middle of the night because she thought that somebody might have used a towel in the bathroom and she had to put it in the washing machine immediately. This aspect of her habit was particularly annoying to the husband, because the noise of the washing machine prevented him from sleeping. The woman did not have this problem when she visited her mother's house, which she did regularly, or other people's houses, nor did she have this problem in hotel rooms when the couple went on vacation. At home, however, the husband would sit by himself every evening and read the newspaper or watch television; then he would go to bed and continue watching television by himself, eventually falling asleep alone while the wife was still busy cleaning. He was 20 years older than the wife and, although he said that he cared about his wife and wanted to help her, he was very disagreeable and obnoxious to the therapist, insisting that he did not want to participate, that this was her individual problem to solve. He was somewhat annoyed at having paid for 5 years of psychoanalysis and for behavior modification and several experiences of the encounter and growth variety without results. The husband also objected to the fact that the couple had to drive 2 hours to come to the sessions. Obviously, the therapy would have to be extremely brief if it were to involve the husband.

A humorous ordeal is particularly appropriate to brief therapy and might succeed where other approaches have failed. Given the information provided in the first interview, it was postulated that the wife spent her time cleaning compulsively to avoid being with her husband. If this were so, it would follow logically that, if the consequence of exaggerated cleaning would be for the wife to have to be closer to her husband, then the situation would be reversed and she would clean less in order to avoid him. Based on this hypothesis, the therapist gave the couple two directives: a short-term intervention designed to introduce an element of playfulness into the relationship and a long-term recommendation that could continue to be effective without a continuing therapeutic involvement.

The first intervention was to tell the couple that every day for the following 2 weeks the wife would purposefully leave something in the house uncleaned. When the husband came home in the evening, he would search the house and try to discover what it was that she had not cleaned that day. If he discovered it, he would win and she would make dinner for him as usual. If he lost, he would take her out to dinner. However, it was important to insure the wife's truthfulness; for this purpose, before the husband came home, she was to record the item that she had not cleaned on a little slip of paper and stick the paper in her bra between her breasts. The husband had to find out whether he had won or lost by finding the slip of paper and reading it. In this way, the problem of compulsive cleaning would lead to the husband's fondling of the woman's breasts. This was a daring directive to give to a couple that was quite rigid and unimaginative. However, even though they might not follow the suggestion, the mere giving of the directive had introduced playfulness and sexual connotations into the situation. During those 2 weeks, the wife also was to make a detailed description of her cleaning and keep a log of the time she spent at it to use as a baseline for the next intervention.

In the next interview, the third, the husband said that he understood that the therapist wanted him to take a firmer position in relation to his wife and that he was planning to do just that. He had searched the house, failed to discover what she had not cleaned, and found the slip of paper a few times; he had not done this every day, but the couple had frequently gone out to dinner. The therapist reviewed the time log that the wife had brought to the session and proposed the following to the couple: A housekeeper works 8 hours a day; the wife was working now as a housewife and housekeeper since she had quit her job; therefore, it would be normal for her to clean 8 hours a day, but no more than that, as any hired housekeeper would. The husband said that only 5 hours a day of cleaning could possibly be necessary, but the couple finally agreed on 8 hours of cleaning during the week and 2 hours on weekends and holidays, as would be normal for a housekeeper. The wife said that that would be normal for another woman but not for her.

Then the therapist said that she had a cure and that if the couple followed her instructions the problem of compulsive cleaning would be solved--but they had to promise to follow her directive before she would tell them what it was. The couple refused to promise, so the therapist gave them the directive anyway. Every day the wife was to stop cleaning at 5:00. (She had reported that she never started before 9:00 a.m.) She then would shower and dress to look nice for her husband. When he came home, there would be no more cleaning; the wife instead could read, needlepoint, or do whatever she liked. She was only allowed half an hour to do the dishes after dinner. If she spent any time cleaning beyond that, the husband would force her to get into bed with him to watch television (which was what he enjoyed doing in the evening), and she would have to stay in bed with him until they fell asleep. If the husband preferred, instead of watching television together in bed, the punishment that he could enforce would be that the two would go out together either that evening or the next. The wife said that this would not work, and the husband said, "Excellent, I understand, excellent!" He commented that he had known all along that he should have taken a firmer position with her and that for this it was not worthwhile to come to therapy.

With this the couple terminated the therapy. They were followed up with phone calls every 3 months for the next 9 months, and they reported that the wife was cleaning only from 9:00 to 5:00 and for only 2 hours on weekends, Some days she preferred to go out and did not clean at all. However, the wife emphasized, the improvement had nothing to do with the therapy.

SYNTHESIS

In the case of the insomniac, Erickson knew that the man thought that he should wax the floors but did not want to do it. In the case of the compulsive cleaner, it was suspected that the woman thought she should spend more time with her husband but did not want to do it. The case of the insomniac is most similar to the story of the man with the cough in that in both cases a worse alternative to the symptom is offered (castor oil and waxing floors). In the case of the compulsive cleaner, a worse alternative is also offered (to get into bed with the husband or to go out with him); but this alternative is precisely the one behind the symptom--the one that, in the therapist's view, the woman had construed the symptom in order to avoid. She could not be with her husband because she had to clean. The therapist turned cause and effect around and proposed that if she cleaned she had to be with her husband. The purpose of the symptom was defeated.

Passing the ball is a well-known theory of mental health. If anything upsets you, you should immediately tell your story to others until you find someone who is willing to be more upset about it than you are. At that moment, you will feel good once again and be able to go about your business. Often a therapeutic intervention consists of arranging to pass the ball, as in taking turns.

Sometimes, however, the same goal can be accomplished with a contract. For instance, when a single mother and her son agree that every time the son brings home an A the mother will go out on a date, the problem has been passed to the mother. The problem has become the mother's loneliness rather than the son's academic difficulties. When an anorectic agrees that if the father does not drink she will eat, but if the father drinks she will starve herself, the ball has been passed to the father and his alcoholism becomes the issue. The humorous effect of these approaches is related to passing the ball, but the therapeutic effect consists of solving the original problem that was expressed through the symptomatic behavior, which was itself a misguided attempt at a solution (in the case of the student, the child's concern about the mother's loneliness; in the case of the anorectic, the anorectic's concern about her father's alcoholism).

REFERENCES

Allen, S. (1981). *Funny People.* New York: Stein & Day.

Erickson, M. (1954). Indirect hypnotic therapy of an enuretic couple. *Journal of Clinical and Experimental Hypnosis, 2,* 171-174.

Frankl, V. (1960). Paradoxical intention: A logotherapeutic technique. *American Journal of Psychotherapy, 14,* 520-535.

Haley, J. (1963). *Strategies of Psychotherapy.* New York: Grune & Stratton.

Haley, J. (Ed.). (1967). *Advanced Techniques of Hypnosis and Therapy: Selected Papers of Milton Erickson.* New York: Grune & Stratton.

Haley, J. (1976). *Problem-Solving Therapy: New Strategies for Effective Family Therapy.* San Francisco: Jossey-Bass.

Jackson, D. D. (1963). A suggestion for the technical handling of paranoid patients. *Psychiatry, 26,* 306-307.

Landau-Stanton, J., and others. (1982). The extended family in transition: Clinical implications. In F. Kaslow (Ed.), *The International Book of Family Therapy.* New York: Brunner/Mazel.

Lederer, S., & Jackson, D. D. (1968). *The Mirages of Marriage.* New York: Norton.

Madanes, C. (1980). Protection, paradox and pretending. *Family Process, 19,* 73-85.

Madanes, C. (1981a). Family therapy in the treatment of psychosomatic illness in childhood and adolescence. In L. Wolberg & M. Aronson (Eds.), *Group and Family Therapy.* New York: Brunner/Mazel.

Madanes, C. (1981b). *Strategic Family Therapy.* San Francisco: Jossey-Bass.

Marquard, R. (1977). *Jokes and Anecdotes for All Occasions.* New York: Galahad Books.

Minuchin, S., Rosman, B., & Baker, L. (1978). *Psychosomatic Families.* Cambridge: MA: Harvard University Press.

Montalvo. B. (1973). *A Family with a Little Fire* [Videotape training film]. Philadelphia, PA: Philadelphia Child Guidance Clinic.

Penn, P. (1982). Multigenerational issues in strategic therapy of sexual problems. *Journal of Strategic and Systemic Therapies, 1,* 1-13.

Selvini Palazzoli, M., Cecchin, G., Prata, G., & Boscolo, L. (1978). *Paradox and Counterparadox*. New York: Aronson.

Selvini Palazzoli, M., & others. (1980). Hypothesizing-Circularity neutrality: Three guidelines for the conduct of the session. *Family Process, 19,* 3-12.

Zeig, J. (1980). Symptom prescription and Ericksonian principles of hypnosis and psychotherapy. *American Journal of Clinical Hypnosis, 23,* 16-33.

THE USE OF
RATIONAL HUMOROUS SONGS
IN PSYCHOTHERAPY

Albert Ellis

Dr. Albert Ellis is, above all else, a rational man. His thoughts are cogent, incisive, and reassuring. In a world loaded with irrationality, his Rational Emotive Therapy (RET) brings a sense of proportion and cognitive clarity to the lives of those seeking psychotherapeutic help. In this stimulating chapter, we find that Dr. Ellis can shoot from the hip, as well as from the vocal cords. His use of humor in psychotherapy illustrates the role of emotional expression in RET, and how humor can be productively combined with "straight-line" therapeutic work to trigger both cognitive and emotional change for the patient's benefit. The chapter also demonstrates how therapeutic interventions can be greatly facilitated when humor is used as a refreshing reference point for introducing and anchoring cognitive structures.

Dr. Ellis is a distinguished clinical psychologist and the architect of Rational Emotive Therapy (RET). In 1985, he was the recipient of the American Psychological Association's Distinguished Professional Contributions to Knowledge Award. He is Executive Director of the Institute for Rational Emotive Therapy in New York City. His publications include Humanistic Psychotherapy: The Rational-Emotive Approach (1973) and Overcoming Resistance: Rational-Emotive Therapy with Difficult Clients (1985).

❊   ❊   ❊

THEORETICAL PERSPECTIVE

Although humor can be appropriately and effectively employed in almost any kind of therapy--even those, like psychoanalysis, that take the therapist and the client much too seriously!--it is particularly appropriate to rational-emotive therapy (RET). In fact, if I didn't have such a fine sense of humor myself, and were I not able to laugh uproariously at myself while I foolishly (and unfunnily) practiced psychoanalysis for several years, I surely would have never originated RET. And had I not been able to take the not so humorous barbs of RET opponents with a huge bucket of salt for many years, RET would never have survived, and certainly not have become as popular as it now is.

Rational-emotive therapy, at its very core, deals with the asinine overseriousness of humans that tends to drive them, as Alfred Korzybski (1933) once beautifully said, *un*sane. Its basic theory says that, when people have what we call "emotional" problems, they largely create them with their own crooked, irrational thinking. They tend to give profound significance to the events of their lives, which, to be healthy and happy, they had better well do! Yet they also give themselves, others, and the conditions under which they live *exaggerated*--or almost totally unhumorous--significance, thereby foolishly upsetting themselves. Foolishly? Yes, and quite *needlessly*.

The theory and practice of RET holds that we would rarely disturb ourselves seriously about anything when (a) all of us stop whining and screaming when we don't get our "needs" (meaning, our taffy) fulfilled; (b) when we rigorously (not rigidly!) stay with our strong desires and preferences and refuse to idiotically escalate them into dogmatic and absolutistic shoulds and musts; and (c) when we therapists remain flexible scientists who hold interesting hypotheses rather than doctrinaire "facts" and dogmas. We would then make ourselves, when faced with unpleasant conditions, decidedly sorry, regretful, frustrated, and concerned--but not panicked, depressed, enraged, self-pitying, or (especially) self-denigrating! We would stubbornly refuse to upset ourselves severely, and particularly refuse to hold onto our *mishigas* about anything--and I mean *anything*.

To help clients (and members of the general public) excavate and annihilate the irrational beliefs by which they largely create their "emotional" disturbances, RET uses a large variety of cognitive, emotive, and behavioral methods (Ellis, 1962, 1971a, 1973; Ellis & Becker, 1982; Ellis & Grieger, 1977; Ellis & Harper, 1975; Ellis & Whitely, 1979). General or unspecialized RET is synonymous with cognitive-behavior therapy (CBT) and is, in fact, the grandfather of CBT. Since I originated RET early in 1955, it has been used, along with CBT, with tens of thousands of clients. The RET approach has been widely disseminated in many talks, workshops, articles, books, cassettes, and films. Moreover, RET has a notably good research record: over 200 controlled experiments show that it is significantly more effective with disturbed individuals than are other forms of psychotherapy or waiting list groups (DiGiuseppe, Miller, & Trexler, 1979; Ellis, 1979; McGovern & Silverman, 1984). Secondly, over 250 additional studies indicate that the tests of irrationality--such as those developed by Jones (1958) and Sharkey and Whitman (1977)--that have been devised from the original main irrational beliefs that I posited in 1956 (Ellis, 1958, 1975), can consistently differentiate more disturbed from less disturbed individuals who take these tests (DiGiuseppe et al., 1979; Ellis & Whiteley, 1979).

Assuming that RET often (not always!) is effective, and assuming that it works because rational-emotive therapists directively and vigorously show clients their specific irrational beliefs while teaching them how to strongly challenge these beliefs and replace them with rational coping statements, then it can be presumed that these results follow from therapists seriously talking with their clients and inducing them to do what RET calls Disputing. Simply put, the ABC theory of RET says that whenever people desire to succeed at something or to win the approval of others, and when Activating Events (A) occur in their lives that tend to thwart them, and whenever they feel anxious, depressed, hostile, or self-downing at point C (Consequence), they mainly *make themselves* disturbed at point B--their irrational Beliefs. Therefore, according to RET theory and practice, they had better clearly identify their irrational Beliefs in order to logically and empirically Dispute them at point D. When clients significantly improve in the course of RET sessions, this is presumably what occurs.

RET Disputing is notably cognitive, and consists of examining, questioning, and challenging clients' (and other peoples') self-defeating Beliefs. But it is also distinctly emotive and uses many evocative, dramatic, experiential methods of helping people to Dispute their irrationalities. Disputing also invariably emphasizes behavioral methods in that virtually all clients are encouraged, instructed, and pushed to do homework assignment activities or other forms of *in vivo* desensitization that effectively contradict and Dispute their unrealistic and illogical ideas about themselves, about others, and about the world.

When, in the dim, dead days of my youth, I foolishly practiced classical psychoanalysis and psychoanalytically oriented psychotherapy, I rarely used humor in my explanations or interpretations. Freud forbid! But when I started to do RET in 1955 I soon found that almost all the irrational Beliefs that my clients fervently held, and with which they were royally befuddling or befogging themselves, had a clear-cut humorous, ironic, and undelightfully perverse quality. I discovered, for example, that almost all my nutty clients ironically held a highly mistaken idea: that they could control and change others. They simultaneously held on to another lulu of an idea: that they had virtually no control over and could not ever importantly change themselves.

Even more humorously, the vast majority of my clients devoutly believed that other people, by the mere use of words, gestures, and attitudes, could magically get into their guts and make them feel hysterical or enraged. My clients ended up believing that they could do nothing, absolutely nothing, to minimize or stop these self-sabotaging feelings!

Well, the list went on and on. I began to see that virtually all strongly held irrational beliefs that accompany and largely create human disturbance are silly, and I also came to recognize the even more hilarious and cockeyed fact that billions of humans all over the world imbibe, create, and maintain similar idiocies. Practically all these people are desperately striving, under conditions that are often hellishly rough, to make themselves happy and effective. Yet, lo and behold! With a rare degree of innate and acquired talent they are creatively unscrewing themselves!

TECHNIQUE

As I clearly noticed the almost incredible ironies and inconsistencies of human disturbance, I soon began to point these out to my clients (and friends!). I showed them that when they were furious at other people they ludicrously became obsessed with people whose behavior they despised. Moreover, when they made themselves panicked about succeeding, they almost invariably consumed so much time and energy with their worrying that they seriously interfered with their succeeding. I found that these forms of Disputing people's irrational Beliefs often (not always!) worked well, and I kept using them more and more in RET.

At the same time I began to use other forms of humor quite consistently in my individual and group psychotherapy sessions (Ellis, 1977a). Thus, when my clients insisted that they automatically or unconsciously kept overeating or smoking against their own wills, and when they denied that they used any Beliefs (at point B) to make themselves act self-defeatingly, I would say something like, "What do you keep telling yourself immediately before you cram that stuff down your gullet and into your craw? 'I hate food? I just eat to keep up my strength? I'll fix my dead mother by showing her that I can eat all I want without getting fat?' Or do you mean to tell me that the food automatically jumps out of the refrigerator, onto your plate, into your mouth and forces you to swallow it?" Using humor in this manner--and taking care to only attack my clients' *behaviors* and never their *personhood*, I began to get excellent results. Not that I made humor the core of my RET techniques, but I normally included it as one of the vivid and forceful techniques, along with some very serious discussion, teaching, and active Disputing of clients' irrational *must*urbation (Ellis, 1977a, 1977b).

As I was increasing my use of humor in RET, I also used serious and comic song lyrics to help clients overcome their irrationalities. My hobby for many years-- indeed, since I was 16--had been the composing of songs, and especially the setting of new lyrics to famous tunes, such as melodies of Tchaikowsky, Grieg, Johann Strauss, Jr., Victor Herbert, and Rudolf Friml. So when I became a rational-emotive therapist I wrote a number of songs that (I imagined) cleverly ripped up people's self-sabotaging ideas and helped them acquire self-actualizing philosophies. For example, one of my fairly serious songs was this one:

*ACHIEVING RATIONALITY
(Tune: *Oh, Susanna!* by Stephen Foster)

When I give up reality and start to go berserk,
At greater rationality, I work, work, work, work,
   work!

---

*This lyric and all the other lyrics in this chapter are copyrighted by the Institute for Rational-Emotive Therapy.

Emotional totality most properly includes
A lot of rationality, as well as loony moods.
I go crazy if I just sit and shirk,
Achieving rationality means work, work, work,
    work, work!

I used these humorous and serious songs, giving them
to my individual and group therapy clients and having
them sing them many times to themselves until the songs'
messages sank in and reinforced the other rational-
emotive self-messages. As far as I could tell, I often obtained excellent therapeutic results with these songs.

Then a landmark in my life as a therapist accidental-
ly occurred. I was invited by my associate, Dr. Robert A.
Harper, to appear on a symposium, *Humor, Play, and
Absurdity in Psychotherapy*, at the American Psychological
Association's Annual Meeting in Washington on
September 3, 1976. Along with papers presented by
Harold Greenwald and Will Schutz, I presented a paper on
Fun as Psychotherapy, showing how humor is used in RET.
I included in my paper several of the rational humorous
songs I had been composing since 1973. Somewhat to my
surprise, I was the hit of the convention--not for my
Bronx-accented baritone, but for the fact that I had the
guts to sing in public at an otherwise highly conventional
convention.

I saw that the humorous songs went over much better
than my previously used serious song lyrics. Consequently, I began to use them more and more with my clients
and my public audiences, and also made them available in
the form of a song book and a cassette recording published by the Institute for Rational-Emotive Therapy.
The rest is history. I now rarely give a talk or workshop
without requests for and inclusion of some of these rational humorous songs!

There are many ways of using rational humorous
songs in RET and in other forms of psychotherapy. My
associates and I at the Institute for Rational-Emotive
Therapy in New York use the songs in the following
ways:

1. When they first come for psychotherapy, all the
   clients at our clinic are given a packet of RET
   articles, such as *How to Maintain and Enhance Your
   Rational-Emotive Therapy Gains* (Ellis, 1984), and
   "Showing Clients That They Are Not Worthless

Individuals" (Ellis, 1965). Included in this packet is a double-faced sheet containing 16 song lyrics set to well-known tunes such as Strauss's *Beautiful Blue Danube*, Friml's *Rose Marie*, and Lady Scott's *Annie Laurie*.

2. From time to time, clients who are anxious are given homework assignments of singing to themselves, a number of times per week, an anxiety-attacking song. Clients who are depressed agree to take the assignment of singing to themselves a depression-attacking song. Perfectionistic clients may take this rational humorous song to sing to themselves:

PERFECT RATIONALITY
(Tune: *Funiculi, Funicula* by Denza)

Some think the world must have a right direction,
And so do I; And so do I!
Some think that, with the slightest imperfection
They can't get by--and so do I!
For I, I have to prove I'm superhuman,
And better far than people are!
To show I have miraculous acumen--
And always rate among the Great!

Perfect, Perfect rationality
Is, of course, the only thing for me!
How can I ever think of being
If I must live fallibly?
Rationality must be a perfect thing for me!

Depressed clients may take the homework assignment of singing to themselves, several times during the week, either or both of these antidepression songs:

WHEN I AM SO BLUE
(Tune: *Beautiful Blue Danube* by Johann Strauss, Jr.)

When I am so blue, so blue, so blue,
I sit and I stew, I stew, I stew!
I deem it so awfully horrible

That my life is rough and scarable!
Whenever my blues are verified
I make myself doubly terrified,
For I never choose to refuse
To be so blue about my blues!

I'M DEPRESSED, DEPRESSED!
(Tune: *The Band Played On* by Ward)

When anything slightly goes wrong with my life,
I'm depressed, depressed!
Whenever I'm stricken with chickenshit strife,
I feel most distressed!
When Life isn't fated to be consecrated
I can't tolerate it at all!
When anything slightly goes wrong with my life,
I just bawl, bawl, bawl!

3. In the course of RET group therapy and marathons, the group members are often encouraged to sing some rational humorous songs together--to liven the proceedings, to give them a lift, and to serve as a shame-attacking exercise for some group members (Ellis, 1971b). In RET shame-attacking exercises, people are encouraged to do foolish or "shameful" acts, such as singing aloud when they have a god-awful voice. By doing so, they can work on giving up their self-downing thoughts and feelings, so that they no longer perfectionistically feel ashamed.

4. I also use rational humorous songs in the RET workshops I conduct for the public, such as the infamous Friday Night Workshops I conduct every week at the Institute for Rational-Emotive Therapy. In the course of this workshop, I demonstrate actual sessions of RET with members of the audience who volunteer to have a public session and agree to talk to me and the other members of the audience about their personal problems. I often have the entire group sing out some of the rational humorous songs in unison, thus introducing them to the principles of rational-emotive therapy. Workshop members are also given a sheet of these songs to take home with them and to use for therapeutic purposes on their own.

5. RET clients (and readers of RET-oriented articles and books) are encouraged to compose their own rational humorous songs. They are further encouraged to use such songs for themselves and with their friends to help spread some of the sensible and sane philosophies of living promoted by RET.

PERTINENT USES

As noted above, RET is used with many different clients, particularly neurotics who have severe problems of anxiety, depression, hostility, self-pity, and self-downing. It is also commonly employed with people experiencing behavior problems such as addiction, procrastination, avoidance, shyness, and various kinds of low frustration tolerance or short-range hedonism (Ellis, 1962, 1985: Ellis and Knaus, 1977). It does not pretend to cure psychotics but is often helpful in getting schizophrenics and manic-depressives to accept themselves and their serious limitations more fully so that they can function more effectively in their social and work lives.

Rational humorous songs are used in RET with a wide variety of clients, including some highly disturbed individuals. But they have their limitations when employed with psychotics who may lack almost any kind of a sense of humor, and who may interpret them iatrogenically, such as paranoid schizophrenics.

Some of the common neurotic syndromes with which the songs have proved most helpful (with examples of suitable songs used in these cases) are these:

1. For clients with abysmally low frustration tolerance or discomfort anxiety:

WHINE, WHINE, WHINE
(Tune: Yale *Whiffenpoof Song*
composed by a Harvard man in 1896!)

I cannot have all my wishes filled--
    Whine, whine, whine!
I cannot have every frustration stilled--
    Whine, whine, whine!
Life really owes me the things I miss,
Fate has to grant me eternal bliss!
Since I must settle for less than this--
    Whine, whine, whine!

MAYBE I'LL MOVE MY ASS
(Tune: *After the Ball* by Harris)

After you make things easy and you provide the
gas;
After you squeeze and please me, maybe I'll move
my ass!
Make my life nice and breezy, fill it with sassa-
fras!
And possibly, if things are easy, I'll move my ass!

2. For clients with hang-ups about the past:

LET'S LEAVE THE OLD FOLKS AT HOME
(Tune: *Old Folks at Home* by Stephen Foster)

Let us suppose my goddamned mother filled me
with pap.
I listened and I let her smother--and carry on her
crap!
Let us suppose my crazy father called me a shit.
I heard it and I let it bother--and I still do my bit!
Sure my childhood was confining, full of lousy
strokes.
Now I am still depressed and whining, far from
my goddamned folks!
Though my past was rather stinking, I am free to
roam.
So let me change my nutty thinking--and leave the
old folks at home!

3. For clients who are love-slobs and who feel that
they must--yes, absolutely must!--be approved by
others:

I AM JUST A FUCKING BABY!
(Tune: *Meet Me in St. Louis, Louis* by Kerry Mills)

I am just a fucking baby, drooling everywhere!
How can my poor life Okay be if you do not
care!?
If you tell me No or Maybe, you will quarter me
and slay me!
For I am just a fucking baby!--please take care,
take care!

I AM JUST A LOVE SLOB!
(Tune: *Annie Laurie* by Lady Scott)

Oh, I am just a love slob, who needs to have you
    say
That you'll be truly for me forever and a day!
If you won't guarantee forever mine to be,
I shall whine and scream and make life stormy,
And then la-ay me doon and dee!

4. For clients who are irrationally hostile:

LOVE ME, LOVE ME, ONLY ME!
(Tune: *Yankee Doodle*--Unknown folk song)

Love me, love me, only me or I'll die without you!
Make your love a guarantee, so I can never doubt
    you!
Love me, love totally; really, really try dear;
But if you demand love, too, I'll hate you till I
    die, dear!

Love me, love me all the time, thoroughly and
    wholly;
Life turns into slushy slime 'less you love me
    solely!
Love me with great tenderness, with no ifs or
    buts, dear.
If you love me somewhat less, I'll hate your
    goddamned guts, dear!

5. For clients who refuse to accept reality:

GLORY, GLORY HALLELUJAH,
PEOPLE LOVE YA TILL THEY SCREW YA!
(Tune: *Battle Hymn of the Republic*
--Unknown folk song)

Mine eyes have seen the glory of relationships
    that glow
And then falter by the wayside as love passions
    come--and go!
I've heard of great romances where there is no
    slightest lull--
But I am skeptical!

Glory, glory hallelujah! People love ya till they
   screw ya!
If you'd cushion how they do ya, then don't
   expect they won't!
Glory, glory hallelujah! People cheer ya till they
   boo ya!
To recover when they screw ya, then don't expect
   they won't!

6. For clients who have secondary symptoms of disturbance, and who upset themselves about their
   upsetness:

BEAUTIFUL HANG-UP
(Tune: *Beautiful Dreamer* by Stephen Foster)

Beautiful hang-up, why should we part
When we have shared our whole lives from the
   start?
We are so used to taking one course,
Oh, what a crime it would be to divorce!
Beautiful hang-up, don't go away!
Who will befriend me if you do not stay?
Though you still make me look like a jerk,
Living without you would be too much work!

I WISH I WERE NOT CRAZY!
(Tune: *Dixie* by Dan Emmett)

Oh, I wish I were really put together--
Smooth and fine as patent leather!
Oh, how great to be rated innately sedate!
But I'm afraid that I was fated
To be rather aberrated--
Oh, how sad to be mad as my Mom and my Dad!

Oh, I wish I were not crazy! Hooray! Hooray!
I wish my mind were less inclined
To be the kind that's hazy!
I could agree to really be less crazy--
But I, alas, am just too goddamned lazy!

CLINICAL PRESENTATION

In the following case the use of rational humorous
songs was particularly effective. Dinah (fictional name)

276

came to see me for rational-emotive therapy after 7 years of psychoanalytic and Gestalt therapy, neither of which had helped alleviate her chronic severe depression. At the age of 33 she was almost continually depressed because her work as a teacher of emotionally disturbed children was full of frustrations and because she never had been able to maintain a meaningful relationship with a man. She had already been left by two husbands who found her to be unusually angry and depressed. Antidepressant medication helped her briefly; yet whenever anything went wrong in her vocational or love life, she reverted to severe feelings of depression and to thoughts about suicide.

I used several RET cognitive methods with Dinah--especially the Disputing of irrational Beliefs, the repetition of rational coping statements, cognitive distraction, and the reframing of her "horrors" as "inconveniences." I also used a number of emotive-evocative methods with Dinah including shame-attacking exercises, the use of very forceful self-statements, and recorded self-dialogues. Another emotive-evocative method I used was rational emotive imagery (Maultsby & Ellis, 1974), in the course of which she would imagine some of the worst things that might happen to her and make herself feel *only* appropriately sad and disappointed and not inappropriately angry and depressed.

Included in the behavioral RET homework assignments I used with Dinah were antiprocrastination assignments, and the employment of reinforcements when she did her promised lesson plans as well as self-imposed penalties when she avoided doing them.

This comprehensive cognitive-emotive-behavioral RET approach soon began to help Dinah, but her progress in overcoming her feelings of depression was slow. Finally, when she almost desperately asked for something *extra* to do that we had not already tried, I suggested that she vigorously sing to herself one or more of my rational humorous songs, at least 10 times a day. I also suggested that she sing some of these songs aloud (as shame-attacking exercises), and that she teach them to others.

At first, she thought that the use of rational humorous songs was a crazy idea and balked at implementing it. But I persuaded her to try this assignment experimentally for 3 weeks. She reluctantly agreed and started singing the songs to herself unenthusiastically for the first few days. To her surprise, they really reached her gut, and she often burst out into hilarious laughter when singing them. This so reinforced her that she soon found herself singing them with great gusto--sometimes silently, sometimes aloud to herself, and sometimes to her friends and relatives.

After 10 days, Dinah reported:

> I truly began to see the real irony of my depression and my over-rebelliousness. I saw how utterly childish I was to anger myself at my depressed mother--to demand that a nut like her act un-nuttily! And I fully realized that, just like she frequently upset herself, I whined and yapped about things I couldn't change--like those pathetically disturbed kids I teach. How ridiculous! I even began to understand--though this was very hard for me--that being loved by a man would be nice and soothing, but that it wouldn't change *me* as a person, nor give *me* the extreme pleasure of actively and creatively loving. And what especially got through to me was the point you have made several times--that who *needs* a needy person? And that the more I depressed myself about not being adored, the less lovable I made myself! For who enjoys a *whiner*?

Thereafter, Dinah still had her problems and from time to time again she made herself depressed and angry. But she did this much less frequently, intensely, and prolongedly. By regaling her students and friends with my rational humorous songs, she also found that she significantly helped some of them--which gave her a new and antidepressing vital absorbing interest.

Some of the songs that helped Dinah were included above, especially: *When I Am So Blue*; *I'm Depressed, Depressed*; *Whine, Whine, Whine*; and *I Am Just a Fucking Baby!* One more song that particularly helped her overcome her lifelong habit of procrastinating was this one:

OH, HOW I HATE TO GET UP AND GET GOING!
(Tune: *Oh, How I Hate to Get Up in The Morning*
by Irving Berlin)

Oh, how I hate to get up and get going!
Oh, how I love to procrastinate!
For the hardest thing I know

Is to hear the whistle blow,
"You gotta get on, you gotta get on,
You gotta get on and stop slowing!"

Someday, I promise that I will get going--
Someday, but never, of course, today!
I think I'll still procrastinate
And always get my ass in late,
And piss the rest of my life away!

SYNTHESIS

RET is, of course, hardly the only school of psychotherapy that almost routinely uses humor. As I previously noted (Ellis, 1977a, p. 3), "my therapeutic brand of humor consists of practically every kind of drollery ever invented--such as taking things to extreme, reducing ideas to absurdity, paradoxical intention, puns, witticisms, irony, whimsy, evocative language, slang, deliberate use of sprightly obscenity, and various other kinds of jocularity." But, as shown in other chapters of this volume, many nonRET practitioners also liberally use fun and frolic in their therapy.

I can safely say that RET uses humor on principle, not merely for practical reasons. It teaches that emotional disturbance does not stem from giving value or significance to things but from giving them *exaggerated* or *sacredized* importance. What we usually call neurosis largely follows from people demanding and commanding that (a) "I absolutely MUST do well and be approved by significant others!" (b) "You HAVE TO treat me kindly and fairly!" and (c) "The conditions under which I live unconditionally SHOULD be nice and easy!" Lots of luck on any or all of these Jehovian commands!

RET hypothesizes that if people consistently look at things skeptically, scientifically, flexibly, and humorously they will usually not make themselves seriously anxious, depressed, or enraged. Lots of luck on that one, too!

Humans *will* be human--that is, screwed-up and fallible. To help them be less disturbedly and more enjoyably human, RET advocates heavy doses of logic and humor. Why? Because, once again, neurosis largely consists of taking things *too* seriously. Thus, according to RET, when people make themselves feel anxious and angry, they do the following:

- Highly exaggerate the significance of things.
- Fail to see their light or funny side.
- Criticize not only their own and others' *acts* and *deeds* but thoroughly damn *themselves* and other *people*.
- *Overgeneralize* and see things in black and white, all-or-nothing terms.
- Awfulize and catastrophize about problems and inconveniences.
- Frame things in absolutistic, dogmatic, necessitous, *mus*turbatory ways.

What are the most effective antidotes to awfulizing, catastrophizing, I-can't-stand-it-itis, and shithood? Rationality and empiricism, says RET, and, of course, humor. What are some of the main cognitive, emotive, and behavioral advantages of using humor in rational-emotive therapy? First, here are a number of cognitive advantages:

1. Humor helps clients laugh at their failings and train themselves to refuse to take anything *too* seriously.
2. It relieves the monotony and overseriousness of some of the grave and heavy aspects of therapy.
3. It tends to help clients gain objective distance with respect to their self-defeating behaviors and makes it easier for them to acknowledge and attack their self-sabotaging.
4. It distracts disturbed people from some of their intensely anxious and depressed thoughts and feelings, makes them temporarily feel better, and allows them to be able to concentrate on the processes of change.
5. It punctures clients' grandiosity, which may be a basic cause of their emotional problems.
6. By nicely revealing human foibles, it shows clients how incredibly fallible they and others can be.
7. Humor exaggerates and counterattacks the overly serious exaggerations that lead to disturbances.
8. It gives alternative ideas and plans that help puncture overgeneralizing and black-and-white thinking.
9. It pithily presents realistic and rational philosophies, such as Mark Twain's observation, "My life has been filled with terrible misfortunes--most of

which never happened!" and Oscar Wilde's homily,
"Anything that's worth doing is worth doing badly!"

10. It is largely incompatible with the categorical im-
peratives and absolutistic musts that lie behind
most neurotic disturbances.
11. It interrupts and tends to break up old ingrained
and rigid habits of thinking.
12. Humor activates a philosophy of joy and happiness
that constitutes the basis for sane living, including
a philosophy of striving for long-range as well as
short-range pleasure.
13. It helps people see that they *can* control and
change their disruptive feelings, deal with their
practical problems, and have good options in the
present and future.
14. It paradoxically indicates that bad things can have
good aspects and that good things can have bad
aspects.
15. It can be used as an effective teaching device by
therapists to help get RET concepts across to
clients.
16. If people take a humorous attitude toward their
disturbances, they can accept the *challenge* of
seeing things unawfulizingly, of reframing "horrible" events differently, and of seeing the "good" aspects of "bad" things.

Humor, when used in RET, also has many emotive,
evocative, and dramatic advantages, such as these:

1. It shows how life, despite its hassles, can be quite
hilarious and enjoyable.
2. It distracts clients from their painful feelings and
gives them immediate constructive pleasure. It is
often incompatible with emotional pain and distress.
3. As Fry (1978) has shown, humor enhances creativity and spontaneity, which themselves constitute
rational goals of therapy.
4. RET-oriented shame-attacking exercises can be
done humorously--as when clients yell out the stops
in subway trains or buses or tell a stranger, "I just
got out of the loony bin. What month is this?"
Humor like this shows people that nothing is truly
"shameful" and that they can fully accept them-

selves even when others think they are acting very foolishly.

5. Humor particularly interrupts and destroys the feelings of rage and hostility that create much internal and external havoc in our world (Dworkin & Efran, 1967; Frenkel, 1971; Whitaker, 1975).

6. Humor can add a sense of play to life as well as to psychotherapy.

7. It can often provide more interesting and more dramatic ways of making rational points than are provided by grave discussion and debating. With humor, RET practitioners can often display more dramatic ways of teaching rational arguments.

8. By using humor, therapists can let their clients see them as people rather than as mere "professionals." In this respect, humorous interactions can often help therapists' relationships with clients.

9. Through humorous sallies, therapists can often manage to be more hard-headed and confronting than they would otherwise effectively be.

10. Humor has an emotive-persuasive quality that non-humorous rational persuasion may lack.

11. Evocative humorous language (such as that frequently used in RET) can get over to people more incisively and tellingly than dry-as-dust language. When a little old lady client says to me, "I feel worthless," and I reply, "Oh, you really feel like a total shit!" she tends to hear me much better-- for I am using the strong kind of language that she may use, not socially, but to herself.

Finally, RET-oriented humor can be effectively used as part of RET's behavioral methods. When so used, it has these action-oriented advantages:

1. It dramatically and incisively interrupts clients' old dysfunctional behavior patterns.

2. It can often be repeated, especially in the form of RET's rational humorous songs, so that it finally affects or "conditions" clients favorably.

3. When people keep using RET humor, especially its humorous songs, humorous messages tend to become unconsciously assimilated into their thoughts, feelings, and actions. These people then tend to "buy" the rational ideas embedded in this humor and explicitly or implicitly tend to act on these

ideas. This form of assimilation is similar to the process that occurs when the ideas incorporated in popular songs, which are often irrational, tend to "catch" people and to motivate their behavior.

4. Humorous statements and songs can strongly interrupt and interfere with clients' self-defeating obsessions or compulsions, thus helping to get them started on new tracks. As Fay (1977) notes, humor gives people a greater sense of freedom.

5. If clients take a humorous attitude toward some of their self-defeating behaviors, they can often get themselves to perform "terrible" and "horrifying" acts--such as riding on trains or elevators--that they phobically think they "cannot" face doing.

6. By showing people how foolish they appear to others, humor can motivate them to change their self-sabotaging habits and behaviors.

7. As Fry (1978) has shown, humor often stimulates people to cope with and overcome negative stress.

In conclusion, let me say that rational-emotive therapy makes the use of humor an integral part of its therapeutic armamentarium. In the process of doing so, it holds these truths to be self-evident:

- That masturbation is good and delicious but *must*urbation is evil and pernicious.
- That shouldhood almost inevitably leads to shithood.
- That lack of humor tends to create emotional tumor.
- That absolute "truths" are almost absolutely false-- and most probably disturbing.
- That overgeneralizations are generally overdone.
- That self-esteem (rather than self-acceptance) is one of the greatest of human disturbances.
- That there are no human subhumans.
- That just about all people seem to be FFHs--fallible fucked-up humans.
- That life, for virtually all of us, is spelled H-A-S-S-L-E; but that, with clear and flexible scientific thinking, we can stop making HASSLES into HORRORS.
- That nothing is awful or awe-ful--only, at worst, a pain in the ass.

- That if you want to start winning you'd better stop whining.

REFERENCES

DiGiuseppe, R. A., Miller, N. J., & Trexler, L. D. (1979). A review of rational-emotive psychotherapy outcome studies. In A. Ellis & J. M. Whiteley (Eds.), *Theoretical and Empirical Foundations of Rational-Emotive Therapy* (pp. 218-235). Monterey CA: Brooks/Cole.

Dworkin, E. S., & Efran, J. S. (1967). The angered: Their susceptibility to varieties of humor. *Journal of Personality and Social Psychology, 6,* 233-236.

Ellis, A. (1958). Rational psychotherapy. *Journal of General Psychology, 59,* 35-49.

Ellis, A. (1962). *Reason and Emotion in Psychotherapy.* Secaucus, NJ: Citadel Press.

Ellis, A. (1965). Showing clients they are not worthless individuals. *Voices, 1,* 74-77. (Rev. ed.: New York: Institute for Rational-Emotive Therapy, 1983)

Ellis, A. (1971a). *Growth through Reason.* North Hollywood, CA: Wilshire Books.

Ellis, A. (1971b). *How to Stubbornly Refuse to be Ashamed of Anything* (Cassette recording). New York: Institute for Rational-Emotive Therapy.

Ellis, A. (1973). *Humanistic Psychotherapy: The Rational-Emotive Approach.* New York: McGraw-Hill.

Ellis, A. (1975). *How to Live with a "Neurotic"* (rev. ed.). New York: Crown Publishers.

Ellis, A. (1977a). Fun as psychotherapy. *Rational Living, 12,* 2-6. (Also: Cassette recording. New York: Institute for Rational-Emotive Therapy.)

Ellis, A. (Singer). (1977b). *A Garland of Rational Songs* (Cassette recording). New York: Institute for Rational-Emotive Therapy.

Ellis, A. (1979). Rational-emotive therapy: Research data that support the clinical and personality hypotheses of RET and other modes of cognitive-behavior therapy. In A. Ellis & J. M. Whiteley (Eds.), *Theoretical and Empirical Foundations of Rational-Emotive Therapy* (pp. 101-173). Monterey, CA: Brooks/Cole.

Ellis, A. (1984). *How to Maintain and Enhance Your Rational-Emotive Therapy Gains.* New York: Institute for Rational-Emotive Therapy.

Ellis, A. (1985). *Overcoming Resistance: Rational-Emotive Therapy with Difficult Clients.* New York: Springer.

Ellis, A., & Becker, I. (1982). *A Guide to Personal Happiness.* North Hollywood, CA: Wilshire Books.

Ellis, A., & Grieger, R. (1977). *Handbook of Rational-Emotive Therapy* (Vol. 1). New York: Springer.

Ellis, A., & Harper, R. A. (1975). *A New Guide to Rational Living.* North Hollywood, CA: Wilshire Books.

Ellis, A., & Knaus, W. (1977). *Overcoming Procrastination.* New York: New American Library.

Ellis, A., & Whiteley, J. M. (Eds.). (1979). *Theoretical and Empirical Foundations of Rational-Emotive Therapy.* Monterey, CA: Brooks/Cole.

Fay, A. (1977). *Making Things Better by Making Them Worse.* New York: Hawthorne.

Frenkel, R. E. (1971). Clinical management and treatment of rage. *New York State Journal of Medicine, 71,* 1740-1743.

Fry, Jr., W. F. (1978, March). Humor, health, and hanging in, or out, or on--as the case may be. *Humor Events and Possibilities,* pp. 1, 3.

Jones, R. (1968). *A Factored Measure of Ellis' Irrational Belief System with Personality and Maladjustment Correlates.* Unpublished doctoral dissertation, Texas Tech University, Lubbock, TX.

Korzybski, A. (1933). *Science and Sanity.* San Francisco: International Society of General Semantics.

Maultsby, Jr., M. C., & Ellis, A. (1974). *Technique for Using Rational Emotive Imagery.* New York: Institute for Rational-Emotive Therapy.

McGovern, T. E., & Silverman, M. S. (1984). A review of outcome studies of rational-emotive therapy from 1977 to 1982. *Journal of Rational-Emotive Therapy, 2,* 7-18.

Sharkey, C. T., & Whitman, V. L. (1977). Development of the Rational Behavior Inventory: Initial validity and reliability. *Educational and Psychological Measurement, 37,* 527-534.

Whitaker, C. (1975). Psychotherapy of the absurd: With special emphasis on the psychotherapy of aggression. *Family Process, 14,* 1-16.

THE "CONSPIRATIVE METHOD": APPLYING HUMORISTIC INVERSION IN PSYCHOTHERAPY*

Michael Titze

In this chapter, Dr. Michael Titze presents a novel European concept of therapeutic work derived from a singular combination of Alfred Adler's teleoanalytical approach and Viktor Frankl's logotherapy. In examining the childhood origins of neurotic behavior, Titze concludes that children develop neurotic tendencies when their healthy expressions of aggressiveness are met by unhealthy counter-aggression from adults (parents, educators). Consequently, many patients harbor a fear of counter-aggression from authority figures that can result in an over-respect for authority, a continuous repression of emotional reactions including anger, or a distortion of aggression under the guise of characterological defenses and acting-out patterns. In attempting to resurrect the patient's assertiveness, Dr. Titze utilizes the patient's private logic to create a humoristic inversion of roles wherein the therapist may be seen as a fallible and democratic individual toward whom the patient can express dissent or disrespect without fear of punishment. This humoristic inversion of the therapist's presumed grandiosity allows the patient to voice assertiveness appropriately while experiencing a lifting of normative constraints via the introduction of humor. Of course, such an inversion cannot occur in a haphazard manner. It needs to be structured by the therapist based on his or her theoretical framework and clinical training. It also requires that the therapist moves beyond the stance of "therapeutic abstinence" in order to understand and function within the patient's own reality, using humor as a balancing variable.

*I am deeply grateful to Dr. Viktor E. Frankl, Vienna, who opened my eyes to recognize the healing power of humor! I am also greatly indebted to my co-worker, Dieter B. Kragl, Bremen, who has significantly contributed to the application of humor in counseling.

287

As he "conspires" to bring humor into psychotherapy, Dr. Titze manages both to inspire and to challenge some of our assumptions about psychotherapeutic work.

Dr. Titze is a clinical psychologist in private practice in Tuttlingen, West Germany. His publications include two clinical volumes authored in German, Lebensziel und Lebensstil (1979) and Heilkraft des Humors. Therapeutische Erfahrungen mit Lachen (1985).

      ✴   ✴   ✴

THEORETICAL PERSPECTIVE

When I began my professional career as a clinical psychologist, I was especially interested in paradoxical interventions. Such interventions seemed to be particularly effective for unraveling the puzzling behaviors of some of my patients. My first effort was to compile everything in the literature that fell under the category "paradoxical." I found that Alfred Adler, as early as 1914, had used paradoxical strategies to treat patients. Two early students of Adler, Rudolf Dreikurs and Erwin Wexberg, further developed these techniques into a systematic therapeutic method called *antisuggestion* (Dreikurs, 1944; Wexberg, 1929).

My research also led to my discovery that Viktor E. Frankl, a well-known exponent of modern psychotherapy, was one of Adler's close associates in the 1920's. In one of my early publications, I compared the specific rationales of the Adlerian *antisuggestion*, Frankl's *paradoxical intention*, and the innovative contributions of the Palo Alto group (Titze, 1977). I began to particularly appreciate Frankl's work, and now see him as the original mentor of humoristic psychotherapy.

At that time, unfortunately, I did not accept the connections between paradoxical methods and the realm of humor. My daily work in psychiatric hospitals and in private practice constantly involved people suffering from severe psychological disturbances. They were passive, depressive, self-destructive, and humorless. Classical therapeutic methods derived from behavior therapy and psychoanalysis seemed ineffective, so I began to use paradoxical methods. Despite some consultants' comments that such methods might have dangerous and uncontrollable effects, I found that even severely disturbed patients were not nearly as traumatized by these interventions as expected, even when such paradoxical interventions were explicitly meant to be shocking and provocative.

> Once in a group therapy session a young woman wept away intensively without any restraint. (In this respect, Adler used to speak of "water power"). All group participants were evidently deeply impressed and struck with this expression of weakness and helplessness. I instinctively realized at that moment that the compassion of the other patients and nurses at hand was not very helpful for the patient. Thus, I said to one of the nurses: "Go and get an old tin bucket, so that she can fill it up with her eye-piss!" Everyone was shocked at my use of such strong language, particularly the patient in question. Completely scandalized, with her eyes wide open, she stared at me. The flood of tears dried up. Feeling completely assured of the consent of her comrades, she had a go at me and screamed: "What a mean guy you are! How dare you insult an ill woman like me!" My reaction was "hyperbolic" in Frankl's sense of the term: "You are right. I am the meanest ass in the world. Now I have the deepest guilt. I think I am just going to cry. So let's fill the bucket together with our precious liquid!"

The entire group, including the patient, laughed uproariously, which showed me the important connection between aggression and the self-liberating power of laughter. Years later, I commented on the aggressive roots of many humor genres in a monograph concerning the special importance of laughter in therapy (Titze, 1985a). The reasons why I no longer apply such a provocative form of humorous intervention, however, will be explained later.

THE PRECONDITIONS FOR BEING MENTALLY INSANE

Especially stimulated by the works of Adler and Freud, I finally realized the power of humor for invalidating the inhibitions and constraints that dominate the emotions of psychologically disturbed people. These self-defeating inhibitions can be traced to certain cultural ideals of education that promote rigid conformity to what Freud called the "reality principle," and what I call the "normality principle." This implies forced efforts by adult educators to make children obey those who set the rules concerning good behavior. Failure to conform elicits negative responses from those adults with whom the children interact.

Thus, most children are regularly confronted with both open and hidden forms of aggressiveness perpetrated by adults who have power over them. Subsequently, children have difficulty learning to appropriately express their aggressive potential.

Ethologists like Eibl-Eibesfeldt (1970) and Lorenz (1966) have clearly pointed out the importance of aggressiveness as a precondition of assertive conduct for every creature, including man. Alfred Adler also made the "striving for power" a central theme of his theory of personality. Innate aggressiveness that is inhibited through socialization may lead to misguided forms of aggressive behavior. When such behavior is directed against the environment and consists of antisocial tendencies, it is often labeled as "psychopathic." Psychopaths are irresponsible and unstable in their attitudes toward life. They are predominantly hedonistic and show no concern for those against whom they may direct aggressive and often destructive behavior.

Neurotics, on the other hand, are restrained in their assertive attitudes against their social environment and tend to direct aggression against themselves in a self-defeating manner. I am convinced that those who are forced to give special consideration to implicit moral standards in the course of their socialization process, within the context of strict educational measures, end up taking things especially seriously in their later life. A characteristic fear of negative consequences (punishment) constitutes one of the most important motives of their regressive actions. In his theory of the "superego," Freud assumed that the "censor," emanating from the internalized normality principle, is a particularly inflexible force that intensifies the individual's feelings of guilt. Obsessional neurosis represents a clear instance of how strictly and scrupulously conscience sets its demands. No wonder neurotic individuals display a typically serious and humorless self-expression. They quite literally have nothing to laugh about! Further theoretical considerations on this topic have been presented elsewhere (Titze, 1979c; 1984).

COMING TO UNDERSTAND THE IMPORTANCE OF AGGRESSION

From this theoretical substructure I formulated my specific therapeutic intentions. Because neurotics have difficulty coping with their own aggressiveness, the therapist would not be advised to confront them directly with aggression. This difficulty stems from having repeatedly faced counter-aggression during their early development. The therapist should therefore avoid being identified with persons who have exercised power and superiority over the patient by not bringing aggression into the therapeutic relationship. If the therapist tries to provoke the patient in order to modify his or her behavior with regard to certain normative expectations (cf. Farrelly & Matthews, 1981), the result could be a struggle for power between patient and therapist, and these well-known phenomena of resistance and negative transference may evoke detrimental forms of aggression in the patient. Consequently, I have tried to find ways of promoting my patients' assertiveness without expecting them to be adjusted to certain normative expectations.

MULTIPLE THERAPY

Dreikurs's (1950) innovative technique of *multiple therapy* has been particularly helpful. It involves two therapists, which allows the patient to experience different roles (role casting). One therapist becomes the patient's opponent (*advocatus diaboli*), while the other takes the role of a good and caring ally. The extraordinary possibilities provided by this form of therapy have been most effective (Titze, 1979a).

Once a psychiatrist on a psychiatric ward asked for consultation in the case of an extremely negativistic patient. This man had decided to reject all food offered to him by the nurses. So I informed the psychiatrist about multiple therapy and eventually convinced him to join me in applying this method. We both met the patient, who was extremely emaciated, in the psychiatrist's office. He did not take any notice of us and sat

291

down with his face turned toward the wall. I previously instructed the psychiatrist not to take heed of the patient but to inform me in his presence about the negative sides of his conduct. The psychiatrist then told me in a low voice (people usually listen more carefully if one is talking about them in a low voice, for this is perceived as a kind of threatening conspiracy against themselves) that the patient had refused to take any food for a long time and that he had beaten the nurses when they tried to feed him. Furthermore, he reported other negative aspects of the patient's conduct.

After he had spoken in this way for about ten minutes, I interrupted him harshly: "Shut up," I shouted, "I can't stand listening to you gossip about this pleasant and brave man! You insolent guy, how dare you violate the dignity of this man in such an impertinent manner! Do you know what I would have done if I were in his place? In addition to what he did in his bold fight for his human rights, I would have puked in my bed."

Suddenly the patient, who had not paid any attention to us yet, looked at me and said: "That's exactly what I did long ago!" I then turned my back to my co-therapist to address the patient. Now it was my turn to speak very softly, making suggestions to him about how to tyrannize the nurses and the doctors in the future. I believe that this session represented my first implementation of the "conspirative method."

THE CONSPIRATIVE ALLIANCE

Unlike my previous directive form of therapeutic confrontation (cf. p. 2), in the session above my attitude towards the patient was not provocative. Instead, I orchestrated an aggressive atmosphere for the patient by instructing the psychiatrist to criticize and blame him. This inevitably evoked counter-aggression by the patient. However, his behavioral repertoire did not include suitable patterns that would allow him to act aggressively in a constructive and overt way. We can assume that the patient's inability to act assertively is somehow connected to his premorbid development, that is, the interactional patterns in his early socialization. In fact, there was evidence that during his childhood the patient had been prevented from counteracting properly to the aggressive behavior of others, which probably explains his pattern of self-defeating aggression. His acute refusal of food reflected this pattern and seemed to provide the most vital expression of his negative attitude towards life. The attending staff had treated the patient's refusal of food as merely maladjusted behavior, which led to a combative relationship with him. This little spark of active assertiveness should have been nurtured, not extinguished, in order to restore the lost *élan vital*.

When I role-played the patient's position, I became his substitute in assertiveness by attacking the psychiatrist as the most powerful representative of the repressive ward. Note that I used strong language in my intervention-- expressions that are usually connected with strict taboos. Effective jokes use such expressions in order to generate the liberating power of laughter in the audience. Real laughter arises, as pointed out by Hobbes (1968), Koestler (1964), and Paul (1963), when a person who seems to be threatening to another is brought down. This "inversion of grandiosity" is one of the most important stimulants for laughter.

By vicariously showing the kind of aggression the patient had been unable to activate on his own, I decisively facilitated my conspirative alliance with him. However, I was not yet aware that many years earlier Jackson (1963) had treated paranoid patients in a very similar way! When the patient remarked that he had vomited in his bed before, he was beginning to interact with me, and I was able to conspire with him. The stage was set for us to start chatting about all those marvelous wicked things he had not yet dared to talk about. It was rather unimportant that I was the one to verbalize his aggressive thoughts, because the patient was emotionally engaged. I had noticed him smiling faintly, which signaled to me that he felt fully understood and accepted by another person.

THE CONSPIRATIVE METHOD

Following this experience, I was ready to gradually and systematically work out the preconditions for the conspirative alliance method. It no longer seemed particularly useful or necessary to use a multiple therapy setting. The second therapist, in his or her function as the

293

"advocatus societatis," has a disturbing effect. Because the second therapist symbolizes the internalized censure of conscience, the patient may have difficulty acting freely. It became increasingly evident that the conspirative alliance could only unfold efficiently through confidential dialogue. Thus, I practice accepting my patients' needs as much as possible: I try to accept their "unknown goals" (Adler, 1927), "their hidden reasons" (Dreikurs, 1971), and their lifestyle. Because I fully identify with the patient's genuine problems, I can mirror them through concrete actions and verbalizations, thereby showing patients how to accept themselves.

I consistently try to strengthen those components of the patient's self that constitute the "young child within" (Adler, 1927). It is this realm of one's basic personality where Freud's "pleasure principle" dominates and where the so-called "primary processes" originate. These motivational processes generate exactly those rule-less, irrational, irresponsible, egoistic, or affectlogical (Ciompi, 1982) tendencies that predominate not only in the thoughts and actions of infants and lunatics, but also in the creative dynamics of humor and jokes. I try to promote those processes that produce the liberating humoristic reaction which occurs when a rebellion against reality constraints (Freud, 1905/1960) takes place. By keeping the censures and self-reproaches of conscience away from the patient's basic personality, the "young child within" can come forth. The following example clearly demonstrates this point:

> Once a patient complained that he possessed certain weaknesses of character which "with the best will in the world" he simply could not overcome. He confessed, rather shamefully, that he masturbated, drank, smoked, and talked about other people behind their backs. In a seemingly unaffected voice, I asked him what was wrong with these behaviors, to which the patient replied: "Of course, you can't imagine things like that! You as a doctor just don't have problems like that!" Whereupon I countered: "What do you mean, problems? I jerk off several times a day and gain tremendous relief and liberation from it. Then I thoroughly enjoy smoking cigarettes. And when I get to my favorite bar in the evening, I

regularly get pissed and say nasty things about my associates!"

My response had broken several social taboos in one stroke, inevitably challenging the patient's rigid conscience yet also triggering a liberating effect on the young child within him.

First, of course, he expressed his incredulity by being amazed and indignant: "I absolutely can't believe that *you* would do things like that. You are simply kidding me!" Now it was my turn to put myself in his place in order to help him accept himself and have the courage to be imperfect: "Are you trying to suggest to *me* that it isn't good? *I* get a lot of fun out of it and *I* don't mind admitting it. But please, do not inform anyone about that, you know. It's simply my private business and has absolutely nothing to do with therapy. What I'm telling you, I wouldn't, by any means, have told all those feeble-minded dummies having no fun in their lives! *Make sure, therefore, not to talk to anyone else about this.* That's really confidential, you know!"

The application of the conspirative formula, as figured out above for the first time, made the invalidation of the pretended augustness of my professional status credible for the patient. If I had not applied this formula, the patient might have thought that I was merely pulling his leg. Despite my "superior" professional position, I voiced fears of social criticism similar to his, and thus became a kind of fellow-sufferer.

THE THERAPEUTIC RELEVANCE OF EQUALITY

Over-respect for the superiority and augustness of authorities stems from fear of negative sanctions for one's own assertiveness. It represents one of the most important components of the feelings of inferiority as described by Adler. Every form of psychopathological disorder is, I am convinced, based more or less on those feelings of over-respect for authority. Such an attitude supplants the liberating element of disrespect that, according to Freud (1928, 1905/1960), is the precondition for humoristic phenomena and healthy self-assertiveness. It is one of the central paradoxes of psychotherapy that the therapist must not be a "therapist" in order to efficiently apply the type of interventions mentioned above. The ability to transcend the therapist role is not related to the therapist's *function* as a helping person, but only to his or her professional role assessment! An effective therapist inevitably gives up the superior position derived from professional status ("expert," "guru," "master").

This "social equality," as advocated by Rudolf Dreikurs (1971), allows the patient to identify with the therapist as a model for self-accepting assertiveness only when he or she can view the therapist as an *imperfect* person--someone who has certain weaknesses yet can still have fun in life. Occasionally, it may even be useful for the therapist to humiliate himself or herself regarding his or her professional role. That is more regularly the case if the therapist is dealing with severely disturbed patients suffering from acute depressions or psychotic disorders.

> A depressive patient who could not get up in the morning did not appear for the first interview at my office at the appointed time. When he came late to the next session, he excused himself by saying that he was "always half there" in the morning.
>
> I did not take any notice of this (obviously hitherto efficacious) excuse but declared: "Well, you couldn't have done anything better than show me what a little nobody I am! Normally I sit here fat and complacent behind my desk and I'm used to people trotting in here punctually to the second. This morning as I was foolishly sitting around here, after a long time I really did feel like a twit. And yet I can't really be angry with you. I find it very plucky of you not to fall in with all the shitty conventions of society. I think I have learned something from you!"
>
> After a long silent lapse during which the patient was looking at me with unbelieving astonishment, I continued, "I implore you not to tell anyone about my emotional lapse which you have experienced right now!"

Because of this conspirative intervention, many things happened. In the patient's view, I had forgotten my role as a therapist, and by doing this I demonstrated to him that I was as imperfect as he was. Furthermore, I also introduced the subject of aggression without involving any of the counter-aggressions that the patient had learned to fear so much. By using the conspirative formula, the patient's anticipation of counter-aggression was invalidated.

The patient was at first unprepared to enter into this alliance; obviously, he was still too distrustful. After a long period of silence, he finally asked if I was angry with him. I answered: "Angry, *I* should be angry with you? But that is totally illogical! I'm doing okay. I make a pile of money without making a special effort; everyday I watch people humiliate themselves in front of me and generally I have the feeling of being a great guy. And then look at you: persecuted by bad luck, tormented and looked down on by mean and vulgar people! So why should I be angry with *you*? Quite the opposite: How on earth do you work it that things are bad for you and good for me and other slobs? Today you really brought it home to me that you are not such a poor wretch after all but that you possess something like human dignity. Because *I* was the one who waited for you today, I suddenly realized who was dependent on whom! But, for heaven's sake, don't tell anybody about what just happened between us!"

In the follow-up, and still in line with the conspirative alliance, I declared that if I were he, I would deal with the "other slobs" in the same way. In other words, I would fail to keep appointments at the employment office, would not turn up for invitations, and so on. I thus vicariously lived out for the patient that forbidden assertiveness he only dared to activate under the guise of his pathology. In this instance, I was making use of the technique of sarcasm, such as revelling in the idea of how fine it was to make fools of other people. Finally, I used strong language that, once again, proved to be very appropriate for bringing up aggression-related issues.

TECHNIQUE

I developed the conspirative method to help manage manifold problems that occurred during therapeutic work. Therapists trained in analytical or depth psychology procedures face various difficulties in addressing relationship problems occurring in therapeutic interactions. On the other hand, the conspirative method takes advantage of the genuine possibilities that arise from adopting a humoristic approach towards life and the world. This approach often generates an inversion of normative constraints, in many respects similar to creating a good joke (Koestler, 1964). Accordingly, the therapist can get acquainted with the young child within the patient, which constitutes the specific field of work for analytic psychotherapy.

Direct confrontation with the unconscious core of personality is a great challenge to the therapist, because the phenomena of transference and countertransference may be involved. Because humoristic inversion usually includes those aggressive or disrespectful tendencies that are crucial to living assertively, the central theme of aggression inevitably arises during the analytical therapeutic relationship. Confrontive and provocative techniques must be critically and carefully handled to avoid reinforcing a patient's sense of powerlessness and inferiority. In my experience aggression can be productively dealt with only when social equality, as facilitated by the conspirative setting, has been achieved.

TRAINING IN DEPTH PSYCHOLOGY

The conspirative alliance method demands subtle intuition and a level of skill that comes from comprehensive analytical training, and it should be reserved for individual rather than group psychotherapy. In my own work, I favor the teleoanalytical approach of Adlerian psychology (Titze, 1979c), enriched by the findings of Frankl's logotherapy. I am convinced that the unconscious causes and motives of human behavior stem from the "conflicts of conscience," where internalized censure is at work with its inhibiting and self-defeating effects, especially for the neurotic.

PERTINENT USES

The process of humoristic inversion, as facilitated by the conspirative method, can release the patient from those unwholesome normative constraints that he or she believes to represent perfectly adapted adult behavior. Addressing the patient in abstract and conventional language would reinforce this image of the normal adult, so humoristic therapy uses exactly the kind of concrete language and figurative expressions that children and humorists use. The conspirative therapist does not aim at personifying a stance of therapeutic abstinence as demanded particularly by orthodox psychoanalysis. He or she would not merely pontificate on the causes of the patient's problems in an emotionally detached manner. Rather, by being sincerely attuned to the patient's frame of reference, the therapist constantly tries to promote the patient's ability to gain distance from his or her unpleasant and painful feelings. Frankl (1978) has demonstrated that this self-liberating attitude can be best achieved by means of a paradoxical intervention. In this method, the "awful distress" that patients usually suffer is not merely analyzed in the framework of a conspirative alliance but can eventually be seen from a humorous angle. The patient and therapist thereby unite in "tragic optimism" that marks the attitude of the real humorist (Frankl, 1967). When the conspirative method is handled with true empathic care and skill, it can be used with many neurotic and psychotic patients and is especially helpful for paranoids. The conspirative method might be contraindicated in working with antisocial personalities (psychopathic disorders). Because these individuals are primarily motivated by the pleasure-principle, that is, the needs of the young child within them, a method constructed for invalidating restraints might be counterproductive. The following example, nonetheless, illustrates the effectiveness of the conspirative method even for a patient experiencing behavioral dyscontrol problems.

I was once attacked by a hyper-aggressive dissocial woman who was treated in a closed psychiatric ward. She had punched her fist into my face, so that my glasses fell to the floor. (I admit that it was not easy for me to keep my self-control and remain relaxed). Yet it was clear to me that this woman, who had suffered so much from other people's aggression, would have been reinforced anew in her antisocial attitude if I had grown furious. Moreover, expression of fear and insecurity on my side would have been just as disadvantageous, as this might have reinforced the patient's destructive aggressive patterns.

For these reasons I turned away from her to ask a nurse to take the patient to my office. Violently punching and slapping several ward members, she was eventually forced to go there. This had caused so much sensation within the ward that, in a short period of time, a crowd of people gathered in front of my office door.

After having tugged the patient into my office, I dismissed the nurses and locked the door. Furiously spitting, the woman got ready to start another attack. Now was the time to initiate my conspirative maneuver. So I turned to her whispering: "For God's sake, I need your help badly! Before I entirely lose face in this ward and become the laughing stock of everyone here, I must do something to regain respect. Otherwise, I can pack up my bags! That's why I ask you to scream for help as loudly as you can. At the same time we should both clap our hands to make people think I'm beating you up. But this absolutely has to remain our secret!"

Puzzled, but signaling fun, the patient spontaneously agreed to take part in this mad show. This marked the beginning of a mutually positive relationship and later allowed us to have numerous rather constructive talks.

CLINICAL PRESENTATION

Years ago, a suicidal patient came to see me unannounced. I had treated this man a few years earlier in a psychiatric hospital. He was presently suffering from severe depressions and had decided to kill himself that very day. Work, family, leisure time--in short, his whole life--seemed senseless and unbearable to him. He stood there in front of me, speaking very softly. He stressed that all therapists, including me, had completely failed in helping him. Consequently, he had come to my office not to seek treatment but simply to say goodbye.

In his bag he had a rope for hanging himself. He also brought along his Last Will and Testament. Bursting into tears, he read his last message to his wife and children. For his wife, should she decide to marry again, he wished a better and, especially, a more courageous man than he had been. Further, he urgently admonished his children not to allow a competitive society to dispirit them. When he started to read the last part, where he begged his family not to entirely forget him, he completely broke down.

I waited for a couple of minutes, and then responded, "You've totally convinced me that your life isn't acceptable for you anymore. As a therapist I actually shouldn't tell you this because it is certainly illegal and, furthermore, somehow a surrender in the face of your tremendous difficulties. That's why I ask you urgently not to tell anybody, especially your wife, what I'm just going to tell you now: You should do what you decided to do! Firstly, you will overcome all the miseries of your life. Secondly, you will demonstrate to everyone the tragedy of your existence, and, last but not least, think of the guilt of those people who did you wrong. Anyway, it will be too late for them! But I object to one point: If you kill yourself right away, people will think of you as a dead loss, unable to cope and compete with others in society. Your children will feel pity for you and will say that their father was too weak and too good a man to get along in life! Your enemies and competitors will say, ' We always knew he was a weakling. Now he backed out of life!' So let me make you a proposal: Give yourself 1 more month in order to square away the accounts you still have with other people. Do everything you didn't dare to do up to now because of fear and for other reasons. Having only 1 more month to live, you can, without further problems, afford to be ruthless and severe. In your final 4 weeks of life you can treat all the loony bastards you can't stand in quite a brutal way. When you take your final step after 1 month, people will remember you as a strong and tough person. If you agree, and I'm convinced you will, come back after exactly 1 month from now. Then it will be me with whom you will have your last chat. There will be a bottle of brandy on this desk, so we can have a drink together. It will be an honor for me, after all, to fulfill that task for you which is normally due to a priest!"

Shortly after I had started talking to him, the patient had raised his head and stopped crying. He seemed to be puzzled, yet listened very carefully to me. When I eventually presented my hand to him in order to seal the contract, he did not take it. I accepted this and accompanied him to the door. Finally I said, "All I told you now is strictly confidential and has to remain a secret! Don't tell anything to anyone, especially not to your wife. Nevertheless, I want to see her tomorrow. I will then find out if you kept the secret."

The patient's wife came in the next day with a bouquet of flowers. She was quite enthusiastic, smiling happily as she reported that her husband had come home the day before in a completely different mood than his usual one. She told me that he had grinned and even laughed like he had not done for many years. Furthermore, she said that her husband had gone to work voluntarily that morning. He had been so frolicsome the day before that he had stayed up with her long after midnight to talk while drinking a bottle of wine.

I did not comment on her report but asked her sternly, "Did your husband inform you about the conversation we had yesterday?" "No, not directly," she answered. "That means he did!" "No," she replied, "not really, but please tell me what happened yesterday."

Seriously and decisively, I said, "I am not permitted to give away a secret. I can only say as much as this: Imagine that you are the wife of a sailor bound for a very long voyage in exactly 1 month minus 1 day. What would a sailor's wife do in such a short period of time? Think about this very thoroughly and try to act appropriately to this very situation! But I can't tell you more." After this short conversation, I asked her to return in exactly 1 month and then dismissed her.

This intervention clearly illustrates the conspirative method. The patient had come in with a problem he considered too grave to bear. So everyone normally would think that the therapist ought to act "very therapeutically." Yet, simultaneously, the patient had clearly indicated that in his case a "therapeutic" approach would be unsuccessful. (Recall that the patient had accused all therapists who had ever treated him of having failed totally.) If I had acted "therapeutically," I would have been working in total opposition to the patient. What else, but "It is not as bad as you think," or, "You should think it over once more," and so on, could I, from a conventional standpoint, have told him? However, when I pretended to have surrendered in that very field where I was supposed to be the expert, he could then experience an unexpected victory.

In this way I used the patient's "private logic" (Adler, 1927) so that I would be able to "walk in his own shoes"

(Titze, 1985a). Obviously, the patient had low self-esteem resulting from defeats in his life tasks (work, family, and communal activities). Consequently, my goal was to restore his self-reliance and anchor a recognition of his own worth. My procedures countered his feelings of powerlessness by encouraging him to prove to posterity what a strong and courageous person he was. By doing so, the patient trusted me to be on his side and not in opposition to him. Furthermore, the way that I expressed my surrender as a therapist offered him an opportunity to regain prestige and superiority.

Although my procedure was not therapeutic in a conventional sense, it surely followed the unusual and perplexing strategy of humoristic inversion as it operated within our conspirative alliance. Now the patient was no longer an outsider with respect to his suicidal intentions. On the contrary, he had gained an enthusiastic supporter who not only wanted to make a contract with him but even hoped to get the chance of acting as a priest. The patient must have recognized that all this was very peculiar as his wife told him that she, too, had received secret and unusual information during her session with me.

One month later the whole affair came to an interesting resolution. On the appointed date the patient came in, bringing along his diary entries concerning the last month. (These entries were printed in full length in Titze [1979b].) He reported on the recent developments in his life. Above all, he told me that he had succeeded at following his own way. He had simply told others, disrespectfully, what he thought of situations he did not enjoy or appreciate. He had also avoided trouble and self-defeating forms of anger by doing things completely on his own, whereas he had previously always insisted on the help and assistance of others. "Consequently, I couldn't get annoyed," he reported to me. Altogether, he had decided to carry on with life. We agreed upon an appointment for a joint therapy session for himself and his wife in 1 more month. Yet, instead of coming in, his wife called and informed me that there was no need for a session as far as she and her husband were concerned. She reported that they were getting along quite well. I agreed, and she ended the conversation with the comment, "Nevertheless, it must be nice for you if people can do without your help!"

SYNTHESIS

Psychotherapy has made far too little use of the theoretical and methodological implications connected with the phenomenon of humor. Consequently, a main objective of this chapter has been to examine some therapeutic applications of humor.

The humorous therapist--who may appear paradoxical or even crazy (Jackson, 1963)--can have rapid and direct access to the sphere of unconscious and irrational events within the psyche, designated as "primary processes" (Freud, 1905/1960), or, as I prefer to say, the "young child within the patient." The therapist then, quite logically, becomes the expert in a particular type of *weltanschauung*, which produces its own logic and its own symbolic codification (Ciompi, 1982; Titze, 1985c). Inevitably, such a therapist will gradually begin to think and to speak differently from the normal, everyday person. He or she will learn to see the world through the eyes of the young child that the patient once was, and will decipher it from this perspective. He or she will also use a corresponding "parabolic" (figurative, concrete) language, which is even stronger than normal colloquial speech, thereby inevitably reaching the young child within the patient and becoming an ally. To facilitate this process, the therapist must provide the following conditions:

1. Create an atmosphere of empathy.
2. Focus on experiences related to the here and now.
3. Identify unconditionally with the patient's needs and expectations,
4. Become a model for assertive acceptance of exactly those needs and expectations.
5. Reflect to the patient in a conspirative way how he or she can be assertively self-accepting.
6. Finally, stimulate the patient to gain a life attitude that may be correlated to "the wisdom of the fools," which takes nothing seriously (Titze, 1985a).

We are undoubtedly just beginning our exploration of the highly promising therapeutic possibilities offered by humor, and numerous perspectives in this therapeutic arena may be considered (Salameh, 1983). Any therapist taking into account the fascinating realm of humor cannot help becoming a true humanist (O'Connell, 1976) and will therefore stop treating patients as objects and join hands with them under the auspices of real equality.

REFERENCES

Adler, A. (1927). Zusammenhange zwischen Neurose und Witz. *Internationale Zetschrift für Individualpsychologie, 5,* 94-96.

Bergson, H. (1911). *Laughter: An Essay on the Meaning of the Comic.* New York: Macmillan.

Ciompi, L. (1982). *Affektlogik.* Stuttgart: Klett-Cotta.

Dreikurs, R. (1944). The technique of psychotherapy. *Chicago Medical School Quarterly, 5,* 4-7.

Dreikurs, R. (1950). Techniques and dynamics of multiple psychotherapy. *Psychiatric Quarterly, 24,* 788-799.

Dreikurs, R. (1971). *Social Equality.* Chicago: Henry Regnery.

Eibl-Eibesfeldt, I. (1970). *Ethology: The Biology of Behavior.* New York: Holt, Rinehart & Winston.

Farrelly, F., & Matthews, S. (1981). Provocative Therapy. In R. Corsini (Ed.), *Handbook of Innovative Psychotherapies* (pp. 678-693). New York: Wiley.

Frankl, V. E. (1966). *Man's Search for Meaning.* New York: Washington Square Press.

Frankl, V. E. (1967). *The Doctor and the Soul.* New York: Bantam Books.

Frankl, V. E. (1978). *The Unheard Cry for Meaning.* New York: Simon and Schuster.

Freud, S. (1928) Humour. *International Journal of Psychoanalysis, 9,* 1-6.

Freud, S. (1960). *Jokes and Their Relation to the Unconscious* (J. Strachey, Trans.). New York: Norton. (Original work published 1905)

Hobbes, T. (1968) *Leviathan.* Harmondsworth: Penguin.

Jackson, D. D. (1963). A suggestion for technical handling of paranoid patients. *Psychiatry, 26,* 306-307.

Koestler, A. (1964). *The Act of Creation.* London: Hutchinson.

Lorenz, K. (1966). *On Aggression.* New York: Harcourt, Brace, and World.

O'Connell, W. E. (1976). Freudian humour: The eupsychia of everyday life. In T. Chapman & H. Foot (Eds.), *Humour and Laughter: Theory, Research and Applications* (pp. 313-329). London: John Wiley & Sons.

Paul, J. (1963). *Vorschule der Ästhetik.* Munich: Hanser.

Salameh, W. A. (1983) Humor in psychotherapy: Past outlooks, present status, and future frontiers. In P. E. McGhee & J. H. Goldstein (Eds.), *Handbook of Humor Research. Vol. II. Applied Studies* (pp. 61-88). New York: Springer-Verlag.

Titze, M. (1977). Ist die "paradoxe Intention" eine individual-psychologische Technik? *Zeitschrift für Individualpsychologie, 2,* 103-112.

Titze, M. (1978). Die "konspirative Methode" der Teleoanalyse. *Partnerberatung, 15,* 145-149.

Titze, M. (1979a). Das "Sicherungsparadoxon" und seine individual-psychologische Behandlung durch zwei therapeuten. *Partnerberatung, 16,* 8-12.

Titze, M. (1979b). Der Einmonatspakt. *Partnerberatung, 16,* 196-201.

Titze, M. (1979c). *Lebensziel und Lebensstil.* Munich: Pfeiffer.

Titze, M. (1984). Individualpsychologie. In H. Petzold (Ed.), *Wege zum Menschen* (Vol. 2, pp. 7-100). Paderborn: Junfermann.

Titze, M. (1985a). *Heilkraft des Humors. Therapeutische Erfahrungen mit Lachen.* Freiburg: Herder.

Titze, M. (1985b). Konspirative Methode. In R. Brunner, R. Kausen, & M. Titze (Eds.), *Wörterbuch der Individualpsychologie* (pp. 236-237). Munich: Reinhardt.

Titze, M. (1985c). Denken. In R. Brunner, R. Kausen, & M. Titze (Eds.), *Wörterbuch der Individualpsychologie* (pp. 67-69). Munich: Reinhardt.

Wexberg, E. (1929). *Individual Psychological Treatment.* London: The C. W. Daniel Company.

"THAT'LL BE FIVE CENTS, PLEASE!": PERCEPTIONS OF PSYCHOTHERAPY IN JOKES AND HUMOR

Edward Dunkelblau

Dr. Edward Dunkelblau provides us with an illuminating change of pace. His chapter does not follow the format adopted for the other chapters. His goal is not to elucidate his clinical approach, but rather to use popular jokes to illustrate some of the underlying concerns that patients frequently harbor about psychotherapy. These concerns tend to center around the aspects of cost, length and effectiveness of treatment, and patient/therapist relationship themes. Such concerns may partially reflect the patients' emotional dilemmas in seeking help for very personal issues from someone about whom they know very little. We believe that it is acceptable for patients to question the therapeutic bottom-line. Their legitimate concerns deserve appropriate attention. It is also acceptable for therapists to use patient questions as fuel for therapeutic exploration of patient motivation and wishes in seeking treatment, and for examination of the patient's relationship patterns. Humor may at times facilitate the exploration of these sorts of issues.

Dr. Dunkelblau is a clinical psychologist on the staff of Forest Hospital in Des Plaines, Illinois.

*   *   *

The way society views the practice of psychotherapy is sometimes reflected by the prevalent humorous characters in the media and by the popular jokes of the time. This chapter examines some possible anxieties, conceptions, and misconceptions about psychotherapy that these jokes and stories address with the goal of sensitizing the profession to such concerns.

With the proliferation of numerous styles of psychotherapy and the increased numbers of people utilizing psychotherapeutic services, there has been an increase in jokes about psychotherapists, clients, and the process of therapy. These humorous views of the therapeutic experience reflect some societal expectations and concerns surrounding this still somewhat secretive and mystifying experience. Popular societal views of the therapist range from the bumbling, reflective persona of Bob Newhart to the direct, incisive comments of Charlie Brown's therapist, Lucy. Lucy's therapeutic interventions are, of course, always followed by the matter-of-fact request, "That'll be five cents, please." Examining these jokes and stories yields a greater understanding of common anxieties and concerns about therapy.

THE COST

Lucy's five cents seems reasonable for a fee, but the cost of therapy is one area where society's concerns and fears are reflected in amusing stories or jokes. For example, there is the maxim that the neurotic builds castles in the sky, the psychotic lives in them, and the therapist collects the rent. It is said that in the olden days therapists put patients in the madhouse; now they put them in the poorhouse. Woody Allen (1964-1968) has commented that he and his therapist disagreed about how to claim the money he spent for his therapy on his tax return. The doctor suggested that the costs should be listed under medical expenses and Woody felt they should be listed under entertainment. It seems that they finally compromised and listed the therapy costs under religious contributions. Another joke relates that a man goes to a therapist on Park Avenue. He goes into an office and sees two doors in the office. The first door says "male," the second says "female." He goes through the "male" door, then sees two more doors; one says "introvert," the other says "extrovert." He goes through the "introvert" door and sees two more doors. One says "income over $20,000," and the other says "income under $20,000." He goes through the "under $20,000" door and finds himself back on Park Avenue.

Stories like those above highlight a societal concern about the expense of seeking therapeutic help. Moreover, other worries bring to the fore the principles and morality of the therapist, a person who profits by other people's psychological distress and whose only concern may be personal financial gain. Consider the following stories:

A patient says to his therapist, "Thank you doctor for curing my kleptomania. Is there anything I can ever do to repay you?" The doctor replies, "Well...If you ever relapse, could you pick up a video recorder for my son?"

A man consults a therapist and states, "Doc, I'm suicidal; what should I do?" The doctor replies, "Pay in advance."

DISTRUST

This worry about therapist exploitiveness is not restricted to the topic of therapy fees. Jokes and anecdotes also depict other variations of the exploitive, self-serving therapist.

Jack Benny (cited in Spalding, 1976) once spoke of when he went into analysis and was told to talk about all that he knew. Sometime later he found his analyst doing his act in Philadelphia. Another patient asks her therapist, "Doctor, can't you kiss me?" The therapist responds, "Of course I can't kiss you. Why, I shouldn't even be lying here next to you!"

Whether gains are in the financial, show biz, or sexual gratification area, these jokes reflect society's fears or skepticism about the ideally understanding, humanitarian therapist. The therapist continues to take a beating with regard to his or her character in the following joke:

A man calls his therapist in the middle of the night, awakening the doctor out of a sound sleep. The client says, "Doc, you have to help me. I just swallowed a whole bottle of tranquilizers--what should I do?" The perturbed doctor says, "Relax, have a few drinks and get some sleep."

Since trust and empathy are the cornerstones of therapy, these personifications of the therapist reflect patients' ongoing concerns that their trust may not be well-founded. Consider the therapist portrayed in the "Mary Hartman, Mary Hartman" television show (Lear, 1976). He would be reassuring about the unconditional acceptance of therapy and would prod, encourage, and cajole his clients to "open up" and reveal their innermost thoughts and fears. Yet upon hearing these thoughts, he would scowl, look disgusted, and state that this was "the sickest thing" he had ever heard. Other therapists are equally unfeeling:

> A patient consults a therapist and the therapist says, "I'm afraid my good man that you are schizophrenic." The alarmed man responds, "I want a second opinion." The therapist replies, "OK...you're ugly too."

> Two therapists are talking and one says to the other after finding out that he had just seen nine clients that day, "Boy you must be exhausted listening to all of those people." The other therapist responds, "Who listens?"

These portrayals reflect not only concern about the therapist's response to the client but also the fear of many individuals that their problems and inner life are so dull or disquieting that "even a therapist" would be bored, disgusted, or unable to help.

THE INCREDIBLE CLIENT

The other side of the question, "Can the therapist help me?" is the belief that only "crazy people" go see therapists. Many jokes and anecdotes characterize what I call the incredible client: a person unlike the "normal" individual, a person who has very unusual concerns that only a therapist can understand. A sampling of these jokes follows:

Patient: Doc, my wife thinks she's a refrigerator.
Doctor: Well, how is that a problem?
Patient: See, she sleeps with her mouth open, and the light keeps me awake.
Doctor: So you think you are a dog, eh? How long has this been going on?
Patient: Since I was a puppy.

> A man went to a therapist's top floor office, and was so insecure that he would go into the elevator and say, "Penthouse, please--if it's not out of your way."

A man walks into a therapist's office with his ear stuffed full of tobacco. The therapist says, "My good fellow, you need me!" The guy says, "I sure do--Do you have a match?"

THE IMPOSSIBLE SOLUTION

Just as there is a concern about the incredible nature of people seeking therapy, there are also worries about whether therapy can offer a solution. It sometimes happens that the very reason or symptom for which a person seeks help makes it difficult for him or her to receive it. The enactment of the problem with the therapist precludes the solution:

A woman seeks out a therapist and says, "Doc, I have a terrible problem with my memory." The doctor replies, "How long have you had this problem?" The woman responds, "What problem?"

A client tells his therapist, "Doc, nobody pays attention to me." The doctor replies, "Next!"

A client says to his therapist, "Doc, you have to help me make more friends, you fat slob!"

If the problems preclude a solution and if clients come expecting relief, just what can the therapist provide? Woody Allen (1975) has written a delightful short story entitled "The Kugelmass Episode," focusing on the apparently unending demands that the client's needs place on the therapist. In short, Kugelmass, the client, has so many expectations that his analyst suggests that he needs a magician instead of an analyst. Kugelmass does seek a magician, yet ends up bemoaning the woes brought on by the fulfillment of his own wishes. The magician then suggests to Kugelmass that what he really needs is not a magician but an analyst.

DEFINITIONS OF THE THERAPEUTIC PERSONA

As mentioned earlier, Woody Allen isn't sure if the therapist is a magician, entertainer, or religious figure. The protagonist in the television production of the play,

Come Along with Me (Finfer, Miller, & Woodward, 1985) states, "I dabble with spirits, the supernatural, psychiatric advice...that sort of thing." Others have described the therapist as an ambivalence chaser or as someone who tells you what you already know in words that you can't understand. Another perspective defines the male therapist as the one who watches everybody else when a good-looking woman enters a room. Finally, Copans (cited in *Insights*, 1985) describes the therapist as a person who begins work at 8:00 a.m. sharp and ends at 6:00 p.m...dull.

PSYCHOTHERAPEUTIC OUTCOME

No matter what the definition of the therapist, one of the most pressing questions in our society regarding psychotherapy seems to be, "Can it work?" and "How long will it take?" What is probably the most popular psychotherapist joke today reflects these concerns:

Question: How many psychotherapists does it take to change a light bulb?

Answer: Only one, but it takes a long time, and it really has to want to change.

In the movie *Sleeper* (Allen & Brickman, 1973), Woody Allen, after finding out that he has been in suspended animation for 200 years, comments, "I would almost be through my analysis by now."

Many individuals are concerned about whether therapy will be helpful to them or whether they will like the way they end up. One story describes a man who, when asked if he was satisfied with the way his therapy turned out, responded that he was dissatisfied: "Last year I was Abe Lincoln, this year I'm nobody!" Here the person's symptoms have been successfully treated, but he is not satisfied with the result. The flip side also yields a joke:

Friend: So you say that you used to think you were a French poodle?

Patient: Yes, that's right.

Friend: Did that therapist you saw help you back to health?

Patient: He sure did, just feel my nose.

312

The final story here highlights a concern of both professionals and the society at large that psychological problems may be more refractory than we realize:

> A woman enters the therapist's office in despair. She says that her husband believes he is dead and can't be convinced otherwise. She then brings her husband in and the therapist finds that in fact the man believes he is dead. At that point, the therapist places the man in front of a mirror and instructs him that for the next 3 hours he is to repeat out loud, "Dead men don't bleed," which the client proceeds to do. After the allotted time, the therapist returns and pricks the man's finger with a pin so that a trickle of blood is seen. He then says, "Now, what does that prove?" The man then turns to the mirror and begins repeating, "Dead men do bleed!" (Spiegelman, 1975)

By heeding the popular stories, jokes, and characterizations of the way society views the therapeutic process, we can discern the worries, expectations, and fears that society has about our profession. Our awareness of these feelings about our profession can help us become more attentive, empathic, and hopefully more responsive to the patient's sensitivities. Once we understand this information, we can develop educational programs to help disseminate accurate data about therapy to the public. As illustrated in this essay, topics such as "what it is," "what it costs," "how long it takes," "how it affects others," and generally "what is reasonable to expect" are all areas to be addressed. These jokes and stories highlight psychotherapy as a human enterprise. Psychotherapists are not perfect; internal change or growth is relative, and patients need to make personal sense of their therapeutic experiences to discover how what they learned is personally relevant in their own lives. These concepts should also be understood.

Another message of this essay is to encourage us as a profession to maintain a sense of humor about what we do, because humor can benefit us as well as our clients. The worries and sensitivities raised by those around us are valid and should be attended to. Many of the worries and questions are serious, and the answers are not simple or readily available. Yet in the immortal words of Charlie Brown, spoken while hanging up-side-down, tangled in a tree with his kite, *"Good humor makes all things possible."*

REFERENCES

Allen, W. (1975). *Side Effects.* New York: Random House.

Allen, W., Brickman, M. (Authors), & Allen, W. (Director). (1973). *Sleeper* [Film]. Los Angeles, CA: United Artists.

Allen, W. (1964-1968). *The Nightclub Years 1964-68* (Record No. UAS-9968). Los Angeles, CA: United Artists Records.

Finfer, J., Miller, M., & Woodward, J. (Authors). (1985). *Come Along with Me* [American Playhouse Television Show]. New York: WNET Television.

Insights (Volume VI, No. 1). (1985). Belle Mead, NJ: Carrier Foundation.

Lear, N. (Producer). (1976). *Mary Hartman, Mary Hartman* [Television]. Los Angeles, CA: TAT Productions.

Spalding, H. (1976). *The Best of American Jewish Humor.* New York: Jonathan David Publishers.

Spiegelman, A. (1975). *Breakdowns.* New York: Belier Press.

CONCLUSION

Because of the fluid, ongoing nature of the subject matter, this book has been more difficult to conclude than most. There is no clear-cut end to the topics of humor and psychotherapy, as these twin topics involve deeply noted commitment and exploration in the lives of both editors with inextricable connections to our professional pursuits: In our professional identities, we live humor and psychotherapy. It would seem more true to the meaning of our lives that the book would go on and on, a seemingly endless ribbon of experiences, ideas, observations, judgments, and anecdotes--more a series of periodicals than a solitary volume.

Yet the issue runs even more deeply. It is understandably difficult for us to separate that which applies to career life from total life experience. And beyond this, we both hold powerfully to the view that humor and therapy are two significant aspects of life as a whole. We assume that our readers, like ourselves, consider humor and therapy to be important parts of the human experience, to be sources of much value, richness, benefit, comfort, and relief of anguish. After all, reading a book of this size and complexity demands no small degree of commitment. Humor and therapy can be presumed to be significant ingredients of our readers' lives, and they can understand and forgive our editorial reluctance to conclude.

Our belief in the importance of psychotherapy may not seem to be a very controversial issue throughout most of the modern world. However, despite the widespread acceptance of psychotherapy as one of the more positive contributions that humans can offer to each other, this acceptance is relatively thin: Many people would rank psychotherapy lamentably low on their lists of priorities. Most of the time they may not see the need for its contributions, or they may hold crystallized beliefs that the benefits of therapy are limited and/or mixed. Hence, the acceptance of psychotherapy has become a fragile given in our times. However, this is clearly not the case for those of us engaged in the healing professions. By and large we not only do psychotherapy, but we also deeply believe in it, along with a much larger group of individuals that includes those nonpractitioners who are motivated to push beyond the obstacles of inertia and various practicalities, such as finances, to add this volume to their libraries.

Humor is another matter, and is so much more complicated. Humor is appealing, infectious, recreational, and delightful; one can usually go on and on with it. However, another consideration contributes to the necessity of this extended commentary on understandings and forgivenesses. Along with humor's traditional, deep-rooted position as one of the foundation-blocks of human culture, it is commonly regarded as a frivolity--an important frivolity, perhaps an essential frivolity. This may seem contradictory until we factor in the wide recognition of stress reactions as the undesirable consequences of too much unrelenting seriousness in life. When this recognition is added to the formula, frivolousness can become essential.

Consequently, whether seen as essential or not, the "frivolous" reputation of humor tends to work against its acceptance as a serious subject of scientific inquiry. It even seems paradoxical to consider seriously studying humor. Yet we personally take humor quite seriously and are committed to its professional study. We believe that its importance extends beyond its entertainment value, its cathartic benefits, its function as a social lubricant, or its stimulatory and informative role, although all these aspects are honored by common usage. We believe that humor is bound up in the very nature of being human--a portion of the psychobiological reality of each human being, part of the human essence. We believe that all humans carry within their genetic templates the potential to develop a sense of humor, and for each of us that potential is realized in one fashion or another. Each person has his or her own, though somewhat unique, sense of humor.

Our hesitancy to conclude this book also goes beyond professional and personal dedication to the subject matter. The production of this book has taken several years, and editorial association with the contributors has gone through different stages. Lasting personal relationships have become established.

Another factor in the concluding equation concerns the scientific information and clinical experience that cannot be contained here. There is no doubt in our minds that more material on the subject could and should be published, some of which we may possibly include in a subsequent volume.

Nonetheless, every ending ultimately brings a sense of perspective and proportion. However this book may be judged by professionals, critics, and the general audience, it has been a spicy and creative slice of our lives. Together with our contributors, we have generated a new entity out of our time and energy. Like good therapy and good humor, the production of this book has been a creative experience. We hope our joint efforts will contribute to bettering the human experience, opening new possibilities for both practitioners and their patients, and adding options for those struggling to cope with their challenging environments. Moreover, we hope this book will finally help to establish humor as a legitimate therapeutic tool, and will serve as a catalyst for more extensive clinical research in this area of study.

In addition to the research that is needed, training in humor technology must be established on an extended format throughout the world. This education program for clinicians and other professionals has begun in several isolated institutions, but is very limited compared to what we envision for the future. If the interest contemporaneously being expressed from many directions is a true indicator, training in humor techniques and usage will grow into a sizable activity.

We anticipate that this growth of training will extend into many different settings. Professional workshops will present information and skills to a wide range of practicing clinicians. Psychotherapy students and interns will receive instruction in humor techniques and their proper applications. Graduate schools and continuing education programs will be organized and will present opportunities for professionals to begin integration of humor technology and philosophy into their career personae. The exploration of humor issues for satisfaction of advanced degree requirements will be expanded beyond its present status. We are sure that various mechanisms for humor training will be devised and put into use. We view growth of humor training as inevitable and desirable. We look forward to it with excitement and know that we will be stimulated by any opportunities to participate in this development. If only we could somehow capture and share here the excitement, innovation, and creativeness of that educative process.

We can also expect that increased, more skillful, and more well-informed use of humor in psychotherapy will affect clinicians and therapists both professionally and personally, especially in the area of professional burnout. There is no denying the devitalizing, depressing, and demoralizing impact of burnout on the lives of many professionals. Among health care personnel, nurses appear to be most affected, probably because they are in closest continuing contact with patient suffering. Numerous remedial approaches are offered and recommended to offset, diminish, or treat burnout. Most are effective at relieving symptoms but leave the cause of the distress untreated. Short of drastically revising the nature of the health care professional's role, preventive measures could focus on altering the underlying attitudes that engender burnout. We strongly expect that increasing use of humor in therapy would add such a preventive element. As more humor techniques are introduced into therapeutic transactions, we can expect less and less burnout to be observed and reported. Boredom, depression, fatigue, disenchantment, cynicism, ennui, negativism, irritability, inefficiency, carelessness, absenteeism, scornfulness, apathy, flatness, nastiness, lack of empathy or sympathy-- underlying all these familiar symptoms of burnout is the bankruptcy of morale that destroys motivation and erodes confidence. There are several causes of morale deficiency, but frustration of problem-solving behaviors and orientation is probably most common in health care. Once humor is well-accepted and widely utilized in treatment, burnout may eventually become an archaic syndrome whose widespread oppressiveness will gradually disappear.

Introducing more humor into therapeutic contexts represents what psychiatrist George Vaillant in his book, *Adaptation to Life*, has named "a Mature Adaptive Mechanism." Vaillant analyzed data from a 40-year life development study of a selected sample group of individuals included in the Harvard Grant Study. He characterizes "mature mechanisms" as being "common among healthy individuals from adolescence to old age, and they can be conceptualized as well-orchestrated composites of less mature mechanisms." They are integrative, convenient, adaptive, and desirable. Vaillant considers humor to be "...one of the truly elegant defenses in the human repertoire. Few would deny that humor, like hope, is one of mankind's most potent antidotes for the woes of Pandora's box."

Vaillant uses the term "coping mechanism" interchangeably with "adaptive mechanism," which returns us to possibilities aimed against morale destruction and burnout. The coping is directed against morale-destroying frustrations by effectively preventing their occurrence, diminishing their impact, and/or hastening their resolution. Coping opposes frustration, protects motivation and confidence, and sustains morale. We can expect increased humor usage to enhance the results of therapy, help in coping with clinical frustrations, and thereby improve morale. Many chapters in this book discuss and document the validity of this expectation. This direct benefit will, hopefully, be considerable and will touch the lives of many people "on both sides of the desk."

Beyond this direct benefit, the coping value of humor will also spread into the therapeutic milieu. Humor's therapy value, and its beneficial psychological and physiological impacts on individuals engaged in mutual mirth, can profoundly affect individual life experience. Therapists and other health care personnel will find humor increasingly effective in preventing, diminishing, and resolving frustration, thereby expanding personal coping capacities and minimizing burnout. The foregoing considerations concern the therapist's external relationships. However, another set of considerations concern his or her relationship with self. Internal factors such as unrealistic expectations, impatience, deficiencies of humility, and desperation can also produce frustration. By influencing and modifying the therapist's general attitude, the use of humor will affect his or her attitude towards self. For example, a humorous approach in self-appraisal is one of the most effective methods for diminishing pomposity that, because of its unrealistic nature, inevitably contributes to frustration and eventual destruction of morale. Humor teaches humility; laughing at one's own foibles and gradiosities will help prevent burnout.

To summarize, this improved internal and external coping due to the use of humor can result in the following: (a) greater career gratification due to more effective therapy tools, thus leading to better results; (b) more positive interactions and better team morale among therapists; and (c) greater and more realistic self-acceptance. These tendencies are all mutually enhancing and directed against burnout. The specific creativity of humor is found in the formal structure of each humorous item or instance. Each occasion of humor represents a discovery by its participants, and this discovery involves the realization of a relationship between two or more entities that had not been recognized previously. In this way each humorous item slightly or even significantly expands our view of life, thereby conforming to the traditional definition of creativity.

Humor also conforms to creativity in a broadly philosophic way. Arthur Koestler produced a massive tome, entitled *The Act of Creation*, in which he used humor as a major prototype of creativity. Koestler introduced a multitude of elements that he considered necessary to any extended discussion of creativity. These elements included conscious and unconscious and the relationship between the two, differences between rationality and irrationality, the nature of thought, and a logic arguing that basic principles of creativity have application at all levels of biologic organization. Koestler's hypotheses have been debated for several decades. The least that can be said is that his themes are provocative and stimulating, and are themselves examples of creative thought. At most, Koestler has proved humor to be profoundly creative.

Whether we concentrate on humor's creativity in a specific, epistemologic sense or in a philosophic sense relating to the biologic organization of life, this tendency actively alters the mental functioning of those involved in humor. Thinking is expanded, thus facilitating an enlarged concept of the world and providing an enlarged base for all future thought and understanding. This experience is stimulating and exciting; it encourages and presents hope for further mental adventures. Greater wisdom enhances the ability to productively deal with obstacles that might have otherwise caused frustration, thus creating a confidence that challenge can be met more competently. A new spirit of enthusiasm is inculcated. This creative element in humor stimulates, encourages, expands, gives hope, and even entertains. The creativity of humor joins with the benefits of improved coping in therapeutic contexts, adding to the artillery against burnout.

Considering the various results of using therapeutic humor in health care, we can project an important alteration of therapist character throughout the health care fields. We may not be able to predict the specific nature of these alterations, yet we can imagine some general changes in therapist style when humor techniques are studied and increasingly used in the therapy experience. These include (a) more personal humility, (b) more inner confidence, (c) less defensive negativism and pessimism, (d) greater appreciation of the value of therapy for individuals and for human life in general, (e) greater awareness of the teaching value of therapy principles for dealing with life problems and challenges not specifically identified as clinical, and (f) greater awareness of how therapy principles can teach prophylactically, helping to prevent life difficulties before they gel. Dare we hope that these enhancements, these expansions, may combine to establish a foundation for some future evolutionary jump in human psychology? Not an utterly bizarre consideration, given the potent nature of the changes we are contemplating and given the extremely important and dedicated roles throughout the world of the people involved in these changes--be they therapists, healers, health care professionals, holistic treatment experts, practitioners of preventive medicine, or others dedicated to the betterment of the human condition.

In conclusion, let us examine the significant impact humor may have on the following mental health frontiers:

1. On the academic frontier, we can see that humor will affect both undergraduate and graduate training in the mental health fields. Alongside classes in psychodiagnostics or hypnosis, new classes can be offered in humor and adjustment, humor and psychotherapy, the clinical use of humor for different emotional problems and psychopathologies, humor in child therapy, humor in family therapy, humor in group therapy, the place of humor in different theories of psychotherapeutic work, and other related topics. As this volume

321

indicates, a corpus of knowledge already exists in these areas to warrant educational exposure to this clinical sphere by students in the mental health fields.

2. On the clinical supervision frontier, psychotherapy supervisors can better address supervision issues with increased access to the personal resources of their students and interns when humor is allowed to leaven the supervisory relationship. The supervisor's use of humor can facilitate clinical supervision in the following ways: (a) The supervisor's humor signals to the student that he or she is interacting with a compassionate, malleable, and tolerant individual, therefore encouraging genuine student self-disclosure and honest expression of problematic issues in a freer atmosphere. (b) The use of humor prevents supervisor burnout and inoculates students against future burnout as it allays their tensions about dealing with severe emotional problems. Of course, this does not imply that students are encouraged to ignore the reality of human distress but simply to understand it from an additional angle. (c) Humor can motivate the student to learn and not feel intimidated by the sizable amount of information he or she needs to grasp in order to do psychotherapy effectively. (d) The humorous supervisor is modeling a responsive and constructive therapeutic persona for the student, who in turn will model the constructive aspects for his or her patients.

3. On the continuing education frontier, humor can offer new therapeutic possibilities for both beginning and advanced therapists. Our experience in conducting humor training workshops suggests that most individuals can achieve at least a moderately helpful level of therapeutic humor use. The skilled clinical use of humor (like the skilled clinical use of hypnosis or biofeedback) requires training. There are attitudinal blocks to surmount. There are distinctions to be made between the therapeutic use of humor and its harmful abuse. There are patient factors to be considered. There are specific humor creation techniques to be learned. All these variables can be productively addressed in professional workshop training experiences, which we anticipate will become more avail-

able to clinicians in different clinical contexts. We should note at this juncture that the purpose of training in the clinical use of humor is not to transform psychotherapists into comedians--humor alone is not sufficient to effect comprehensive therapeutic change. Rather, clinical humor training is designed to open new therapeutic vistas and present new clinical tools in addition to the clinician's existing competencies.

4. On the clinical frontier, this volume clearly substantiates the relevance of humor in the numerous arenas of psychotherapeutic work. As humor takes its proper place in psychotherapy, two developments could ensue: (a) The therapist's clinical persona will undergo a positive transformation. The untenable position equating solemnity with effectiveness will be dropped--an examination of everyday experiences readily reveals that individuals joke about what is most serious to them (sex, anxiety, relationships, death), and that humor typifies a higher form of seriousness than the one represented by superficial formality or solemnity. Therapists will be able to use humor more freely in their everyday work without feeling that their credibility is undermined. (b) The use of humor can show the therapist's human side to his or her patients and help modulate the professional therapist's public image as unresponsive and detached. Both therapists and the therapeutic enterprise may then be perceived more realistically and with less fearful apprehension by the public.

5. On the personal frontier, the introduction of humor would reduce the occurrence of burnout, would provide therapists with an effective antidote to stress and frustration, and would encourage a richer (more colorful, less self-critical) attitude toward oneself. Interpersonal dealings with colleagues, friends, and family would become more rewarding. Overall, the infusion of humor would vivify and illuminate the therapist's personal and interpersonal world.

6. On the social frontier, the use of humor as a mode of initiating social contact and as a form of social entertainment could help bridge the interactive gap between individuals. If we concur with the premise that the rampant onslaught of alcoholism

and drug addiction is a shocking indication of the current level of interpersonal alienation in our society, spanning all age categories and socio-economic groups, then we can begin to imagine the salubrious effects of humor's compassionate message on interactions between parents and children, teachers and students, employers and employees. When appropriately used, humor constitutes non-harmful clean fun that conquers boredom, lubricates interactions, and draws people closer. Healthy humor would then become an acceptable component of the social etiquette. Humor courses would eventually be included in grade school and high school curricula to teach children and teenagers how to successfully use humor in their social interactions. Adult education classes would be offered to adults, families, and the elderly to facilitate the development of humor skills. Humor workshops would bring the benefits of humor to the workplace for the enhancement of productivity and improvement of interactions between employees, managers, and consumers.

7. On the creative frontier, humor can liberate us from the complacent jadedness that corrodes resourcefulness and ultimately stunts the development of inventive solutions. As we engage in humor, we begin to break free from everyday limitations. We feel less stymied by our assumed intellectual or emotional constraints. Our thinking is expanded beyond the realm of monotony. New possibilities begin to unfold. New ideas begin to sprout. New ways of resolving therapeutic dilemmas begin to bloom. New approaches for dealing with particularly resistive or challenging patients begin to emerge. The results of such a widening of horizons can only be fruitful to both therapist and patient.

8. On the research frontier, further study is needed in the physiology, psychology, sociology, and anthropology of humor, with special focus on the clinical implications of these findings. For example, the intriguing and intricate matrix of catecholamine production during the humor response could be clarified. In-depth cross-cultural studies could be conducted on the role of humor in different cultures and how humor is used to

facilitate social adjustment in various cultural contexts. The effect of humor on altering self-concept could be scrutinized. The effectiveness of different humor techniques for different patient populations would be investigated. The structure of the psychological templates that different individuals use to decode humorous messages would be analyzed. New psychodiagnostic instruments using humorous stimuli would be developed and standardized. New humor technologies aimed at developing a healthy sense of humor or at using humor to modify specific maladaptive behaviors would be researched. In this respect, an interdisciplinary coordination of research efforts could integrate and correlate findings in different disciplines. A professional journal on humor and therapeutic change could be launched. The results of such endeavors would be extremely interesting and would significantly improve our knowledge of human behavior.

9. On the theoretical front, humor would become an integral part of our conceptualization of psychotherapy. If it is agreed that unobtrusive humor is an expression of mature emotional adjustment, a successful human coping mechanism, and a tool to help patients move from a stilted unidimensional yes/no position to a wider multidimensional perspective whereby various constructive alternatives to emotional problems can be considered, then it becomes important that humor be a component of the "learning package" that psychotherapists impart to patients throughout psychotherapeutic work. More theoretical work would be needed on humor as a paradigm of human change and how humor is similar to or different from other change processes. The unifying influence of humor as well as its distinctive efficacy in different theories of personality change would deserve further elaboration.

The very nature of this volume persuades us that humor is a potent connective baseline among theories and individuals, bridging various therapeutic approaches. This book is about humor, but it is not only about humor. It represents, in fact, a state-of-the-art compendium of psychotherapeutic theories and techniques, a comprehensive panorama of contemporary psychotherapeutic developments. Indeed, our hope is that this work will generate new connective baselines in the reader's clinical and personal perspective, all in good humor.

APPENDIX: HUMOR AND PSYCHOTHERAPY–A COMPREHENSIVE CLINICAL BIBLIOGRAPHY

Abelson, R. P., & Levine, J. (1958). A factor analytic study of cartoon humor among psychiatric patients. *Journal of Personality, 26,* 451-466.

Ames, F. R., & Enderstein, O. (1975). Ictal laughter: A case report with clinical, cinefilm, and EEG observations. *Journal of Neurology, Neurosurgery & Psychiatry, 38,* 11-17.

Anzieu, D. (1980). Une passion pour rire: L'esprit. *Nouvelle Revue de Psychanalyse, 21,* 161-179.

Arieti, S. (1950). New views on the psychology of wit and the comic. *Psychiatry, 13,* 43-62.

Assagioli, R. (1973). Cheerfulness: A psychosynthetic technique. *Psychosynthesis Research Foundation, 33,* 12-21.

Assagioli, R. (1974). Smiling wisdom. *Human Dimensions, 3,* 20-22.

Banmen, J. (1982). The use of humour in psychotherapy. *International Journal for the Advancement of Counselling, 5,* 81-86.

Barchilon, J. (1973). Pleasure, mockery and creative integrations: Their relationship to childhood knowledge, a learning defect and the literature of the absurd. *International Journal of Psycho-Analysis, 54,* 19-34.

Bateson, G. (1953). The role of humor in human communication. In H. Von Forester (Ed.), *Cybernetics.* New York: Macey Foundation.

Bateson, G. (1969). The position of humour in human communication. In J. Levine (Ed.), *Motivation in Humour.* New York: Atherton Press.

Bateson, G. (1979). *Mind and Nature.* New York: Bantam.

Bergler, E. (1937). A clinical contribution to the psychogenesis of humor. *Psychoanalytic Review, 24,* 34-53.

Bergler, E. (1956). *Laughter and the Sense of Humor.* New York: Grune & Stratton.

Bishop, B. R., & Stumphauzer, J. S. (1973). Behavior therapy of thumbsucking in children: A punishment (time-out) and generalization effect: What's a mother to do? *Psychological Reports, 33,* 939-944.

Blank, A. M., Tweedale, M., Cappelli, M., & Ryback, D. (1983). Influence of trait anxiety on perception of humor. *Perceptual & Motor Skills, 57,* 103-106.

Bloch, S., Browning, S., & McGrath, G. (1983). Humor in group psychotherapy. *British Journal of Medical Psychology, 56,* 86-97.

Bloomfield, I. (1980). Humour in psychotherapy and analysis. *International Journal of Social Psychiatry, 26,* 135-141.

Bolk-Weischedel, D. (1978). Alterations in the untreated partner of the patient during analytic psychotherapy. *Zeitschrift für Psychosomatische Medizin und Psychoanalyse, 24,* 116-128.

Brenman, M. (1952). On teasing and being teased: The problem of moral masochism. *Psychoanalytic Study of the Child, 7,* 264-285.

Brill, A. A. (1911). Freud's theory of wit. *Journal of Abnormal and Social Psychology, 6,* 189 ff.

Brill, A. A. (1940). The mechanism of wit and humor in normal and psychopathic states. *Psychiatric Quarterly, 14,* 731-749.

Brody, B. (1976). Freud's analysis of American culture. *Psychoanalytic Review, 63,* 631-377.

Brody, E. B., & Redlich, F. C. (1953). The response of schizophrenic patients to comic cartoons. *Folia Psychiatrica Neurologica at Neurochirurgica Neerlandica, 56,* 623-635.

Brody, M. W. (1950). The meaning of laughter. *Psychoanalytic Quarterly, 19,* 192-201.

Brown, J. R. (1978). Ritual and gestalt: The gestalt group in high relief. *Gestalt Journal, 1,* 68-74.

Brown, J. R. (1979). *Back to the Beanstalk: Enchantment and Reality for Couples.* LaJolla, CA: Psychology & Consulting Associates Press.

Buckman, E. S. (1980). The use of humor in psychotherapy. *Dissertation Abstracts International, 41*(5-B), 1715.

Burbridge, R. T. (1978). The nature and potential of therapeutic humor. *Dissertation Abstracts International, 39*(6-B), 2974.

Burns, W. J., & Tyler, J. D. (1976). Appreciation of risqué cartoon humor in male and female repressors and sensitizers. *Journal of Clinical Psychology, 32,* 315-321.

Cassell, J. L. (1974). The function of humor in the counseling process. *Rehabilitation Counseling Bulletin, 17,* 240-245.

Cattell, R. B., Cattell, A. K. S., & Hicks, V. (1952). *IPAT Humor Test of Personality.* Champaign, IL: Institute for Personality and Ability Testing.

Cattell, R. B., & Luborsky, L. B. (1947). Personality factors in response to humor. *Journal of Abnormal and Social Psychology, 42,* 402-421.

Chapman, A. J., & Foot, H. C. (Eds.). (1976). *Humour and Laughter: Theory, Research, and Applications.* London: Wiley.

Chapman, A. J., & Foot, H. C. (Eds.). (1977). *It's a Funny Thing, Humour.* London: Pergamon.

Chatterji, N. N. (1952). Laughter in schizophrenia and psychotic disorders. *Samiska, 6,* 32-37.

Childs, A. W. (1976). A tale of two groups: An observational study of targeted humor. *Dissertation Abstracts International, 36*(11-B), 5860.

Cohn, R. (1951). Forced crying and laughing. *Archives of Neurology and Psychiatry, 66,* 738-743.

Corbin, H. (1971). Mystique et humour chez Sohrawardi, Shaykh al-Israk. In *Collected Papers on Islamic Philosophy and Mysticism* (pp. 16-38). Montreal: McGill University Press.

Coriat, I. H. (1939). Humor and hypomania. *Psychiatric Quarterly, 13,* 631-688.

Cousins, N. (1979). *Anatomy of an Illness as Perceived by a Patient.* New York: Norton.

Daniels, E. B. (1974). Some notes on clowns, madness and psychotherapy. *Psychotherapy and Psychosomatics, 24,* 465-470.

Davison, C., & Kelman, H. (1939). Pathologic laughing and crying. *Archives of Neurology and Psychiatry, 42,* 595-643.

329

Deikel, S. M. (1974). The life and death of Lenny Bruce: A psychological autopsy. *Life Threatening Behavior, 4,* 176-192.

Deleuze, G. (1969). *Logique du Sens.* Paris: Editions de Minuit.

Derks, P. L., Leichtman, H. M., & Carroll, P. J. (1975). Production and judgment of "humor" by schizophrenics and college students. *Bulletin of the Psychonomic Society, 6,* 300-302.

Dewane, C. M. (1978). Humor in therapy. *Social Work, 23,* 508-510.

Domash, L. (1975). The use of wit and the comic by a borderline psychotic child in psychotherapy. *American Journal of Psychotherapy, 29,* 261-270.

Dooley, L. (1934). A note on humor. *Psychoanalytic Review, 21,* 49-58.

Dooley, L. (1941). The relation of humor to masochism. *Psychoanalytic Review, 28,* 37-46.

Druckman, R., & Chao, D. (1957). Laughter in epilepsy. *Neurology, 7,* 26-36.

Ecker, J., Levine, J., & Zigler, E. (1973). Impaired sex-role identification in schizophrenia expressed in the comprehension of humor stimuli. *Journal of Psychology, 83,* 67-77.

Eidelberg, L. (1945). A contribution to the study of wit. *Psychoanalytic Review, 32,* 33-61.

Eisenbud, J. (1964). The oral side of humor. *Psychoanalytic Review, 51,* 57-73.

Ellis, A. (1977). Fun as psychotherapy. *Rational Living, 12,* 2-6.

Ellis, A. (1983). Rational-emotive therapy (RET) approaches to overcoming resistance: II. How RET disputes clients' irrational, resistance-creating beliefs. *British Journal of Cognitive Psychotherapy, 1,* 1-16.

Emde, R. N., & Koenig, K. L. (1969). Neonatal smiling and rapid eye movement states. *Journal of the American Academy of Child Psychiatry, 8,* 57-67.

Epstein, S., & Smith, R. (1956). Repression and insight as related to reaction to cartoons. *Journal of Consulting Psychology, 20,* 391-395.

Fabry, J. (1982). Some practical hints about paradoxical intention. *International Forum for Logotherapy, 5,* 25-29.

Feldmann, S. (1941). Supplement to Freud's theory to wit. *Psychoanalytic Review, 28,* 201-217.

Ferenczi, S. (1911). The psychoanalysis of wit and the comical. In *Further Contributions to Psychoanalysis.* London: Hogarth.

Ferguson, S. M., Schwartz, M. L., & Rayport, M. (1969). Perception of humor in patients with temporal lobe epilepsy. *Archives of General Psychiatry, 21,* 363-367.

Fisher, H. (1976). A credo for responsible group therapy with hospitalized adolescents. *Clinical Social Work Journal, 4,* 121-126.

Frankl, V. (1966). *Man's Search for Meaning.* New York: Washington Square Press.

Freud, S. (1928). Humor. *International Journal of Psychoanalysis, 9,* 1-6.

Freud, S. (1960). *Jokes and Their Relation to the Unconscious* (J. Strachey, Trans.). New York: Norton. (Originally *Der Witz und seine Beziehung zum Ubewussten.* Deuticke, Leipzig, & Vienna. [1905].)

Friedman, H. J. (1971). Comment on "The destructive potential of humor in psychotherapy" by Kubie. *American Journal of Psychiatry, 128,* 118.

Fry, W. F., Jr. (1968). *Sweet Madness: A Study of Humor.* Palo Alto, CA: Pacific Books.

Fry, W. F., Jr. (1971, Winter). Laughter: Is it the best medicine? *Stanford Medical Alumni Association, 10,* 16-20.

Fry, W. F., Jr. (1979a, August). *Catharsis and Arousal: Humor as a Paradigm.* Paper presented at the American Psychological Association Annual Convention, New York, NY. (Abstract available from author)

Fry, W. F., Jr. (1979b). *Using Humor to Save Lives.* Paper presented at Annual Convention of the American Orthopsychiatric Association, Washington, DC. (Abstract available from author)

Fry, W. F., Jr. (1980). *Humor and Healing.* Paper presented at the University of California Healing Brain Symposium, San Francisco, CA. (Abstract available from author)

Fry, W. F., Jr. (1984a). Laughter and health: Special report. *Encyclopaedia Britannica Medical and Health Annual.*

Fry, W. F., Jr. (1984b). *Learning with Humor.* Paper presented at Fourth International Conference on Humor and Laughter, Tel Aviv, Israel. (Abstract available from author)

Fry, W. F., Jr., & Allen, M. (1975). *Make 'em Laugh: Life Studies of Comedy Writers.* Palo Alto, CA: Science and Behavior Books.

Fuller, R. E. (1972). Headshrinker: The psychiatrist in cartoons. *Bulletin of the Menninger Clinic, 36,* 335-345.

Goffman, E. (1974). *Frame Analysis.* New York: Harper & Row.

Goldsmith, L. (1979). Adaptive regression, humor and suicide. *Journal of Consulting and Clinical Psychology, 47,* 628-630.

Goldstein, J. H. (1982). A laugh a day: Can mirth keep disease at bay? *The Sciences, 22,* 21-25.

Goldstein, J., & McGhee, P. (Eds.). (1972). *The Psychology of Humor.* New York: Academic Press.

Golub, R. R. (1979). An investigation of the effect of use of humor in counseling. *Dissertation Abstracts International, 40*(6-B), 2837.

Gordon, A. (1947). Cataplexy. *Diseases of the Nervous System, 8,* 11-14.

Graham, L. R. (1958). The maturational factor in humor. *Journal of Clinical Psychology, 14,* 326-328.

Granfield, A. J., & Giles, H. (1975). Toward an analysis of humor through symbolism. *International Journal of Symbology, 6,* 17-23.

Greenwald, H. (1975). Humor in psychotherapy. *Journal of Contemporary Psychotherapy, 7,* 113-116.

Grossman, S. A. (1970). The use of sexual jokes in psychotherapy. *Medical Aspects of Human Sexuality, 4,* 35-46.

Grotjahn, M. (1945). Laughter in dreams. *Psychoanalytic Quarterly, 14,* 221-227.

Grotjahn, M. (1949). Laughter in psychoanalysis. *Samiska, 3,* 76-82.

Grotjahn, M. (1950). Laughter in psychoanalysis. In S. Lorand (Ed.), *The Yearbook of Psychoanalysis* (Vol. VI). New York: International University Press.

Grotjahn, M. (1951). The inability fo remember dreams and jokes. *Psychoanalytic Quarterly, 20,* 284-286.

Grotjahn, M. (1957). *Beyond Laughter.* New York: McGraw-Hill.

Grotjahn, M. (1966). Laughter in group psychotherapy. *Brief Communications,* 234-238.

Grotjahn, M. (1970a). Jewish jokes and their relation to masochism. In W. H. Mendel (Ed.), *A Celebration of Laughter.* Los Angeles: Mara Books.

Grotjahn, M. (1970b). Laughter and sex. In W. Mendel (Ed.), *A Celebration of Laughter.* Los Angeles: Mara Books.

Grotjahn, M. (1970c). Laughter in psychotherapy. In W. Mendel (Ed.), *A Celebration of Laughter.* Los Angeles: Mara.

Grotjahn, M. (1971). Laughter in group psychotherapy. *International Journal of Group Psychotherapy, 21,* 234-238.

Grotjahn, M. (1972a). The qualities of the group therapist. In H. I. Kaplan & B. J. Sadock (Eds.), *New Models for Group Therapy* (Vol. xii, p. 281). New York: E. P. Dutton.

Grotjahn, M. (1972b). Sexuality and humor: Don't laugh. *Psychology Today, 6,* 50-53.

Grotjahn, M. (1972c). Smoking, coughing, laughing and applause: A comparative study of respiratory symbolism. *International Journal of Psychoanalysis, 53,* 345-349.

Haggard, E. A. (1942). A projective technique using comic strip characters. *Character and Personality, 10,* 289-295.

Haggard, E. A., & Sargent, H. (1941). Use of comic strip characters in diagnosis and therapy. *Psychological Bulletin, 38,* 714.

Haley, J. (1963). *Strategies of Psychotherapy.* New York: Grune & Stratton.

Hand, I., & Lamontagne, Y. (1974). Paradoxical intention and behavior techniques in short-term psychotherapy. *Canadian Psychiatric Association Journal, 19,* 501-507.

Hankins-McNary, L. (1979). The use of humor in group therapy. *Perspectives in Psychiatric Care, 17,* 228-231.

Hanly, C. (1977). An unconscious irony in Plato's Republic. *Psychoanalytic Quarterly, 46,* 116-147.

Harper, R. A. (1984). The goal is the process: To enjoy. *Psychotherapy in Private Practice, 2,* 21-26.

Harrelson, R. W., & Stroud, P. S. (1967). Observations of humor in chronic schizophrenics. *Mental Hygiene, 51,* 458-461.

Hartmann, G. W. (1934-1935). Personality traits associated with variations in happiness. *Journal of Abnormal and Social Psychology, 29,* 202-212.

Herth, K. (1984). Laughter: A nursing Rx. *American Journal of Nursing, 84,* 991-992.

333

Heuscher, J. E. (1980). The role of humor and folklore themes in psychotherapy. *American Journal of Psychiatry, 137,* 1546-1549.

Hickson, J. (1977). Humor as an element in the counseling relationship. *Psychology, 14,* 60-68.

Hickson, J., & Hammer, E. F. (1975). Humor and the counseling relationship. Psychology imagery: The artistic style in the therapist's communications. *Art Psychotherapy, 2,* 225-231.

Holmes, D. S. (1969). Sensing humor: Latency and amplitude of responses related to MMPI profiles. *Journal of Consulting and Clinical Psychology, 33,* 296-301.

Holt, E. (1916). Wit and humor. In D. Robinson (Ed.), *Readings in General Psychology.* Chicago: University of Chicago Press.

Holt, R. R. (1960). Cognitive controls and primary processes. *Journal of Psychological Research, 4,* 105-112.

Hom, G. L. (1966). Threat of shock and anxiety in the perception of humor. *Perceptual and Motor Skills, 23,* 535-538.

Hooff, J. A. R. A. M. van. (1972). A comparative approach to the phylogeny of laughter and smiling. In R. Hinde (Ed.), *Nonverbal Communication.* New York: Cambridge University Press.

Horowitz, L. S. (1957). Attitudes of speech defectives toward humor based on speech defects. *Speech Monographs, 24,* 46-55.

Horowitz, M. W., & Horowitz, L. S. (1949). An examination of the social psychological situations of the physically disabled as it pertains to humor. *American Psychologist, 4,* 256-257.

Hoult, T. (1949). Comic books and juvenile delinquency. *Sociology and Social Research, 33,* 279-284.

Huber, A. T. (1974). The effect of humor on client discomfort in the counseling interview. *Dissertation Abstracts International, 35*(4-A), 1980.

Huizinga, J. (1955). *Humo Ludens: A Study of the Play Element in Culture.* Boston: Beacon.

Humes, J. C. (1974). *Podium Humor.* New York: Harper & Row.

Hurrell, J. D. (1959). A note on farce. *Quarterly Journal of Speech, 45,* 426-430.

Hyers, C. (1974). *Zen and the Comic Spirit.* Philadelphia: Westminster.

Isager, H. (1948). Factors contributing to happiness a-mong Danish college students. *Journal of Social Psychology, 28,* 237-246.

Jablonski, B., & Range, B. (1984). O humor e so-riso? Alsumas consideracoes sobre os estudos em humor [On humor and laughter: Various considerations of studies of humor]. *Arquivos Brasileiros de Psicologia, 36,* 133-140.

Jackson, H. J., & King, N. J. (1982). The therapeutic management of an autistic child's phobia using laughter as the anxiety inhibitor. *Behavioural Psychotherapy, 10,* 364-369.

Jacobson, E. (1947). The child's laughter: Theoretical and clinical notes on the function of the comic. *The Psychoanalytic Study of the Child, 2,* 39-60.

Jacobson, E. (1971). On the child's laughter and the function of the comic. In *Depression.* New York: International Universities Press.

Jankélévitch, V. (1964). *L'ironie.* Paris: Flammarion.

Kadis, A. L., & Winick, C. (1973). The cartoon as therapeutic catalyst. In H. Mosak (Ed.), *Alfred Adler: His Influence on Psychology Today.* Park Ridge, NJ: Noyes Press.

Kahn, E. M. (1984). Group treatment interventions for schizophrenics. *International Journal of Group Psychotherapy, 34,* 149-153.

Kaneko, S. Y. (1972). The role of humor in psychotherapy. *Dissertation Abstracts International, 32*(9-A), 5344.

Kant, O. (1942). Inappropriate laughter and silliness in schizophrenia. *Journal of Abnormal and Social Psychology, 37,* 398-402.

Kanzer, M. (1955). Gogol - A study on wit and paranoia. *Journal of the American Psychoanalytic Association, 3,* 110.

Kaplan, H. B., & Boyd, I. H. (1965). The social functions of humor on an open psychiatric ward. *Psychiatric Quarterly, 39,* 502-515.

Kazrin, A., Durac, J., & Agteros, T. (1979). Meta-meta analysis: A new method for evaluating therapy outcome. *Behaviour Research & Therapy, 17,* 397-399.

Kelling, G. W. (1971). An empirical investigation of Freud's theory of jokes. *Psychoanalytic Review, 58,* 473-485.

Killinger, B. E. (1978). The place of humour in adult psychotherapy. *Dissertation Abstracts International, 38*(7-B), 3400.

Klein, J. P. (1974). On the use of humour in counseling. *Canadian Counsellor, 8,* 233-239.

Klein, J. P. (1976). Rationality and humour in counseling. *Canadian Counsellor, 11,* 28-32.

Koch, M. (1955). Constitutional variants of wittiness. *Psychotherapy and Medical Psychology, 5,* 203-214.

Kramer, H. C. (1954). Laughing spells in patients after lobotomy. *Journal of Nervous and Mental Diseases, 119,* 517-522.

Kris, E. (1938). Ego development and the comic. *International Journal of Psychoanalysis, 19,* 77-90.

Kris, E. (1940). Laughter as an expressive process. *International Journal of Psychoanalysis, 21,* 314-341.

Kubie, L. S. (1971). The destructive potential of humor in psychotherapy. *American Journal of Psychiatry, 127,* 861-866.

Kuhlman, T. (1984). *Humor and Psychotherapy.* Homewood, IL: Dow Jones-Irwin.

Labrentz, H. L. (1974). The effectiveness of humor on the initial client counselor relationship. *Dissertation Abstracts International, 34*(7-A), 3875.

Lacroix, M. (1974). Humorous drawings and directed-reverie therapy of children. *Etudes Psychothérapiques, 15,* 17-27.

Lazarus, A. (1971). New techniques for behavioral change. *Rational Living, 6,* 2-7.

Lee, J. C., & Griffith, R. M. (1963). Forgetting jokes: A function of repression? *Journal of Individual Papers, 19,* 213-215.

Levin, M. (1957). Wit and schizophrenic thinking. *American Journal of Psychiatry, 113,* 917-923.

Levine, J. (1961). Regression in primitive clowning. *Psychoanalytic Quarterly, 30,* 72-83.

Levine, J. (1969). *Motivation in Humor.* New York: Lieber-Atherton.

Levine, J., & Abelson, R. (1958). A Factor analytic study of cartoon humor among psychiatric patients. *Journal of Personality, 26,* 451-466.

Levine, J., & Redlich, J. (1955). Failure to understand humor. *Psychoanalytic Quarterly, 24,* 560-572.

Loewald, E. (1976). The development and uses of humor in a four-year old's treatment. *International Review of Psycho-Analysis, 3,* 209-221.

Lukas, E. (1982). The "birthmarks" of paradoxical intention. *International Forum for Logotherapy, 5,* 20-24.

Malamud, D. I. (1980). The laughing game: An exercise for sharpening awareness of self-responsibility. *Psychotherapy: Theory, Research & Practice, 17,* 69-73.

Manuel, E. A. (1962). Bagobo riddles. *Asian Folklore Studies, 21,* 123-185.

Maranda, E. K. (1971a). The logic of riddles. In P. Maranda & E. K. Maranda (Eds.), *Structural Analysis of Oral Tradition.* Philadelphia: University of Pennsylvania Press.

Maranda, E. K. (1971b). Theory and practice of riddle analysis. *Journal of American Folklore, 84,* 51-61.

Maranda, E. K. (1976). Riddles and riddling: An introduction. *Journal of American Folklore, 89,* 127-138.

Marcos, L. R. (1974). The emotional correlates of smiling and laughter: A preliminary research study. *American Journal of Psychoanalysis, 34,* 33-41.

Martin, J. P. (1950). Fits of laughter (sham mirth) in organic cerebral disease. *Brain, 73,* 453-464.

Martirosyan, V. V., & Sayamova, A. A. (1969). Laughter as the equivalent of epileptic attack. *Zhurnal Nevropatologii i Psikhiatrii, 69,* 569-570.

Maslow, A. (1968). *Toward a Psychology of Being.* New York: Van Nostrand.

Meerloo, J. A. M. (1966). The biology of laughter. *Psychoanalytic Review, 53,* 189-208.

Megdell, J. I. (1984). Relationship between counselor-initiated humor and client's self-perceived attraction in the counseling interview. *Psychotherapy, 21,* 517-523.

Mendel, W. M. (Ed.). (1970). *A Celebration of Laughter.* Los Angeles: Mara Books.

Messenger, J. C. (1960). Anang proverb-riddles. *Journal of American Folklore, 73,* 225-235.

Messer, S. B., & Winokur, M. (1980). Some limits to the integration of psychoanalytic and behavior therapy. *American Psychologist, 35,* 818-827.

Mettee, D. R., Hrelec, E. S., & Wilkens, P. C. (1971). Humor as an interpersonal asset and liability. *Journal of Social Psychology, 85,* 51-64.

Miller, L. D. (1970). Humor as a projective technique in occupational therapy. *American Journal of Occupational Therapy, 24,* 201-204.

Mindess, H. (1971). *Laughter and Liberation.* Los Angeles: Nash Publishing.

Mindess, H. (1976). The use and abuse of humor in psychotherapy. In A. J. Chapman & H. C. Foot (Eds.), *Humour and Laughter: Theory, Research, and Applications* (pp. 332-341). London: Wiley.

Mindess, H., & Turek, J. (Eds.). (1982). *The Study of Humor.* Los Angeles: Antioch University Press.

Minuchin, S., & Fishman, H. C. (1981). *Family Therapy Techniques.* Cambridge, MA: Harvard University Press.

Moody, Jr., R. A. (1978). *Laugh After Laugh: The Healing Power of Humor.* Jacksonville, FL: Headwaters Press.

Mozdzierz, G. J., Macchitelli, F. J., & Lisiecki, J. (1976). The paradox in psychotherapy: An Adlerian perspective. *Journal of Individual Psychology, 32,* 169-184.

Murray, H. (1934). The psychology of humor. *Journal of Abnormal and Social Psychology, 28,* 341-365.

Myers, L. (1962). *Psychiatric Glossary: A Cartoon View of the World of Psychiatry.* New York: Dutton.

Nadal, J. (1974). Subjective living, fantasy, and myth. *Etudes Psychothérapiques, 15,* 9-14.

Nies, D. C. (1982). A role of humor in psychotherapy: Reduction of dating anxiety in males. *Dissertation Abstracts International, 43*(6-B), 1993-1994.

Niesenholz, B. (1983). Solving the psychotherapy glut. *Personnel & Guidance Journal, 61,* 535-536.

Nietz, M. (1980). Humor, hierarchy, and the changing status of women. *Psychiatry, 43,* 211-223.

Nussbaum, K., & Michaux, W. W. (1963). Response to humor in depression: A predictor and evaluator of patient change? *Psychiatric Quarterly, 37,* 527-539.

Oberndorf, C. P. (1932). Kidding. *International Journal of Psychoanalysis, 13,* 479.

O'Connell, W. E. (1964a). Multidimensional investigation of Freudian humor. *Psychiatric Quarterly, 38,* 97-108.

O'Connell, W. E. (1964b). Resignation, humor, and wit. *Psychoanalytic Review, 51,* 49-56.

O'Connell, W. E. (1965). Humanistic identification: A new translation for Gemeinschaftige Fuehl. *Journal of Individual Psychology, 21,* 44-47.

O'Connell, W. E. (1968a). Humor and death. *Psychological Reports, 22,* 391-402.

O'Connell, W. E. (1968b). Organic and schizophrenic differences in wit and humor appreciation. *Diseases of the Nervous System, 29,* 275-280.

O'Connell, W. E. (1969). Humor: The therapeutic impasse. *Voices, 5,* 25-27.

O'Connell, W. E. (1971). Adlerian action therapy. *Voices: The Art and Science of Psychotherapy, 7,* 22-27.

O'Connell, W. E. (1972). Frankl, Adler and spirituality. *Journal of Religion & Health, 11,* 134-138.

O'Connell, W. E. (1976). Freudian humor: The eupsychia of everyday life. In A. J. Chapman & H. C. Foot (Eds.), *Humour and Laughter: Theory, Research, and Applications* (pp. 313-329). London: Wiley.

O'Connell, W. E. (1981). Natural high therapy. In R. Corsini (Ed.), *Handbook of Innovative Psychotherapies* (pp. 554-568). New York: Wiley.

O'Connell, W. E., & Bright, M. (1977). *Natural High Primer.* Houston: Natural High Associates.

O'Connell, W. E., & Covert, C. (1967). Death attitudes and humor appreciation among medical students. *Existential Psychiatry, 6,* 433-442.

O'Connell, W. E., & Peterson, P. (1964). Humor and repression. *Journal of Existential Psychology, 4,* 309-316.

O'Connell, W. E., Rothaus, P., Hanson, P. G., & Moyer, R. (1969). Jest appreciation and interaction in leaderless groups. *International Journal of Group Psychotherapy, 19,* 454-462.

O'Connell, W. E., & Worthen, R. (1969). Social interest and humor. *International Journal of Social Psychiatry, 15,* 179-188.

Olson, H. A. (1976). The use of humor in psychotherapy. *Individual Psychologist, 13,* 34-37.

Orfanidis, M. M. (1972). Children's use of humor in psychotherapy. *Social Casework, 53,* 147-155.

Papp, P. (1982). Staging reciprocal metaphors in a couples group. *Family Process, 21,* 453-467.

Paskind, H. A. (1932). Effect of laughter on muscle tone. *Archives of Neurology and Psychiatry, 28,* 623-628.

Peters, C. B., & Grunebaum, H. (1977). It could be worse: Effective group psychotherapy with the help-rejecting complainer. *International Journal of Group Psychothera-py, 27*, 471-480.

Peterson, J. P. (1981). The communicative intent of laughter in group psychotherapy. *Dissertation Abstracts International, 41*(8-B), 3194.

Peterson, J. P., & Pollio, H. P. (1982). Therapeutic effectiveness of differentially targeted humorous remarks in group psychotherapy. *Group, 6*, 39-50.

Peto, E. (1946). Weeping and laughing. *International Journal of Psycho-Analysis, 27*, 129-133.

Pines, L. N. (1964). Laughter as an equivalent of epilepsy. *Soviet Psychology and Psychiatry, 2*, 33-38.

Plass, P. (1972). Freud and Plato on sophistic joking. *Psychoanalytic Review, 59*, 347-360.

Plaut, A., Newton, K., & Zielen, V. (1971). What do we actually do? Learning from experience. *Journal of Analytical Psychology, 16*, 188-203.

Poland, W. S. (1971). The place of humor in psychotherapy. *American Journal of Psychiatry, 128*, 635-637.

Potter, E., & Goodm, R. E. (1983). The implementation of laughter as a therapy facilitator with adult aphasiacs. *Journal of Communication Disorders, 16*, 165-169.

Prerost, F. J. (1976). Reduction of aggression as a function of related content of humor. *Psychological Reports, 38*, 771-777.

Prerost, F. J. (1983). Promoting adjustment to college: A counseling technique utilizing humor. *Personnel and Guidance Journal, 62*, 222-226.

Pustel, G., & Siegel, L. (1973). Humor products of high grade institutionalized retardes. *Art Psychotherapy, 1*, 67-68.

Pustel, G., Sternlicht, M., & Siegel, L. (1972). The psychodynamics of humor as seen in institutionalized retardates. *Journal of Psychology, 80*, 69-73.

Redlich, F. D., Levine, J., & Sohler, T. P. (1951). A mirth response test: Preliminary report on a psychodiagnostic technique utilizing dynamics of humor. *American Journal of Orthopsychiatry, 21*, 717-734.

Reich, A. (1949). The structure of the grotesque-comic sublimation. *Bulletin of the Menninger Clinic, 13*, 160-171.

Reik, T. (1949). *Listening with a Third Ear*. New York: Farrar & Strauss.

Rey-Pias, J. M. (1972). Gelastic epilepsy (laughing seizures). *Schweizer Archiv für Neurologie, Neurochirurgie und Psychiatrie, 111*, 29-35.

Roback, A. A. (1943). *Sense of Humor Test* (2nd ed.). Cambridge, MA: Sci-Art Publishers.

Roberts, A. F., & Johnson, D. M. (1957). Some factors related to the perception of funniness in humor stimuli. *Journal of Social Psychology, 46*, 57-63.

Roberts, J. M., & Forman, M. L. (1971). Riddles: Expressive models of interrogation. *Ethnology, 10*, 509-533.

Robinson, D. (1983). Laughing fit. *Health, 15*, 19.

Robinson, V. M. (1977). *Humor and the Health Professions.* Thorofare, NJ: Slack, Inc.

Roecklelein, J. E. (1969). Auditory stimulation and cartoon ratings. *Perceptual and Motor Skills, 29*, 772.

Roncoli, M. (1974). Bantering: A therapeutic strategy with obsessional patients. *Perspectives in Psychiatric Care, 12*, 171-175.

Rose, G. J. (1969). "King Lear" and the use of humor in treatment. *Journal of the American Psychoanalytic Association, 17*, 927-940.

Rosen, V. (1963). Varieties of comic caricature, and their relationship to obsessive compulsive phenomena. *Journal of the American Psychoanalytic Association, 11*, 704-724.

Rosenheim, E. (1974). Humor in psychotherapy: An interactive experience. *American Journal of Psychotherapy, 28*, 584-591.

Roubicek, J. (1946). Laughter in epilepsy, with some general introductory notes. *Journal of Mental Science, 92*, 734-755.

Rule, W. R. (1977). Increasing self-modeled humor. *Rational Living, 12*, 7-9.

Sachs, L. T. (1973). On crying, weeping and laughing as defenses against sexual drives, with special consideration of adolescent giggling. *International Journal of Psychoanalysis, 54*, 477-481.

Safko, S., & Klimo, Z. (1972). Casuistic contribution to the problem of pathological laughter. *Ceskoslovenska Psychiatrie, 68*, 32-34.

Safranek, R. A. (1982). Humor as a moderator for the effects of stressful life events. *Dissertation Abstracts International, 43*(2-B), 534.

Salameh, W. A. (1981). *Personality of the Comedian: The Theory of Tragi-Comic Reconciliation.* Unpublished doctoral dissertation, University of Montreal.

Salameh, W. A. (1982, August). *From Discordant Childhood to Creative Adulthood: The Making of Stand-Up Comedians.* Paper presented at The Third International Conference on Humor, Washington, DC.

Salameh, W. A. (1983). Humor in psychotherapy: Past outlooks, present status, and future frontiers. In P. McGhee & J. Goldstein (Eds.), *Handbook of Humor Research. Applied Studies* (Vol. II, pp. 61-88). New York: Springer-Verlag.

Salameh, W. A. (1984a, April). Inviting Alice (and Allen) to humorland: On bringing humor into psychotherapy for fun and profit--Part I. *Academy of San Diego Psychologists Newsletter*, 1-8.

Salameh, W. A. (1984b, May). Inviting Alice (and Allen) to humorland: On bringing humor into psychotherapy for fun and profit--Part II. *Academy of San Diego Psychologists Newsletter*, 1-9.

Salameh, W. A. (1984c, August). *Humor as a Facilitative Therapist Trait in Psychotherapeutic Work.* Paper presented at the 92nd Annual Convention of the American Psychologist Association, Toronto, Canada.

Salameh, W. A. (1985a). *Humor Immersion Training*™ Paper presented at the Fourth Annual World Humor Membership Conference, Tempe, Arizona. Abstracted in D. L. F. Nilsen & A. P. Nilsen (Eds.). (1986). *Humor Across the Disciplines* (pp. 284-285). Tempe, AZ: Arizona State University.

Salameh, W. A. (1985b, June). *Humor Immersion Training*™--*A New Technology for Humor Development.* Paper presented at The Fifth International Conference on Humor, Cork, Ireland. Abstracted in D. MacHale (Ed.), *Book of Abstracts of The Fifth International Conference on Humor* (p. 94). Dublin, Ireland: Book Press Limited.

Salameh, W. A. (1985c, August). *Integrative Short-Term Psychotherapy (ISTP)--A New Clinical Approach.* Paper presented at the 93rd Annual Convention of the American Psychological Convention, Los Angeles, California.

Salameh, W. A. (1986a). *The Stress Reduction Handbook: 10 Steps to Emotional Fitness.* San Diego, CA: Southern California Psychological and Consulting Associates.

Salameh, W. A. (1986b). The effective use of humor in psychotherapy. In P. A. Keller & L. G. Ritt (Eds.), *Innovations in Clinical Practice: A Source Book* (Vol. 5, pp. 157-175). Sarasota, FL: Professional Resource Exchange, Inc.

Salameh, W. A. (in press-a). Humor as a form of indirect hypnotic communication. In M. Yapko (Ed.), *Hypnotic and Strategic Interventions: Principles and Practice.* New York: Irvington.

Salameh, W. A. (in press-b). *Humor Immersion Training*™ *Manual: The Definitive Workout Manual for Exercising Your Humor Muscles.*

Schachter, S., & Wheeler, L. (1962). Epinephrine, chlorpromazine and amusement. *Journal of Abnormal and Social Psychology, 65,* 121-128.

Schafer, R. (1970). The psychoanalytic view of reality. *International Journal of Psycho-Analysis, 51,* 279-297.

Schafer, R. (1972). The psychoanalytic view of reality: II. *Psyche, Stuttgart, 26,* 952-973.

Scheflen, A. E. (1978). Susan smiled: An explanation in family therapy. *Family Process, 17,* 59-68.

Schienberg, P. (1980). Therapists' prediction of patients' responses to humor as a function of therapists' empathy and regression in the service of the ego. *Dissertation Abstracts International, 40*(8-A), 4501.

Schimel, J. (1978). The function of wit and humor in psychoanalysis. *Journal of the American Academy of Psychoanalysis, 6,* 369-379.

Schneider, H. (1967). Irony and defense. *Psychotherapy & Psychosomatics, 15,* 326-338.

Schwartz, B. E. (1974-1975). Telepathic humoresque. *The Psychoanalytic Review, 61,* 591-606.

Scogin, F., et al. (1983). Humorous stimuli and depression: An examination of Beck's premise. *Journal of Clinical Psychology, 39,* 165-169.

Senf, R., Huston, P. E., & Cohen, B. D. (1956). The use of comic cartoons for the study of social comprehension in schizophrenia. *American Journal of Psychiatry, 113,* 45-51.

Shaw, C. R. (1961). The use of humor in child psychiatry. *American Journal of Psychotherapy, 15,* 368-381.

Simon, R. K. (1977). Freud's concepts of comedy and suffering. *Psychoanalytic Review, 64,* 391-407.

Sloane, H. (1978). *Humor in the Creative Process.* San Francisco: Institute of Psychosynthesis.

343

Smith, C. M., & Hamilton, J. (1959). Psychological factors in the narcolepsy-cataplexy syndrome. *Psychosomatic Medicine, 21,* 40-49.

Smith, E. E., & Goodchilds, J. D. (1959). Characteristics of the witty group member: The wit as a leader. *American Psychologist, 14,* 375-376.

Smith, E. E., & Goodchilds, J. D. (1963). The wit in large and small established groups. *Psychological Reports, 13,* 273-274.

Smith, R. E. (1973). The use of humor in the counter-conditioning of anger responses: A case study. *Behavior Therapy, 4,* 576-580.

Speigel, D., Brodkin, S. G., & Keith-Speigel, P. (1969). Unacceptable impulses, anxiety and the appreciation of cartoons. *Journal of Projective Techniques and Personality Assessment, 33,* 154-159.

Speigel, D., Keith-Speigel, P., Abrahams, J., & Kranitz, L. (1969). Humor and suicide: Favorite jokes of suicidal patients. *Journal of Consulting and Clinical Psychology, 33,* 504-505.

Spencer, H. (1860). The physiology of laughter. *Macmillan's Magazine, 1,* 395-402.

Sperling, S. J. (1953). On the psychodynamics of teasing. *Journal of the American Psychoanalytic Association, 3,* 458-483.

Stanton, A. H. (1978). The significance of ego interpretive states in insight-directed psychotherapy. *Psychiatry, 41,* 129-140.

Starer, E. (1961). Reactions of psychiatric patients to cartoons and verbal jokes. *Journal of General Psychology, 65,* 301-304.

Stearns, F. R. (1972). *Laughing: Physiology, Pathophysiology, Psychology and Development.* Springfield, IL: Thomas.

Stern, M. (Ed.). (1981). Humor in therapy [Special edition]. *Voices, 17*(3).

Strother, G. B., Barnett, M. M., & Apostolakos, P. C. (1954). The use of cartoons as a projective device. *Journal of Clinical Psychology, 10,* 38-42.

Tarachow, S. (1949). Remarks on the comic process and beauty. *Psychoanalytic Quarterly, 18,* 215-226.

Taubman, M. T. (1980). Humor and behavioral matching and their relationship to child care worker evaluation and delinquency in group home treatment programs. *Dissertation Abstracts International, 41*(5-B), 1896-1897.

Ullman, L. P., & Lim, D. T. (1962). Case history material as a source of the identification of patterns of response to emotional stimuli in a study of humor. *Journal of Consulting Psychology, 26,* 221-225.

Urewitch, M. (1975). *Comedy: The Irrational Vision.* Ithica, NY: Cornell University Press.

Van den Aardweg, G. J. (1972). A grief theory of homosexuality. *American Journal of Psychotherapy, 26,* 52-68.

Van den Aardweg, G. J. (1973). The factor "complaining," neurosis and homophilia. *Psychologica Belgica, 13,* 295-311.

Van Hemert, N. A. (1975). Semantic transformations in the structure of the intellect model and cartoons. *Nederlands Tijdschrift voor de Psychologie en Haar Grensgevieden, 30,* 113-138.

Vargas, M. J. (1961). Uses of humor in group psychotherapy. *Group Psychotherapy, 14,* 198-202.

Vasey, G. (1875). *The Philosophy of Laughter and Smiling.* London.

Ventis, W. L. (1973). Case history: The use of laughter as an alternative response in systematic desensitization. *Behavior Therapy, 4,* 120-122.

Vranjesevic, D. (1977). Gelastic epilepsy. *Psihijatrica Danas, 9,* 555-559.

Warkentin, L. (Ed.). (1969). Humor in therapy [Special edition]. *Voices, 5*(2).

Waye, M. F. (1979). Behavioral treatment of a child displaying comic-book mediated fear of hand shrinking: A case study. *Journal of Pediatric Psychology, 4,* 43-47.

Weinstein, E. (1974). The neurology of humor. *Mount Sinai Journal of Medicine, 41,* 235-239.

Whitaker, C. (1975). Psychotherapy of the absurd: With a special emphasis on the psychotherapy of aggression. *Family Process, 14,* 1-16.

Wieck, D. T. (1967). Funny things. *Journal of Aesthetics & Art Criticism, 25,* 437-447.

Winterstein, A. (1934). Contributions to the problem of humor. *Psychoanalytic Quarterly, 3,* 303-316.

Wolfenstein, M. (1953). Children's understanding of jokes. *The Psychoanalytic Study of the Child, 9,* 162-173.

Yörükoglu, A. (1974). Children's favorite jokes and their relation to emotional conflicts. *Journal of Child Psychiatry, 13,* 677-690.

Yorukoglu, A. (1977). Favourite jokes of children and their dynamic relation to intra-familial conflicts. In A. J. Chapman & H. C. Foot (Eds.), *It's a Funny Thing, Humour* (407-411). New York: Pergamon.

Yorukoglu, A., & Silverman, J. S. (1963). Responses of psychiatric patients to a battery of cartoons and jokes. *Psychiatric Communications, 6,* 9-16.

Zigler, E., Levine, J., & Gould, L. (1966). The humor response of normal, institutionalized retarded and noninstitutionalized retarded children. *American Journal of Mental Deficiency, 71,* 472-480.

Zuk, G. H. (1964). A further study of laughter in family therapy. *Family Process, 3,* 77-89.

Zuk, G. H. (1966). On the theory and pathology of laughter in psychotherapy. *Psychotherapy: Theory, Research and Practice, 3,* 97-101.

Zuk, G. H., Boszormenyi-Nagy, I., & Heiman, E. (1963). Some dynamics of laughter during family therapy. *Family Process, 2,* 302-314.

Zweben, J. E., & Miller, R. L. (1968). The systems games: Teaching, training, psychotherapy. *Psychotherapy: Theory, Research and Practice, 5,* 73-76.

Zwerling, I. (1955). The favorite joke technique in diagnostic and therapeutic interviewing. *Psychoanalytic Quarterly, 24,* 104-115.

AUTHOR INDEX

Author Index

Subject Index